A Private Spy

'A colossal addition to our knowledge of the writer whom Ian McEwan has said "will be remembered as perhaps the most significant novelist of the second half of the twentieth century in Britain" . . . a richly rewarding experience for the reader . . . these letters are full of trails to follow, and stories to chase'

Matthew d'Ancona, Tortoise

'Unsurprisingly, he was a brilliant correspondent. Revelations tumble out . . . These engaging letters are edited with great fairness and sensitivity by a family member, his son Tim Cornwell'

Andrew Lycett, *Mail on Sunday*

'Sensitively edited by his son Tim . . . the letters show how hard he worked to get the fiction right'

Blake Morrison, *Guardian*

'Well written and entertaining'

Adam Sisman, *Spectator*

'Even letters where he is firing a publisher or an editor are masterpieces of sensitivity and charm'

Jon Smith, *Irish Independent*

John le Carré was born in 1931. For six decades, he wrote novels that came to define our age. The son of a confidence trickster, he spent his childhood between boarding school and the London underworld. At sixteen he found refuge at the University of Bern, then later at Oxford. A spell of teaching at Eton led him to a short career in British Intelligence (MI5 and MI6). He published his debut novel, *Call for the Dead*, in 1961 while still a secret servant. His third novel, *The Spy Who Came in from the Cold*, secured him a worldwide reputation that was consolidated by the acclaim for his trilogy *Tinker Tailor Soldier Spy*, *The Honourable Schoolboy* and *Smiley's People*. At the end of the Cold War, le Carré widened his scope to explore an international landscape, including the arms trade and the War on Terror. His memoir, *The Pigeon Tunnel*, was published in 2016, and the last George Smiley novel, *A Legacy of Spies*, appeared in 2017. He died on 12 December 2020. His posthumous novel, *Silverview*, was published in 2021.

Tim Cornwell was born in 1962, the third son of David Cornwell (John le Carré) and his first wife, Ann Sharp. He was a journalist for various British newspapers in Washington and Los Angeles in the 1990s. After twelve years in the US he moved to Edinburgh, and from 2001 to 2012 he was deputy foreign editor then arts correspondent of the *Scotsman*. After leaving the paper, he worked as a freelance arts journalist specialising in the Scottish Colourists and in Islamic art. He died in May 2022.

A Private Spy

The Letters of John le Carré

Edited by Tim Cornwell

PENGUIN BOOKS

PENGUIN BOOKS

UK | USA | Canada | Ireland | Australia
India | New Zealand | South Africa

Penguin Books is part of the Penguin Random House group of companies
whose addresses can be found at global.penguinrandomhouse.com.

Penguin
Random House
UK

First published by Viking 2022
Published in Penguin Books 2023
001

Copyright © Viereck Ltd, 2022

The acknowledgements on pp. xiii, 649–52 constitute an extension of this
copyright page

The moral right of the author has been asserted

Typeset by Jouve (UK), Milton Keynes
Printed and bound in Great Britain by Clays Ltd, Elcograf S.p.A.

The authorized representative in the EEA is Penguin Random House Ireland,
Morrison Chambers, 32 Nassau Street, Dublin D02 YH68

A CIP catalogue record for this book is available from the British Library

ISBN: 978–0–241–99455–9

www.greenpenguin.co.uk

For Noah

Forgive this long scribe, but sometimes letters are more fun.

– le Carré to his stepmother Jean Cornwell, 4 June 2009

We all write too few letters these days.

– to Al Alvarez, 16 September 2016

Contents

x

List of Illustrations and Picture Credits

Insets

1. David Cornwell with his parents, grandparents and great-grandparents.
2. David Cornwell with his parents and brother.
3. Ronnie Cornwell in close proximity to the Duke of Edinburgh.
4. David and Tony Cornwell as children.
5. Jeannie Cornwell.
6. The Sherborne School Junior Hockey Team.
7. Reginald Stanley Thompson.
8. Ronnie, Jeannie, David and Tony Cornwell.
9. David skiing.
10. David and Ann.
11. David and Charlotte Cornwell.
12. Vivian Green.
13. David's drawing of Ann.
14. John and Miranda Margetson's wedding.
15. Sir Victor Gollancz.
16. *New York Times* bestseller list.
17. Graham Greene.
18. The Cornwell family in Greece.
19. Le Carré and his sons drawing together.
20. Le Carré and Richard Burton.
21. Susan Kennaway.
22. Sydney Pollack.
23. Jane Cornwell.
24. Robert Gottlieb.
25. Le Carré and Jane working on *Tinker Tailor Soldier Spy*.
26. Le Carré and his family at Tregiffian.
27. Le Carré and Alec Guinness on Hampstead Heath.

Text Illustrations

Picture Credits

The majority of images have been reprinted by kind permission of the Cornwell family; other credits are below.

Insets: 6, courtesy of Sherborne School; 7 and 15, © National Portrait Gallery, London; 12, © Deborah Elliott; 14, reprinted by kind permission of the Margetson family; 17, Pictorial Press Ltd/Alamy Stock Photo; 18, Jean-Claude Sauer/Paris Match via Getty Images; 20, *Daily Mail*/Shutterstock; 21, Susan Vereker; 22, Steve Schapiro/Corbis via Getty Images; 24, George Etheredge; 26, Ben Martin/Getty Images; 27 © BBC; 28, Pascal Parrot/Sygma/Sygma via Getty Images; 29, reprinted by kind permission of the Greenway family; 31, © Stuart Franklin/Magnum Photos; 35, Getty Images; 36, Judith Herrin; 37 and 39, Dave M. Benett/Getty Images; 38, Anton Corbijn/Contour by Getty Images; 40, © Tom Jamieson; 42, reprinted by kind permission of the Ink Factory; 44, reprinted by kind permission of the Musharbash family; 45, reprinted by kind permission of the Geller family; 46, © Sean Smith.

Text illustrations: p. 90, Simon Bingham; p. 348, Jeff Danziger editorial cartoon used with permission of Jeff Danziger, CounterPoint Syndication and the Cartoonist Group. All rights reserved.

Introduction

'I hate the telephone. I can't type. Like the tailor in my new novel, I ply my trade by hand. I live on a Cornish cliff and hate cities. Three days and nights in a city are about my maximum. I don't see many people. I write and walk and swim and drink.' So wrote my father, in a 1996 article-cum-letter, sent to his long-time editor Bob Gottlieb and others, called 'Talking to My American Publishers'.

I am writing these few words of introduction from the same Cornish cliff. Yesterday a wind was whipping round the stone walls, shaking and swaying the hardy skimmia and veronica bushes of my father's garden, with a sea as fierce as I've seen it, twisting the rollers into white crests. But now the place is bathed in brilliant winter sunshine, bouncing off a rippled ocean, with a magpie hopping on the lawn.

In 1969 my father took on a row of three derelict cottages and an adjoining hay barn, converting and expanding them over fifty years, adding his library and writer's studio and creating his own artist's garden, with hidden lawns and sculptures and thick hedges of giant hewn stone.

'I have very much hibernated down here, see almost no one,' he wrote to his stepmother Jeannie in 1972, after he bought the buildings and about a mile of untamed cliff from a local farmer. 'And work seven or eight hours a day on a new book, just a thriller to mark time . . . I get up at seven each morning to a ninety mile an hour gale that hasn't stopped for four days, and only the bloody power cuts for company – except that I like it very much and enjoy my work, and the fields and the sea, and the potato farm that is part of the place.' The book, 'just a thriller', was *Tinker Tailor Soldier Spy*.

My father, who died of pneumonia after a fall in December 2020, was brave in the way he spoke for what he believed in, brave in the places and subjects he tackled in his writing, and brave in the way he faced illness. He invented a language for the cancer he long fought, though it wasn't the cancer that took him. He built a Wodehousian language of medicine, coded like his language for the spies: the prostate doctor was the Rear Admiral; gruelling check-ups were 'the sheep dip'; and doses of a lethal radioactive medicine were 'getting nuked'. He was brave in the way he cared for my stepmother, Jane, already ravaged by cancer as he died, and who followed him two months later.

'Vile weather here: murderous north easterly, sleet and rain, very cold,' he emailed to me a week before he died. It was often our best way of communicating; an email or two brought always a sharp observation, a smile, a line of words to treasure. 'That's after a long spell of sunshine and autumn. We're OK, but Jane is having a tough time with the chemo . . . I fell down in the bathroom like an idiot and cracked a rib, which makes me very grouchy.'

This book of John le Carré's letters, and occasional emails, is intended to share the more private voice of a man widely considered one of the greatest post-war novelists. He elevated the spy into the realm of literature, enticing readers into the characters, the language and the labyrinthine conspiracies of his secret world. There is one obvious omission from the collection: it contains only a smattering of letters to his lovers, of whom there were quite a few throughout his life. It seems that he was mostly attracted – romantically and otherwise – to people of consequence and agency, and inevitably also to those whose anguish was somehow akin to his own. The son of an abusive father and a mother who, for good and sufficient reasons, abandoned him and his brother when he was five, he was predictably wayward in his relationships: inconstant, needy, desperate to please – yet desperate also to retain his own sovereignty over his heart, lest something on which he depended suddenly evaporate. It's tempting to say that genius is complex, but probably truer that trauma is simple. He cannot have failed to inflict emotional wounds in his turn, but a part of him was perpetually and ferociously on watch against the reflection of his father in his own actions. However that may be, he was as scrupulous in keeping his romantic correspondence covert as he was in recording the rest, and our archive contains little that is enlightening on that score.

Le Carré – which is what I call him in this book – produced internationally acclaimed novels in every decade, from *The Spy Who Came in from the Cold* in 1963 to *Agent Running in the Field* in 2019, as well as the posthumous novel, *Silverview*, in 2021. His writing defined the Cold War era and spoke truth to power in the decades that followed, though never – or almost never – putting polemic above a good story. Graham Greene called the younger le Carré the author of the best spy story he'd ever read; Philip Roth and Ian McEwan placed his works among the most important of the twentieth century.

My father spent sixty years in the public eye, after *The Spy Who Came in from the Cold* hurtled him from MI6 agent masked as a junior diplomat to global bestselling author of a Cold War publishing sensation. A scholar of French and above all German literature, he knew from early on that his letters would be treasured, archived, potentially publicised, misused, misquoted or sold.

In a letter in these pages my father describes F. Scott Fitzgerald as the 'writer's ultimate writer', a verbal conjuror who can 'keep the light on in the dark', 'make a rainbow out of black and white'. But to his one-time lover Susan Kennaway, he wrote that three quarters of Fitzgerald's letters 'are self-conscious crap, injurious to him and his art alike, and if anybody ever went raking in my desk for that stuff, I hope to God I'd managed to burn it in time'.

There are letters in this book in which David Cornwell is writing intimately and freely, while in others John le Carré is having a good look over his shoulder and laying down his legacy for posterity, as well as having some literary fun. If not self-conscious, thoroughly self-aware. 'I have decided to cultivate that intense, worried look and to start writing brilliant, untidy letters for future biographers. This is one,' he wrote to Miranda Margetson, while still serving at the British Embassy in Bonn, enclosing a caricature of himself doing just that (see p. 109).

The author of twenty-five novels, my father was a prolific and conscientious letter-writer, from thank-you letters to answering fan letters. The backgrounds of those with whom he corresponded spanned politics, literature, publishing, the arts and his former profession as a spy. The actor and author Stephen Fry and the playwright Sir Tom Stoppard are represented in these pages; so are the former London station chief of the KGB and the former head of MI6. So are the members of his close family, particularly in his early-adult years.

My father was a gifted illustrator who, as a young man, considered a career as an artist. This book includes examples of early drawings, caricatures, and illustrations for books and magazines. They are of mixed quality and might be dismissed as juvenilia, but when my father visited Russia in 1993 he was delighted to find that Pushkin's manuscripts, like some of his own, were occasionally covered in racy doodles – in Pushkin's case, of nymphs playing snooker. Once, left alone in London with several thousand sheets of paper to sign for his US publisher, he chose to illustrate them instead – initially with spies and dogs, but, as his boredom increased, the figures became distinctly risqué. He illustrated his early letters, and for his whole life wrote his manuscripts, his letters and his signature in a distinctive, fluent hand. The last letter in this book, written two weeks before he died, to his old friend the journalist David Greenway, covers four handwritten pages.

Stephen Fry first wrote to my father in 1993, as an admiring fan, and this was the beginning of an intermittent correspondence. 'Those letters, though – such care and engagement in them,' he wrote after my father's memorial. 'Kindly, sharp, detailed – I can almost hear those eyebrows rustle slightly – what a courtesy it is to share so much observation and insight with someone you know so little.'

As a boy I joined my father as we cut through our stretch of the new Cornish coast path in the early 1970s, running just under the house. The Cornish landscape and the weather rolling off the Atlantic are offstage characters in my father's letters, Wagnerian motifs. Cornwall was a place he used for intense writing stretches, and where he went to ground after publication – though also to entertain, and as a backdrop for interviews and photographs.

'I arrived here yesterday – huge, running skies, black cloud, brilliant sun, then daft, sloping showers that catch you in the ear just when you think you might perhaps build another wing,' he wrote to Sir Alec Guinness in 1981. 'We have been stuck down here all winter, and stuck in most senses: huge storms, on and on, rain, running fog, then huge storms again,' he wrote to his lifelong friend John Margetson in April 1994. 'The result is, I've written ¾ of a very muddy, fog-laden book, very introverted and strange, but I'm rather pleased with it, at least so far.' The novel was *Our Game*.

Guinness came to stay here; so did many of the recipients of the letters in this book, from the writer Nicholas Shakespeare to the actor Ralph Fiennes (drenched along with le Carré in a rainstorm), to the head of the German secret service, August Hanning. George Smiley and Ann walked here on the Cornish coast path, 'the worst time Smiley could remember in their long, puzzled marriage', with a nameless shadow of betrayal. In an early draft of *Tinker Tailor Soldier Spy*, Bill Haydon retired here.

My father wrote the vast majority of his letters by hand – typically signed 'As ever, David'. Some were dictated or typed from his drafts – business letters to agents, or to publishers, or letters to newspapers. Sometimes he seemed to treat them like writing exercises; others were fire and forget, a kind of personal Snapchat, with a sense that handwritten letters were safer, more private, less sensitive to hacking or reproduction.

For a number of years my father exchanged letters with Willard J. Morse, a Maine obstetrician, picking him out as a correspondent for no discernible reason, sharing lacerating and highly quotable opinions on Princess Diana, Tony Blair and Gordon Brown. These letters started to appear in internet auctions, saucy enough for headlines in the *Guardian* and the *Daily Mail*. 'Please don't worry about the publication of my letters,' he wrote to his friend Anthony Barnett, founder of openDemocracy, in December 2018. 'They were written in privacy to a man I never met, a retired US army medic who became disenchanted with his country under Bush junior, settled in the Bahamas and poured his soul out to me in a steady stream of letters over several years. I wrote to him with equal frankness. I don't keep correspondence, or copies of my own letters, so have no idea any more what exactly passed between us. His heirs decided to make money out of them, and seem to have done so. Agent and lawyer alike want me to proceed against the heirs. I don't need the hassle. And I wrote what I wrote. Finis.'

My father was fiercely aware, however, how his words might be used, and never handed out quotes lightly. Writing to him in 2009, retired lecturer Michael Hall noted how my father had carefully avoided putting anything in their correspondence that could be used as an endorsement of Hall's two books. Hall wrote of the pike in the ponds on Hampstead Heath, with 'one wily old veteran who will not be caught, whatever bait you run past his nose'. 'A wily old Pike thanks you for your wily letter, and was much entertained,' my father wrote back.

This book draws heavily on the main archive of my father's correspondence, now mostly destined for the Bodleian Library, Oxford; it was assembled over several decades, kept by his secretaries and his wife Jane and first put into order in the late 2000s. He did not routinely retain copies of outgoing letters unrelated to business matters, though some early exchanges, for example with Sir Alec Guinness, were carefully copied and kept. The archive is self-curated; my father was making the calls on which letters to file, and which to burn. It has been supplemented by the return of collections of early letters, in particular to his first wife, my mother, Ann; and to the Reverend Vivian Green, his schoolmaster and Oxford mentor, who married them. The correspondence with my father's stepmother Jeannie, second wife to his father, Ronnie, lent by her granddaughter Nancy, was a particular revelation; she was an early confidante of the famously motherless le Carré, whose mother, Olive, had left when he was five.[1]

In the research for this volume, I harvested copies of le Carré letters as best I could from libraries, archives, publishers, agents, family and above all friends. My late godfather Sir John Margetson, one of

---

1. Le Carré's brother, Tony, believed their ages to be six and four respectively when their mother left.

six men on my father's MI6 training course, was a correspondent for over sixty years.

My parents' marriage ended painfully, but my mother kept all my father's letters over twenty years, from about 1950 to 1970; they are a remarkable resource on his early life. The same cannot be said about the very sad destruction of certain groups of letters – in particular, my father's letters to his first American publisher, Jack Geoghegan, a vital promoter of *The Spy Who Came in from the Cold*. His stepson sent my father these letters after Geoghegan's death in 1999, and he later shocked Adam Sisman, his biographer, by telling him he had destroyed them. The two men had a close and complex relationship, but that record of it is now lost.

One of my father's oldest and closest friends – his best friend, in his words – was John Miller, the Cornish painter, former architect, and once my father's agent in MI5. Miller's paintings cover a wall at the family home in Cornwall – he first led le Carré to the site – and after his death in 2002 my father wrote to the director John Boorman: 'I never knew I could miss a friend so much.' John Miller treasured my father's letters – 'Those will be valuable one day,' he joked, nodding towards them – but sometime after his death they were destroyed, it appears, by his partner, Michael Truscott, who has also since died.

Almost all the letters to the aid worker Yvette Pierpaoli, who had a long involvement with my father, and to whom *The Constant Gardener* is dedicated, were burned by Yvette's daughter after her death, in the kitchen sink. Yvette had kept them preciously; her daughter felt my father had been so important in her life that 'whatever they had between them had to stay that way'.

Rainer Heumann, described in the *Independent*'s obituary of 1996 as 'the most powerful literary agent in Europe', had a long and close relationship with my father, but it appears the letters to him were destroyed after Heumann's death. According to colleagues at Heumann's Mohrbooks Literary Agency, Heumann's letters were kept at home; he and his wife, Inge, died without legal heirs, and items of no apparent sales value in the estate were dumped.

There is perhaps one more 'What if?' related to my father's letters:

the papers of his own father, Ronnie Cornwell, conman extraordinaire, who makes appearances in my father's fiction in *The Naive and Sentimental Lover*, *Single & Single* and, above all, *A Perfect Spy*.

According to Ronnie's last secretary, Glenda Moakes, my father told her he had destroyed many of Ronnie's papers after his death in 1975. Le Carré, in his 2002 *New Yorker* article, 'In Ronnie's Court', describes 'a stack of brown boxes that my father always carted round with him when he was on the run'. In *A Perfect Spy*, Rick Pym, the conman character based closely on Ronnie, has a green filing cabinet. Moakes remembers that Ronnie too had filing cabinets; if they included letters from my father, they have gone.[2] The one apparent surviving letter to Ronnie from my father is included in this collection, as is a group of later letters to his mother.

John le Carré, predictably, received more than his fair share of crank mail. For each letter of the alphabet in the le Carré archive of correspondence there is a separate file marked 'difficult people'. 'What the hell do I do with this one?' my father wrote about a weird and rambling letter from a fan, who told how he had gone mad on a bus and declared *The Little Drummer Girl* to be the finest love story since *Pride and Prejudice*.

One fan submitted a book that appeared to be a thesis about an early internet discussion list. 'Oy – What on Earth?' he wrote on it to my stepmother Jane, using his favourite nickname for her, 'Oysters'. On another letter, addressed in 1994 'To the Great Writer, David Cornwell' at his home address in Cornwall, he notes: 'File under our category of deranged people – he writes and writes and I never answer.'

Mostly, answer he did. 'It is hard to describe the pleasure I derive from the occasional letter from a faithful reader who, overcoming either sloth or inhibition, has the grace to put his thoughts on paper,' he wrote on 29 January 2010 to Ronojoy Sen, writing from Assam, India, to thank him for two and a half decades of 'making the English language come so wonderfully alive', and the 'exquisite new

---

2. Le Carré later assumed they were 'just burned'.

subtleties with each joyful reading' of *The Honourable Schoolboy* in particular.

In 1986, when a British couple wrote about wanting to start a le Carré fan club, it was Jane who replied. 'Sometimes, he has to cut himself off from the rest of the world and I often answer letters for him,' she wrote. 'The thing is that, although sometimes we get quite a lot of letters, they are usually more than just requests for signatures. We have often thought of having a standard letter where you mark the answer you want to give but we've never been able to bring ourselves to do it. It's so impersonal and unfriendly. So in the end one of us usually answers with a proper letter.'

My father's typical working routine was to write early in the morning, walk in the afternoon, and deal with correspondence and other matters later in the day. Letters would be turned around in two or three days, seldom left for more than a week.

In 2011 Jonathan Turner wrote to my father in an effort to find out something about his own father, Edward, who had died mysteriously young and was rumoured to have had an intelligence background. He was startled to get a warm reply almost by return of post, though without anything that promised to breach the Official Secrets Act. 'I met no Turner in my time there, but that means nothing. Your simplest course these days is just to ask them,' my father wrote sympathetically, about 'your Papa,' suggesting Turner try the personnel department at the Secret Intelligence Service (SIS) in Vauxhall. (I myself have received similar inquiries from people hoping John le Carré could solve a family mystery.) It was his standard answer, though sometimes he might carefully offer more. In *The Secret Pilgrim*, George Smiley finds himself fielding a similar question from a set of grieving parents, and what he ultimately chooses to tell them says a great deal about the man who created him. In *A Legacy of Spies*, it is the children of spies who come demanding answers about the casualties of the Cold War.

The le Carré literary estate made the decision to publish a volume of my father's letters that would appear not long after his death. The publication of *Silverview* in 2021 and a planned documentary feature project with the director Errol Morris suggested the time was right. My elder brother Simon, as literary executor, kindly set me on what became a journey in my father's company, and I thank him and the reader for allowing me to treasure that, whatever the result. It was a privilege to take it on, and a challenge, as my own modest career has been as a journalist, and not as an academic or biographer. But I came to know him much better, particularly as a young man; and regret that I did not spend more time asking him simpler questions about his life.

I did not set out to select and edit with any particular slant, or story to tell. The letters chose themselves. There's a review on the back of Norman Lewis's book *Naples '44*, my favourite of the many books my father gave me: 'One goes on reading page after page as if eating cherries.' That simile has stayed with me. I would hope every letter here could be eaten separately: fresh, crisp, colourful, tart; or soft, juicy, rich, a little rotten. As much as possible, the letters are published in full; some edits are made for brevity, relevance, and occasionally to protect identities or feelings, as these are mostly private letters being printed soon after my father's death.

Too often in the last months I have simply enjoyed them myself, forgetting that I was supposed to be editing, gone exploring instead. The process of selection began simply by choosing the best, most readable, individual letters; they began to dictate a narrative structure, which was then augmented. There has never been a dull day amid my father's words.

Being John le Carré's son has been part of my identity since boarding school, when his maroon Rolls-Royce came rolling up a country drive very like that of Jim Prideaux's school in *Tinker Tailor Soldier Spy*. As a twelve-year-old I read the book in a large-print version, and later wondered which of we sons was Roach. My father came to speak at a school club, and I asked if he'd ever seen a man killed on the Berlin Wall.

This book was always going to be incomplete; I could not hazard a guess as to the number of letters my father wrote. In the files in Cornwall, incoming letters that were kept, and mostly only from the last three decades, are often marked simply 'replied by hand'. There are correspondents overlooked, and there are significant letters that will be discovered in future years, one hopes – such as those that might exist among my father's Palestinian contacts in the Middle East, written when he was researching *The Little Drummer Girl* (where my own inquiries into archives have so far gone nowhere), or among the journalists he knew in South-East Asia.

The records of outgoing letters are generally thin until the 1990s, when my father's frequent use of the fax machine for his most important letters meant originals were kept at home, while photocopiers were ever more accessible. 'I abhor the telephone and have taken the somewhat eccentric decision to live by the fax and the mail, which at least restores the dignity of the written word!' he wrote to his old Sherborne schoolmate Gerald Peacocke on 3 August 1994.

My father continued to send handwritten letters by fax until the mid 2000s; he learnt to type with two fingers in order to send emails from his laptop and iPad. 'This is my day to become an emailist,' he announced to his half-sister Charlotte on 17 May 2006. But he continued to handwrite letters. The journalist Luke Harding, who immediately framed the note my father sent praising his book *Collusion*, posits that le Carré was 'the last great letter-writer of the twenty-first century'. He was an orderly correspondent from the beginning; it was as rare for letters to be undated as it was for them to be illegible. His handwriting aged: I still remember it from the 1970s, its flowing, even joyous form on the front of an envelope; late in life it moved scratchily downward to the right side of the page.

My father lived an eventful life, and relationships seldom followed an even keel; letters to important correspondents – of which one or two might appear here from a group of thirty – are often almost novellas in themselves. They form conversations over time, or interrupted dialogues.

In the publishing industry my father demanded high standards of publishers and agents – 'demand' is very much the word – and changed them more than once. It was in his gift to form high-intensity relationships fast, with men and women. People who believed themselves intimate friends seemed to fall in or out of favour as they ran up against an author who had moved on from South-East Asia, or the Middle East, or Panama, one with multiple claims on his time.

'I cannot promise to be available to you socially,' he wrote coldly to Vladimir Stabnikov – who had helped to facilitate le Carré's first trip to Moscow – after the Russian took umbrage at being steered away by Jane. 'I am presently immersed in a new book, and writing is nothing if it is not obsessive. None of my friends expects intimacy of me when I am in this state.' This to someone whom he would describe two years later as a man whose 'cultural knowledge, erudition and humanity has impressed me since the day I met him'.

The character of Ronnie Cornwell haunts these letters, as it does the novels. My father remained amazed to the end of his life at the things Ronnie got up to – including, for example, the new details of his early crimes and punishments that were discovered by le Carré's biographer, Adam Sisman. He was still wrestling with Ronnie's shadow in his very late letters to his brother, Tony. What one finds in the early letters is Ronnie in real time, unadorned by later recollection, interacting with the young le Carré. He moves in and out of the first twenty-five years of my father's adult, letter-writing life. The stories, the drama, the pain that sometimes seemed too exotic to be true were not exaggerations or fabrications.

Ronnie Cornwell appears to have thought he taught my father the art of writing, though he boasted of never reading books. C. B. Wilson, who knew Ronnie in Singapore, wrote to my father: 'He had a very good control of the English language and would write a most polished letter. He felt he had passed on this ability to you.' Among the letters to Jeannie Cornwell is one from Ronnie written in October 1974, a year before he died. 'I am sure that I do not have to tell you, how deeply touched I was with your telephone call yesterday morning and the purpose for which it was made,' he began. 'Quite apart from what may be the ultimate outcome, of what we may decide to do, it is good to know that there exists that concern for each other's welfare and I hope you will take it for granted that mine for you will be just as great as yours for mine and that is the nicest way to put it.'

The letter concerned a mysterious picture that Jeannie had found in the house, which he urged them to get valued by Sotheby's or Christie's. 'We could either know that you were sitting on a gold mine or had to face up to the fact that it was a slag heap after all,' Ronnie wrote, wisely. Quickly he moved hopefully into dividing up the proceeds of the as-yet-undiscovered masterpiece: fifty per cent in trust for their children, Jeannie to receive the income. 'As to the remaining 50 percent I would like to utilise this for my needs which are urgent at the moment,' he wrote, though of course promising a solicitor's undertaking it would be returned after a promised £1 million property deal went through. 'If I may for a moment dwell upon the reasons for the difficulties I am going through they arise not through any lack of realities but purely due to liquidity, by that I mean short of actual cash.'

The letter is an exercise in Micawberish self-parody. With banks reluctant to increase overdraft facilities, Ronnie explained, he had had to get rid of his horses, perhaps his offices, and his apartment in Chelsea. Meanwhile he'd had lunch with the head of the Rank Organisation, trying to offer him the rights to the latest le Carré book, though its author would have nothing to do with him. Little wonder that my father so loved Charles Dickens, that we both loved *David Copperfield*; he bought me two antique sets.

Characters pick themselves out in this volume. The last book that my father gave me was the biography of Graham Greene by Richard Greene. Greene was a fleeting presence in my father's life, rather than a friend – 'We met in Paris & Vienna &, very briefly, in London,' he wrote to Alan Judd – but he constitutes another motif in the correspondence. Greene provided the key author's quote for *The Spy Who Came in from the Cold*. Aiming for a satirical spy novel in *The Tailor of Panama*, my father wrote in the book's acknowledgements that 'without Graham Greene this book would never have come about. After Greene's *Our Man in Havana*, the notion of an intelligence fabricator would not leave me alone.'

The two men clashed publicly in the 1960s over Kim Philby. Le Carré wrote an introduction to the book by the *Sunday Times* Insight team, *Philby: The Spy Who Betrayed a Generation*, in which he described the MI6 mole as 'vain, spiteful and murderous'. Greene, who had worked under Philby at SIS and counted him as a friend, penned a riposte in the *Observer* against such a 'vulgar and untrue' depiction. He likened le Carré to E. Phillips Oppenheim, the best-selling pre-war author of easy-reading genre fiction. (Ironically, le Carré had also likened his adventures to those of E. Phillips Oppenheim, in an illustrated letter to my mother describing his days in spy training camp.)

They made up their quarrel. In 1974 le Carré wrote to Greene after his research visits to South-East Asia, to praise the astonishing accuracy of mood and observation in *The Quiet American*, published twenty years before. Outwardly careful of criticising Greene, however, in private he would be increasingly scornful of his Catholicism, his politics, of 'He who lived in Antibes and fell in love with Central American dictators.'

Kim Philby is also an inescapable presence in the letters. My father did not take kindly to certain literary journalists, but Philby was the only man I remember him to have truly hated. In 1989 he ruled out any meeting with Philby on a trip to Moscow; but told his guide, John Roberts, that one day 'I'd like to meet him for zoological reasons', as if Philby were some poisonous reptile.

The uncomfortable relationship with England and its politicians is also explored. My father accepted major awards from France, Germany and Sweden, but declined any honours from the British state. He refused to have his work put forward for literary prizes, and turned down political and royal honours. In his letters, Prime Minister Tony Blair is the 'arch-sophist' and 'intuitive liar'; Boris Johnson the 'Etonian oik'. Only Margaret Thatcher was somehow admirable.

My father wrote to my mother, Ann, from Austria in 1950, of the 'grey indifference of England'. 'I'm sick of England and English institutions, I'm sick of our neuroses and the flesh-eating and the infantilism,' he told her in 1966 – though his sickness had as much to do with the marriage as with the country. He had just published *The Looking-Glass War*, one of his grimmest tales of a British intelligence operation, a novel he deliberately draped in failure. 'Englishness & the box – well, we are <u>all</u> born into boxes, but the Brits perhaps more so than most, which makes them (for me) so interesting – and quaintly universal – to write about,' he wrote to his brother, Tony, in 1999.

Inevitably in this book I found myself in the footsteps of a master – Adam Sisman, my father's biographer. Sometimes I specifically followed his trail to letters. At other times I lighted upon a particularly illuminating passage in a letter – only to find that my choices were the same as his, which was part frustration and part reassurance, in that he had chosen the very letter to extract at length in his book.

My father took against the biography; his supposedly private comments about the book and its author, spread liberally around, amounted to a full-blown campaign. I was unable to read the biography with clear eyes when my father was alive. Rereading it, I feel the full strength of Sisman's erudition, his painstaking research. I've read others' words on its shortcomings, but it found favour with critics, and is a reference book on my father on which I could not but rely, particularly for the early periods of his life. I have tried in this book to use the letters, and my father's own writing, as my principal source, but Sisman's work has always been there as roadmap and backstop.

My father wrote in one early letter that he believed he would be dead when the biography was published; in later correspondence with Sisman he asked for it to be delayed until then; and, by agreement, the book was altered and made acceptable for publication while he lived. He had, after all, negotiated an agreement with one putative biographer, the writer Robert Harris, that the account of his life after 1972 would be published only after his death. 'I think it was a real mistake,' one old friend said to me of the Sisman biography. 'He had lots and lots of secrets.'

Many of those secrets concerned what he called his untidy love life. But I for one had urged him to set a biography in motion, at the last as a means of interviewing the key players, including himself, while they were still alive.

My father mostly covered the tracks of his untidiness. A few years ago I went to visit a woman whom I remembered with vivid, warm affection from my early childhood, who had bounced me on her knee as 'little Timbo'. 'He was a one,' was all she told me. 'He was a one.' When I asked my father about the woman, a couple of years before his death, he told me coldly it was none of my business. He had flirtatiously signed first editions to her worth hundreds if not thousands of pounds today.

I have included here the letters to James and Susie Kennaway, though my father objected to their use by Sisman, because I think they mark a watershed in my father's life: a liberation from his marriage to my mother and a (possibly) more naive self. And we see his love letters in full flow.

It would be tempting to make this book a group of celebrity exchanges. But my own interest harks back to the 1950s and 1960s, the making of le Carré, although my father never talked, or wrote directly, about his intelligence career, speaking of his loyalty to his sources, and to their children.

The only collection of letters that my father gave me was *Yours, Plum*, by P. G. Wodehouse, published in 1990. Two copies of the longer *P. G. Wodehouse: A Life in Letters*, from 2011, were on a cupboard shelf in the Cornwall offices. There was one set of Wodehouse outside each of the two main bedrooms in the house. It was a delight to find the references to Wodehouse dotted through the letters, more and less obviously. (My father wrote of the MI6 spy Nicholas Elliott that he 'looked like a P. G. Wodehouse man-about-town, and spoke like one'.) When my father packed his suitcase for the hospital, *Wodehouse: The World of Jeeves*, the first omnibus of Jeeves and Wooster short stories, was the one volume he took with him. 'I don't feel any power loss yet,' he wrote to the producer Eric Abraham, about writing, in 2006, 'but it waits, I am sure, like P. G. Wodehouse's Fate, just around the corner, armed with a stuffed eel-skin.' Or to the director Sydney Pollack in 1994: 'As Wodehouse would say, I spit myself of age.'

As well as a caricaturist, my father was a famous mimic, a gift remembered by his schoolfriends; his father would call on him to perform. Alec Guinness was a party piece, while a lunch companion remembered being in stitches over his imitations of a past director of MI5. One of my memories is of a dinner at the British ambassador's residence in Bern, after my father had taken me on a tour of his old stamping grounds as an impoverished student. He sat next to a titled European lady, and after she left had captured not just her voice but her attitude, her mannerisms, a little of her soul.

As children, we had the joy of my father reading in his many voices. Our favourites were Sir Arthur Conan Doyle's stories of Caribbean pirates, or the Napoleonic stories, and of course Sherlock Holmes – we thrilled in horror at the scream of 'The Speckled Band', or at the footsteps of a gigantic hound. And he drew – the ceiling of my childhood bedroom was a procession of river creatures, smiling water snakes, a frog and fishes; a dashing pirate guarded my door.

Collecting my father's letters has been an easy task; he left an enormous reservoir of love, admiration and good will. One of the abiding qualities in my father's letters is his generosity of spirit – whether addressed to an emerging author or to a twelve-year-old boy asking how to be a spy. Recipients have been equally generous in sharing them.

My father played games with names in his books, doffing his hat to friends. Sarratt, where his old friend Dick Edmonds lived, became his MI6 training school. Zelide, a designer label on the clothing in *The Little Drummer Girl*, was named for the wife of his friend Rex Cowan. My university girlfriend's name, and perhaps a bit of her character, for Magnus Pym's wife in *A Perfect Spy*. The name of my mother, Ann, for Smiley's wife, glamorous and unfaithful, a sly joke.

My father learnt German from the age of thirteen, from his Sherborne schoolmaster Frank King, who played his boys old gramophone records of Romantic German poetry. After he left Sherborne early for Bern University – which was the closest place to Germany where he could feasibly study – German language and culture became a constant companion on his literary journey, his second soul, to which I have tried to pay tribute in the choice of letters. German, he told *Der Spiegel* in 1989, had 'the fascination of the forbidden. At that time I absolutely refused to speak English and to identify myself as an Englishman.'

The German journalist Yassin Musharbash, who has generously helped with translations for this volume, suggests that German for the teenaged le Carré – on the run from both his father and his rigidly upright public school – represented something of his own that no one could take away, a source of confidence and pride. 'Changing into German is like putting on a tail suit,' le Carré told his Swiss friend Kaspar von Almen in 1955. After 1968's *A Small Town in Germany*, postulating the rise of a new nationalism, he became a public figure in German discourse.

The last place I looked for letters should have been the first. In eight months of tracking down my father's letters, I had never gone through his studio or his desk. They remained almost as they were the day he died: left alone, perhaps as a future le Carré museum. We began a cautious search. For the most part, drawers and shelves were remarkably uncluttered, even empty; my father did not hold with messy desks. But in the lower-left-hand drawer, there was a wad of manuscript sheets tied together with string.

It was my father's account of his MI6 training course, dating from December 2006 – a handwritten manuscript that was transcribed, printed and reworked by hand, again and again. The title was 'Postcards from the Secret Edge'. It was a draft version, though with more detail, of what would become Chapter 1 of *The Pigeon Tunnel*, published in 2016. 'We were a class of six, all men, of varying ages, skills, and experience . . . most of us had done time in other branches of intelligence before being selected. One had been a special soldier in Oman, another was a Chinese expert, I myself was a defector from our own hated rival service, better known as MI5.'

My father told me no more of his intelligence work than he did those people who wrote to him, surprisingly often, asking for information about people, mostly parents, whom they thought might have worked for MI5 or MI6. But the training course had a particular fascination for me. His fellow trainees included my godfather, who subsequently left SIS to pursue a distinguished diplomatic career. Another was Rod Wells.

I knew my father admired and revered Rod Wells, about as much as he hated Kim Philby. He was humbled by Wells's courage under torture by the Japanese, who had caught him constructing a secret radio. There are no records of letters to Wells, but, when my father visited him in Australia many years later, he wrote, in the family visitors' book, 'The old lion's heart beats as ever.' It was an admiration that perhaps had a later echo in my father's fascination with the case of Murat Kurnaz, the Guantanamo survivor who inspired the character of Issa in *A Most Wanted Man*.

Just as the publication of *The Spy Who Came in from the Cold* was a fulcrum of my father's life, so too was his MI6 course. It ended, as he has recorded in *The Pigeon Tunnel*, with the new recruits being told by the weeping head of their training course that George Blake had been exposed as a Soviet spy. A succession of British betrayals followed – Burgess and Maclean, Philby. 'It is only recently that I have come to realise how closely my brief career in British Intelligence coincided with the most convulsive years of its history,' he wrote in the manuscript. 'With each revelation that hit the newsstands, with each British double-agent, real or imagined . . . I had a growing awareness of how much I had witnessed, without being aware of it. But that isn't quite true either. I had been aware.' The sensational scandal of Philby's defection to Moscow was playing out in newspapers before the publication of *The Spy Who Came in from the Cold*.

From that moment, my father's experience of MI6 was stained with betrayal and futility. And it was also as a fresh recruit to MI6 that he received the news that *Call for the Dead* had been accepted for publication. The private spy was on course to become the public writer.

Tim Cornwell
May 2022

Note on Tim Cornwell

1 June 2022

Our brother Tim was the curator of this book – it is his formidable journalistic integrity which governs its route and tone. He ordained a strict objective approach, largely without editorial comment, but we believe he would forgive us this one personal interjection.

Tim collapsed and died of a pulmonary embolism shortly before 9 p.m. last night. We have no idea what happened. It is incomprehensible. He was a funny, loving, gentle fellow who suffered for years from depression and other ills, but did his best to meet his troubles with what he had. The book you hold in your hands is his legacy as well as our father's. He dived into the archive even when it hurt, assembled narrative from chaos, and is responsible for all that is excellent about the collection. We're so proud of him for it.

So long, Tim. We'll miss you so much.

Simon, Stephen and Nick Cornwell

Note on the Text

My father is referred to as John le Carré throughout this book. Of course in his early years there was no John le Carré, only David Cornwell, and he signed his letters almost invariably as 'David'. However, given that for sixty years he was known in public as John le Carré, I made the decision to keep to le Carré in the notes and introductions to the letters.

I have chosen and edited this selection as both the author's son and as the book's editor. My choices are surely more rooted in le Carré's family than another editor's might be. In that context, however, I have tried to edit as objectively and unobtrusively as possible, and in the third person, except in the case of a single letter that was sent to me as a schoolboy, and a moment I witnessed around the dining table.

Le Carré was a prolific letter-writer. In order for the book not to become truly unwieldy many letters had to be excluded. Of course, selection is always a subjective business, but, on the whole, decisions were dictated by whether the letter illuminated the period, the subject or the writer himself – either his work or the relationships that meant a great deal to him. Inevitably there will be correspondents who do not agree with the editorial decisions made but that comes with the territory of a book of this nature and a writer like John le Carré.

In transcribing the letters, we have treated the manuscripts as sacrosanct, and included le Carré's errors and peculiarities. This approach will make for some inconsistencies, but it is intended to provide the most authentic and fluid rendering of his voice. Le Carré was unpredictable in his use of accents, often adding them to words such as 'suede', 'role' and 'elite', with a European flourish; we have retained these. We have silently corrected five place names that were misspelt: Siena, Lots Road, Albemarle Street, Pailin and Caneel Bay.

SCHOOLDAYS

I hated English boarding schools. I found them monstrous and still do, probably because I began my boarding school career at the age of five, at a place called St Martin's Northwood, and did not end it till I was sixteen, when I flatly refused to return to Westcott House, Sherborne, on the solid grounds that I would take no more of such institutions.

– in the new 1991 introduction to *A Murder of Quality*

I wrote to Stalin during the war, while I was at prep school. I promised to do all I could to encourage the opening of a second front, though I was not sure what this meant. I wrote to him again telling him how awful the school regime was, and how I had been beaten unjustly.

– in the *Sunday Times*, 10 November 1985

Le Carré moved from his first school, St Martin's, to board at St Andrew's Pangbourne in 1939, close to his eighth birthday. He wrote at the age of thirteen to his future housemaster at Sherborne School, Reginald Stanley Thompson, described in his obituary for the Old Shirburnian Society as a man of 'unusually strong convictions' and 'profound Christian faith'.

TO R. S. THOMPSON

St Andrew's School
Near Pangbourne
Berks.

24 June 1945

Dear Mr Thompson,

Thanks so much for your letter; I am very much looking forward to coming to Westcott house next term. I can quite believe what you say about lunch!

We have played several matches and have a good few to come. Our first match was against Elstree School, and owing to rain and some poor batting we were just unable to force a draw in their favour. The second was against Bradfield B House Junior Colts which we won easily. The next, yesterday, was against Ludgrove School, which we won easily once again, though after some absolutely frightful fielding!

Do you see much of Philip Simons?[1] I suppose not.

---

1. Philip was a pupil at St Andrew's Pangbourne, but his surname was Simms. He was eight months older than le Carré, so went to Sherborne a year before him. He was in School House at Sherborne, hence le Carré's comment that Thompson probably didn't see much of him. He later worked in the tea industry in Calcutta.

I fully appreciate what you say about the 'birth' of a new house and I will do my very best to help establish a good reputation.

My brother Anthony, whom you saw, if you remember, a long while ago, won a scholarship to Radley about two years ago, and is now flourishing in the first eleven.

Could you please tell me some of the routine and coustoms of your house, so that I shall be sufficiently prepared for next term.

Yours sincerely,
David Cornwell

~

Le Carré's stepmother, Jean Cornwell – always known as Jeannie – went with the thirteen-year-old le Carré to Sherborne. On 22 November 1945 she wrote to Mr Thompson: 'He tells us in his rather staccato letters that he has never seen so much work in his life which has to be done as he puts it "at all costs". In the role of the wicked stepmother I am delighted that he now has to put his nose to the grindstone, and also has to work things out for himself without the guidance of his elder brother.

'I'm glad you find him a friendly and likeable person because I am convinced that your influence on David will be invaluable. Needless to say he wraps me around his little finger and I have to guard constantly against spoiling him!'

Le Carré's adult letters to Jeannie would show a remarkable intimacy and warmth. The fortunes of his father, Ronnie Cornwell, track through his letters to her, as would the fortunes of his own marriage.

Born in November 1916, Jeannie went to an upmarket girls' school and became a studio announcer and manager for the BBC's European Service during the Second World War, a job that included reading bizarre coded messages over the airwaves to the Resistance in Europe. The upshot of a hectic wartime private life, lived under the existential threat of German bombs, was marriage to Ronnie Cornwell in December 1944. She lived through the Great Crash, and she lived through Ronnie's crashes.[2]

In a 1986 interview for the publication of *A Perfect Spy*, le Carré said he received 'no encouragement to read' at home until a stomach operation at the age of seven, when 'a lady who later married my father read me *The Wind in the Willows*'. Jeannie would have been twenty-two. 'I asked her to read it again and she must have read it two or three times,' he continued. 'After that, I read the book myself and everything seemed to fan out from there ... A year later, the same lady took me to John Gielgud's *Hamlet* and that was my introduction to live theatre.'

Ronnie, by contrast, boasted of reading no books – telling his sons he was educated in the 'University of Life' – and discouraged his children from reading them.

Le Carré left Sherborne at the age of sixteen, with the support of his father and the fierce opposition of R. S. Thompson. There was an angry confrontation when he came to collect his belongings from the school.

---

2. Rupert Cornwell's remarks at Jeannie's funeral.

TO R. S. THOMPSON

Tunmers
Chalfont St Peter
Bucks.

Thursday morning
[n.d. but summer 1948]

Dear Mr Thompson,

I am very sorry if I misinterpreted your attitude on Tuesday afternoon, but in view of what had previously occurred you must admit that it was certainly understandable. My omitting to notify you of my arrival was a breach of manners which I deeply regret, but the truth was that, also in view of what had occurred, it seemed to me very difficult to say simply 'I shall be coming down on such-and-such a date to collect my possessions; please make all necessary arrangements.'

If I may, I should like to come down once more to say a slightly more conventional 'goodbye' in the style that I was anticipating on Tuesday afternoon. Would next Saturday be convenient? I would like to leave on the 5.20 or the 6.45 (if they run on Saturday) as I have a friend staying over the week-end.

Yours sincerely,
David

~

On 21 September 1948 Ronnie wrote to Thompson to report that he had 'been giving this matter of withdrawing David from Sherborne the most serious consideration'. The Sherborne archives are rare in containing letters from Ronnie, who later claimed his son learnt the art of letters from his epistolary style.

'I do not disguise the fact that the terms of your letter to me gave me the greatest anxiety and I had to ask myself whether, after all, I was doing the right thing in sending David to Switzerland for the twelve months University Course and taking him away from Sherborne,' Ronnie Cornwell wrote.

'You refer to his mental and spiritual immaturity and I agree wholeheartedly with you that he is at a particularly delicate stage in his life. On the other hand you must not misunderstand me when I say that my first consideration in this matter must always be David, and what you have been good enough to say in your letter amounts to practically the same thing. I am satisfied from what he has told me that whatever would be within his power to give the school during the next twelve months, and whatever they may have to give him, it would be a desperately unhappy year for him. Knowing him as I do I must acquit him entirely of the allegation of cowardice, and I was rather inclined to take the view of a used expression that he was "born young". You said he was impulsive and I know that, too, to be true, and I think that if one is fair to that aspect of the matter much of that impulsiveness could be traced to a desire to acquire knowledge, and with that knowledge some degree of power. I agree with you entirely that he has infinite possibilities and I admit they may be for good or for ill. So it is with other boys, and having given this matter much serious consideration with a full sense of the heavy responsibility which must inevitably rest upon my shoulders finally, I have decided, so far as the visit to Switzerland is concerned, to give the boy his head as I believe in him completely. I sympathise with him in many of the things which he has found irksome during the time he has been at Sherborne. But in fairness to him, you must agree with me, judging by results, that he has not altogether wasted his time from a scholastic point of view. In view of all the circumstances, therefore, he will go off to Switzerland about the 15th or 16th of next month, and he will not be going entirely as a stranger. I have a number of friends there and I have no doubt that he will find other friends on his own account.'

Le Carré long described 'running away' from Sherborne to Bern, but it's clear that Ronnie had a larger hand in this than he described – though his father failed to come through for both school and university fees.

The Reverend Vivian Green was Sherborne's chaplain and a history master. While he did not teach le Carré, who was already specialising as a modern linguist, he vividly remembered shaking hands with the boy when he left.

In October 1948 le Carré left for Bern.

The manner of le Carré's departure from Sherborne, and the falling-out with Mr Thompson, continued to trouble both school-boy and schoolmaster; and both would describe it as the result of the tension between le Carré's home life, the high-wire existence of 'Ronnie's Court', and the Anglican orthodoxy of Thompson's Sherborne.

On 2 May 1952 Thompson wrote his assessment of le Carré in a lengthy reference letter for the rector of Lincoln College, Oxford: 'I regretted his leaving very much indeed and did my best to stop it, but unsuccessfully. It was all the result of an unsatisfactory home back-ground working unhappily on a very sensitive mind. It was the case of a miniature Faustus story. The boy found a disturbing contrast between his very material home background and what he experi-enced at school. He was afraid that he would "lose" his family, which he did not want to do. So he thought that the only thing to do was to leave the place which was causing the conflict within him. That is what he told me, with a good deal of distress, and I have no reason to doubt its truth, because it made sense from my own observations. He came down at the end of the holidays to collect his things and annoyed me extremely by "creeping" into the House and trying to get away without seeing me. I found this out and saw him and we had a very sharp interview, which ended unsatisfactorily, largely my fault. However, I wrote to him afterwards and amongst other things told him I would always do anything for him that I could.

'He is an extremely sensitive boy, artistic and a poet – he won the School Prize poem at the age of 16 – and he has a good brain. Perhaps by now he has steadied down, at any rate I hope so, for he has it in him to do very well at anything to which he gives his mind with conviction. He strikes me as the sort who might become either Archbishop of Canterbury or a first rate criminal!'

Le Carré would speak in the documentary *The Secret Centre*[3] of a 'savagely orthodox and brutal early education'. He said: 'The actual gulf between Sherborne and its very High Church orthodoxy as it then was, and the chaos of domestic life and the terribly funny rackety scenes we lived in, that gulf became unbridgeable and absurd and I found myself tending to both extremes so that I went off and stayed with the Anglican Franciscans at Cerne Abbas for one bit of the holiday, because I really wanted to immerse myself in the meanings of Christianity, I wanted to commit to the extremes of the teachings of the school I was in. On the other hand I then suffered a complete revulsion from the Christianity and the orthodoxy and I began to think that I was the plaything of ridiculous forces, on the one hand this rackety criminality, on the other hand this toffee-nosed high-school style and I fled it really.'

Four years later, as le Carré prepared to go to Lincoln College, Oxford, there was another exchange of letters with Thompson. The two would remain in touch until 1968.

---

3. BBC Two, 26 December 2000.

TO R. S. THOMPSON

Tunmers
Chalfont St Peter
Bucks.
Jordans 3152

5 May 1952

Dear Mr Thompson,

Many thanks for your letter, which, as you may imagine, caused me no little thought. I have of course always known that you would be prepared at any time to help me any way you could. Furthermore I have often thought of coming to see you, not because I have regretted leaving early but because the idea of returning to the place of such unbearable moral conflict has always had a magnetic fascination.

I believe now, more than ever, that what I did was right, though I am sorry that it caused such pain. I have <u>not</u> – as you once suggested – chosen Mammon rather than God. I chose the natural rather than the unnatural; the free rather than the repressed, for the choice was mine as I think you always knew. I have experienced in the years since I left Sherborne so much – pleasant and unpleasant, good and bad, elating and depressing. If I have lingered longer in the 'Courts of the Devil', as you would call it, than I have in others, then it was because I was appalled, not enticed. I found what I always looked for – a basis of comparison, a <u>broader</u> foundation on which to form ones views.

I remember the Headmaster devoted a whole term's scripture to the study of Buddhism. Surely in the light of that fact alone my argument is at least more reasonable?

Neither have I lost from an academic point of view – I studied in Bern most of the things I might have done at Sherborne.

So I am 'neither black nor white' – but I can say that I have begun to study <u>the need</u> for something, whether I believe in it or not. For in all conscience, the need is there. Surely we have

<u>time</u> to view things objectively? Or must we as immature children, lost in fantasy, be forced into a creche of such fabulous implications? I wish I could start from the beginning! But I am happy to come round to belief in something in my own time, as the result of my experiences – in other words, I want to think it out for myself.

If you will accept me on that basis then I will be delighted to see you again. But I could not endure again, yet, what I went through before, for it nearly drove me mad.

Forgive me if I seem to be quoting improbable conditions, but I believe you will understand a little of what I am trying to say.

Yours ever
David

SKI RACER

I took part in the Lauberhorn Race when I was an English bloody fool and nearly killed myself.

– to Bernhard Docke, by email, 20 December 2007

Le Carré later explained his nine months at Bern University as a stepping-stone to German culture, in the closest place to Germany where he could study; but he formed a lasting relationship with German Switzerland as well. Through his Swiss fellow student Kaspar von Almen, he made his first visit to Wengen, the mountain village that hosts the famous Lauberhorn Ski Races, and where le Carré was recruited to the Downhill Only Club, training British ski racers. He built a chalet there in the 1960s.

Bern was also a stepping-stone for le Carré's life in the secret world, where he was recruited by British intelligence to carry out minor tasks as a student, to attend left-wing gatherings and 'to act as a mule in some operation of which I knew nothing'.[1]

For all his bitter recollections of Sherborne School, it was le Carré's German master, Frank King, an officer in the Military Intelligence Service during the war, who had infected him with the German bug. 'He spoke excellent German and he always reminded us in German class, as everyone was demonising Germany with justice, that there was another Germany, an enduring one and a much older one and a wise and loveable Germany,' le Carré recalled. 'And this got into my head and when I fled my public school I insisted on going to Switzerland. Germany was still under occupation and that was not a feasible project.'[2]

At Bern University, he remembered German-Jewish tutors and the company of exiled German children who formed a kind of German caucus. 'I assumed German identity and German culture as a replacement of my own. That's where it began.'

Le Carré never advertised his past either as a ski racer or an illustrator. In later years he skied gently with an upright, graceful, old-fashioned style and never tried to match his sons for speed. At a time when ski racers averaged speeds of about 50 mph over

1. 'Berliner Salon' at the German ambassador's residence, London, 3 March 2020.

2. ibid.

downhill courses, with wooden skis and fixed cable bindings, he skied the Lauberhorn Race; he hit the bank of a railway bridge and was laid out unconscious in Wengen's Eiger Hotel.

The nineteen-year-old le Carré wrote from the slopes to his future wife Ann Sharp, the daughter of a senior officer in the Royal Air Force. They first met in St Moritz in January 1950, when he was eighteen and she seventeen, and Ronnie – she would recall – 'was using David as bait for the daughter of a possible client'. Ten months later they arranged to meet again, at a weekend dance at an RAF group captain's house. Le Carré was by then in the army and going to Austria in the Intelligence Corps. 'After that, well, David wrote letters,' she said, in a personal memoir.

Both le Carré and Ann were looking for shelter from torturous home lives – Ann, from her father, Bobby, an irascible, womanising, compulsively brave flier and veteran of Bomber Command.[3] As a child she had counted bombers out and in from an airfield, flying missions to Germany.

Le Carré skied with his friend Dick Edmonds in the Downhill Only Club in Wengen. And it was for the *Downhill Only Journal*, with Edmonds as editor, that he made many of his illustrations, as well as for the department store run by Edmonds's father.

Julie Kentish-Barnes knew the DHO team in Wengen and began a warm friendship with le Carré that would continue to Oxford. He was 'bar none the best looking thing you have ever seen. They wore white cable stitched sweaters, [with the] blue sky, blue eyes it was devastating. I nearly swooned when I saw them,' she remembered.[4]

Kentish-Barnes's parents adored le Carré, and he embraced them in turn, writing to her years later that 'the happiest days of my late childhood (early manhood) were spent in your house, and on your tennis court and in your swimming pool'. He designed a logo for the family's nursery garden business, Waterers, to go on apple boxes, for

---

3. Air Commodore A. C. H. 'Bobby' Sharp retired from the RAF after an affair with his secretary and went to work in Washington for a defence contractor. He subsequently divorced Ann's mother, and died, aged fifty-one, in 1956.

4. Interview with Tim Cornwell.

twenty-five pounds; it was an apple with a maggot coming out, captioned 'British to the core'. The firm used it for years. Kentish-Barnes drove a 1936 Ford 8, which had a bug deflector; 'He painted a terrific bug with wings on the front of it,' she said.

Le Carré was happy skiing in Wengen, Kentish-Barnes believed, at a distance from his father's talk of 'my Rolls and my silver'. But he drew dark pictures, as well as his skiing sketches. Decades later le Carré would parlay his skiing days into a film script, 'Schüss', intended for his son Stephen, a gifted skier, screenwriter and film-maker. But the sport had changed. 'Skiing,' he wrote to Kentish-Barnes in 2016, 'looks awful now: too fast, too easy, too crowded, and too badly behaved. I'm so glad we had the best of it.'[5]

The drawings for Dick Edmonds would be used in a montage at le Carré's memorial at Micklefield Hall, the Edmondses' family home, on 19 October 2021.

TO ANN SHARP

Palace Hotel
Wengen
Oberland
Switzerland

18 December 1950

Please note new address. D.

My darling,
'Après-ski' – that wonderful feeling of tiredness after a day's ski-ing, when every muscle aches and shivers. Fatigue, mentally and physically, combined with the satisfaction of having achieved something. And today we have achieved something – for in a temperature of 17°–20° below zero we made four runs of five miles odd, and the snow was blowing with a hard, cold

5. To Julie Kentish-Barnes, 14 March 2016.

Le Carré provided illustrations for the *Downhill Only Journal* in Wengen.

wind that bit into our clothes and bodies. Your goggles clog, and your eyebrows grow stiff and icy, and eventually your trousers grow stiff too, so that every time you bend your knee, it grates against frozen material, like canvas. You can only see a few yards, and you don't know where you are, but you follow the chap in front of you, but keep clear of his track, and woe betide you if you fall. One of the team lost a ski today – it came off on a sharpish turn and went straight on 150 yards down hill and we never found it.

And then to return to the Hotel, sit down by the fire and talk about it all, to tell stories of the day's skiing, of how this corner is with the new snow, or that gully or hill. Net result of the day – one chap with a twisted ankle and another with one ski – and everyone pleased with himself and apprehensive about tomorrow. But tomorrow can wait.

And yet the feeling of loneliness, a sinking empty sort of feeling in the stomach, the knowledge that something is missing and that that something is you – this alone spoils – but only in a way – a perfect day. Yet the stupid thing is, I am happy that that is the case!

Darling, I will see you soon – I must. I will ring up on Christmas Eve at 8.30 British Time and tell you how everything is.

It is conceivable that your letters addressed to c/o DHO Team may take some time to reach me, as the Club-office here is not open yet. But Hotel Palace, Wengen will get me direct from now on.

God bless, my darling; I love you with all my heart
David

to ANN SHARP

Palace Hotel
Wengen

20 December 1950

My darling Ann,

Today we started jumping in earnest – but only 15–20 yards. Each day we will do four or five jumps from now on as part of our training. Believe it or not, it is the most wonderful sensation in the world, for on reaching a certain height you feel as if the <u>air</u> is carrying you – you float as smoothly as a bird. Aesthetically, it is the most satisfactory side of ski-ing perhaps. The sun came out this morning for the first time, and we spent the first half of the day skiing in brilliant sunshine, with new snow up to the knees and higher. It was wonderful, my darling, like riding on the crest of a high wave, with blue sky above and foaming sea below. That is real skiing, that is where the mind, as it were, overflows and inspires the body to achievement – all of which sounds rather stupid, but once you have done it you can never forget it. That is why perhaps I want you with me here more than anywhere else. We raced again at midday – that is, were timed over certain stretches of 5–7 miles, and we all of us did quite well. No injuries! Our team is already depleted from 10 to 6, so we are now 'at minimum strength'.

I received a wire from Tony,[6] and he arrives here tomorrow – it will be very pleasant having him here although I don't quite see what he is going to do. Then after Christmas he is going to Grindelwald, near here, to a chalet for 2 weeks, so he should enjoy that.

Again, as at the end of every day, every muscle aches and ties itself into knots – and today we have done more actual ski-ing than before. In the afternoon – slalom (between sticks)

---

6. Anthony 'Tony' Cornwell, le Carré's brother, older by two years.

and jumping. This evening we all had massage – which always makes me giggle.

Darling Ann, I will try desperately hard not to break anything, for I do so want to see you again soon. But if necessary I will hobble round Europe with both feet in plaster, if only to be with you for a while. I love you, my darling – you seem to have become my life-blood, the foundation of all my hopes and ambitions.

David x

O darling I don't want to stop writing to you – for it seems the only time when I can tell you I love you – and I do so desperately and sincerely. Does it then seem stupid that I tell you this in every letter and with every breath? My dearest darling Ann, I love you, I love you.

～

TO ANN SHARP

Palace Hotel & National Wengen

10 January 1951

My darling,

I've been to Zurich for several days on business. This morning I trained again with the team for the first major international meeting which is on Saturday – and had a frightful fall, the result of which is that I am once again in bed, having twisted some muscles in my left thigh. It had to come sooner or later. I may only be in bed for a day or two – in which case the doctor says he can bind up my thigh and I may be able to race on Saturday after all.

Oh my darling, darling Ann, I need you desperately, as I have never needed anyone. Please, please tell me when you are

'Ja, Ja schnow very good next year.'

coming. Write to Rosemary again, if necessary, but please find out, darling, and let me know. It is not long now.

Thank you for your letters – they make me very happy.

The course for Saturday's race is nothing short of amazing. One of the Italian team broke his leg today and knocked himself out. The Norwegian team is here and they go <u>telemarking</u> down the slalom course!

The German Team is also training and they look pretty good. The Americans are chronic and the French are brilliant. The Swiss Team is stolid and will probably win – they know the course like the back of their hand. The course is supposed to be faster than ever before. We have had no snow for ten days so you can imagine it is quite icy.

Sorry my writing is a bit groggy, but I have just been given some pills to make me sleep. But I want to talk to you so much, to think of you & imagine I am holding you in my arms, and you are pressing up against me as if you were really a part of me. I want to dream of your deep, soft eyes and of your voice. To think for a second you are here, talking to me. To suppose you are sitting here beside me.

It won't be long now, darling. Sorry this is rather a peculiar letter – I'll stop now & get it posted. I'm getting up on Friday. Darling, I love you terribly

David

∼

Back in Britain for his National Service, le Carré did his basic training in the regular army, and was selected for the Intelligence Corps.

TO ANN SHARP

The Intelligence Corps Depot
Maresfield Camp

[n.d.[7]]

Ma chère Véronique,

A little letter to amuse, because although I love you no less than usual, but perhaps a little more, it's in a quiet contented way this evening.

Today D. played spies and was caught and put in prison. Escaped in true E. Phillips Oppenheim[8] by laying out an Other Rank guard and removing his braces & tying him up, and stealing his revolver. Masqueraded as a publican from Doncaster. All rather fun, but cut my hand a little in the fight.

But as I was tying up the soldier with his braces, and keeping him still by putting my knee between his legs, he looked up at me and said 'Excuse me sir, but is this <u>all</u> part of the exercise?' All rather sad.

Anyway, I was recaptured – and taken for reinterrogation – which really was rather tough because I was

1 stripped
2 struck
3 confined to Barracks

But I never got my clothes back – so I am writing to you in a state of nature.

Comme toujours
David

---

7. Le Carré wrote to Ann from Maresfield Camp in 1950, which is the likely year for this letter, but also in August 1953 and September 1954.

8. Edward Phillips Oppenheim, 1866–1946, a popular English novelist whose stories 'were peopled with sophisticated heroes, adventurous spies, and dashing noblemen' (britannica.com). Ironically, Graham Greene would liken le Carré's writing to Oppenheim's in their 'passage of arms' over Kim Philby.

Ma chère Véronique,

A little letter to amuse, because although I love you no less than usual, but perhaps a little more, its in a quiet contented way this evening.

Today D. played spies. And was caught and

put in prison. Escaped in true E. Phillips Oppenheim by laying out an Other Rank guard and removing his braces & tying him up, and stealing his revolver.

Masqueraded as a publican from Doncaster. tel rather fun, but cut my hand a little in the fight.

But as I was tying up the soldier with his braces - and keeping him still by putting my knee between his legs, he looked up at

~

*In 1951 le Carré was serving in Austria as a military intelligence offi-
cer.[9] He was based at the Palais Meran in Graz, and drew on the
experience in* A Perfect Spy. *He arrived in the country less than two
years after the release of Graham Greene's* The Third Man, *set and
filmed on location in Vienna.*

TO ANN SHARP

[Postmark] 30 March 1951

Darling,

I received your letter this morning – thank you very much.
New address – POSTLAGERND (i.e., Post Restante) GRAZ
(HAUPTPOST) STYRIA AUSTRIA. Please just put 'D.
Cornwell'. I am going to Venice for a few days soon – leav-
ing Vienna tomorrow morning, and going through the Russian
zone by car. I am spending today walking around Vienna again.
There is a Communist meeting tonight I shall attend. They are
very interesting.

Food here is excellent and cheap. Gin is 3d per glass, beer
sixpence a pint, Brandy 4d a tot. Just for interest. I'm not
exploiting the situation more than usual.

Life is very good – opera and intrigue. What could be more
entertaining?

---

9. 'In Graz, Austria, as a National Service officer in field security during the quadri-
partite occupation of the country, I ran my first very own messenger boy: a twinkly,
blue-eyed Austrian scoundrel called Freddy with a motorbike and a quick tongue,'
le Carré told an audience at the Southbank Centre in 2017. 'Freddy traded porno-
graphic photographs for military gossip with Russian sentries guarding the Soviet
airbase at Wiener Neustadt. It is not widely known but, between us, Freddy and I
averted a third world war.'

Do you want a secretarial job in Vienna? There is always a chance I could get you one. Perhaps it wouldn't be quite the thing with the family.

Love to all – at least to you, Darling. Must fly, believe it or not. Sometimes one has to work.

David

~

TO ANN SHARP

[Austria, presumably Graz]

[Postmark] 2 April 1951

<u>Sorry – only paper. D.</u>

It has been a warm spring day and a cool summer evening; the weeping willows are rich and green now, and the birch trees silver and shiny in the sun. I travelled down here three days ago in the same compartment as thirty Russian soldiers – the long carriages, that have no partitions. We smoked cigarettes together, but they refused to speak to me, or even say 'Goodbye' when they got out of the train. This afternoon I climbed a hill outside Graz – which is a very beautiful town – and saw the whole fields of red slate rooves spread out underneath me, and the river winding through, and smoke coming up from the chimneys. No people, just the buildings. It seemed impossible that this is the home of practically every underground political movement in Austria, was the seat of Nazism in 1939, is a hot-bed of Communism now, and the up & coming breeding ground for international intrigue of every discription. All you could see was the smoke & the rooves & the river. The sun was warm and bright and everything so peaceful. Funny really. I hope to be able to pick up any letters you have written me to-morrow, but am not sure when I can write again. Probably soon though. Darling, I love you. You cannot know how much I want you. I am lonely, and at night I long and yearn for you beyond words. And during the day, I suddenly stop and think of you and imagine your face close to mine, and your eyes looking into mine, and I wish like anything you were here. I love you darling, I love you.

Must stop.
D.

P.S. Got the photos yet?

~

to ANN SHARP

Corinthia[10]

Midday, Monday [23 May 1951]

Darling,
Today, sun and a fresh fall of snow on the Dolomites, a cold sharp wind. A smell of Spring, and 'Vermouth Syphon'. This evening, the night train to Vienna, and with luck by tomorrow morning I should have further news of where I shall go next, for I am still 'en route'.

I wish you were here – it is very beautiful. A small, unspoilt village, with a pub, a couple of shops and a group of houses with wooden walls and steep grey rooves. Cobbled streets, and the vigour and happiness of a real spring day. The river and the lake & the mountains. The fields look young and green, as if they were breathing in the warm sun and letting the wind run across them like spray over the side of a ship. You would never

---

10. Presumably Carinthia, the federal state of southern Austria.

think that this land had ever been a battlefield, that these cottages had been pill-boxes, and the rivers tank traps. This is no country for soldiers and war. Rather, for music and painting, for poetry & happiness.

I wonder how Vienna will look now – will the trees that run along the broad streets be in bud yet, the river swollen from the melted snow?

O darling – this is life! I only hope I will continue to think so. I only wish that above all you were here to see it with me.[11] To see this happen – this great transformation from the grey indifference of England to the bewitching colours and the bright rebirth of Spring in Austria. You could half close your eyes and look into the sun, and perhaps you would see, as I do, the myriad of colours, like a live rainbow, or sun on a painted parasol outside a French café in the Champs Elysées. You could drink the air in these clean, smokeless cities, and laugh at nothing, as I do. But one day we will see it, both of us, together. We can wait till then.

Oh I know this is nonsense – it can't all be true. But sometimes I feel as if I had woken up from hibernation in England, and cleared my lungs of the soot of 'dark satanic mills' to breathe again the beauty and the peace of the outside world. And the more I enjoy & love it, the more I miss you, my darling, who are the only person who could ever enjoy and love it with me – who could swim in this great lake of pretence. It must all be an illusion – but I claim for both of us the right to dream until we wake. For wake we must – and I fear that more than death – and believe me, I am afraid to die too.

God bless
David

---

11. The couple met again when le Carré stayed with Ann's family for a weekend on home leave in the summer of 1951.

OXFORD AND MARRIAGE

And at Oxford, while studying German – by which I mean of course the translation of the Bible into Gothic by the fourth-century bishop Wufila – I had posed as a crypto-Communist and selflessly offered myself to a visiting cultural attaché from the Soviet Embassy in London: so just the sort of young, idealistic, bourgeois leftist that any decent KGB talent spotter would have leapt at.

– 'An Evening with George Smiley', Southbank Centre,
7 September 2017

I wasn't just broke, but – halfway through my second year – seriously insolvent, since my father had recently made one of his spectacular bankruptcies, and his cheque for my term's fees had bounced. And though my College was behaving with exemplary forbearance, I really saw no way to remain in Oxford for the rest of the academic year.

But that was to reckon without Reggie,[1] who drifted into my room one day, probably with a hangover, shoved an envelope at me and drifted out. It contained a cheque made out to me by his Trustees, large enough to pay off my debts and keep me at university for the next six months.

– 'To Reggie with thanks', Chapter 34, *The Pigeon Tunnel*

---

1. Reginald Bosanquet, at New College, Oxford, future journalist and ITN's *News at Ten* anchor.

Le Carré was interviewed for admission to Oxford in 1952 by the Reverend Vivian Green, the former Sherborne master who was now senior tutor at Lincoln College. He became le Carré's mentor and lifelong friend, the Oxford don who gave him the 'inner life' of the bookish George Smiley.

Le Carré's Oxford years saw his marriage to Ann Sharp, amid the continuing misadventures of his father, Ronnie, the future model for Rick Pym of *A Perfect Spy*. At his home Tunmers, in Chalfont St Peter, Ronnie 'entertained the Australian test team, patronised Arsenal, bought racehorses, dressed in dapper fashion and lived lavishly', wrote Vivian Green, inhabiting 'the never-never land of floating companies and speculative adventures'.[2]

In future letters to his stepmother Jeannie, le Carré twice referred to an 'Oxford novel', which he was writing in the wake of *The Spy Who Came in from the Cold*. It has not been traced.

---

2. 'A Perfect Spy: A Personal Reminiscence' by Vivian Green, in Alan Bold's *The Quest for le Carré* (1988).

TO ANN SHARP

40 St John Street
Oxford

6 October 1952

Darling –

Arrived here this evening to find your letter waiting for me, but alas no writing paper with which to reply. Giving way to indecent haste, I am using this prosaic and strictly practical foolscap, for which please forgive me.

I have spent three days phoning to Switzerland and Paris with no success; three foolish, dabbling days with neither start nor finish, ambition nor achievement.[3] But that is over and done with, for henceforward I am a strictly intellectual beast with rapidly growing hair and an exotic taste for Saudi-arabian[4] cigarettes with gold spats. One rather inhibiting factor is that I have to wear – according to the College and University Statutes – 'dark lounge suit, white shirt, white tie, black shoes, gown and mortar board' for the matriculation ceremony which is shortly to be held in my – and other people's – honour. Oxford is full of all the colours in the rainbow just now – a crazy time with golden and rust-coloured leaves on the trees and swirling winds that come tumbling down the streets as if they were running away from each other – it is getting cold too, with a bite in the evening air not unlike St Moritz at dusk after a sunny day. The whole of Nature seems to have made up its mind to wake people up at the end of the Summer. I think there's a smell of Christmas in the air.* I wish people sold hot chestnuts on the streets as they did in Bern. Then I think I would have all I wanted!

---

3. Le Carré had gone to Switzerland with an alleged Rothschild baroness to reclaim a chest of treasures, on one of Ronnie's wild schemes.

4. An old-fashioned usage.

Played golf with Tony yesterday evening. Terrible! Tony has become far more human I think, and seems to have overcome a great deal of his American influence.[5] Foreigners are a menace, aren't they?

And yes I do think of you, darling – in a dozen different ways and for a dozen different reasons. Sometimes I wonder how I can ever be without you – sometimes in gratitude for your love. Sometimes I'm worried, for there must be shadow where there is light; and sometimes I am even frightened by how much you know about me! But you know that I love you.

I seem to have written a terrible amount – but, if you enjoy reading it, I owe it to you, for I have not written for a long time.

I have the drawings here with me – but I cannot do any fashion plates for the moment. I will try and send them* to you for use as samples. I hope it works, your plan.

Now – God bless darling
David

[*at the bottom of the letter*] *I've said that before
*The drawings

∾

TO ANN SHARP

Lincoln College
Oxford

26 May 1953

---

5. Tony Cornwell, his elder brother, had been offered a scholarship to Bowdoin College in Maine, and he took it up in place of what would have been his last year at Cambridge University. Ronnie's cheque for Tony's Cambridge fees had also bounced.

Darling,

Thank you a thousand times for your letter. I feel a free man again. I have given up the production of a German play I was producing – the cast was hopeless and so was I. As always, I seem to be assailed by a fit of guilt when I write to you – I still have sent you no drawing,[6] and the frequency with which I write is vague and hopelessly undependable.

We are having a sudden and fierce heat wave which has caught everyone on the wrong foot. But somehow it has driven me quite mad. I can't work, I have no desire to do anything but drink iced beer. I wish you [were] here because I happen to feel terribly amorous – a biological phenomenon resulting from the tropical climate which has descended on us.

What is happening here? Oh yes – Eights week and garden parties by the river, May Balls and Coronation Dances, Oxford covered in red, white and blue, and awful cut-out photographs of the Queen. There is Coronation beer, Coronation tooth-paste and Coronation licensing laws. I don't think I shall go to London for the Coronation, though. London is a swarming mass of little people dressed in ribbons, it's fearfully hot and smells of fish and chips. Vice flourishes too over the Coronation – more girls in the streets than ever before, more spivs selling nonsense souvenirs and forged tickets, more hypocritical shop keepers exploiting patriotism. And above the shouting and the giggling of the crowds, the microphones of patriotic cant lift their pompous voices – in the newspapers, on the wireless, in cinemas and television. Behind them come the men who must work hardest of all – little men with bald heads who crouch over ledgers and budgets twenty hours a day, and scratch away with long quills. They make sure that the raison d'etre is not forgotten – that money is not sacrificed but won. What a far better investment it is not to sell the Crown Jewels,

---

6. While le Carré once had ambitions to be a commercial artist, encouraged by Ann, he would eventually focus single-mindedly on his writing, though he continued to draw for children and grandchildren, including murals and caricatures for his children's bedrooms.

but to line them for view on a queen's head, for dollars, francs, pesetas, rupees, marks, obols or what you will.

What a pity that a national gift for tradition has become a national opportunity for dishonesty.

On June 5th I have been invited to a Girl's School Dance from an unknown agency! Quite funny. I'm simply dying to go. I shall cause chaos if I'm given half a chance. I'm going with Robin Cooke.[7]

Went out drinking to the Trout last night. Going up to London this evening for a cocktail party at the Soviet Embassy.[8] More anon.

I love you darling –
David

~

TO VIVIAN GREEN

Oxford Canning Club[9]

14 October 1953

Dear Mr Green,

I wonder if you would like to reply to a paper I am reading to the Canning Club this term? The paper is an attempt to trace

7. Robin Cooke was le Carré's friend from Sherborne School and an Oxford contemporary. In the summer of 1952 the two men went on tour selling copies of the *Cricketer* magazine, then owned by Ronnie.

8. For MI5, le Carré was posing as a left-wing sympathiser in part to persuade the Soviet intelligence services to recruit him. The effort failed, but le Carré later joked about his repeated viewings of *Battleship Potemkin* with Soviet Embassy officials. Ann was not indoctrinated into le Carré's MI5 work until 1954.

9. The Oxford Canning Club was founded in 1861 to promote and discuss Tory principles. Le Carré was also a member of the Communist Party and the Gridiron Club. 'It was possible to be eccentric, in those days,' he said, at the 'Berliner Salon' in March 2020.

the reflection of German Literature since its earliest stages on the German Nation in its most recent development. Much of it will be in lighter vein, and it can scarcely be a comprehensive effort, since it only lasts 35–40 minutes. If you reply, you will be expected to speak for 20–25 minutes.

The date would be the Wednesday in the sixth week of term. Could you let me know fairly soon what you feel about this, so that I can have the programmes printed?

Yours sincerely,
David Cornwell

～

At the age of twenty-one,[10] *the young le Carré saw his mother for the first time in sixteen years. She revealed a series of distressing details about her former husband's criminal past and portrayed him as a dangerously charming conman. Le Carré confronted his father and, shortly afterwards, fled Tunmers, Ronnie Cornwell's Buckinghamshire home, to stay with his friend Nigel Althaus at his family's sixteenth-century rectory. He wrote two letters on 7 April 1954: an illustrated one to Ann, and another, very different in tone, to Vivian Green.*

TO ANN SHARP

Yew Place
Farnham Royal
Bucks.

[Postmark] 7 April 1954

---

10. Le Carré maintained in *The Pigeon Tunnel* and elsewhere that he met his mother at the watershed age of twenty-one after 'sixteen hugless years'. Ann's private memoir pins the date at February 1954, making him twenty-two.

Darling [*illustration of mouse*]

Staying with Nigel Althaus[11] in a big and beautiful [*house*] with trees, and a farm with sleepy pigs. We play [*tennis*] in the [*rain and rainclouds*] and it has been raining jolly hard, too.

A long letter from Tony saying that he is doing much much better, earns 80$ a week and is very happy – hopes to have a [*illustration of a car*] or rather a [*illustration of fast car*] very soon.

So perhaps we'll all go out in it one day [*four people in an open-top car: see next page*].

So very much love from
<u>Maggot</u>

<u>Beware of the bandits</u>
[*Illustration of a bandit and a young woman: see p. 47*]

∾

TO VIVIAN GREEN

Yew Place
Farnham Royal
Bucks.

As from: 11 Lincoln Road
Oxford

7 April 1954

Dear Mr Green,

I went and saw my father and told him everything my mother had told me that was relevant – namely just about everything except the actual circumstances supposedly surrounding his

11. Nigel Althaus won scholarships to Eton and Magdalen College, Oxford, before joining his father and grandfather in the City.

Darling

Staying with Nigel Blotham in a big and beautiful [house] with trees, and a farm with [pig] sleepy pigs. We play [tennis] O in the [garden] and it has been raining jolly hard, too.

A long letter from Tom saying that he is doing much much better, earns 80 £ a week and is very happy — hopes to have a [car] or rather a [car] very soon.

So perhaps will all go out in it one day

first marriage. After an awful lot of ducking and emotional side-tracking he said 'so what?' I told him that I wanted to be independent of him, at least for a few years, and that I considered this meant financial independence too. He was terribly upset, and said that the irony of his life was that everything he had done for us (my brother & myself) had separated us further from him, that just at the very moment in his life when he most needed my companionship, he should be denied it, etc., etc.

However, if I decided to leave home, he would sell the estate and divorce my stepmother. The second of these threats was only inferred – 'and Jean must go too, David, she must go.'

I told him I considered his marriages had both broken up as a result of his own actions, and that he couldn't rely on me to hold the second one together.

The position now is that I am taking whatever money he will give me to stay on at Oxford, with no obligation whatever. I don't think this position will last long – but I don't think he will attempt anything at all risky to get me back into the home. The thing that staggered him really was my apparent disinterest in the ultimate promise of plenty, the fact that I had negotiated with Kemsley's[12] and was prepared to go down immediately if there was no way of staying on at Oxford, rather than be on the end of a rope.

At the moment, therefore, things are still in the wind, but it's a very much clearer and better wind than before, and I can see the possibility, sadly, of living away from home with an allowance until I finish at Oxford.

Yours ever
David

P.S. I feel I should repeat my gratitude to you for all your help and advice. I really don't know what I should have done without

---

12. Kemsley Press, the newspaper group that included the *Sunday Times*. Le Carré had been given an introduction by MI5.

the assistance of yourself and Sir James Barnes.[13] I do believe that the light is shining through the trees a bit, and that before long things will be settled at least for the time being. So thank you very much indeed for everything. D.

~

July 1954 saw Ronnie's spectacular and very public bankruptcy. 'Made £15,000 In a Day – Man Now Owes £1,359,000' read the headline in the London Evening News. *'A forty-eight-year-old London property dealer who formed sixty companies and bought about four thousand properties admitted in the Bankruptcy Court today that he had contingent liabilities of £1,359,000.'*

TO VIVIAN GREEN

Intelligence Corps Centre
Maresfield Camp
Nr Uckfield
Sussex

[n.d. but likely October 1954[14]]

Dear Vivian,
Thank you so much for your card, and for consenting to marry Ann and myself.
    I have just spent a terrible two weeks at home – so much so that I am positively relieved to find myself back in the army for

---

13. Sir James Barnes, who shared interests with Ronnie in Arsenal football club, had helped to find le Carré a place at Lincoln College.

14. In October 1954 le Carré was lecturing at the Intelligence Corps Centre at Maresfield Camp on German intelligence services 1939–45, and Germany and Germans in general.

OXFORD LEFT

SPECIAL PEACE ISSUE

TRINITY 1954   **1,000 PRINT**   **SIXPENCE**

1,500 SIGNATURES TO OXFORD APPEAL

THE Oxford Appeal for disarmament and the abolition of the Hydrogen Bomb is now gaining momentum. As we go to press about fifteen hundred signatures have been collected. So far the best response has come from St. Hilda's, Exeter, St. Cath's, Ruskin, Somerville, Jesus, Lincoln—and Balliol.

Since the beginning of term there has been widespread support in the University for an Oxford contribution to the world-wide efforts to preserve world peace. The very broadness of the movement in Oxford is an indication that new sections of opinion have become aware of the great danger to peace and the necessity for unified action —the only way by which peace can be preserved. And unity of action has been achieved. A mere catalogue of the O.U. Hydrogen Bomb Campaign Committee will demonstrate this: Charles Taylor (Chairman, Oxford Secretary, World University Service); Michael Pike (Ex-Editor of "Cherwell"); Anthony Thwaite (Editor of "Isis"); Nicholas Waterhouse (Ex-Editor of "Oxford Tory"); Jeremy Isaacs (Chairman, O.U. Labour Club); Ralph Samuel (Ex-Secretary, O.U. Communist Club); Donald Matthew (Chairman, O.U. Student Christian Movement); Raghavan Iyer (President of the Union); Gordon Snell ("Isis" Editorial Staff); Adrian Mitchell (Secretary, O.U. Poetry Society); Stella Aldwinckle (Chairman, O.U. Socratic Club). Further, the actual text of the petition was proposed by Mr. Michael Heseltine, a prominent member of OUCA. The desire from all sides for a common point of action was shown by the compromise reached which resulted in the present text. Indeed the only real opposition has come from New College's extreme Right-Wing clique (Bingham, Mac-Beth, Hall) and their satellites.

The most hopeful effect of the campaign has been the sudden realisation among undergraduates that politics is not another (and a nastier) game, but must be the concern of every human being, if we are to escape universal catastrophe. The petition and the meeting, the articles and the editorials upon the issue, the discussions in J.C.Rs and bars, have welded the campaign firmly into Oxford's consciousness. Cynicism, that greatest threat to the intellectual integrity and the future of Oxford, is on the retreat. Anthony Thwaite wrote in "Isis": ". . . no longer is it true that 'the best lack all conviction,

"the natural but unreasoning fear" (the counter-petition leaflet).

1

Le Carré would furnish illustrations for the *Oxford Left*, as he worked to infiltrate and inform on Communist sympathisers at Oxford, including Stanley Mitchell, its editor, with whom he attempted to find a reconciliation more than forty years later.

two weeks. I won't bore you with details – but the conclusions I have come to are these –

That if I stay at Oxford another year, I shall have to be dependent on my father to a certain extent – during the vacations at least. That every time I take money from him, or even a meal, I am acquiescing to his way of life, and weakening my own position. That as long as I stay in England I shall not be able to get away from him. No one who is anything at all can live with him – Communist, Christian or what you will, for his very existence is a complete mockery of any moral consideration. So much is surely undeniable. We are also both aware of the doubtful morality of postponing this issue.

But it is not so much this last point that troubles me, as the fact that if I live with him or under him for another year, I shall be quite incapable of coming to any moral decisions whatever. It was you – whose wisdom I respect more than anyone's – who mentioned in your last letter that Ann & I might be able to give to our children what we had both been denied. Having made a stand, and having tried to shake myself out of a state of indifference, I find I have slipped back into that horrible state where I have no more resistance to his demands or his way of life. What do I do if he offers me five pounds, and I know that he has not only borrowed it from someone else, and owes it thousands of times over to people much more deserving than I, but also has refused the same sum to my step mother for housekeeping?

I suppose I am making issues out of things over which I have no control, but really – if ever one should act as one feels, and as one thinks is right, then why not here? Nothing, frankly, is worth the price; yet what else can I do? I am not exaggerating – things are in a terrible state at home – one of my step-mother's aunts had a cheque for £1000 returned 'account closed', in proposed repayment of an unsecured loan of her entire savings. She has £28 left. The loan was made in Spring, & was to be repaid entirely by the end of September. The Ansorges, who live opposite, are owed £2,500. He is retired ICS[15] – the figure constitutes the majority of his capital. He (Father) has mortgaged my step-mother's family laundry without the knowledge of the family of directors, who signed the whole thing away. My step mother discovered this by accident three or four weeks ago, and so it goes on & on & on. And so after too much thought and too much banking on the future, I have written to Kaspar[16] and Lothar Schreuers[17] asking them to find me a teaching job in Switzerland. If one can be found that offers any prospects at all, then I shall go down from Oxford, teach, draw and take an eventual doctorate at Bern.

I am only too aware of the great disadvantages of not having a degree, but Oxford isn't everything – to me the present state of affairs at home is everything and I must do something about it, or sink. I've always wanted to become a Christian, and try & live like one. Ann is a very religious girl and I think together we could manage. I know it's all very impulsive and silly, and probably immature too, but what else can I really do? There is the additional temptation of this offer from 'Kemsleys' – but again, I am committing myself to something I don't really want to do. Finally, if I don't do as I think I should now, I never will.

So Vivian please forgive me, after all you've done, and try to understand. I always felt that you were in a false position anyway – advising as a tutor and helping as a Christian, if you see what I mean. That sounds rude but it isn't meant to be a bit – quite the reverse.

The Bears[18] will not suffer from this anyway. I've done a fair amount on them, and wherever I am, I shall certainly complete the drawings in as short a time as possible; I read the story to

---

15. Indian Colonial Service.

16. Kaspar von Almen, his friend from Bern.

17. Lothar Schreuers lived above le Carré in Bern.

18. Le Carré was working to illustrate an unpublished book by Green called 'The Bears', in which Alpine bears foil an exploiting capitalist's plan to dam a beautiful valley.

the 2 children and they both (5 & 8) absolutely loved it. I do too. Charlotte said my bears looked like kangaroos in silhouette, which is quite true so I've changed them a bit.

As soon as I hear from Kaspar or Lothar I will let you know. Until then I see little point in telling the College – I shall no doubt forfeit the term's deposit and cause a great deal of inconvenience besides, if I can find a job, but I'm afraid I cannot prevent this. But until I am 100% certain of going down this term, I see no advantage to be gained. Similarly our arrangements for getting married are also in the melting pot, and we had better see you about this some time.

I am here until Saturday morning, when I shall be coming to Oxford.

Yours ever,
David

~

Von Almen's family owned hotels around Wengen.

TO KASPAR VON ALMEN

Intelligence Corps Centre
Maresfield Camp
Nr Uckfield
Sussex

3 October 1954

My dear Kaspar,
When I was in Switzerland last summer, we talked about the possibility that I would be able to get a job as a teacher somewhere in Switzerland. The situation at home has become so unbearable that I have been thinking in all seriousness of moving to

Switzerland with my beloved (I got engaged two weeks ago – you don't know the woman I'm afraid). Even though my dad has gone bankrupt to the tune of £1¼ million, we both – Ann and I – have means enough to stay in Switzerland for at least three months, and if it came down to it, longer than that. We'd live in Bern I think as that would be the easiest place to find a job.

You said that you might be able to introduce me to someone who would need an English teacher (European literature also a possibility, especially German). If it's still a possibility I would be extremely grateful if you were able to do something.

This is not an uncalculated and foolish flight from nothing – but a seriously considered plan to get away one and all from things over here, and begin a new life. I will take on <u>any</u> academic job I am offered to begin with. You know I can do other things besides – I can teach drawing, produce English plays, take part in school sport or anything like that. My fiancée can also teach if necessary, and we can make things work, I know.

The price I am paying must be weighed against this – I shall not have my university degree <u>but</u> after two years at Oxford, I shall I think be able to take my degree at Bern; I shall have the preliminary knowledge and the time to do this.

Kaspar – if you can help me find a job for three years I believe I can make things go well. Money is <u>not</u> the problem. The problem is to live happily with my wife away from the degrading publicity of the present court case, to live an intelligent life. I am miserably tired of trying to live for the future indefinitely. I want to live for the present.

I am not going to make any Teutonic outcries about friendship. If you can help in finding me a job then you know that you will have our gratitude.

And – when you have both met Ann and got to know her – perhaps we shall have a chance of entertaining you & Erica in Switzerland, a pleasant thought.

If however you can't help, don't please worry and I'll find something somehow. Vivian Green will, I think, also be able to advise me on this.

I am doing 2 weeks camp at present, an annual cross to bear, for the gold has long worn off the gingerbread.

Write as soon as you can to

Lincoln College
Oxford
England

Ever
David

~

On the heels of Ronnie's bankruptcy, le Carré was reaching for the security of marriage to Ann – whose father's womanising had led her own parents to divorce. 'I don't think anyone is as well equipped to combine the task of mistress and wife for D as you,' he wrote to her from Maresfield. 'I adore you, angel mouse, and you are very beautiful.' With Green's help he made the decision to leave Oxford for a year and teach at Edgarley Hall, near Glastonbury, since 1945 the junior school of Millfield School.

TO VIVIAN GREEN

9 St John Street
Oxford

29 October 1954

Dear Vivian,

I feel I must write and let you know that had it not been for your help and your friendship, I do not think I would have found anywhere near so satisfactory an answer to the present problem. I won't indulge in one of those awful Tutonic eulogies – but I do feel very deeply how much I owe to your help and understanding, and I want to thank you very much.

I know that Ann and I will find the peace we are looking for, and although it may be a bad way for me to go about becoming a Christian, i.e. waiting till things are sorted out, and then considering the whole problem peacefully, it will perhaps have a more permanent effect than a dramatic conversion in times of trouble.

But I 'feel' better than I 'think', and when the peace and freedom which I think the next year will bring have made their mark, I believe that faith too will have been re-born. All of which is horribly expressed, and leaves quite the wrong impression on re-reading.

Anyway, I am very, very pleased that it is you who will conduct the wedding service. Incidentally, it will also be a chance for you to meet papa! It's infuriating – Ann's mother insists on a 'full wedding', and the only hope is that she won't be able to afford it, because neither Ann nor I want anything but to <u>be married</u>. As it is I see a strong danger of driving away from [a] reception of 100 strong with confetti, and drunken cries of 'here comes the bride', etc., following us into the distance. Heaven forbid. But ghastly wedding receptions are a 'déformation professionelle' of all – even the nicest mothers-in-law.

The Maharajah of Baroda's private secretary has been on to father for several days, I hear, and father is dining with the Maharajah tomorrow night. I expect it's to do with his wife's jewelry.[19] But what? Don't forget to read the next instalment of the Rake's Progress: 'The Strange Mission to the Maharanee.'

My love to the bears. And thank you again, very, very much.

Yours ever
David

---

19. The Maharani of Baroda, Sita Devi, had become famous for her luxurious lifestyle and her fabulous jewels; she was known as the 'Indian Wallis Simpson'. Her extravagant travels with the Maharaja, deposed in 1951 by the government of India, were widely reported; they stayed at the Waldorf Astoria in New York or the Dorchester in London. The Baroda treasury, from which the couple transferred many items, included the nineteenth-century Baroda pearl carpet, made of 2.2 million pearls, and the Brazilian Star of the South pink diamond necklace; the Maharani's personal collection ranged from bejewelled anklets to a 1948 cigarette case of yellow gold, rubies, sapphires, emeralds and diamonds.

~

Le Carré and Ann were married on Saturday, 27 November 1954, at St Luke's Church in Redcliffe Gardens, London.

TO VIVIAN GREEN

Cumhill Farm
Pilton
Nr Shepton Mallet
Somerset

13 December 1954

Dear Vivian,

Two weeks have passed since you married Ann and myself, and still I have not written to thank you. It is hard [to] find suitable words to express our appreciation of the way in which you conducted the service, that you made it a really memorable day for us, and Ann and I both felt most strongly that we had become part of a triple, not a dual, union. From the moment you began, it seemed that only we three were in the Church – Ann, myself and you as God's minister, and what we fully expected to be a gruelling and frightening affair assumed a very different character.

All is going almost alarmingly well. We went to Bristol that evening, and on Sunday afternoon went on to Pilton, to find to our bitter disappointment that there was not a stick of furniture in the place, as the van – which was due on the previous Wednesday, and had then been promised for the Friday – had not arrived. However, our landlord provided the basic essentials, and on Wednesday morning (whilst I was at School) the van arrived from London via Exeter, which even I know to be a surprising detour. Apart from forgetting the middle part of the spare bed (springs, mattress and frame), a nest of tables and a standard lamp, and being unable to get the double bed up the stairs (and incidentally leaving it in a decomposed state in the Farmer's Hall) they did a quick and efficient job. Ann had been cooking on an upturned electric fire, but we then managed to borrow an oil stove from the farmer, and became modernised. Soup, stew and boiled eggs were our staple diet. I can recommend the combination.

But by the end of the week a cooker had arrived & been installed, the workmen's feet sinking deep into the semi liquid floor-paint of the kitchen, laid ten days before, and recommended by the iron-monger for its qualities of quick drying on stone surfaces.

But now there is a sudden calm, and in a surprisingly short time really we find we have really rather a delightful home at a minimum cost, and a beautiful village to live in, with what must be, from the outside at least, as fine a village church as any in England.

Saw Robin yesterday! He was in very cookish form. Have you noticed the strong resemblance between Robin and Clovis Sangrail?[20] He was staying with sister Rosemary and psychiatrist brother in law Percy at Wells (Mendip Mental Hospital). This was the second time I have seen him down here, but the first since the wedding.

We have a bed for you here any time you wish – two beds in fact, both complete – and Ann's cooking, though not yet comparable to that of Madame of La Gouille, is certainly passable. The country is lovely here, and there are any number of walks to be made. But in any event I do hope to see you some time during the Christmas Holidays – as I told you, on Christmas Eve, before lunch, we are having a small wine party, and your family and yourself will be more than welcome. I expect we will be providing something in the way of a light

---

20. Cooke had a wicked sense of humour. Le Carré compares him here to Clovis Sangrail, a languid, acid, calculating young Englishman in the darkly satirical short stories of Saki, H. H. Munro.

lunch, so there will be no difficulty there. But on the other hand, I remember that you run to a very tight schedule over Christmas, so perhaps another time would suit you better – we are away over the New Year, but otherwise are here most of the time.

You will be pleased to hear that I am planning on returning to Oxford if it is at all possible; I do not see what should prevent, unless it is an unexpected arrival of family, or something of this kind!

Ann joins me in sending my regards, and in thanking you most deeply for a wonderful start to married life. She emphasises that you should come and see us soon!

We are, I must confess, very happy indeed, and I see no earthly reason why this state of affairs should not continue.

Yours ever
David

~

Le Carré wrote to von Almen in both English and German, swapping languages in different paragraphs. He spelt Kaspar with a 'K' when writing in German and a 'C' in English.

TO KASPAR VON ALMEN

Bread Street,
Pilton, Shepton Mallet
Somerset

[n.d. but likely early 1955]

My dear Kaspar,
I was very happy to get your letter this morning, and decided to reply right away, and in German, even though this language

which has become foreign to me, no longer flows through my rotten quill the way it once did.

My answer will be long and will go deep. I will try to tell you for the first time and in all seriousness the events of the last two years, and if some of it you are hearing for the second time, please put up with it, as it is all a part of the whole.

Which sounds absurdly pompous, and a <u>very</u> selfish way to carry on a correspondence, but since you have been good enough in the past to dry my rather un-British tears and listen to my hard-luck stories, and above all to provide the most invaluable support and advice, I owe this to you at least. Particularly since the story has a happy ending!

First of all I must thank you for your letter [*in English*] (changing to German is like putting on a tail suit) [*returns to German*] and assure you that the long time I had been waiting for it has only served to increase my joy at its arrival. I can't believe though that your sense of guilt led you to write this letter: the often-whipped dog no longer has the strength for such an opus. [*in English*] (As for setting a theme for our correspondence, I can conceive nothing more monotonous – don't you realise that you and I are the two most interesting topics in the world?) Now I am going to choose one of these two topics – not the <u>most</u> interesting I am afraid – and, to answer your questions, must discuss it for the remainder of a very long letter.

Now listen carefully to me Caspar, for I am about to do not only an un-British thing but something unique and very intimate. Those wild letters from a wild pen that swooped on you like the great black chuffs of Scheidegg and laid unquestioning claims on your good heart (more than helpfulness) represent a 'crise' – an emotional 'crise' – produced by circumstances of which you have no inkling. [*switches back to German*] Suffice it to say, that my father has revealed himself both through his police-related and his private affairs to be an infinite, darkest swindler. [*in English*] The clothes I wore, the food I ate and the books I read were bought with the money this had

provided. Little old ladies in the Midlands had provided every
penny of their savings towards some lunatic scheme which
never existed – honest good Bürgers [citizens] had been <u>legally</u>
robbed and ruined, whilst I fattened and grazed on their pastures. This I know is an emotional standpoint, but there are
times when it is wiser to weep, and (on Ann's shoulder, thank
God) I wept. I felt not so much humiliated as socially in debt to
those who lay crippled in my father's fearful wake. You must try
and understand the essential reality of this feeling, and realise
the extent of my father's evil doing. Add to this the fact that I
had no moral machinery to cope with such a shock, that I am,
as Grillparzer[21] would have it, too small to love or hate and too
large not to feel. And so I sauntered, drifted, from camp-bed
to camp-bed, from friend to acquaintance, right through the
'long vacation' (June–Oct) of 1954. (Roland Reinacker came
over then & I saw him for a while in London.[22]) 'A word of
thunder swept me away,' as Faust[23] said, and like him, 'I feel like
a dwarf' in the world. Vivian Green, the chaplain and senior
tutor of my college, was of immense help and, thank God, kept
in touch with me on our return from Switzerland (it was whilst
we were there that the bankruptcy business became public).
Ann and I, who had intended to wait until Oxford was finished, eventually decided that, where-ever the uncertainty of
the moment might end up, we would get married at once and

---

21. Austrian dramatist Franz Grillparzer.

22. Le Carré met Roland Reinäcker, whose parents lived in Essen, when he was a
Bern student.

23. A later letter to von Almen from Oxford is littered with references to the writers le Carré studied in four years of German literature, Goethe prominently among
them. In 2020 he named the 'greatest film of my life': the Faustian drama *Mephisto*,
directed by István Szabó and starring Klaus Maria Brandauer as a German actor who
traded integrity for fame under the Nazis.

    Fans have speculated on the source of le Carré's pen name – with little result, as he
usually claimed to have forgotten it. The nineteenth-century French author Michel
Carré wrote the libretto for Gounod's opera *Faust*, based on Carré's play *Faust et
Marguerite*, raising the slim possibility of a Goethe connection.

damn everything until we had done so. I secured a loan of £300 to clean up my debts at Oxford, we were married on 26 November, had a honeymoon of one night, and on the Monday I was back at the school where I was teaching, our problem solved in one respect, and our fortunes, for better or for worse, tied. Since then we have been very happy.

Now the news. A grant (County Scholarship) provides us with enough for a last year at Oxford in October providing that Ann does a certain amount of work.

We have a small cottage in Somerset which we rent at an extremely small sum, it is beautiful country and there is room for you both when you come. We have rooms in Oxford when you come there too, if ever this is of any service to you both.

Your invitation to come & stay with you in the spring or autumn is something we treasure very much – and suggest you stay with us here first and that we return <u>with</u> you – possibly in autumn '56. I have taken to painting commercially and have made a little money, and this helps to keep us going. I want to find a teaching post after Oxford & teach painting and languages.

We are sending you a wedding photograph. This has been ordered, and I expect it will be ready in about a fortnight. I thought, despite your protests, a nice glossy Tatler photograph was what you really had your eye on.

Our very best wishes to you both – and you, Caspar, behave yourself.

As always –
David

P.S. Call this letter 'confession of an unpretty soul' from Wilhelm Mesters Wandeljahre.[24]

---

24. Le Carré may be making a joke here. The original title of Goethe's *Wilhelm Meister's Journeyman Years* is *Wilhelm Meisters Wanderjahre* (literally, his 'Wandering Years'). Le Carré appears to have deliberately misspelt it as *Wandeljahre*, underlining the 'l' and changing the meaning to 'Years of Changing'.

~

Cooke and le Carré were schoolfriends from Sherborne, where they called each other 'Tig' at David's insistence.

TO ROBIN COOKE

> *52 Beechcroft Road*
> *Oxford*
>
> 7 October 1955

1 Malta Cottages
Bread Street
Pilton
Nr Shepton Mallet

My dear chap how are you?

Having at last received a letter from you to Bread Cottage (prick)[25] which has been redirected by the entire postal force of Somerset, I write to tell you that we are in Oxford struggling my dear to complete my sadly neglected academic course before plunging into the world of Commercial Art in July. I have been seeing publishers & people & have been assured by unprejudiced birds that my book illustration is well above average & will make me a living. Am getting me a reputable agent through a most fortunate introduction, shall do a bit of part-time teaching in case things go wrong but am quietly optimistic re the outcome. The Little Woman (or my Lady Wife – whichever you prefer) is flourishing & we have a couple of rooms (& a spare bed in one of them for you darling), & we make do somehow as the bishop said. Sweetheart, come & stay a weekend here, it

---

25. A term of endearment.

won't cost you anything for food & accommodation & we'd love to see you. How about it?

If you want to use our cottage in Somerset for a night, a week end, a week, a month, it's all complete & equipped with whatever you want, but let me know a day or two in advance so that I can have it aired before you go down. You can take any guests you like. Absolute privacy guaranteed ...

Please come & see us or something – it really is high time we met again. Come & see us here or something.

Ann sends her v. best love & hopes to see you soon. Write write write.

Love
Tiggy wig

~

TO KASPAR VON ALMEN

> *13a Polstead Road*
> *Oxford*
>
> After 20 August:
> *Wheatbutts*
> *Eton Wick*
> *Eton*
> *Windsor*
>
> [n.d. but likely June 1956]

Dear Kaspar,
[*in German*] Heartfelt thanks for your letter – or rather your decorated card. I've finally finished my Finals, but I don't need your ever-welcome help this time as I have – God knows how – got a job at Eton, and as a German teacher. The term begins on the 20th September but of course we need to move

in well before that, as we have to furnish and equip our new house.

I won't get the results of my Finals until the 28th July, after my viva voce exam.

If you could put your highly developed anglophobia to one side for two weeks and are thinking about a holiday trip with your Erika, you should really come over and see how the pointy-nosed, chinless and gooseberry-eyed British lords[26] are brought up. You know that Eton and Windsor are close to each other and a lot about it is inexpressibly beautiful. A lot, of course, is lousy.

The photos we had of us together have disappeared. But one day . . .

It's funny, I studied your literature for four years but in the end it's really only three writers that relate to me – Goethe, Kleist, and Büchner. Keller and Storm in small doses only. Do you think this is due to an incomplete understanding of the language, a lack of feeling? Can you, for example, rave about Hebbel, Grillparzer, Hauptmann, and Fontane? I have to stick to my native arrogance and admit that little about German poetry touches me, except for the soul itself, which breathes out from the pure romantic (Novalis, Heinrich von Ofterdingen) as it does from the strictest classic (Tasso or Iphigenie);[27] a dark, unmistakable, demonic earnestness, which is basically dangerous and suicidal in its effect – an illness that probably reaches its highest fever with Nietzsche.

[*in English*] So much for the Teutons. I seem to be falling into their habit of tedious introspective criticism. I've also decided that the only role for a British Germanist is to rescue the Germans from their own critics.

---

26. The German reads '*spitznasigen, kinnlosen, stachelbeeräugigen britischen Lords*'.

27. Refers to *Torquato Tasso* and *Iphigenie auf Tauris*, both by Goethe.

We thought vaguely of coming to Switzerland in early September, in which case we will certainly call on you – is this still your high season?

Love to Erika and your beautiful children, whose stoic good-health Ann much admires. I'm sure you'll find Ann far too nice for me.

I just get nastier and nastier.

Salutations,
Ever
David

ETON

And after Oxford, in an attempt to go straight, I had spent a couple of years teaching German at Eton.

– 'An Evening with George Smiley', Southbank Centre,
7 September 2017

The most bizarre encounter I had with a former pupil was meeting one dead drunk on the corner of a street in Pimlico, where he had laid out the family silver on a folding table and was trying to sell it to passers-by.

– to Dr Hugh Cecil, his former German pupil, 12 March 2009

'His father had designed him for the Foreign Service,' Vivian Green wrote, but, as he prepared to leave Oxford, le Carré 'was attracted by the possibility of teaching, more especially if this involved art'.[1] After the Lincoln rector Sir Walter Oakeshott wrote to several schools on his behalf, Eton offered a job teaching the top class in German and a lower grade in French. Four months' holiday a year, his wife Ann told a relative, would allow him 'to paint what he likes and not necessarily for the money'.[2] The few paintings by le Carré known to survive include a garishly coloured portrait of Ann.

The class-ridden, claustrophobic quality of the fictional Carne School was the later setting of *A Murder of Quality*, where George Smiley investigates the brutal killing of a schoolmaster's wife. 'I had begun a novel set in a public school,' le Carré wrote in *The Pigeon Tunnel*. 'For background I was using Sherborne, where I had been a pupil, and Eton, where I had been a schoolmaster.' Certainly some of the Eton staff believed le Carré had modelled the most unsavoury characters in the book on people he disliked especially in his time there.[3]

1. 'A Perfect Spy: A Personal Reminiscence', in Alan Bold's *The Quest for le Carré* (1988).

2. Ann Cornwell to Lynn Sharp, 2 May 1956, Tim Cornwell's private archive.

3. William Waldegrave, Baron Waldegrave of North Hill, provost of Eton College, to le Carré, 18 September 2017.

TO VIVIAN GREEN

13a Polstead Road
Oxford

26 June 1956

Dear Vivian,

Many thanks for your letter and the press cutting, to which I shall reply. Ann and I went and saw our 'cottage' at Eton. This is quite unbelievably charming – with 5 bedrooms, 2 bathrooms and three living rooms – two small and one v. large. 17thC cottage, detached, in its own large garden, with a double garage. Reconditioned from top to toe, with the decorators just having left – large kitchen, with 2 sinks, new boiler & gas cooker! The rent is £90 p.a. deducted at source. So apart from furnishing it, and attacking the overgrown garden, there is nothing to be done. The cottage overlooks a green, and could be in the middle of the country: pond & ducks, and cows grazing.

So we're pretty lucky – the bursar assured me that some married masters lived in semi detached red-brick houses, mostly with little or no garden.

Our money has come & is paid in to our accounts, but apart from being measured for a suit at Hall's and Ann indulging in one or two 'follies' we haven't done anything rash. In fact we're a bit nervous. It seems unreal to have £2000 instead of £20 in our account.

[. . .]

What a blessing we came back to Oxford! Hope to see you for the first week-end in August. Saw the Marslands[4] at Eton – he seems a new man. Thank goodness his wife hates cricket!

Ever,
David

---

4. Geoffrey and Fiona Marsland. He played first-class cricket for Oxford University.

~

TO VIVIAN GREEN

Wheatbutts
Eton Wick
Windsor

24 October 1956

Dear Vivian,

Many thanks for your letter – I am sorry not to have replied earlier, but life here is terribly hectic and most unnerving – I'm not a bit sure I can stand the Eton pace! I don't think I've ever met <u>so</u> much arrogance. However, it's all right as long as you preserve the strength to resist. In other ways – socially, and from point of view of accommodation, we are extremely lucky. There are <u>some</u> very sticky people, but a lot of awfully nice ones too – and obviously you can pick your company. But the boys are collectively quite frightful and individually variable and rather unnerving.

[. . .]

Geoffrey & Fiona [Marsland] have been very sweet to us, and I think he is much improved. He's terrifically 'keen' here and plays all manner of games & is much admired by the boys. I think they find life awfully expensive – as we do – and are always 'in the red'.

I've got some good teaching and some rock-bottom. But 50% French & 50% German – the German is quite good. My delight is the division of complete beginners, who are picked and sorted for brightness – I've got the brightest & they are <u>very</u> good, & seem to learn by themselves. I've also got the 6 best German boys once a week to correct their essays, which are very clever – clever and crammed with idiotic careless mistakes. They're brilliant at the literature and hopelessly behind at the language, with the odd exception.

Ann sends her love – she is very well and happy. We've got a splendid new dog which you must meet.

Will write again soon, but must make the post with this before school.

Ever
David

~

In this letter le Carré appeared to be attempting italicised handwriting.

TO VIVIAN GREEN

Wheatbutts
Eton Wick
Windsor

[n.d. but February 1957, four weeks
before Simon was due]

My dear Vivian,
You must forgive the long delay in writing – our time has been so full recently with brother Tony's visit and preparing for the arrival of the baby that my correspondence has fallen sadly behind. Ann's baby is due within the next four weeks now and we have been getting a room ready to receive it. Will you be Godfather (in companionship with Robin)[5] as well as Christen the Baby? We both hope you will be able to. I am afraid, incidentally, that our Christmas cards never got sent either because of Tony's premature arrival two days before he was expected, and we have been gradually writing around to apologise to everyone!

---

5. Robin Cooke.

The Easter Half began on Jan 22nd and has been distinguished for me by the acquisition of 'pupils', to whom one is mentor etc., and as I only have three I have plenty of time to hear their tales of woe! But of the three boys I have, two, on being questioned about their future careers, replied that they were going to 'manage the estate'! The other is going into father's business. (His father's – not mine!) Birley[6] has also resurrected a 'Reheboamite' meeting for Junior masters and himself, the first of which he held early in the Half. So many junior masters – particularly of 6 or 7 years' standing – seem to have complaints (is this always so?) to make, and Birley (whom I admire very much malgré tout) was extraordinarily patient and tolerant, although, as you probably know, his great and probably only failing is to talk incessantly and ineffectually when ever he gets a chance. Naturally as Headmaster he gets a good few chances, particularly in Chambers.

In many ways, without all the nervousness of starting from scratch, it has been very pleasant to begin the Half. The thing that sticks in my throat more and more however is the 'Herrenvolk' doctrine that is encouraged in the boys by the ruling body of masters, the free use of comparison with the 'oik'[7] classes, etc., and the 19thC conviction of the efficacy in every sense of the 'gunboat doctrine'. At the same time there is a curious lowering of standards among the aristocracy e.g. Lord C. Spencer Churchill (aged 16) tells me that he spends his evenings with father glued to the television, watching parlour games, and a contemporary of mine on the staff who spent the holidays tutoring him at Blenheim says that at family dinners the meal is served one end of the table by the flunkeys and the 'Telly' is plonked the other end for the Duke to 'look in'.[8] (I

6. Sir Robert Birley, appointed headmaster at Eton in 1949, a passionate anti-apartheid campaigner nicknamed 'Red Robert'.

7. In the last letter in this volume, le Carré refers to Boris Johnson as an 'Etonian oik'.

8. From these inauspicious beginnings, Charles 'Nutty' Spencer-Churchill, youngest of five children of the tenth Duke of Marlborough, kept racehorses, lent his name

suppose inevitably, there is also a very considerable amount of perversion in evidence, and I have even heard a housemaster mention it with jocularity in connection with his own house! Nigel Althaus, an old Etonian of my age, tells me that there is an actual 'tradition' that in this respect the needs of the 'bloods' must be served by the smaller boys.)[9] On the other hand, there is astonishing liberalism in many ways – not the least of these being the number of boys who are so terribly bad at games that Sherborne would have had a fit, and whose lives remain unimpaired by this handicap.

There is an infuriating tradition of not being enthusiastic about anything, or surprised. Hence discussions on painting for instance are somewhat limited by the extent to which a boy will confess himself impressed. And to be impressed by anything a 'beak'[10] does is pretty 'wet' anyway. I gather from housemasters that old E. parents actually urge boys to 'mob up' masters when they come here to show them their place & teach them perspective.

[. . .]

Impending parenthood finds me intrigued, apprehensive and extremely nervous. We do hope you will be able to manage the Christening – I'll try and come over to Oxford whilst Ann's in nursing home and then we can arrange a day. And we do hope you will be Godfather.

Ann sends her love.

Yours ever,
David

~

<hr>

to a line of men's suits and handled publicity for Blenheim. He died in 2016.

9. Le Carré recalled to Julie Kentish-Barnes in 2016 that he was warned by a 'weird' fellow master 'that boys would flirt with me and I shouldn't reciprocate: I was <u>just</u> married!'

10. Eton slang for 'teacher'.

"Ashley's Pater's got Agriculture and Fisheries!"

Undated early illustration from the le Carré archive.

Le Carré had already visited the Cerne Abbas Friary of St Francis from Sherborne School. His dear friend and former MI5 agent, the artist John Miller, later conducted a 'Looking, Seeing and Drawing' course there every year. Le Carré's words here contrast markedly with his later views on faith, including his letter of wishes for his funeral arrangements, explicitly ruling out any 'mumbo-jumbo'.

Ronnie had triggered another emotional crisis for le Carré. 'Indeed my reaction against him (with Ann's assistance) was so strong that it drove me in the third year of our marriage to seek counsel and absolution in an Anglican monastery, where I had nothing but the silliest advice,' le Carré wrote to Dr Bockner, a psychiatrist he consulted in 1968. 'I was trying at that time, as I have tried off and on throughout my life, to embrace religion. Ann, again, was the model. The monk who advised me has since gone off his head.'

TO ANN CORNWELL

The Friary
Cerne Abbas

Monday night
[n.d. but likely early 1957[11]]

Darling,
This is the end of my first day here, and I am writing again so soon because I have already reached a state of mind hard to express – a kind of spiritual preparedness, not necessarily enthusiastic, not necessarily even Christian – though predominantly so. And so I am using you my darling as a kind of diary, and if it is a very selfish one at least it is for you to read. And if it wanders & is formless forgive me. I urgently want you to share – though not yet to discuss – what I feel.

---

11. Undated, but while le Carré was at Eton, after Simon was born on 7 March 1957; he refers to 'you both'.

The services – I have attended 3 so far – are of an extraordinary beauty, being very simple yet high church, with mediaeval – or what I imagine to be mediaeval – intonations of the psalms & hymns. Father Gregory started talking to me after 7.0 Evensong, and we went for a walk all round the friary in the mist. He began to explain the nature of faith – 'Father I believe, help thou my unbelief' and relationship between prayer and faith. He made it seem logical that one should pray for faith while having none. The very feeling of insufficiency & waste (which I have had so strongly) is an aid to this type of prayer and frequently precedes apostolic vocation. 'Some Christians die at 90 without <u>faith</u>.'

Father Gregory is extremely intelligent and pleasant, and (as a maths graduate from Cambridge) has a very tidy mind which doesn't permit of silly generalisations. He is a Jew I think, only about 28, very humble and awfully pleasant. He is going on holiday for 2 weeks (which is what they get a year) tomorrow but is being posted to Cambridge & will come and stay with us from there. Incidentally, he says one <u>is</u> entitled to choose a congenial church (as some are 'dead' spiritually) to visit, although later on we might consider returning to a 'dead' church with a conscious mission. He says one often has to look for a long time! He also feels that if I feel as I do about Eton then I should stay & change it perhaps – or at least consider that as a line of thought. He also thinks I might have a shot at Borstal boys of which more later.

There have been a lot of children around but they are going tomorrow. I see Father Denis Marsh tomorrow.

We have to do a job for the whole morning or afternoon. I hope I'll get printing but fear it may be gardening . . . !

Darling I'm not suddenly getting religion nor will I turn monk & leave you both in the snow. I just feel, perhaps for the first time, that I am near to finding a way of life and a real faith. Whatever happens I shall share everything with you, & that shall be one of my greatest delights.

God bless you –
David

[*On a last page le Carré illustrated the letter.*]

Golly, it's <u>pouring</u> down. I have rather taken to lino cuts as a hobby. I can always do them at home & get the Brother Printer to do them here for me.

I forgot to bring my nail scissors & only managed to borrow some last night & now I've cut them my fingers feel all funny.

Ho ho, po.

Much love always to you and Flea.[12]

David

---

12. 'Flea' was le Carré's nickname for Simon.

Ronnie's mother, Bessie, had died.

TO VIVIAN GREEN

> *Wheatbutts*
> *Eton Wick*
> *Windsor*

> 29 November 1957

Dear Vivian,

So sorry to wrest you from the pleasures of the SCR[13] last night – after I rang you Jean rang and rather put on the pressure, but in such a circuitous way that I completely 'missed the point'. 'What would I do about my father – would I write to him for instance?' to which I replied 'Yes, I would write him a comforting letter' and I have done so. I have said I would like to be at the funeral on Monday but have doubts about being able to get away – which is true as Trials & Certificate are on. In fact, I don't think I shall go and feel no incentive. I was very fond of the old lady, etc., but feel I can honour her at a distance.[14] No doubt very callous. So in fact, until the next crisis, I don't suppose there will be any trouble, or danger of seeing him.

[. . .]

The crisis before this was just about the limit. He sailed to USA to see Tony (he is <u>still</u> an undischarged bankrupt), & two days before going, a brand new Ford Popular – about £500 – was delivered by a friend of his & left in the garage. When I got the papers & things, with a covering letter, I found that every

---

13. Senior Common Room, at Lincoln College, Oxford.

14. Ronnie's mother, Bessie, le Carré's grandmother, had died. She was 'pure Irish', Tony Cornwell remembered. 'It would be a bit of a stereotype, but probably a correct one, to surmise that that is where the Blarney came from.' Bessie's roots would entitle le Carré to the Irish citizenship he acquired at the end of his life.

thing was in my name except the purchase, which was in his secretary's name, & it had been bought on the H.P. in Wales!

The number plate was R.C.4! (Jean's new Hillman is R.C.3 & his two Ford Zephyrs are 1 & 2.)

The next afternoon I ran it straight back to a Henley garage & wrote him a note saying where it was. He wrote to me from the Queen Mary absolutely heartbroken, etc., that I had not accepted this gift 'which had no strings attached – it had been something he had <u>always</u> wanted to do & never been able, etc., etc.'

I wonder what the next thing will be. I <u>expect</u> it will be a personal illness or breakdown and ailing father will send for errant son.

I feel rather like the man in 'Lucky Jim' with all those different faces,[15] & can't otherwise whip up any enthusiasm, remorse, affection or <u>anything</u> for him any more.

Do hope to see you soon – Simon is growing apace & Ann is blooming & happy.

Love from us all – in haste.
Ever
David

P.S. Eton is just about murdering us – still wildly expensive and maddeningly Etonian. We're all too broke, too comfortable, too smug. Bah!

---

15. Jim Dixon, the title character of Kingsley Amis's *Lucky Jim*.

LONDON

And somehow or another, instead of reading those great big broadsheets on the train going up and down to London, I just began writing in a little notebook.

– in a Q & A for his American publisher Scribner, 6 January 1999, on the publication of *Single & Single*

The contemporary record in letters from le Carré about his years in the intelligence services is for obvious reasons thin. There are veiled references in letters to Ann and little more. In one letter to Jeannie Cornwell, who had read coded wartime messages over the BBC, he mentions the possibility of secretarial work with people he knew.

Le Carré served at a time of dark betrayals, with the public exposure of the Foreign Office spies Guy Burgess and Donald Maclean, and the Soviet double agents George Blake and Kim Philby, spanning his years in intelligence from 1948 to 1963. I vividly remember my mother at the dining table, suddenly and furiously insisting it was Donald Maclean who blew my father's cover, not Kim Philby, as is commonly said. She was probably being more argumentative than accurate: Maclean had no knowledge of the MI6 personnel from his position in the Foreign Office, unlike Philby, who was in the service. Le Carré in a 2010 interview said his betrayal by Philby was one reason why he had avoided meeting him on a visit to the Soviet Union in 1987.[1]

Outwardly he maintained the fiction, until the mid 1970s and beyond, that he was a schoolmaster and diplomat. Only many years later would he write to Tom Bower, for example, that 'I lived through the big betrayals while I was still inside the tent, and the tent itself was in a state of decay.'[2] The problem with le Carré, one MI6 colleague observed, was that he had never experienced a successful operation in the service.

Where there was not betrayal, there was suspicion, aimed at le Carré's MI5 chief Sir Roger Hollis and his MI5 controller and colleague George Leggett; both men were interrogated in the hunt for a Soviet mole inside MI5. Leggett was exonerated but so traumatised

---

1. Le Carré's attitude to Blake and Philby shows in his 12 April 2012 letter to Roger Hermiston.

2. Email to Tom Bower, 29 June 2019.

by the experience that he left the service early, and le Carré later hired him as a fact-checker.[3]

After what seemed an unlikely interlude at Eton, le Carré moved back into the secret world and joined MI5 in the spring of 1958, and two years later MI6. The Cornwell family lived in Great Missenden in Buckinghamshire for a year, before moving to London. Le Carré began to write on the London commute.

'The small back room contained six desks and was called F4. The figure 4 indicated that we ran spies,' was how he described his MI5 office, on the third floor of Leconfield House in Curzon Street, in London's West End. 'The letter F indicated that our target was Communist subversion in all its perceived variations. F4's remit was to recruit spies of both sexes, to motivate, befriend, brief, counsel, debrief, pay and welfare them.'[4]

Betrayals aside, his time there brought enduring memories and friendships. For years after he claimed it was the discipline of 'Foreign Office' summaries that taught him how to write. 'I miss the Office, always have done – both Offices – in their way. In a sense they are the only places, apart from writing,' he wrote, sixty years later.[5]

In MI5 le Carré worked for two years with John Bingham, Lord Clanmorris, himself a published thriller writer. 'If Smiley had an origin physically it was a man I worked with as an agent runner within MI5 called John Bingham,' he recalled. 'John was my controller really, he was a very seasoned old spy and I was very grateful for his guidance.'[6] Bingham was published by Victor Gollancz, where le Carré took his own first novel, *Call for the Dead*. Bingham gave a

---

3. The exposure of the Cambridge Five drove fears in the mid 1960s that there were further Soviet-penetration agents in both MI5 and MI6. Peter Wright was chairman of the FLUENCY Working Party aimed at tracking them down. He wrote of his investigation of Hollis, and other mid-level operatives, in his 1987 book *Spycatcher*, which the British government fought to suppress.

4. 'An Evening with George Smiley', Southbank Centre, 7 September 2017.

5. To Alan Judd, 18 May 2019.

6. At the 'Berliner Salon', German ambassador's residence, London, 3 March 2020.

quote for the book: 'Mr le Carré is a gifted new crime novelist with a rare ability to arouse excitement, interest and compassion.'

In 2000 le Carré wrote an introduction to Bingham's first novel, *My Name is Michael Sibley*, published in 1952. Bingham, he said, had come to regard le Carré's work as an act of betrayal, in which Britain's intelligence services are portrayed alternately as 'murderous, powerful, double-crossing cynics' and 'bumbling, broken-down layabouts'.

The Clanmorris family kept a sketch of Bingham by le Carré, drawn when the two men worked together. 'When I came to write Smiley, I tried to give him the same faint air of loss that John carried around with him,' he wrote. 'There was something quixotic as well as shrewd about him . . . He was a superb listener.' Bingham, wrote le Carré, 'understood and loved police work': in *Call for the Dead*, Smiley finds in Inspector Mendel 'the same reserves of patience, bitterness and anger' he has seen in policemen all over the world.

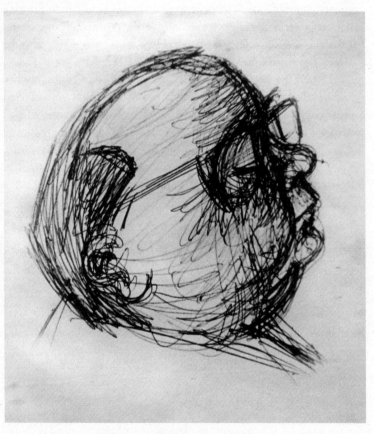

Le Carré's sketch of his MI5 colleague John Bingham.

In a group of hastily written letters in an envelope marked '6 May 1959', le Carré, now employed by MI5 in London, wrote to Ann in Buckinghamshire of being 'absurdly uprooted'. He was very busy 'trying to close off a big case' and added: 'Sometimes I wish you c̲d̲ see something of my work. I've finished an immense report today I was rather pleased with. Dearest love, aren't I vain!' In another he wrote: 'Oh darling heart where have you gone? I have a great deep wound that I feel all the time.'

TO ANN CORNWELL

[Postmark] 6 May 1959

Dearest little Ann,

This is that long letter you talked about. Sitting alone in Peter's[7] rather gloomy sitting room contemplating the gas ring cooking the water to make some Nescafé. Have just spoken to you on the telephone & feel LOW. Have scoffed at nearby scruffy caffy with little joy but some effect, and thought deeply of To [Tony] & how lonely it must have been for him – all those meals alone, so little to talk to or talk of except needing love. I wonder how many people are <u>really</u> independent & self contained – the best extrovert thriller style.

How's the play going now I wonder?[8] It was really quite funny watching you alternate between spontaneous pleasure and spontaneous rage at my suggestions! I feel just a little like Dorian Gray among these antiques and fine things! Intermission for coffee. Kettle boiled.

---

7. Former Squadron Leader Peter de Wesselow, an MI5 colleague with a distinguished career as a Bomber Command pilot.

8. Ann always wanted to be a writer of stories and poetry, and, presumably, here a play; le Carré sometimes edited them. The couple had performed in amateur dramatics in Somerset.

Went to Sotheby's this morning with Peter and it was just like going to the Louvre: there's a staggering sale tomorrow of Utrillos, Piccassos and 19thC impressionists (Degas, Monet and Vlaminck mainly). Peter sniffing about like a little bloodhound – we both hated the Rouault and Dufy thank heaven and Peter of course had to tell everyone what nonsense they were! Catalogue was only 3d – entry free – & there was a <u>mass</u> of fine things (furniture, silver and curios as well).

After lunch returned to the office to find pandemonium raging and had to closet myself with F in Philip's[9] absence. Lecture this morning on six.

When I arrived last night Peter said I looked b. miserable and took me straight off to the Bicyclette for dinner on him, and then to TM's, former member of the office, now retired,[10] & a very Oliverish[11] amateur painter who is now pro. but rich. His brother Guy was head of the Ops section in the war and recently died, remember? He owns a Poussin which hangs on the wall of his drawing room with stunning simplicity – you just look at that familiar reproduction & then realise it isn't a reproduction. His mistress (old Austrian lady) embroiders altar pieces! And so between them they lick the platter clean . . .

When I do all these things and see how many fascinating, live and stimulating places & people there are to be seen I long to bring you up to London to live here – take a tiny unfurnished flat and a new lease of youthful energy. I feel you've nursed me through a period of stagnation, hopelessness & moribundity, and that in return for being a burned up old bear for so long, I should pull you up here & go young & gay again. Darling, this isn't just the spring – what do you think of it? I want to go with you to all the newest and loopiest theatres, go

---

9. MI5's F Branch was charged with counter-subversion at home. Philip is currently unidentified.

10. Name redacted.

11. Their Eton friend Oliver Thomas, an impressionistic landscape and portrait painter, became director of art at Eton in 1959.

to beastly little night clubs, listen to the fruits in Hyde Park. For the first time since Father happened I feel the world is our oyster and we should feed the cancers of mind and imagination with all London's loopiness and wisdom – this isn't To-ish[12] drivel darling but it's what I've been wanting to say to you for some time – in brief, let's cut down on the business of living & get help. We're too young and too (let's say it) intelligent to be buried and mouldy and darling do you agree?

I should love Flea to be in on all this – and to have more bears abroad. Tell me what you think. We don't have to move tomorrow, but next Spring perhaps, if you agreed. Nor do we have to move period. Just let's <u>talk</u> about it without losing our fluff over it till we've thought more.

Darling I love you
    Napiolion[13]
    D

∾

to ANN CORNWELL

[Postmark] 20 July 1959

Darling little heart,
You may well wonder why I didn't write over the week end. I was D O – and in fact on duty non stop from 10am on Saturday to 12 midday on Sunday with one of the biggest fiascos the office has

---

12. Le Carré had given Ann Tony's 'very stream of consciousness' novel 'The Tree Farm' to read at Eton. Neither of them liked it.

13. In later life le Carré had a minor fascination with Napoleon, buying books about his exile at St Helena and the retreat from Moscow, and at least one bust. He twice signed himself 'Napoleon D' to Jeannie.

had to cope with since the great defection.[14] Managed to raise the DG at 1am on Sunday and we opened up the office with all frills by about 4am. Nearly had to go to Chequers to find the Col. off. rep![15] Got no sleep at all – went to Christopher's[16] for lunch when it was all over & slept a bit in the p.m. and then went and looked at the flat which was enormous & super & have bid for it – with rates it is now £7 p.w. but we can have a lodger providing we don't advertise for one & I'm sure I can get a girl from the office. The rooms are vast & there are 7 of them. Enormous & lovely house. More when we meet.

You remember the mad scheme with Reggie?[17] It has fallen through as last time they went down to the water's edge they got the cameras smashed!

Yesterday was <u>boiling</u> here and today too. I do hope you are having lovely weather. Oh I <u>do</u> so miss you – both of you.

[. . .]

I shall be quite exhausted after this week – all hell's let loose here . . . [. . .]

D.

~

In 1960 le Carré went 'across the Park' from MI5 and 'joined the competition' in MI6, as he would describe it. Officially he joined the Foreign Office.

---

14. Le Carré was duty officer when a Commonwealth leader went public over a crude approach by an MI6 officer.

15. Colonial Office representative.

16. Currently unidentified.

17. Currently unidentified.

TO JEAN CORNWELL

62 Overstrand Mansions
Prince of Wales Drive
London, SW11

21 May 1960

Dearest Jeannie,

Thank you very much for your card – hope you had a fine holiday. Ann and the children[18] are going to stay with an aunt of hers in Weston Super Mare in August and I think that's the nearest we'll get to a holiday this year as I've just been appointed to the Foreign Office as from the end of next month. I shall have to go to a charm school[19] and learn to push paper about and then we're hoping for an embassy posting in about April '61. All very exciting – but no holiday.

Father said in a recent letter that he was leaving for America last Thursday (?). I don't know how long he's away for but we wondered whether you'd like to spend a few days here if you had nothing else to do. We would love to have you and on Tuesday next Michael Scott[20] is speaking in Battersea Town Hall and we thought we might all go and hear him. A-Mouse is becoming a militant bomb-banner, to my embarrassment![21]

---

18. Stephen Cornwell was born 29 March 1960. Simon was now three.

19. 'Charm school' may refer to le Carré's SIS training at Fort Monkton. 'A nine months course in the black arts, at a remote castle in the South of England,' he described it in unpublished material for *The Pigeon Tunnel*. 'We had played with radios, codes, secret inks, knives and hand guns. We had explored ad nauseam the minds of traitors, grappled with each other in unarmed combat, and undertaken mock operations in strange towns.'

20. Guthrie Michael Scott was an Anglican priest and pre-war Communist Party sympathiser, a prominent campaigner against apartheid in South Africa and an early advocate of nuclear disarmament in Britain. In 1960 he set up the British anti-war group the Committee of 100 with Bertrand Russell and others.

21. Ann had joined the Campaign for Nuclear Disarmament after watching the powerful post-apocalyptic 1959 film *On the Beach*.

Stephen Mark is prospering and so is Flea. I've also just had a commission from Bell's to illustrate a book on talking birds (not That kind)[22] and when Simon gets his feet out of my paint box I might be able to get down to it.

Could you ring Ann on Monday and let her know whether there's any chance of your coming to stay. And please write and congratulate me on the F.O.

Haven't any idea of what To's up to – his last letter (recd. last week) made no mention of <u>not</u> going back to university but taking a job instead, but seemed quite jolly about la vie maritale.

much love from us all
Napoleon D

~

Hilary Rubinstein, editorial director of Victor Gollancz, had flagged possible legal issues with le Carré's first novel, Call for the Dead, *including with anyone claiming similarity to his superior Maston, a 'nasty piece of work'. At the top of le Carré's answering letter, in red handwriting, is noted: 'Wolf changed to Mundt.' Le Carré's murderous East German villain of* Call for the Dead *and* The Spy Who Came in from the Cold *initially carried the surname of the head of the East German spy service, Markus Wolf – a man whom le Carré would resolutely refuse to meet. He later said he got the name from his lawnmower.*[23]

---

22. *Talking Birds* was a book by Maxwell Knight, a famed MI5 agent-runner who found a successful second career as a naturalist with the BBC. Le Carré supplied twelve illustrations for forty guineas. 'This little book is intended to help those who are interested in talking birds to learn more about them and their varying capabilities,' Knight wrote in the introduction. It had chapters called 'Why and How Do Birds Mimic?' and 'Parrots and the Law'.

23. Markus Wolf called his autobiography *Man without a Face*, for his supposed ability to elude being photographed.

Stand for a Macaw

An illustration by le Carré from *Talking Birds* by Maxwell Knight.

TO HILARY RUBINSTEIN

> *62 Overstrand Mansions*
> *Prince of Wales Drive*
> *London, SW11*

21 January 1961

Dear Mr Rubinstein,

Thank you for your letter of January 13th enclosing a copy of your lawyer's report. May I first apologise on my wife's behalf for addressing you as Miss Rubinstein?

May I take your lawyer's questions one by one? The characters <u>are</u> wholly fictitious, and so is the Secret Service setting – so far as I am capable of judging I know of no Government office at or near Cambridge Circus, but I do not suppose that the Secret Service publicises the location of its offices. My reading on the subject has always led me to the belief that Intelligence work is divided between separate services and you will notice that in my book there is only one service, which I suppose reduces the risk of a chance similarity. I know of no one called Maston or anything like it – but again I don't suppose there <u>is</u> any way of protecting ourselves – no list we can consult, etc. It might be worth looking up Maston in the Civil Service lists, but I doubt it.

There seems to be an East German Trade Delegation in London (Kammer für Aussenhandel) whose address is in Albemarle Street, and whose principal is, unfortunately, called Wolf. Personally, I feel that the commonness of the name and the remoteness of the connection preclude the possibility of a claimant on this account.

The Fountain Café and its proprietor are, to my knowledge, wholly fictitious.

One or two other points occur to me which your lawyer has not mentioned: the Weybridge Repertory Theatre – I don't know whether one exists, but if necessary I suppose we could change it to Weystock. There <u>is</u> a pub called the Balloon in

Lots Road, and there is a pub called the Prodigal's Return in Battersea.[24]

I apologise for the confusion about dates in the text – I should have examined them more closely before submitting the M.S. I shall be returning the proofs on Monday and as far as I know nothing I have done necessitates altering the text from one page to the next. Thank you very much for sending a second copy of the proofs.

Yours sincerely,
David J. M. Cornwell

P.S. Would you like me to return the typescript?

---

24. The Battersea pub in *Call for the Dead* became the Prodigal's Calf.

GERMANY

I wrote the book in a great rush over a period of about five weeks. I wrote it in the small hours of the morning, in my British Embassy hiring in Königswinter, in odd moments at my desk in the Embassy, and even at the wheel of my car as I crossed the Rhine back and forth by ferry, sometimes parked alongside Chancellor Adenauer's huge armoured Mercedes as he made his own stately way to work.

– in the foreword to the Hodder Lamplighter edition of *The Spy Who Came in from the Cold*, 1989

The German influence in le Carré's novels ran from the first to the last. In *Call for the Dead*, George Smiley duels with his German former student from the German university where Smiley worked and spied. *The Spy Who Came in from the Cold* opens and closes on the Berlin Wall. George Smiley is devoted to the work of the seventeenth-century German poet Hans Jakob Christoffel von Grimmelshausen; in *A Perfect Spy*, Grimmelshausen's *Simplicius Simplicissimus* is a key to the secret heart of Magnus Pym. In le Carré's final novel, *Agent Running in the Field*, the main character, Ed, considers he has a German heart.

Le Carré went ahead of the family to his new posting in Germany. Ann and the children remained in London.

To ANN CORNWELL

British Embassy
Bonn
Germany

[Postmark] 7 June 1961

Darling,

Left Brussels this morning at 5 am, having spent an acutely uncomfortable night in a small hotel exactly like the one in 'Genevieve',[1] do you remember? The clock struck, the plumbing went wrong, and above all it was so <u>hot</u> that in desperation I finally got in the car & drove off.

Starting from the beginning, though, I was pitched on to an enormous Autobahn at Ostend which whisked you on the sink or swim principle towards Brussels. Turned off at Ghent (I was past Bruges before I'd even started looking for it) and as I turned became aware of very odd steering: a puncture. Managed to change wheel with the aid of genial Belgian motorcyclist who unscrewed the nuts for me, and had just set about looking for a small hotel when I was accosted by a Roman Catholic priest who had just had a 'panne' and was frantic to get to a reunion in Brussels at 7.30. Of course I had to drive the man to Brussels, and he kept on urging me 'faster, faster', until finally I got annoyed & told him to shut up. We parted company slap in the middle of Brussels in what was evidently the rush hour: he shot into a taxi and I started looking for

---

1. *Genevieve* was a 1953 British comedy caper set around a vintage-car race. A young married couple, played by John Gregson and Dinah Sheridan, share a decrepit hotel room opposite a giant clock with grinding gears and an earth-shaking bell.

somewhere to park. You cannot imagine the confusion, both in Brussels and in my own head, by this time.

Finally found a hole in the rue Neuve for the car & I asked a copper whether I could leave it there all night. He told me that it wd be O.K. provided that I transferred it to the other side of the road at midnight. Then I started looking for a hotel near the car, & discovered the hotel Oxford which is one to avoid. Had a marvellous plate of cold roast beef & potato, & lots of beer & felt better – & so to bed, (after moving the car at midnight!), and a sleepless 5 hours until this morning. Heavy fog either side of Liège, and then a warm rain as far as Aachen. The road from Brussels to Aachen was lousy – pitted and often cobbled (my spare tyre unrepaired of course) and a lot of heavy transport jockeying for position. However Nap. D battled on.[2] After Aachen (where my diplomatic visa produced a comic show of deference) got on to the Autobahn to Cologne which was quite marvellous, I've never known anything like it. You really can do 50 miles in an hour simply by driving at 50 mph for one hour – no hindrances, lights, nothing; but dreadfully dull.

Arrived at the Embassy before lunch (having breakfasted just short of Aachen) and met H of Chancery (Tim Marten) who is a Reggie type of smoothe Wykehamist, and about 50 other people. Instead of sending me straight on to my hotel he insisted on introducing me to half the Embassy – still travel-sore & dirty. Then to my hotel in Bad Godesberg, which is rather super – bathroom attached & so on. Small room but very good. Returned in my brown suit, bathed & refreshed, this afternoon. I've got a nice office looking on to open field.

They really are all out to get us accommodation – this is the first time they've ever not found anywhere in time. This evening I'm going to see what is described as half a house (maisonette I think) with garden & garage which is on Bad Godesberg hill. It may be available, they don't know. If it is, I shall be faced with the v. awkward decision of whether to take it

---

2. Napoleon D, for David.

or hope for something bigger & better: most of the dip. houses <u>are</u> larger than this, & they are very apologetic about it, etc., & leaving me with the choice of whether to take it or gamble on s.th else coming up. On verra. If this one is O.K. & so on, it is vacant from the end of July. I shall look round for a small pension for us, meantime, for July.

Am dining with Marten tomorrow night, and there's an Embassy garden party on Thursday, to which I am summoned with a piece of pasteboard the size of a wall. Must finish now & get this to the post.

Much love
D

~

Le Carré arrived in Germany as his second novel, A Murder of Quality, *was readied for publication.*

TO MIRANDA MARGETSON[3]

> *British Embassy*
> *Bonn*
> *Germany*
> [n.d.]

Dear Miranda,
How very sweet of you. I'm so glad you enjoyed it. Do please come and see us here. Our house is small but very pleasant. The most important thing is the garage, of course, and I am pleased

3. Miranda Margetson, the younger daughter of the painters Sir William Coldstream and Nancy Sharp (later Spender), married John Margetson, one of the six men on le Carré's MI6 training course, in 1963.

room for one guest

Love

The Author

———————

I have
decided to
cultivate that
interest, worried
look and to
start writing brilliant, untidy
letters for future
biographies.
This is one.

to say that the car will be entirely protected from atmospheric changes, falling earwigs and other phenomena of the open air which might damage the paintwork. Ann comes out on Saturday. Bliss.

Thank you again, and do <u>please</u> come – we have ample room for one guest.

Love
The Author
I have decided to cultivate that intense, worried look and to start writing brilliant, untidy letters for future biographers. This is one.

~

TO ANN CORNWELL

British Embassy
Bonn

9 June 1961

Darling,
Ten minutes to write you a better letter than the one I posted to you earlier today. I have finished that Evans/Christie book by L. Kennedy and it really is a harrowing (though hysterical and badly written) affair.[4] Don't read it. Roland[5] rang me today from Essen: we are meeting for dinner tomorrow night, and I shall have some explaining to do!

---

4. Ludovic Kennedy's book *Ten Rillington Place* investigated the case of Timothy Evans, hanged for the murder of his baby daughter on 9 March 1950, and also accused of the killing of his wife. The serial killer John Christie, who lived in the same house, was arrested on 31 March 1953 after the hidden bodies of six other women were found there.

5. Roland Reinäcker, whose parents lived in Essen.

I will try and give you more idea about the house. It is very handy for the naafi,[6] which is in Godesberg, and where you can buy many things at a far lower price than in German shops, but I know that that won't stop you from burrowing in the German market – or I hope it won't! German milk, for instance, is lousy and goes off very quickly, but the naafi get in Swedish milk which is apparently excellent. The house has a tiny front garden and an enclosed back garden – the two together are about the size of our back garden at Missenden. I'll go see it again in a day or 2 and make a plan. Cyril Whitworth, the Counsellor (Admin) is a <u>very</u> kindly and efficient soul. The downstairs floors are wood block and both they and the walls are all going to be done up.

Incidentally – there's a 'pool' of glasses and crockery at the Embassy, and so it isn't vital to have either. I like the Rosenthal[7] china here very much – the unpatterned stuff anyway, the patterns tend to be tasteful flowers – but it's no better than Wedgewood I suppose – they have some rather nice dull lustre-glazes. I've met the panel doctor who is a very nice German who apparently never minds turning out at night (another reason for being this side of the river) and also enjoys a high reputation. There's also an Embassy chaplain, young and rather nice. HE's[8] party was very elaborate yesterday – I'll tell you more when we meet.

I should ring Andrews and Salmon's round about the 12th or 13th and confirm the dates for their visits – as also the Pall Mall.[9] If you get <u>trouble</u> from Jones of Travel Section for any

---

6. NAAFI – the Navy, Army and Air Force Institutes running shops and other facilities for the British Armed Forces.

7. Bavarian porcelain manufacturer. In the 1950s Rosenthal commissioned designs by Henry Moore and the German potter Beate Kuhn.

8. Abbreviation for 'His Excellency', referring to British Ambassador Sir Christopher Steel.

9. Unidentified. A diplomatic friend of the Cornwells suggests London estate agents, with an advert placed in the *Pall Mall Gazette*.

reason, don't forget you can go and <u>see</u> him, which is often effective! But I should keep in close touch with [*illegible*] & co.

I love you
D

~

TO ANN CORNWELL

British Embassy
Bonn

[Postmark] 16 June 1961

Darling –
You ask what news coverage the German press devotes to Eichmann. The German TV ran a 5-serial programme on the 3rd Reich's crimes, and the good papers – Welt, Frankfurter Allgemeine, etc., gave as much coverage – & continue to give – as the Telegraph or M. Guardian.[10] Among the young intelligentsia, it is said, the lesson has been well & truly learnt, & that is certainly the impression one gets from young German FO officials & so on. In the main, though, the Volk is so incredibly prosperous that they are dazzled by their own jewels, and of a pacific disposition: war means no money, lots of taxes & poor food, and to the German man in the street, if he exists, these things are more of a reality, and more to [be] abhorred, than to his British counterpart. I haven't found much to worry about from <u>that</u> point of view. In other ways they <u>are</u> worrying,

---

10. The trial of Adolf Eichmann, who oversaw the deportation of European Jews to ghettos and killing sites, began before a special tribunal of the Jerusalem District Court on 11 April 1961. One of the first widely televised trials, it brought the details of the Holocaust, including survivors' testimonies, to a global audience.

but no[t] quite in the way you fear. That at least is my immature judgement after 10 days here!

No letter from you today. Gloom. Marvellous weather here today. Roof rack is fitted & was foully expensive but now it's done.

> Love love love
> husband D.

~

John Margetson, one of six men on le Carré's MI6 training course, was serving undercover with SIS in The Hague. He had served with the Life Guards in Palestine and with the Colonial Service in Tanganyika. The two men were together when le Carré learnt that Call for the Dead *had found a publisher; they remained lifelong friends.*

TO JOHN MARGETSON

> *British Embassy*
> *Bonn*
> *Germany*
>
> 5 July 1961

My dear John,

I have been meaning to write to you ever since I arrived, but somehow never made it. At last Ann's arrival, and tales of your hospitality, have compelled me to. They arrived safely on Saturday in that fantastic heat wave which in the damp, clamminess of the Bonn climate was almost intolerable. The children were over excited and absolute hell for 2 or 3 days but now they've settled down, Simon's plugged in to a dame school in the British colony until the end of this term (where he is making mayhem) and the prevision is really pretty fair.

My own social round is hectic, and of course Ann can't get out much till the girl arrives.

There is good and bad to relate – work is interesting and by no means chair bound. One's chancery colleagues on the other hand are pretty grim and very inhospitable – no-one's surfaced to show Ann around or anything like that. You can imagine the picture, I think.

The book seems to be making a fair amount of money, which is not to be sneezed at, but anyway our allowances seem adequate and the rumour is they're going up, as the inspectors have just left, and the mark has been up-valued or whatever the word is. Culturally the place is a nonstarter unless you can get to Cologne, Düsseldorf or down to Munich. Scenically it's pretty good – a lot of hilly Rheinland with spiky little castles and shades of Wolfram von Eschenbach.

Ann is writing to you separately. All I want to say is 'thank you' once again very sincerely, and to urge you to come and stay as soon and as long as you can.

Ever,
David

~

to RONNIE AND JEAN CORNWELL

British Embassy
Bonn

8 August 1961

Dearest Jeannie and Father,

Ann and the children arrived at the beginning of July, but we are still waiting for the builders to finish our house. The date for us to move in is now to be August 16th, but we are sceptical. We were in an hotel but the children (Stephen particularly) behaved so foully that we were turfed out. German hotels have no public rooms as we understand them, so we were rather cramped.

Accommodation is terribly difficult here – the Embassy found us a very small but pretty modern house with a garage and garden, and we decided to take it rather than wait vainly for something larger. But we shall always have room for the odd guest!

The Berlin crisis[11] dominates one's life rather, and tends to interfere with leisure, but the surrounding Rheinland is very beautiful, and yesterday we made a successful trip to an 11thC monastry, and a spectacular Schloss, and drank a good deal of Rhein wine out of the barrel, without going more than 20 miles from Bad Godesberg, which is the sort of dormitory spa for Bonn. Ann's 17 y.o. cousin is here as nanny for the children and so far she seems quite reasonable. Simon has a fine new German scooter with inflatable tyres, which puts the premiums up a bit. On the subject of premiums, the roads here are fantastically dangerous – 1,000 people killed a month. My U.K. insurance co. charges £62 p.a. for a worldwide policy based on Germany.

Life here in general is very expensive, and we find it quite easy to run through most of our salary & allowances just entertaining and running the family, but we've opened a honey pot for winter sports. On the other hand whisky is 10/- a bottle and cigarettes bought in bulk work out at 6d for 20, so we can always fall back on the simple things of life.

Tony, I gather, is coming to England first & then out here. There has been a bit of to-ing and fro-ing because Anna doesn't

---

11. About four days after this letter was written, le Carré was at a rally in Nuremberg where West Berlin Mayor Willy Brandt warned of a 'fingertip feeling', a *Fingerspitzengefühl*, about events in his city. Returning late to the British Embassy to file his report, le Carré found the lights blazing. On the morning of 13 August, the border with West Berlin was closed, and East German soldiers began to install barbed-wire fences along the border between West and East Berlin. The first concrete blocks of the Berlin Wall soon followed.

want to come to Germany because it gives her willies. Frankly, it sometimes gives us willies too![12]

Simon fancies himself a dab-hand at German, and makes awful gutteral noises at German children when he plays with them, afterwards asserting proudly 'and they understood what I <u>meant</u>'. His main sources of pleasure are German level crossings, with their great red & white booms, and trams with 'carriages'. I sometimes wish mine were.

Love
David

~

On the same day le Carré wrote to Dick Edmonds apologising for a slow delivery of the latest set of drawings for the Downhill Only Journal.

TO DICK EDMONDS

[HM crest headed paper]

8 August 1961

Dear Dick

Thanks for yr letter. I quite understand the situation & will do my best to let you have stuff by end of August at the latest. We have at present no house, but live gypsy life in hotels, which makes it v. difficult for me to unroll my mat. You may also have noticed that there's a spot of bother going on re. Berlin, & this tends to interfere with one's leisure. However, Russians

---

12. Tony Cornwell's wife Anna Christake Cornwell lived through the German invasion of Greece as a young woman. After her house was bombed, her family fled to the mountains and she joined the anti-Nazi Resistance.

& housing permitting, send the articles (or copies), give me a deadline & let's see.

Love
David

~

TO HILARY RUBINSTEIN

Until Friday:

c/o J. W. Margetson
British Embassy
The Hague
Holland

28 April 1962

Dear Mr Rubinstein,

I have just posted the corrected proof to you. I sent it unregistered and as printed matter to avoid all possible delay, and I hope you will have it by Tuesday morning. There are no substantial alterations, except that I have re-written eight lines two pages from the end, cut out the second paragraph of the foreword and put in a dedication 'To Ann'. Otherwise it's largely a matter of correcting printing errors & standardising punctuation.

To anticipate some of your legal advisor's worries, I might perhaps make a few comments. I do not know whether there is such an organisation as the Public Schools' Committee for Refugee Relief. I think it highly unlikely, but could you please glance in the London telephone directory as a precaution? If there is anything akin, do please change the name as you think advisable. I have altered Vivat Rex Eduardus Sextus to Ave Rex Eduardus Sextus (the crest under the dolphin in, I think,

Ch III) because I gather Sherborne School still sings 'Vivat Rex Eduardus Sextus' in its school song, and has it as one of its school mottos. If Ave . . . is still too near the bone, I suggest 'Regem defendere diem videre'.[13]

I haven't yet got the FO to approve the book, which is a pure formality. If you could lend me or give me a spare proof for this purpose, I'd be most grateful.

Yours ever,
David Cornwell

~

TO JEAN CORNWELL

British Embassy
Bonn

16 May 1962

Dearest Jeannie,

Many thanks for your letter – we are so ashamed of all our omissions; Ann is writing to you at this moment muttering 'coals of fire' to herself. It is no excuse to say we are busy – though we are – or that we have only just come back from Holland or that A-mouse is in pig again (which she is). We just should have written.

We remembered Charlotte's birthday when we returned from Holland – I enclose a little note for her and the little note contains a humble humble apology and a not too humble check so that I hope we can redress our apparent indifference.

---

13. The words *Vivat Rex Edwardus Sextus* ('Long live King Edward the Sixth'), used in a rousing chorus in Sherborne School's song, celebrate its founding by King Edward in 1550. The motto '*Regem defendere diem videre*' ('To defend the king is to see the day') was used in the book.

My new book comes out on July 16th and is called 'A Murder of Quality'. We have done really quite well with the first now, and I have just had a letter (which will probably come to nothing) from Alfred Hitchcock's agent saying that A. H. wd like to make a TV film of it. Did you see, incidentally, that Call for the Dead got 2nd prize in the Annual Award of the Crime Writers' Association? A panel of critics (Symonds, Gielgud & co) gave a gold plated dagger to J le Carré. Hio, hio.

Ann is probably coming over to England in June/July to do some shopping & will be staying at her mother's cottage in Somerset. I think she will take the children. If she has time she'll probably take some driving lessons, as we hope to get her a small car when we move to a larger house the other side of the Rhein at the end of July. She's also going to look for a nanny, as Wendy goes home in June and we want an older bag for the new baby.

Tony wrote only a week ago – the first time for about 6 months I think – to say he was coming to Europe in September perhaps, with Anna & Alex.

I hope that next time you come & see us we shall be in a 6 bedroomed house with hot & cold, and that we shall be able to put you up in comfort.

Alison[14] is here at the moment & she & Ann are going down to Luxembourg tomorrow. I'm giving a lecture on British Foreign Policy to a crowd of 700 in Oberhausen tomorrow night – teenaged schoolchildren. Have to keep the old Adam at bay.

Simon recovers from a nasty attack of gastric 'flu & an even worse attack of temper, Ann mouse's social conscience is all that it should be and Stephen is incredible. We will send you some photographs.

Very, very much love,
D

---

14. Ann's mother, Alison Shacklock.

~

TO JEAN CORNWELL

[? January 1963]

My dearest Jeannie,

Thank you very much for our wonderful presents – mine was particularly welcome because I have become rather a fruit recently and study these things. Have written my third (and last thriller)[15] which Gollancz have accepted with much joy but am still awaiting FO approval, which is rather slow in coming. Am dashing off a little thing about Oxford at the moment – a vignette, my dear.

The new baby[16] is in the pink, eating his victuals without complaint, and prospering in mind & body. Have embarked on the perilous venture of starting up an Embassy school for young nippers – bringing out a teacher & all that – and stand to lose a packet but it looks O.K. Nothing in it for me except an O.B.E. or dismissal. Have also been travelling Germany a good deal lecturing on Common Marketry and so on – great fun. Knowledge-hungry krauts, D with loaded official picture influencing and losing friends. Hio hio.

A-mouse spends a lot of time rolling about on Ministry of Works carpets getting thinner. If only the MOW could see her in almost nothing on <u>their</u> carpets, hammering her behind on the curly Wilton.

Gave Flea a bike for Christmas – he's getting enormous. Ann teaches him herself, & his reading & writing are coming on a pace. Very reflective and soulful; Stevie quite the reverse – we

15. *The Spy Who Came in from the Cold.*

16. Timothy, le Carré's third son, was born on 6 November 1962.

gave him a telephone which works ('<u>NOT</u> you talk! <u>ME</u> talk <u>YOU</u> listen!') There's a little of Napoleon in Stevie.

We would love to see you all again. Conceivably I am bringing a delegation of German MP 's over in February – if so, I'll drop you a line & perhaps you'll all come & have lunch?

Thank you again – love, love to you all
D

∿

TO JEAN CORNWELL

[n.d. but likely spring 1963]

My dearest Jeannie,
Thanks very much for your letter. I have since had a super letter from Rupert – so sorry the children have been poorly. We are going over to Rheinbach on Saturday, where they make glass, to buy something for Elizabeth's birthday[17] – it will probably be a trifle late, therefore, or will you ask her to have patience? Stevie and Simon are being taken to the circus by their ma tomorrow afternoon – great excitement.

Rupert mentioned in his letter that you were toying with the idea of sending Charlotte out for a bit in the summer – why not send both children?[18] We would be delighted to have them. Mouse and I are sneaking off to Normandy and Brittany for May on our own while Ann's ma looks after the children & Nanny – (I passed the F.O. advanced German exam last week, roughly equivalent to an interpretership, which entitles me to an allowance – much joy – sorry, non sequitur) – but as far

17. Unidentified.

18. Jeannie's children and le Carré's half-brother and half-sister, Rupert Cornwell, then aged about seventeen, and Charlotte Cornwell, nearly fourteen.

as I know June and July and August are free. Let me know fairly soon if you cd manage it so that I can put in for a bit of leave. There's a good heated swimming pool not far from us, where they could go & enjoy themselves. There are also girls for Rupert.

I am plodding on with a new novel about Oxford – no bodies in this one – I think at last I can risk one non-commercial venture.[19] Gollancz really do seem to think the one they're bringing out in August is going to clean up.[20] I do hope it does – I think it's awfully good, of course, but then I still find my first two unputdownable. I prefer them to Dickens, for instance, and others who wrote their own instead of reading (buying) mine.

Why not get in the car one week-end and just drive to see us? May I make a concrete suggestion? What about April 19/20/21? Have you got any money left – do you want some?

Love, love,
D

∼

---

19. If le Carré wrote an Oxford novel, referenced in these two letters to Jeannie, it is untraced. In a 1963 letter to Ann's mother he also wrote of starting a 'non thriller' about Oxford and an undergraduate ('noble D [David] in disguise') called Ogilvie. Ogilvie does not appear as a character in any le Carré book until an Ogilvy in *The Night Manager*. In *Tinker Tailor Soldier Spy*, Bill Haydon recommends his friend Jim Prideaux as a Circus recruit when they are both at Oxford.

20. *The Spy Who Came in from the Cold*, his third novel.

to VIVIAN GREEN

British Embassy
Bonn

7 July 1963

My dear Vivian,

I thought you'd be pleased to hear that Paramount has bought my new book (due out in September) for (coyly) a five-figure sum and the Book Soc.[21] has made it a choice for Sep. It's called 'The Spy Who Came in from the Cold' and is a sort of Quiet American story set in Berlin. Coward McCann, the US publisher,[22] have also paid a small fortune for the rights & are aiming at simultaneous publication. If, therefore, you have any chance of visiting us here, make haste, as we may well abandon the FO for the lusher pastures of the Perfecto-Zizzbaum Corporation (P. G. Wodeh_se_).[23] For this reason, all the above is not quite for publication.

Secondly, I shall be in London from July 21st – August 1st, and visiting Oxf_d_ for part of that time, with 4 German star journalists. Any chance that you might be about? COI[24] will, no doubt, be pleased to entertain you – otherwise the P-Zizzb'm will oblige. Muddle, disgrace and royal indifference to national interest seem to characterise the domestic scene at present. Or am I reading the wrong papers?

---

21. The Book Society was founded in 1921, modelled on the American Book-of-the-Month Club. Book choices were selected each month by a panel of judges and generated mass sales.

22. Coward, McCann & Geoghegan, an imprint of G. P. Putnam's Sons. Jack Geoghegan was le Carré's first American publisher.

23. A satirical fictional film studio featured in P. G. Wodehouse's Hollywood stories, narrated by Mr Mulliner.

24. Central Office of Information, the UK government's marketing and information agency.

Please write & let us know your holiday plans. And do come
& see us if you possibly can.

Love from us both
Ever
David

~

TO JEAN CORNWELL

Hamburg

[n.d. but likely 15 October 1963]

Dearest Old Horse,[25]
At long, long last have heard from To who has a new address
(which he had omitted to tell me, and where, apparently, he
receives no mail addressed to his previous flat). He says Father
is covering vast distances by air, appears seldom, gives the
impression of being about at the end of the line, has no money
& so on. Usual To stuff, loaded with doom-tones. I'm only
afraid To will give his all with Ibsen-like compulsion. Father, he
says, is 'poor & sad to see'. Can you beat it? Feels he can't hold
his head up because he's no money, etc., Heartless D. Dear To.[26]
 [. . .]
I thought you'd like to know about the progress of the book.
It got very handsome notices (with the exception of some callow
ape in the Lit Sup who panned it, and M. Richardson – getting
past it. Losing his grip. Poor Richardson – in the Observer

---

25. A Wodehousian manner of address, used by his character Ukridge.

26. Le Carré's tone describing his brother, Tony, here recalls his 1968 statement to
the psychiatrist Dr Bockner: that it was the example of Ronnie Cornwell's malign
influence on his elder brother that made le Carré determined to break with his
father.

who was cool).[27] But the Times, S. Times, Mail, Standard & co did me proud & we've sold around 20,000 in England already, which is quite something. Dell's, the US paperback firm, have paid an all time record for a thriller of $25,000 advance; it's being serialised in the States, Canada, Australia and Norway & so on. It's sold in virtually all European countries except Finland, & the Frogs are doing an immediate paperback issue of 33,000. The net result is that we have cleaned up in a pretty big way and as long as I keep out of England until April '66 stand a goodish chance of keeping ⅔ of the stuff. Not clever D but lucky D. A.T.V.[28] wanted to do a Smiley serial with J le C writing it, but that I really <u>couldn't</u> do. Can you imagine it?

I hope the move is going/has gone/will go successfully and that you won't feel too wrung out at the end of it. Jeannie, do you want a job? I think I could guide you to one or two quite interesting ones – no chance of big money but quite amusing. Don't bother to answer if you're already fixed up.

Ann mouse has become very severe since she's discovered she's married wealth. Not at all sure she approves. It's all right, I suppose, as long as you don't enjoy it. Like sex on Sundays.

love, love to all,
D

In a later undated letter to Jeannie from Hamburg, le Carré writes: 'I have had a letter from To saying Father's absolutely down & out, and also that my mother is too, asking me (dear To) to share the expense of buying her house. As To has no money I think I shall be shamed into doing the whole thing . . .' It appeared his mother was running an orthopaedic business, with her home owned by a company with one of Ronnie's long-time associates as a director. Le Carré asked if Jeannie had the address, 'so that I can go and find out what is going on'.

---

27. Maurice Richardson reviewed *The Spy Who Came in from the Cold* in the *Observer*, 15 September 1963.

28. Associated Television.

~

TO VIVIAN GREEN

British Consulate General
2 Hamburg 13
Harvestehuderweg 8a

14 November 1963

My dear Vivian,

I am coming to London for a week, arriving on Sunday with a German group, and staying at the Hyde Park hotel. Is there any chance of seeing you? I <u>think</u> I could get down to Oxford on the Friday evening, possibly stay the night & return early on Saturday, but I would have to check when I arrive.

I am looking, among other things, for a job, as I am tired of the FO and tired of abroad. I don't really need to earn very much but we would like to buy a pleasant house almost anywhere rural and beautiful, and do something a bit useful. I know this sounds terribly airy-fairy. I had in mind one of the new universities, and wondered if you knew anything about them. I don't imagine I would qualify for Oxford teaching as I have been out of touch with my subject for so long and haven't done any research or anything. Almost anything considered really, provided it enables me to settle Ann and the children in a decent, permanent home not too far from where I work, and to let off political steam without offending anyone – that is, anyone who employs me. I would of course need time to write.

Could you send a card to the Hyde Park Hotel giving me your telephone number?

Ann and the children are fine and send their love.

Any chance of giving you dinner in London on Sunday evening?

Very best wishes – ever
David

WANDERING

Colleagues, chatter, crises, the warmth of human contact, are all grist to your mill, I'm sure; & you c<u>d</u> easily become becalmed & scared without them, as I did.

– to the writer Yassin Musharbash, in 2017, urging him to keep his journalism work until his novels took off

The success of *The Spy Who Came in from the Cold* – and the change of circumstances it wrought in le Carré's life – is almost unfathomable. He moved from a spy in the guise, and on the salary, of a junior diplomat to a writer lionised worldwide, who lunched in New York with Richard Burton and Elizabeth Taylor.

'I couldn't handle it emotionally or whatever you will,' he said. 'I had never had money before, suddenly I was being showered with money. I had lived in the shadows, seriously in the shadows, and suddenly I was having bright lights shone on me, and it imposed stresses on my marriage from which it would never recover . . . it was so extreme from the shaded withdrawn life that I had lead, the unspoken life that I had lead.'[1]

Le Carré's friendship with the writer James Kennaway and his wife, Susan, marked a watershed in his personal life, while he struggled to find a worthy follow-up to his landmark novel of the Cold War.

The novel that followed *The Spy Who Came in from the Cold* was *The Looking-Glass War*, which 'for me remained always much braver and much better and was naturally reviled'. After the success of *The Spy* – and the costly success of the spy mission within it – he deliberately wrote failure into the new novel, around a futile intelligence operation launched by 'The Department' in an attempt to relive wartime glories.

---

1. At the 'Berliner Salon', German ambassador's residence, London, 3 March 2020.

Dick Franks was le Carré's second head of station with SIS in Bonn, serving there from 1962 to 1966. His wife, Rachel, drove the Cornwell family from Bonn to Hamburg when le Carré was reassigned there in the wake of the publication of The Spy Who Came in from the Cold. *As le Carré left Hamburg and the Foreign Office, he was told by his accountant that if he returned to Britain he would risk a huge tax burden. The family sailed from Venice to Crete on 23 March 1964; le Carré had heard about Agios Nikolaos, on the eastern coast of the island, from a man he met in a swimming pool.*

TO DICK AND RACHEL FRANKS

> *Hotel Lato*
> *Agios Nikolaos*
> *Crete*
> *Greece*

> *On the beach*

> Thursday
> [n.d. but likely spring 1964]

My dear Dickie and Rachel,

Germany already seems several light years away. The journey here was a controlled nightmare – you w<u>d</u> have enjoyed it. We had 22 pieces of accompanied luggage. The three most important contained our immediate needs for the next few weeks and got stuck in Ancona because a customs man <u>struck</u> & refused to work on Saturday afternoon. When all else failed I suggested I pay his overtime. If ever you are down that way you may wish to know that the price of a customs man (off season rates) is 3,500 Lire. In Ancona also we were refused permission to board the boat (having arrived at lunchtime) until 8.0pm. It was raining heavily, there was nowhere to leave our luggage. An interesting man management problem arose but we solved it by hiring (at rather more than 3,500 Lire) the electric luggage transporter that zooms up & down platforms. This followed our 2 taxis with our heaviest luggage & a team of voluble advisers, sort of non-carrying caddies who came partly for the ride & partly, as I afterwards learned, to see what happened to the luggage truck as it is only licenced to ply railway platforms.

We arrived at Heraklion at 0530 yesterday in a deluge of rain & were dumped, not a porter in sight, at the seaward end of an enormous breakwater. The city loomed in the background, half obscured by the driving rain. All our luggage surrounded us. We had 78 Km to Agios Nikolaos & still no confirmation of the hotel bookings. Finally 2 enormous American taxis were found & we filled the first with Rhona & luggage (omnivorous boot) & the 2nd with Kinder, Kirche und Küche,[2] me & mother, & set off, without breakfast, children creating. After half an hour of mountain roads, Timothy was wonderfully, gloriously & noisily sick.

So we arrived. The hotel, recipient of 2 letters & 2 telegrams, crouched beside the harbour (fog bound) & no one had ever heard of us. Oh yes, our letters had come (they showed us the file with pride) but what was the good of a letter? Yes, of course they had rooms, they would be prepared. Doom doom. Now the children are in quarantine for mumps.

Now the sun has come out, we have a house (6 rooms, on the shore, all mod cons, £18 a month & we're robbed, beautiful little bay) a maid, some furniture, the children have paddled and we've even met the British community, most of whom look like Fred Clarke.[3] We also remember the kindness of you both and, with sincere appreciation, a lot of other things besides. Thank you too for ringing on Friday – sorry we were out.

---

2. The traditional German slogan for 'children, kitchen, church'. Le Carré often dropped German phrases into his letters to Franks.

3. Fred Clark was an American character actor with a high-domed bald head, a pencil moustache and a gift for sourly comic villainy.

Incidentally, I rang Colchester[4] from Athens & gave him my regards. Schönheitsrep. for H'burg house are not a problem – there don't seem to be any & what there is will be mine.

I leave for USA for week/10 days on April 16th – T.V. appearances, award of some kind, etc., I've signed up that TV contract & they are also making a film of Call for the Dead, don't know who with.

A house here on the coast with 4/5 rooms h & c mod con costs about £1500 at the moment. We think we'll invest. Why don't you? <u>Do</u> come & see us – it's heavenly.

Love from us all, & thanks
David

~

Le Carré and Ann had first met the Scottish writer James Kennaway and his wife, Susan, at Oxford, but in the early 1960s le Carré, now a successful novelist, met the couple again in London. In 1964 le Carré invited Kennaway to Paris to work on a film script of The Looking-Glass War. *Le Carré signed himself variously to the Kennaways as Corncrake, Cornflake and Cornguilt.*[5]

TO JAMES KENNAWAY

Hotel Ambassador Wien

[n.d. but likely 1964]

---

4. Halsey Colchester: diplomat, intelligence officer and priest, he ran the personnel department in MI6 and became vicar of Bollington in Cheshire after his retirement.

5. In a later letter to Buzz and Janet Berger he calls himself and Jane the Corncrows.

Jum,

This will probably get you before the letter I posted from Athens. I've now read 'Tunes'[6] & 'The Bells'. The letter I sent from Athens was not, I think, sufficiently enthusiastic. I can't really remember. I'm full of them, my head's singing – final scene between Jock & his actress made me weep generously. Oh hell. Jum boy you've really, really got it. In a big way. Far bigger than most of us lot. So for Gawd's <u>sake</u> take your silly finger out and give. Write bigger books with more crap in them: the crap is marvellous too (last scene in Tunes of Gl. – glorious, superb bilge – best first novel ever) but oh Jim if you love us at all, <u>write</u>

Your old winger
D

~

TO JEAN CORNWELL

Kytroplatia
Agios Nikolaos
Crete, Greece

15 May 1964

Dearest Jeannie,

Rupert[7] particularly asked me to let him know when I got back from America (where my book is <u>still</u> top of the bestseller list, hio hio) what I knew about Father. Tony[8] and Anna have seen

---

6. *Tunes of Glory*, Kennaway's first and most famous novel. Kennaway was nominated for an Oscar for his screenplay of the 1960 film, starring Alec Guinness as the Scottish major Jock Sinclair.

7. Le Carré's half-brother, Rupert Cornwell, Jeannie's son, now eighteen.

8. Tony Cornwell worked in New York for several advertising agencies, later joining Needham & Grohmann, an agency specialising in hotel, resort and travel advertising, as creative director.

a fair amount of him – Tony lent him 1000 dollars which he still hasn't had back – just a dud cheque. I also saw him once in NY and arranged to have dinner with him but he didn't show up – sent a message instead to say he was going out of town, but I heard from Tony that this was untrue. It was probably my own fault – we met (believe it or not) by sheer chance – he was dining in the restaurant where I was giving a party for my publisher, and after dinner I asked him & his partner over to our table. I was fairly bored about three things – his owing To money, the fact that he has been signing my books 'from the author's father' and the fact that he has been <u>ordering</u> my books on credit representing himself as my father and not meeting the bills, which ended up in a couple of cases with my publisher. So I was fairly short with him (I had a holy terror of his getting into the act, which was a high powered one involving E. Taylor, Burton & co)[9] and also because I found his woman friend so disagreeable. I behaved like a prig, therefore, & he was much as usual! I begged him to write to Rupert, & I told him about yourself, & about the situation with my mother. He was evasive about his own affairs but I gather from To that he has been on his uppers more than once. He looks pretty seedy, I'm afraid. None of us could work out what he is living on, or how he hopes to make out – he has a flat but no furniture, is practically never available there, a woman just takes messages. Tony believes he is on the edge of trouble about credit, but when isn't he? Apparently when he came to NY he was armed with big introductions & began at the Plaza – since then the contacts & the addresses have become increasingly modest. More particularly he has no permit to work – so if they once start looking in to him, To feels, there may be trouble. He was terribly anxious to see me alone, which was why I suggested dinner, but as I say he didn't turn up. I would have tried to do something more if it hadn't been for my engagements and the complications that

9. Elizabeth Taylor and Richard Burton, with the latter to star in *The Spy Who Came in from the Cold*.

arose on the film sale of Call for the Dead, my immigrant status from point of view of TV appearances & finally US Income Tax!

Did you get the pie from Fortnums? Thank you so much for having me.

Rupert can come out as soon as he likes as far as we're concerned. I would love him to be out here by July 1st because I have to go to London & Denmark & A-mouse would welcome his company. I am writing all this to you because I think you should decide how & what to tell him about Father. He does cut a very tragic figure, I should say a fairly desperate one too; Tony, who loves him far better than I, has become pretty bitter about him, about his exploitation of affection and all the rest. Personally – but then I'm biassed – I think Rupert should get on with his own life and with his university course, which is vitally important for him, and cope with Father when he is a little stronger. Just now, I don't believe there is anything any of us can do. He seems to have women friends; I don't know who they are. I don't think Rupert's affection will do anything but upset Rupert.

My impression of Father was that we didn't really exist for him over there. He didn't ask after anyone – I gave him what news I could.

I have asked To to write to Rupert. They seem quite happy. It was awfully hard for me to behave in a normal way because I was being so lionised & it was all so rapid.

My love to you all. Come & see us.
D

∼

Ann was typing The Looking-Glass War, *a bitter novel of failed efforts at spying and failing marriages. A British intelligence agency, The Department, clinging to faded glories of the last war, launches an inept mission to send an agent into East Germany, pursuing flimsy reports of a Soviet rocket build-up.*

TO VICTOR GOLLANCZ

> *Kytroplatia*
> *Agios Nikolaos*
> *Crete, Greece*
>
> 30 May 1964

Dear V. G.,

Thank you for your letter of May 26th. I hope we shall be offering you a manuscript by mid July. The book is finished, is in a messy state and Ann is typing it out painfully as I write.

Once the book is accepted I shall have to make a short trip to Scandinavia and (if I can get in) to East Germany, but that should not take more than a week. I also have to do a little more research on rocketry and wireless transmission but none of these chores affect more than thirty or forty lines of print, and I think it legitimate to offer the book subject to the additional research.

When Ann has typed it, it goes to the Foreign Office for formal approval – that is a courtesy I think worth while – and then for typing by an agency – I want several copies this time – and then to Peter.[10] We shall then (Ann and I) heave a sigh of relief and go on our long delayed tour of Greece.

If you could give me your itinerary, it would be very nice to arrange a meeting somewhere: we would love to offer you both hospitality here, but I fear we shall be taking our holiday at the same time as yourselves.

Best wishes –
Yours ever,
David

---

10. Peter Watt, le Carré's agent.

~

On 10 June 1963 le Carré's publisher Victor Gollancz had approached both J. B. Priestley and Graham Greene with a view to obtaining quotes for The Spy Who Came in from the Cold. *'I think you will find in it an unmistakable (and quite terrible) authenticity,' he wrote.*

Priestley's response went on the front cover: 'A superbly constructed story with an atmosphere of chilly hell.' But Greene delivered the line that would stay with the book for decades to come: Josephine Reid, his secretary, passed on his message that it was 'the best spy story I have ever read'.

When le Carré left his publishing house after the publication of The Spy, *Gollancz reacted with fury, saying the quote he got from Greene gave the book its 'great break'. Greene heard of le Carré's move, and wrote to try to recruit him for the Bodley Head, where he was a director.*

Le Carré's literary relationship with Greene is dotted through his correspondence, and swings from the veneration shown here to later privately scathing remarks about Greene's politics.

TO GRAHAM GREENE

Kytroplatia
Agios Nikolaos
Crete
Greece

4 August 1964

Dear Mr Greene,
Thank you for your letter of July 17th, which reached me today after a long journey.

I wish I could respond to your kind suggestion – in my ignorance I did not even know you were a Director of the Bodley Head, but I fear it is now too late. I can only promise you that if the present negotiations fall through I will get in touch with you.

You have given me an opportunity to write to you, which I have long wanted to do, to thank you most sincerely for your support. I do not need to tell you what this has meant to me, both practically, since it contributed immeasurably to the success of my last book, and morally because there are few writers, living or dead, whose support I would appreciate more. I have just finished another book which, I fear, will not be out much before the Autumn of next year. I will, if I may, send you a copy, not in order to solicit another quote, but because I would enormously like to hear what you think of it.

And I am sorry I cannot at the moment think of coming to the Bodley Head.

Please don't bother to answer this.

Yours sincerely,
David Cornwell

~

TO JAMES KENNAWAY

[n.d. but likely 1964, from Athens]

Cher St Jum,
I have just finished 'the Bells' – it seemed the decent thing to begin on your last book first, and listen you're great. I go all the way with the Hudson Review.[11] You're God.

But: I ask myself one question only – whether a great writer has written a great book. Will you listen while I drift into my

11. Kennaway's *The Bells of Shoreditch* featured in a 'Fiction Chronicle' by Patrick Cruttwell in the *Hudson Review* in the summer of 1964. Kennaway was the 'most intriguing' new novelist to have emerged in Britain in the last ten years, he wrote. *The Bells* was 'a true novel' that shared qualities with Jane Austen. In it, Glaswegian socialist Stella Vass has an affair with amoral financier J. T. Sarson, the boss of her husband, Andrew.

facile critical act? As in your play, you produce one knife so sharp that the others lose their edge a little: the duck, Stella. I think you suffer from jealousy with your characters: 'nobody knows Stella as well as Beeg Jeem does, nobody lays Stella as well as Beeg Jeem does.' If you give her that much force, we can't believe (I can't) that she stops at the end of the road. If you give A that kind of weakness it's hard to believe, etc., I notice, with the nasty, corosive writer's eye, the <u>ingredients</u> of Stella which I believe are unnecessary: she's complete without them. One of these is her socialism, which is not real for you because I don't believe she (or you) give a fuck about politics but only about class and attitudes, so that I feel her resentment should stem from her origin rather than her intellect – probably does. Misread, Cornwell. There were two scenes I didn't dig: the solicitor (hogged the scene, constructed man; writer's nerves. A superb scene without a Big One there) and the Sarson lecture bit. Characteristically, both scenes are superbly written.

Summa summarum: brilliant poetry, brilliant visions, brilliant people, brilliant Jum. Superstructure (Edinburgh shipowner, currency fiddling, politics, smart Trust office) sags, creaks, but who on earth cares? I find it heartening & splendid that after the hamming you have done, you're so <u>bad</u> at hamming; and so <u>bloody</u>, bloody good at writing. People, poetry, and the drama are magnificent. It's as good as I expected. Rarer perhaps. It's less expert than I expected – astonishing. I think you've proved what is bound to be accepted – that you have it in very large quantities. And I am convinced that you will (if you break a few fences) write something bloody soon that will outlive G. Green, C. Snow, Monica Dickens and your admiring mate

John le Carré[12]

---

12. At the time of writing, the only copies of *The Bells of Shoreditch* available on Amazon were second-hand, including several modestly priced first editions from 1963.

❦

Undated, but refers to the twenty-four-hour strike in Austria of 13 February 1965. The Cornwells were staying in Vienna; the Kennaways had taken a house in Zell-am-See, Austria. Le Carré gave instructions for sending covert telegrams signed 'Yours Peter'. In early 1965 he would tell his wife Ann that he and Susan were having an affair – begun, according to Susan, in November 1964.[13]

to SUSAN KENNAWAY

[n.d.]

Darling,

Heaven knows when this will reach you: Austria is in the hands of a strike which includes Post, telegraph, telephone, railways & aeroplanes; and anything else they can think of. At the moment it's for a provisional 24 hours but they have every hope of extending it.

I become more & more hopeless for you, don't I? Dear heart, try to understand a mole too used to the dark to believe in light; if you live, as I have, so long in the dark, you can't always, if you are me, have faith in the light. When I make myself think of what we have now done together, the muddles, the laughter and the companionship, the total ease and warmth of being in your company, the whole futility of my own life becomes unbearable; then I shout your name inside me, and

---

13. The relationship between le Carré and James and Susan Kennaway would inspire two novels: Kennaway's *Some Gorgeous Accident* in 1967, and le Carré's *The Naive and Sentimental Lover*, published in 1971. In 2013 the Edinburgh Fringe saw an unsuccessful theatre production of *Some Gorgeous Accident*. Le Carré, in a letter to the producers, declined to help with any publicity, but added: 'I have long made my admiration for Kennaway's writing clear and, if I have more to say, I shall say it in my own time and in my own way.'

hold your body against me, and laugh and unwind, and live; and even my children round me, ghosts, little written on faces, are no reproach for that happiness. I know how little faith you have in me – sorry, but you said it so often – and I know how little faith I deserve; but if I can still exist for you, keep me, keep me, because I love you.

David

P.S. I will ring <u>Hillie's</u> number next SUNDAY at 10 o'clock your time – if I can. (We are in Bonn then). If you aren't there, leave a message when I can ring you (I'll make it a personal call). For emergencies, I am staying at the Hotel Cäcilienhöhe, Bad Godesberg, near Bonn, W Germany; Tel no. Bad Godesberg 62733. Any telegram signed 'Yours Peter' can come there direct. I get there on Friday.

∾

The only letter to Ronnie Cornwell that is known to have survived was sent to Jeannie Cornwell with a handwritten covering note.

TO JEAN CORNWELL

Jeannie –
Got an enraged letter from father – sent this. Thought you might like to see it.

love D

Wien XIX
Hohe Warte 29
Austria

20 March 1965

Dear Father,

Thank you for your letter and for the copy of the letter you sent to Pitman of the Express. I really am sorry that the article upset you. You must understand that I have a very difficult hand to play in answering journalists' questions about my family background and about yourself. Any newspaper has in its archives enough clippings about you to make a far more embarrassing picture than the one I painted. Robert Pitman is not to blame for whatever you find inaccurate; the article was a pretty faithful report of what I said to him. He is, on the other hand, warmly to be thanked for not making use of more painful material which was already available to him.

The choice in such cases is invidious. If one says nothing, one invites speculation and disagreeable revelations; if one takes the other course as I did, one runs other risks.

After Pitman had left Vienna I telephoned Jean and asked her to warn whoever she could, particularly your sisters and Rupert and Charlotte, that the article would appear, and that it represented the best I could make of a precarious situation. I could not do more.

If you have become shy of publicity I suggest you refrain from writing provocative letters to such skilled newspapers as the Express.

You do not say whose disapproval I have incurred. The only reactions I have had are from Rupert and G. P. Ellard. The former was relieved and the latter fulsome with praise.

I, like you, hope you will be spared for many more years on this planet. It would certainly be poorer without you, and I think this is something which the average reader would have deduced from Pitman's article.

Yours ever,

Robert Pitman's interview in the Sunday Express *of 14 February 1965 did not use Ronald Cornwell's name, but it included details that would become staples of le Carré's future writing about his father.*

In the hands of a skilled interviewer, le Carré gave a detailed chronology of his life at Sherborne, Bern, Oxford and Eton. He included Ronnie's attempts to become an MP, that he owned race-horses and hosted the Australian cricket team, along with the legendary jockey Gordon Richards.

Pitman, an Express *columnist and regular of TV debating shows, interviewed le Carré in Vienna, where he was staying with his family before their return to the UK. Perhaps le Carré's sense of safety in Austria, or the prospect that the* Express *was to serialise* The Looking-Glass War, *encouraged him to open up.*

'When I look back at my life, I am so appalled that the reaction is to keep down the lid,' *he told Pitman. He spoke of his stern Christian grandfather, the mayor of Poole, and suggested his father had reacted against him; he gave a veiled account of his father's business dealings, mentioning a series of large houses in Buckinghamshire; he related how* 'we had it rich and we had it poor . . . the less we had, the more we seemed to spend.' *He had barely seen his father in years, he finally said, but knew he had been signing le Carré's books* 'From the author's father'.

Pitman described le Carré as one of a handful of world writers who could earn £500,000 for a book. Ronnie's feelings, reading of his son growing fabulously – and legitimately – wealthy, can only be imagined.

Le Carré suggested later that the principal effect of his success upon his father was to create in him 'a sense of entitlement'. In a Vienna meeting at the famous Hotel Sacher, he recalled, Ronnie asked his son first for a substantial sum of money as recompense for his school fees, and then to buy him a pig and cattle farm in Dorset. Le Carré refused.

∽

TO SUSAN KENNAWAY

[n.d. but likely mid 1965]

I waited till today to write. In the night I lay awake and hoped the day would come; when I went to bed I said goodnight to you like a prayer, and when the morning did come I said the prayer again and got up & fiddled in the kitchen, still drunk with love and still deeply hurt from the pain. I want to write this, my love, not in the aftermath of seeing you, not in the night or in the early morning, but against a real sky, and all I can see is your face, and the lines I think I have drawn, and the eyes I have made sad; all that I love. Look, this is the truth, what I am going to say. Your marriage is sane and real; I love your marriage and James almost as much as I love you, because I love your way of living and understanding, I despise what you despise, and if you had made a silly marriage, as I have, you wouldn't be Susie.[14] I've failed where you succeeded, I want what you've got, but I don't want to take it away from you, nothing. I don't covet, I swear; I would have done six months ago but now I don't: it was James' year. Nothing you have ever said or done, not a smile or a moment's hesitation, has displeased me since I fell in love with you. I can't pretend that I have not envied James, but I'm not jealous of him; I like the places you live, and your children and your courage, and I believe in your marriage. Because I've mucked things up for myself, and am available, I'm frightened of my own infections spreading. I don't <u>want</u> to unsettle you, break you or hurt you – listen that isn't guilt, or love, but observation: you <u>have</u> created something real and good. Don't let me in. I want to take your

---

14. In 1981 Susan Kennaway, later Vereker, published *The Kennaway Papers*, with notebooks, letters and diaries around James Kennaway's friendship with le Carré and the affair with Susan that followed. In it she wrote that she and le Carré agreed they could not break up two families and live together, although there were dramatic scenes after James discovered their affair. James Kennaway suffered a heart attack and died in a car accident in December 1968, aged forty.

decision for you. I warned you at the start: there's too much to release in me. Don't do it.

But because of everything, I'm not going to give you the choice. I love you beyond everything: I think that. But we start so hopelessly disparate in terms of our needs and our obligations that I cannot see how I can ever express my love in a way that will not destroy the things that make your life. You know I worship you; I really think I love you enough to be brave and leave you. Do you believe that? Please don't doubt me now. The few days with you, all of us together, must secretly have made it plain to you. You said you felt less guilty now you had met Ann. Do you really think I did? Susie, my love, don't cry. You have my heart, my whole love; I don't believe you can doubt that. Find another lover, or don't. Don't philosophize about it (that was my fault, darling) but for the love of Heaven, know what you've got in James. I would marry you, take you away, do all the things you wanted; but I never shall, and you must know that now. Darling heart, my darling Susie, don't dare me any more. Write to me; I love you beyond everything; write to me. Look, I am writing the letter you nearly wrote yourself, or wrote and tore up. It doesn't work my way; you never meant this to happen and I did. That's the truth that we're always told. I've never felt closer to you than now, I have never loved you more, never loved you more than now. Look, I am holding you, as in my heart I will always, close to me. I am trying to love you more than that and send you away. I want to give: that's love. I don't want to take or destroy. I want to give. I love you. If you see any other way, if you can honestly see any other hope, tell me. But I will <u>not</u> destroy what you have. I love you. Don't write a spikey letter. Write. I'll be back on the 9th.

～

TO JEAN CORNWELL

British Consulate General
200 S. Michigan Avenue
Chicago, USA

[Postmark] 29 September 1965

Jeannie love,

I expect you have heard from Ann – if you haven't I must tell you now – that for the time being at least I'm not coming back to England. There isn't anyone else involved – I haven't got another girl or anything – but the tensions between us became intolerable and I'm afraid I've run away. I can't expect you – you, who had no idea that things were not perfect between us – to be anything but shocked and upset. But I have been very unhappy for the last year or two & suddenly I can't take it any more. I don't think the children (yours) need know anything except that I'm abroad writing for an extended time, unless it gets into the papers, which of course it may. Please give Ann a ring if you can – I miss the children terribly, and I'm nice and miserable. Don't write and tell me I'm a pig, I know I am. But I can't change it now.

In case your cup isn't full, the FO has caught up with Father, who has got into the Embassy stream by running up an enormous bill in Djakarta, had his passport confiscated & told the Ambassador it was a temporary problem of liquidity. They want to 'repatriate' him as far as Bangkok because the Indonesians are very angry with him. I'm trying to find out what's happening.

Poor, poor Jeannie, I love you so & I am sorry to cause you all this pain. I'm going off the air for a bit. I'm really not a bad person, isn't it silly. And now I've done something awful.

D

TO STEPHEN CORNWELL

12 October 1965

My darling Stevie,

I love you so much. How are you? I hear your new school is not quite as fine as the school in Chew Magna, but don't worry because soon we'll all be in the Forever House and like old moles in a deep, safe hole. I seem to do nothing but fly round the world in aeroplanes to write the new book. But soon it will all be done and I shall be able to come and feast with all the family for Christmas, and roister with all the boys. Do you know what I saw this evening? An organ player turning his organ and a little chained-up monkey dancing to the music. I didn't think such things were to be seen in London any more. Here is a drawing of the monkey: and of the organ grinder. You could colour it.

Darling Stevie, take care of Timo and Mummy, and be as dear as always.[15] Back soon

Daddy

~

TO JEAN CORNWELL

[Postmark] 14 October 1965

Darling Jeannie,

It was the best letter you ever wrote and I love you so much. Please take care of her because of course I love her – even if it all gets messier, I do somehow love her and I am in agony about the children. I must stay away from her still, both to write and to give it all depth and lasting meaning – I think it's now or never. We

---

15. Stephen was now five years old and Timothy almost three.

player turning his organ and a little chained-up monkey dancing to the music. I didn't think such things were to be seen in London any more. Here is a drawing of the monkey : and of the organ grinder. You could colour it.

Darling Stevie, take care of Timo and Mummy, and be as dear as always. Back soon

Daddy.

couldn't go on like that. At moments I could just call a car and dash to her & the boys, but I have to resist and I will. Don't tell her all this because it's only painful & not easy for her to understand. I'm not God, but she <u>has</u> been sick & wrong – I'm sure of that. She thinks I'm so strong & sure of myself & <u>you</u> know how frightened I am, & insecure, and how writing or painting or having babies is to make order out of chaos – it's what we all do every day.

Darling, darling Jeannie, look after your super grown-up children & look after Ann and my babies & I do love you so.

D

~

TO JEAN CORNWELL

Coxley House
Coxley
Nr Wells
Somerset

30 April 1966

Dearest Jeannie,

How are things? I heard by chance that you were divorcing Father, which made me <u>very</u> happy – I hope it all goes through without fuss.

I'm nice and miserable and would like to have dinner with you one evening soon. Could you manage something in London? Could we make it a little ahead? Monday May 16th, for instance? Come to the flat after work, have a drink & I'll take you on to the Savoy.

I'm sure you don't want anything said about your own affairs & I shan't mention it to the children.

Love,
David

~

Ever since The Spy Who Came in from the Cold, *le Carré recalled in* The Pigeon Tunnel, *he had been the target of Soviet literary invective, 'one moment . . . for elevating the spy to heroic status . . . the next for making the right perceptions about the Cold War but drawing erroneous conclusions . . .*

'From the trenches of the Soviet Literary Gazette, *controlled by the KGB, and* Encounter *magazine, controlled by the CIA, we dutifully lobbed our bombs at each other, aware that in the sterile ideological war of words, neither side was going to win.'*

'To Russia, with Greetings', an open letter to the Moscow Literary Gazette, *was published in* Encounter *in May 1966. The magazine was founded by Stephen Spender and Irving Kristol; its CIA funding was exposed in 1967.*

TO THE EDITOR, *LITERATURNAYA GAZETA*

May 1966

'To Russia, with Greetings'

Sir,

After the publication of *The Spy Who Came in from the Cold* in many languages and countries, I waited hopefully for a reaction from the Communist bloc. The more so, perhaps, because of the widely differing reactions I had already received from readers in America, some of whom charged me with writing a 'pro-Communist' book. My literary agent needed some persuading before he approached the Soviet Union and other East European countries. For the record: Rumania, Bulgaria, Czechoslovakia, and Hungary declined the book without comment. Poland took the precaution of protecting even her publishers from its odious qualities: a Polish publishing house twice reported that it had not received my agent's copy, adding in its second letter the injunction: 'We suppose not to risk again with sending it.' One Balkan editor excised the passages he found most obnoxious and returned the remnants. It was a little like recovering one's shirt from a faulty washing machine.

With profound surprise, therefore, I read the article in your issue of 14 October 1965, in which a Russian critic discusses my work. There are many questions I would ask of your contributor, Mr Voinov, just as he – judging by his bewilderment – would be grateful for my own clarifications. I suppose I would like him to tell me what is the value of reviewing books which his readers will never be allowed to see? What is his purpose in warning them against an evil of which they would otherwise be ignorant? But perhaps I had better be grateful that my work was noticed at all, and confine myself to the content of Mr Voinov's article.

Mr Voinov observes, rightly I think, that I have little good to say of the British power structure, or of the morals of British intelligence, and he notes with commendable accuracy that I have little good to say of the Communist system either. He says – what could be nicer? – that realism and cleverness distinguish my books from those of the late Ian Fleming, and he implies (precisely as the *Daily Worker* has recently implied) that the poison is more deadly.

In the book of mine which occupies the larger part of his review (*The Spy Who Came in from the Cold*) I have equated, in hypothetical terms, the conduct of East and West in the espionage war. I have suggested that they use the same weapons – deceit – and even the same spies (a point Mr Khrushchev made long before I did). To ram the message home, I chose some rather obvious paradoxes. The functionaries in opposing intelligence services feel closer to one another than to their own controllers. A man who is in the pay of *both* intelligence services is a particularly odious ex-Nazi. The central character in the book loves two people and both are Jews: by indulging his decent instincts, he destroys them both. I used Jewish people because I felt that after Stalin and Hitler they should particularly engage our protective instincts.

By these and other means I sought to remove espionage from the sterile arguments of the cold war and concentrate the reader's eye on the cost to the West, in moral terms, of fighting the legitimised weapons of Communism. For this reason, my Western agent is at a loss to defend himself in ideological dispute with his Communist interrogator. The Communist *should* be able to reconcile the loss of innocent life with the progress of the proletarian revolution; Western man can't. [. . .] I suggested that in this respect the Communist argument is clearer than that of the West because it sees the progress of humanity in collective terms. [. . .] For a Communist there is nothing inherently wrong in sacrificing the uncommitted to the course of history. If Mr Voinov doesn't know this, he ought to be reading more solid fare than mine. To a Western man, there inherently is, but he does it all the same. Western inhibitions spring from the Christian and humanist ethic that the individual is worth more than the collective. In espionage as I have depicted it Western man sacrifices the individual to defend the individual's right against the collective. That is Western hypocrisy, and I condemned it because I felt it took us too far into the Communist evaluation of the individual's place in society. Why should that bother Mr Voinov?

In *The Looking-Glass War*, to which he also refers, I tried to deal with a different aspect of the same Western predicament. The ideological deadlock which provided the background to *The Spy Who Came in from the Cold* is replaced by the psychological deadlock of men whose emotional experiences are drawn from an old war. The piping has stopped but they still dance. [. . .] I tried to touch new ground when I discussed the phenomenon of committed men who are committed to nothing but one another and the dreams they collectively evoke. [. . .] Because I chose a Western Intelligence Service as a vehicle for these ideas, do not think, I beg you, that I consider they do not apply elsewhere. I mention this because I have heard rumours that *The Looking-Glass War* may after all be published in the Soviet Union.

I now realise that both these books make an assumption which is anathema to a Communist, and directly contrary to the trend now established by the public relations team of the Soviet Secret Services: that the enemy is not outside us but within, that we fight not looking forward but looking back, not for the future but for the past. The problem of the Cold War is that, as Auden once wrote, we haunt a ruined century. Behind the little flags we wave, there are old faces weeping, and children mutilated by the fatuous conflicts of preachers. Mr Voinov, I suspect, smelt in my writing the greatest heresy of all: that there is no victory and no virtue in the Cold War, only a condition of human illness and a political misery. And so he called me its apologist (he might as well have called Freud a lecher).

James Bond, on the other hand, breaks no such Communist principles. You know him well. He is the hyena who stalks the capitalist deserts, he is an identifiable antagonist, sustained by capital and kept in good heart by the charms of a materialist society; he is a chauvinist, an unblinking patriot who makes espionage exciting, the kind of person in fact who emerges from Lonsdale's diaries. Bond on his magic carpet takes us away from moral doubt, banishes perplexity with action, morality with duty. Above all, he has the one piece of equipment without which not even his formula would work: an entirely evil enemy. He is on your side, not mine. Now that you have honoured the qualities which created him, it is only a matter of time before you recruit him. Believe me, you have set the stage: the Russian Bond is on his way.

With greetings,
John le Carré

When Charlotte Cornwell learnt she was pregnant, having just turned seventeen, her half-brother David was the first one she called, and he guessed before she told him. He wanted to help in any way he could; Ann offered to raise the child. In the event the baby boy was adopted.

TO JEAN CORNWELL

> *Coxley House*
> *Coxley*
> *Nr Wells*
> *Somerset*

> 3 June 1966

Dearest Jeannie,

No one has done more, ever, to earn my admiration than yourself in the last three days. I found myself almost leaning on you.

Darling Jeannie, please don't blame yourself too much. Let me tell you how it always looked from the outside: this is much what I wrote to Rupert today. Charlotte suffered change of a kind Rupert avoided. Rupert kept his status, Winchester and Magdalen, and – because his pride suffered from the internal knocks and deprivations caused by Father – turned himself into a bit of an escape artist. Self preservation became for Rupert a way of life: sartorially, in the choice of a wierd subject, in the leap outward to Greece, in the placing of love in his absent father, in a strongly materialist attitude.[16] Beside this went his love for you, and need for you. At times he found home odious, wanted 'out', but even the escaper had to come back. For Charlotte, the reverse happened. She took on the

---

16. Rupert Cornwell read Modern Greek at Oxford. An award-winning foreign correspondent, he reported for *Reuters*, the *Financial Times* and the *Independent*, from Paris, Brussels, Rome, Bonn, Moscow and latterly Washington; he also worked for spells in London. He was known for his pin-sharp reporting and immaculate copy, with an eye for discerning fact from fraud that notably eluded his father, Ronnie.

responsibility of you, and your love, gave up Father, suffered all the changes on the surface as well as inside, and was concerned more than any of you with staying put, of being part of the new environment, the new (lower) status. (Miss McKay said she was marvellous at school – popular, a good prefect, no trouble, remarkably integrated.) She had no escape, she had the full treatment, and suffered all the upset literally, as it happens, on her own body. I believe what she has done has no more relevance to morality than wetting her bed. The dreadful thing is that nothing you could do could ever give them back a Father, social confidence, or destroy their sense of being incomplete, and nothing you could do will stop, or could ever stop, Charlotte from being the one to suffer. When you say you thought it might happen, were almost waiting for it to happen, I think you simply acknowledged that they had inherited (Charlotte particularly) qualities and circumstances that were bound to collide; and you knew the result would be tragic. To that extent, I agree. I believe you gave everything, did everything you humanly could for your children – without indulgence. You never chained them down or pushed them out; you did, quite simply, all you could, but you couldn't beat the circumstances. To me, she is paying the price for what happened to <u>all</u> Father's children.

I also believe you now have the feeling that it may even be to the good, that the baby is a catalyst, the challenge of truth in some way. That's a belief I share. I'll ring you on Monday; I gather King has been on to you. Dear Jeannie.

love,
D

Charlotte was reunited with her son, Mark Baylis, in 2006.

∾

The Comedians was published in 1966.

TO GRAHAM GREENE

> *Coxley House*
> *Coxley*
> *Wells*
> *Somerset*

[n.d. but likely 1966]

Dear Mr Greene,

I have just finished my second reading of 'The Comedians' and I find it quite excellent – for my taste, your greatest novel. I do hope you realise that that is the common talk of everyone one meets. I would not have bothered you with this letter had I not been disgusted by the Amis review, which seemed to me the cheapest thing I had read for a long time.[17] Why does no one dwell on the construction? There can be few plots in our time which so perfectly <u>move</u> the idea, and few characters which so innocently move the plot. It was, is a really wonderful book. I am too stuck with German ideas I know, but I could not help equating the thesis of the book to that of the Thomas Mann short stories – the notion of the artist and his relation to the citizen. You say quite casually in humanist terms what Mann contrived in mechanical terms; what Mann blared at us with an orchestra you play gently in clear, solitary themes, and having established your distinctions you continually re-arrange them. You have also done strange and marvellous things with motive:

---

17. In 'Slow Boat to Haiti' in the *Observer*, 30 January 1966, Kingsley Amis began: 'After about a hundred pages of Graham Greene's new novel, one begins rather irritably to notice the style.' It critiqued clumsy word order and the use of hyphens, but conceded the lively and angry reporting of Haiti and the Haitians made the book 'compulsory reading'.

'I am behaving like this because people are watching me' is not an easy notion to express!

Although it is a book which will provide critics with endless interpretations (the Germans will run on for ever) it is also wonderfully entertaining. I do believe it is a masterpiece – that is all I am trying to tell you.

Don't bother to reply to this, and please believe that I am neither trying to requite your generosity to me, nor secure it for the future. I am spellbound by a great novel in our own time and wanted to tell you so.

Yours ever,
David Cornwell

~

TO C. P. SNOW[18]

> *Coxley House*
> *Coxley*
> *Wells*
> *Somerset*

21 July 1968

PERSONAL

Dear Lord Snow,

Charles Pick[19] telephoned me today and read aloud your piece on 'A Small Town in Germany.' This evening I was able to read it for myself. I do not know what to say; though you wrote it of course with publication in mind, it had the close, personal quality of a private letter. So if I do not dwell on the more

---

18. The scientist and novelist C. P. Snow was made a life peer in 1964.

19. Le Carré's publisher at Heinemann.

practical advantages, it is not that I have overlooked them; it is that by a mixture of perception and generosity and coincidence you touched me very deeply.[20] The book took me two and a half years, and I wrote it three times, once with a narrator, once without a Leo-figure at all (Turner was an Embassy official) and finally in the form in which you read it. Once I gave it up altogether, and last Christmas I wrote to Pick & to my American publisher to say the book had defeated me, and they should not expect anything from me for some time. All this was doubly upsetting since, like yourself, I don't care to spend too long on a book – the paint gets thick and grey and the subject changes too often. About a year ago, I had considered giving up writing altogether. In addition to all this, I ran into one of those phases of multiple personal misfortune inside & outside my family, and was constantly having to rush off & put out fires. And the longer they waited, the more despondent my publishers became, and the more urgent their requests: 'for your own good, don't you think . . .' and so on. (I exclude Pick from that charge!) Finally, on the first of January, I gave myself four months, took a clean bit of paper and began willy-nilly for the last time. It was, as I say, one of those spells; it is more or less over now and I really don't belong by temperament to the precious school of writers who can only work when they are 'in the mood'. Meanwhile I had behind me the poor reception, in England at least, which greeted my last book, and before me the dubious assurance that a good thriller would recover a declining reputation. All it amounts to now, I suppose, is what the trade calls 'a block', but I took it, as we all do, very tragically at the time.

Perhaps you can understand, therefore, what your piece means to me. Your appreciation alone would have been a great comfort, but in the form it took, it was much more. Turner, banishing doubt with action, giving external form to the

---

20. C. P. Snow had introduced le Carré in an article for the Book of the Month Club as 'one of the most interesting writers alive'.

internal journey, the clear eye & the painful heart, and the need to come out fighting – all the inner things you understood and expressed in your piece were for me the very substance of the book, but I had not expected to hear it said, and I wanted you to know, for your own satisfaction perhaps, how acutely trenchant I felt your observations to be.

As to my reference, a year or two ago, to my debt to C. P. Snow. It was not mere politeness. Rightly or wrongly, I have always responded to a sense of hopelessness in your books. I don't mean pessimism, least of all nihilism. But in your private *échelle des êtres* I am constantly bumping up against people with ambition but no purpose; at the end of the night-walk of all your heroes, after the ghostly change and interchange of people, I have always fancied a lost, bewildered retirement. How will Smiley end his days? Or Turner? I'm afraid in your clubs and corridors, their time served, puzzled and occasionally deeply, if briefly, indignant.

There: it is a travesty, I know, of much of your work, but I thought you would like to know that I was not offering a *coup de chapeau* to a very generous elder writer; I have admired the <u>form</u> of Graham, but never the metaphysics; I have thought I responded to a quality in your own work not easily touched upon, but for me both real and sad.

This is a mess of a letter; I barely dare re-read it. Thank you – at least you can believe in my gratitude if not my critical faculty. And it is not the Good Housekeeping seal for which I am chiefly grateful – though it will enormously help the book – it is the timely and profoundly perceptive understanding which you brought to bear upon my work.

With best wishes to Lady Snow.
Yours ever,
David

~

TO CHARLES PICK

Coxley House
Coxley
Nr Wells
Somerset

2 November 1968

My dear Charles,

Thank you so much for your hospitality, and for the party; I am so sorry about the German boy, but there it is: possibly it will reflect back, certainly it will help Hans Polak,[21] who remains much stimulated by the book's prospects.

I know you are terribly disappointed about the reception the book[22] has received; deep down, you seem to be more depressed than I am. I <u>know</u> it is my best book by far, and I know what I have to do for the future. Equally, it is not a perfect book, and I am one of those writers whose imperfections are a great deal more interesting than their virtues. To be honest, I am even alarmed at how seriously the reviews affect you; and by now the 'Times' will have driven in the extra nail; it is an unanswerable charge, and therefore cheaply made, that I am too rich, too pretentious, too much all the rest. For critics, you <u>must</u> try and realise, I am simply too much altogether: too fluent, too young, and too capable. This is why, after 'The Spy', I recognised, as I believe you must, that personal publicity about me is very ill-advised. We can't have it both ways: I'll give Grosvenor[23] his vulgar copy if you insist, but let's not suppose it will help me to critical recognition. I'll help you make a good go of the launching party, but every big name that is gratuitously attached to mine chimes out another review like

---

21. Hans W. Polak was a co-translator of two of Graham Greene's books.

22. *A Small Town in Germany*.

23. The *Daily Express* journalist Peter Grosvenor wrote the 'New Books' column.

those that have hurt most. This is something Jack[24] and I have learnt at great cost in the States: I <u>am</u> in an extremely equivocal position. A thriller-writer with pretentions? A novelist who hasn't the guts to drop the thriller form? An FO smoothie doing his upper-class PR and inviting the Establishment he lampoons . . . and so on. I have in fact only one identity that will matter to either of us over the next few years: I write in my own way about my own things. At the moment, this is the anti-time; I wish so much that you would see me in this light. Every review that gives me quarter is (to me) a bloody miracle, and this is what I wanted so much to tell you on that Sunday evening. Three books from now, they will have got used to me: but at the moment, they must live uncomfortably with what they have created. But you wanted it <u>now</u> (which is nothing but sympathetic) whereas I look to you to bridge the gap between The Spy and that second-state recognition which I don't think will come for anything up to ten years.

Do you mind my saying all this? I have already taken leave of 'A Small Town' – I must do – but in doing so, I feel I must try to explain the difference (as I saw it) between our two reactions. Personally, I think the sales will ultimately survive the reception, because the book remains 'a good read'. I have nothing but admiration for the way you have all put it together: Roland's editing, Nigel's production & Tim's selling.[25] But I wish very much I could mitigate your own disappointment – while confessing to my own – and I wish I could explain to you my ambivalence about being turned into a public personality. For two pins, if I were pushed, I would stumble into Telly and all the rest of the cheap ways to public acclaim. But my wisest course, and the course in which you <u>must</u> help me, is to see my own writing future in the round, and not expect 'The Spy' every time, and <u>keep quiet</u>.

---

24. Jack Geoghegan, le Carré's US publisher.

25. Roland Gant was the editorial director at Heinemann, Nigel Hollis handled production and Tim Manderson was sales director.

I don't know whether I've written to you or to me – of course I am bitterly disappointed – but it seemed a good time to write because I'm off to the States & you're off to Australia and we have been talking about new books. Probably I won't offer you any of the new stuff until it's ready for book-form; I think with so much going on the next one I'd rather show it to you clean & complete. And I think that until that's done I'll hibernate a little bit. Because only the books will matter in the end, and 'A Small Town', for all its faults, is quite a reasonable one for now.

Ever,
David

So good luck in Australia, have a super holiday, love to the children, and we'll think of you at Christmas.

~

TO JOHN MARGETSON

Coxley House
Coxley
Nr Wells
Somerset

15 June 1969

My dear John,
It is so silly that when people are a long way away, and therefore <u>need</u> a letter, they become ten times as difficult to write to as if they lived next door. (Grammar?) Miranda has written twice to Ann I gather and Ann has not yet replied; I started a long, self pitying letter to you a while ago and thought how oafish to load you up with my headaches when you are sitting on so much trouble out there. So: zero.

Facts first. I finished a 1½ hour television play the other day & am now deep in a new novel which is going fast and quite well. I scripted the film of 'Small Town' and they are to shoot it this Autumn, though they <u>still</u> don't know who's to direct it. They tried a lot of big names but got varying negatives – Karel Reisz[26] told me he thought the script debased the book, someone else said it was professional suicide, & everyone, the studio included, had hysterics except me. Me, I largely abuse myself of the Film industry, as my French editor would say, and have forgotten what <u>was</u> in 'Small Town' anyway, so it's hardly surprising if the script is not like the book. At the end of the day the sales look good – 100,000 in America, 70,000 in England and Frogs & Krauts quite satisfactory.[27] Then when last in Switzerland I decided to build a chalet in the Bernese Oberland whither we could all, or I alone, take refuge from an increasingly rackety world. I'm flying out next Sunday to have a look at progress – it's to be ready by November. [. . .]

Not long ago Father surfaced with a 'This-is-it, seven-thousand-quid-or-I'm-in-the-workhouse' touch. Hale[28] faced the music (I was in Switzerland) and in the end we gave him a thousand in old ones & he promptly pushed off to Madrid and, so far as I can make out, blueed it in a fortnight.

We are enduring a ferocious & wholly un-English wave of dry June heat – yesterday we had some local braves in for Tennis & they bloody nearly killed me. A local architect, calling by to encourage us to add a wing to the Schloss, took one look at us and said he had never seen four such beautiful men gathered on one piece of grass. Tell Miranda.

---

26. The director Karel Reisz had shown interest in both *The Looking-Glass War* and *A Small Town in Germany*. By late 1970 le Carré was working on a screenplay for him of *The Naive and Sentimental Lover*.

27. Expressions such as 'Frogs' and 'Krauts' were very common in Britain in the 1960s. Le Carré often used slang terms to refer to various nationalities from time to time, but most reliably to the French and the Germans – not coincidentally the two foreign languages he spoke fluently and most admired.

28. H. Hale Crosse, le Carré's accountant.

Ann has sold one of the horses and the others are crouched under the lime trees mopping their brows & longing for a Pims. Yesterday I had a fan letter from G. M. Pullen (Mrs) of the Beacon, Willesborough containing the following pearl: 'A protracted convalescence has brought me time to read . . . I have read & re-read your haunting and beautiful words (i.e., my poem 'Night of the March') – but I am sorry to say I cannot understand them.' I have been padding round the rose walk in my summer flimsies wondering what haunting & beautiful reply I can send her.

The boys are in the pink. Simon wrote an infuriated letter complaining of 'saidistic brutality by a young master' so I tore over & bearded the headmaster:

'Ted, don't you think this is rather a worrying state of affairs?'

'Yes. Yes, I suppose it is.'

'I mean, he might end up in court.'

'Yes. Yes, I suppose he might.'

'Or deafen a boy.'

'Yes. Yes I suppose a blow like that could damage an ear quite considerably.'

'I can see the parents acting up a bit. Vaisey's still complaining of dizzy headaches.'

'Yes. Yes but Vaisey's a bit of a sickly boy anyway.'

'Do you think you might <u>speak</u> to Mr Mullion?'[29]

'Yes. Yes I suppose I might. Wherever he is.'

That fixed him. Then Stevie wrote from <u>his</u> school to say that the driver who took him to ballet every week stopped at pubs on the way and got very jolly, but drove rather saucily as a result. We telephoned the school who said yes, they knew about that, they'd had complaints already.

I've gone Conservative. Putting away safe liberal causes was one of the great cathartic moments of my life. The conscience asleep, I can now face anything: Kingsley Amis,

---

29. Simon's headmaster was Ted Vidal. Mullion was not the master's real name.

Francis Chichester and Harold Wilson. I'm supposed to be having dinner with Papandreou[30] at the Hellenic Restaurant, Bayswater, next Wednesday, but I've funked it. Politics is not for me.

When you feel like it, & not until, write me a letter and tell me how you are <u>in yourself</u> as May the charlady says, and perhaps we shall have the pleasure of seeing you here in the Autumn. I miss you very much; real friends are very few.

love,
David

∽

In the late 1960s the young Czech film star Vladimir Pucholt made the startling decision to defect and stay in Britain, hoping to study medicine. An initially sceptical le Carré wrote to the home secretary, Roy Jenkins, on his behalf, and then offered to support Pucholt's medical training if he found a place.

TO VLADIMIR PUCHOLT

California

19 November 1969

Dear Vladimir,
Thank you very much for your letter of 12 October – I am <u>too</u> bad at answering letters but yours took a long time to reach me. It was good to hear about the sailing: I do not think you

---

30. Perhaps a missed opportunity. Andreas Papandreou, assuming it was he, was busy rallying opposition to the Greek colonels who had seized power in 1967, imprisoning and then exiling him. He became Greece's first socialist prime minister in 1981 and a towering figure in its twentieth-century history.

would like California at all. In fact everything I ever read about wicked, decadent capitalists seems to be pretty much realised here!

I would like very much to come up and sail next Summer, even if you sink me.

I am very, very happy that you do not regret your decision, and I would like you also to know that I have great pleasure from the knowledge that I was able to help you.[31] So never feel burdened with gratitude: it constituted one of the more useful moments of a life that (in the depressions of the American film industry) seems very much misused! Thank you for writing.

As ever
David

~

Le Carré wrote XXXOOO at the top and 'best bits sidelined in red'.

to CHARLOTTE CORNWELL

Sancreed House
Sancreed
Penzance
Cornwall

10 January 1970

---

31. Le Carré wrote in *The Pigeon Tunnel* how he used his memories of Pucholt to shape the character of Issa, another young man seeking refuge, in *A Most Wanted Man*. With le Carré's financial help, in 1969 Pucholt passed his 1st MB at Sheffield University and in 1974 qualified with Distinction in Medicine. He was awarded the Gold Medal for Clinical Medicine and Surgery, and the Prize Medal for the Finals. He went on to pursue a successful career in medicine in England and later in Canada.

Dearest Charlotte,

I was very proud of your performance last night: <u>unequivocal congratulations.</u> Buzz and Janet[32] & Jane and me <u>all</u> thought you <u>were just fine.</u>[33]

The position with your equity card is: if a director insists on having you, you get one. But he can't have you unless you've got one, etc. Which means you have to be wanted specifically.

When Karel & I meet again – on Jan 15th to start the film rolling – I will do my own lobbying on your behalf. Buzz, himself among other things a long standing casting director, thought you had chosen a very tough medium indeed – it's where the competition is thickest. <u>Myself, I thought you had a real potential for pathos and comedy, and that if you really worked you could become a great female clown in the Italian tradition,</u> and that you are ready to start work now in character parts. (But you are, alas, doomed to young parts for a long time maybe. Pregnant girl-next-door in TV series, delinquents, all that manure.) That is my frank, unadorned view – and I will back it hard for you in the new year. A lot of idiots are going to offer you advice but do nothing. So I'll try and do something and refrain from offering opinion: BUT: the rest of the cast was, of course, frightful; the production of a banality that passes the imagination; yet it was all drilled & moderately skilled & somehow hung together, like an Army platoon after 8 weeks on the

---

32. The producer Robert 'Buzz' Berger and his wife, Janet, met le Carré in 1969. The producer Herb Brodkin, one of the biggest names in American television in the 1960s, brought Buzz in on a three-picture deal that included *A Small Town in Germany*, and suggested he got to know le Carré. Janet had worked as Brodkin's secretary. They lunched out in April 1969, and Buzz and Janet became friends of le Carré and Jane for fifty years.

33. Charlotte Cornwell, David's half-sister, had begun an acting career which would take her to the Royal Shakespeare Company, the Royal National Theatre and the television musical drama *Rock Follies*, with Rula Lenska and Julie Covington. She was the model for Charlie, the central character in *The Little Drummer Girl*, a left-wing actress of the provincial English stage recruited by Israeli intelligence for a lethal sting operation. The Bergers cannot recall that evening's production.

parade ground. Your own performance, against this, was particularly effective: <u>but I believe that you would have done even
better in better company, and that you have enough magic and
gall and ham rolled into one to make a great light actress.</u>

Whether you make it, God knows, is a lottery. Depends on
you, luck and a little bit on me. This is by way of a promise to
do my little bit for you so that you can add the rest – the considerable rest – and find God, or whatever, and of course <u>lerv.</u>

   love, love
   David x x x x

JANE

. . . and Jane to support, type, never offer editorial advice except by the twitch of an eyebrow or the almost imperceptible curl of the lip.

– to Jean Cornwell, 7 December 2009

Valerie Jane Eustace was born on 28 April 1938 into a comfortable home at South Park, Sevenoaks; she disliked the name 'Valerie'. She was evacuated to Devon during the Second World War after a V-1 flying bomb, or 'doodlebug', fell near her home.

Her father, a dentist, was then posted to Northern Ireland with the army, and she long remembered visiting an American battleship off the coast and tasting ice-cream for the first time.

Jane went to Sherborne School for Girls, where she opened the batting at cricket; she and le Carré later watched cricket assiduously. From Sherborne she went to secretarial college and then to work in publishing; first as secretary to the literary agent George Greenfield, and then as a publicist and foreign rights manager for Hodder & Stoughton.

Jane met le Carré at a literary event in Birmingham in 1968. He called her 'Oysters', shortened to 'Oy', after a German publisher at the Frankfurt Book Fair mispronounced her surname as 'Oystace'. They called each other 'Eejit', and his other nickname for Jane was 'Cow'; their homes had several cow paintings.

Le Carré later moved to Greenfield's agency and to the publishers Hodder & Stoughton. Jane introduced him to Bob Gottlieb, who would become his US editor at Knopf.

The first book Jane worked on with le Carré was *A Small Town in Germany*. 'When the book was in shreds, it was she who helped me piece it together and make something of it,' he wrote to his psychiatrist Dr Bockner. 'I find her compassionate, understanding, and remarkably intelligent.'

Jane had not worked as an editor when she met le Carré, but she typed his manuscripts and became the first reader of his books. The Bodleian Librarian Richard Ovenden noticed a 'deep process of collaboration' between the two, 'a rhythm of working together that was incredibly efficient'. She became his 'crucial, covert collaborator', in the words of their son, Nicholas.

to VIVIAN GREEN

Chalet Chamois
3823 Wengen
Switzerland

9 August 1970

Dear Vivian,

September 6th–13th would be absolutely fine. You could make
the chalet your base for that time if it suited you – there is a
room free all the while. I am trying to finish a book so I shall be
fairly tied up, during the day that is, but I can think of nothing
better than that you should come & stay, walk & we can meet
in the evenings. And anyway, some days I stop before lunch, &
some days I shall run away from school altogether.

I may have a girl staying here, formerly in publishing, now
girlfriend, assistant & what have you – I am fairly sure you will
like her, and she cooks. She decisively post-dates my separation
from Ann, and has a decent quiet. I only mention this in case
you might overlap, which I rather hope you do.

If you would like to come, then, from 6th–13 Sep & use the
house to come & go as you wish, you are extremely welcome,
& I look forward to it very much.

Ever
David

~

*Le Carré was preparing for the publication of a very different kind of
novel,* The Naive and Sentimental Lover.

TO CHARLES PICK

Sancreed House[1]
Sancreed
Penzance
Cornwall

7 November 1970

PERSONAL & CONFIDENTIAL

Dear Charles,

This is a very sad and difficult letter for me to write. I think it is time I had a change of publisher. I have reached a moment in my writing career where, for good or ill, I have taken leave of the type of book that has made my reputation, and as never before I need to have absolute confidence in the way the transition is handled. In the last months, as the book neared completion, I found myself worrying more and more about whether I was really suited – in this new rôle – to the house of Heinemann. The last two books, it seemed to me, had found no real accept-ance outside the framework of 'The Spy' – I even remember your telling me in Paris that had you known me better you wd have perhaps dissuaded me from publishing The Looking-Glass War at all. Just what it is that I fear for the new book I don't know – perhaps that very commercialisation which is also the admirable strength of Heinemann; perhaps a projected misconception of what the book is about; perhaps merely the extension of that losing streak which, critically, has character-ised the last two books. It seems to me that by making a change I stand to win a new image, and that I have, conversely, no

---

1. Le Carré stayed at Sancreed House in West Penwith, Cornwall – with John Miller, his former MI5 agent-turned-artist and Stephen's godfather, and Michael Truscott, a potter – where he partly wrote *The Naive and Sentimental Lover*. He had bought three derelict cottages at Tregiffian, his future home, in October 1969, from a local farmer. As le Carré's marriage ended, Truscott drove his children between Cornwall and Coxley House, which became Ann's home.

old image to lose. You and I have always shared a close and friendly personal relationship; but I must confess to you that I do not have, in my relations with the firm as a whole, the confidence that derives from, and grows with, sympathetic editorial stimulus.

I do not deceive myself that this news will not be a great blow to you; and that it runs against the consideration & hospitality you have always extended to me; not to speak of the very fair & liberal contractual terms on which we have done business. I am sure I am nowhere near your most lucrative author, but I know that I mean a lot to you, and I am very, very sorry to cause you personal distress. Nor do I mean to take a swing at Roland,[2] who has always been gentle and terribly painstaking in our work together. But I believe that, with the great professional wisdom you have always brought to publishing, you will find it in you to agree that when an author feels he needs a change, he should make it.

I don't know, at the time of writing, where I shall go. Not to Tom Rosenthal, though I admire him very much. Perhaps to a smaller house. But wherever I do go, I hope that we shall manage to achieve a decent & honourable separation, in keeping with the way we have worked together, and in defiance of the kind of rancour which seems so much a part of publishing.

Lastly – it really was my decision & mine alone. Perhaps I shall live to regret it; but I certainly shall always know that I took it for myself.

Yours ever
David

~

---

2. Roland Gant, editorial director at Heinemann.

TO JOHN MARGETSON

11 November 1970

Dear John,

It was rude of me not to answer your card, but I didn't quite know what to say. I have changed very much in the last year and I am not very sociable; the new book[3] has not left me much energy, & what there is has gone into coping with the children & the divorce and trying to settle again. Will you understand if I don't come tonight? I do not feel equal to the explanations, not quite yet, & not till the new book is done. I don't seem to be very good at letters.

Please forgive me, and let me surface a little later. Belatedly also: welcome back.

As ever
David

~

TO JEAN CORNWELL

Tregiffian
St Buryan
Penzance
Cornwall

22 October 1971

Dearest Jeannie,

Thank you so very much for the pullover. It makes me look very manly and grown up, which I suppose is what I should be at forty.

---

3. *The Naive and Sentimental Lover.*

I am selling the penthouse & living down here all the time, which suits me best. The book is selling very well & I am so proud of it despite some bitchy reviews. In a few years, noone will ever know how it was received. But I will have my book.

Thank you again. It was sweet of you to do that.

Love,
David

~

The Bergers had given le Carré and Jane hand-embroidered napkins, made by two sisters in Wengen. Le Carré's response seemed touched with Dickensian rhythms from A Tale of Two Cities, *a favourite book.*[4]

TO BUZZ AND JANET BERGER

> *Chalet Chamois*
> *3823 Wengen*
> *Switzerland*
>
> 8 January 1972

Dear Buzz and Janet,
It was too much, it was low, it was mean, we are hopelessly out-manoeuvred; it was lovely, timely and sweet. They made them, those unerring sisters, in the same red as the table cloth, with green, red and black braid, the names in green crosstitch. They delivered them in tissue, gift wrapped, by blushing, breathless messenger; we opened them round the table and a kind of awful silence fell, very unavoidable, and eyes brimmed & we got queer feelings in the throats. You <u>must</u> have felt it. Vivian

---

4. On 20 November 2010 he writes to Professor Owen Dudley Edwards of keeping *A Tale of Two Cities* by his bed.

went very pink, he has taken his home though I forbade it, so he'll have to bring it with him next year.

You have to hear the rest. Two nights before Christmas, Jane fell the full length of the stone staircase, landing on her head. She was bruised & dizzy and after a couple of days up & down here & the doctor prescribing aspirin, we flew her home to Sevenoaks to see her own doctor, who had her thoroughly examined & pronounced her miraculously fit. Therefore Vivian ate the turkey alone, & drank the Christmas claret (B Br & R,[5] despatched specially) and we had a rather rocky time in Kent, pursuing Christmas-bound doctors, who responded gallantly. She was fit enough to receive the children, though, when I brought them out, and all that went _very_ well. But Christmas here was not that great after all! My book[6] came out in the States but I haven't seen any reviews, which I hear were mediocre. I'm sick of reading them anyway, they just annoy me. New book goes okay, penthouse sold, Cornish house dreamy, Chalet empty as a drum after the boys went yesterday and Wengen full of pelvically deformed Gerrards Crossers dressed in IRA linoleum. Saw Carnal Knowledge & hated it, saw 5 Easy Pieces & liked it a lot, but mainly I liked Valdez is Coming and now I want a shotgun like Burt Lancaster.[7]

Quiet here, therefore, with just the occasional rustle of me & Jane wiping our lips. Our love to you, and please let's meet soon. Maybe we'll sneak over,

David

---

5. Berry Bros & Rudd, wine and spirit merchants.

6. _The Naive and Sentimental Lover_ was inspired by the Kennaway affair. 'It was my attempt at a kind of self-mockery, my life was in complete disarray, I'd had this tortuous affair which has been much written about and I tried to portray that in a soul-washing way,' le Carré said at the 'Berliner Salon' in March 2020. 'People said it didn't work and I largely agree with them, but I had a go.'

7. Burt Lancaster plays a Mexican-American sheriff in the Western _Valdez is Coming_.

~

TO JEAN CORNWELL

Tregiffian
St Buryan
Penzance
Cornwall

9 May 1972

Dearest Jeannie,

Jane and I got furtively married last Tuesday and Jane's having a baby. Neither event was unplanned but I feel very happy about it all, and a mysterious & quite productive calm has descended over me. I am continuing to stay down here to work, as my book is going like a bell.

I bought a gorgeous ring for Charlotte's birthday and I will send it to her for this weekend (late). We want very much to get to her play and <u>boy</u> is she doing well.

Baby's due in November.[8] We kept it dark because it didn't seem to be so important somehow – I mean the marriage & the fuss and telegrams, which actually w<u>d</u> have reduced me to a powder, also Jane.

Please tell Rupert: I have bought him a desk. Eddie[9] has it & he can see it when he goes to Ann. If he doesn't like it, he can cash it in so to speak & tell Eddie what he w<u>d</u> prefer. It's country fruitwood, 18th Century.

Love as always,
D

~

---

8. Nicholas Robert Cornwell was born on 26 November 1972.

9. Eddie Nowell, an antiques dealer and close friend.

Eighteen months earlier le Carré had told Jeannie he was working
seven or eight hours a day on a new book, 'just a thriller to mark time'.

TO JEAN CORNWELL

> *Tregiffian*
> *St Buryan*
> *Penzance*
> *Cornwall*

> 26 November 1973

Dearest Jeannie,

It's a hundred years since we communicated – your card from Paris was the last word between us I think – and I'm writing to say that at last my book is finished, and put to bed well wrapped up, & will come out in England in September, & America in June; and that it's a spy story called Tinker Tailor Soldier Spy. Publishers very bonny about it; I'm quite pleased with it; it's long and very professional. The advances, if they mean anything, are larger than they've ever been, so at least it has what they call the confidence of the trade. By the time it comes out, I'll have invested mine in something new. Weary, that's me: a very hard two years.

Nicholas flourishes, so does Jane; we had a holiday in the Bahamas but I was still working so it wasn't the complete flake out we meant it to be; it was lovely all the same.[10] On Sunday we leave for Switzerland (via the South of Spain for a six day sleep) and the boys come out on Dec 28. We'll do our usual thing of losing ourselves in the chalet over Christmas. Simon came down for his half term and showed some talent as a painter – I fixed up lessons for him, and his first effort was ridiculously successful. This time he did a still life which was also quite fair.

---

10. All their lives, le Carré and Jane promised themselves holidays that they never managed to take.

Of course: a while back Jane & I went to the Savoy to celebrate the finish of the working draft; Jane arranged everything, we sat drinking shampoo[11] before tucking into our grouse when who should swarm in, grinning from ear to ear but your ex, my undivorceable vater, with his very lovely lady wife and a paralytic couple of Bournemouth millionaires who were also being prepared for eating, plucking or whatever, Savoy style. They* had a very simple little human problem on their hands: how to kill the three hours between the close of lunch at the Savoy and the opening of dinner at the Savoy, to which, in other company, they were committed at seven. Jane suggested a swim and there was a loud silence. We had a drink with them & went back to our corner, which mercifully was in the other dining room. The Bahamas were extraordinary: never been there before. Colour incredible, population windy but delightful, hotel sinister & Mafia owned.

Jeannie – it's happy-Christmas-time again; we shan't be staging in London on the way through next Sunday; we both feel absolutely wrung out. I think the book's pretty good; it's certainly <u>meant</u> to be. The enclosed cheque is to lengthen your Christmas candle a bit, and comes to you with, as ever, my warmest step-filial love.

Ever
David

[*in the margin*] *Father and Joy

---

11. Le Carré used this vintage slang for champagne well after it went out of fashion.

SOUTH-EAST ASIA AND *THE HONOURABLE SCHOOLBOY*

The Honourable Schoolboy was the first book I wrote on location, and the first, but not the last, for which I put on the non-uniform of a field reporter in order to obtain my experiences and my information. It commemorates the first time I saw shots exchanged in the heat of battle, or succoured a wounded soldier, or smelt the stench of old blood in the fields. It tells therefore of a certain growing up, but also of a certain growing down, for war is nothing if not a return to childhood.

– for Hodder & Stoughton's new edition of *The Honourable Schoolboy*, in 1989

Researching a plot in which Smiley attempts to turn the tables on Karla in South-East Asia, le Carré travelled through north-east Thailand, Laos and Cambodia with H. D. S. (David) Greenway, of the *Washington Post*, nominally working as his photographer.

The British journalist, spy and old Asia hand Peter Simms was a model for the character of Jerry Westerby; sadly, no correspondence between le Carré and Simms, who died in 2002, has survived.

TO JOHN MARGETSON

[n.d.]

My dear John,

In haste: my new book is set in Singapore & Hong Kong & area, and I am heading that way on Feb 17 for at least a month. I am writing a spy story, mainly action, and I'm in search of colour & locations & first hand knowledge of the local tensions; it's no sort of exposé.

Do you know anyone out there who wd touch me with a bargepole?[1] I have one good introduction in Hong Kong, none yet in S'pore, & my embarrassment is that my papa has a horrendous track record there, notably of floating unsure football pools, etc., & was chucked out.

If you have any bright ideas, will you let me know. Off to Spain on Sunday, then to Switzerland.

Love to you all
David

～

TO GRAHAM GREENE

Tregiffian
St Buryan
Penzance
Cornwall

7 November 1974

---

1. John Margetson soon moved from SIS into the diplomatic service. He served in Saigon from 1968 to 1970.

Dear Graham Greene,

After our passage of arms over Philby[2] a while back, it is a little difficult for me to write to you. But I should hate you to think that the dispute either soured my gratitude to you for your help and encouragement ten years ago, nor – for what it's worth – my admiration for your work. I am moved to write by my visits to the Far East this year, & particularly to Indo China: 'The Quiet American', which I re-read in Saigon, seems to me still as fresh as it did nineteen years ago, and it is surely still the only novel, even now, which does justice to its theme. But the sheer accuracy of its mood, and observation, is astonishing. The book seemed more real on location, even, than away from it. I was really very moved, and felt I had to tell you. It is, of course, all quite hideous now in Saigon. Phnom Penh is still beautiful, but not for much longer, and the rest of Cambodia is heart breaking.

That is all I have to say, really. Your work has been a constant inspiration to me, and whatever our differences I wanted to thank you for it, and for your example. I hope that your biographers will not forget your generosity to new writers, of whom I was lucky enough to be one. But in case they do, let me again record my own thanks.

Yours sincerely,
David Cornwell

Greene replied that he had never considered their 'passage of arms' a serious one 'and I am sorry that you ever gave it a second thought'.

∽

2. Le Carré had written the foreword to a book by the *Sunday Times* Insight team, *Philby: The Spy Who Betrayed a Generation.* He cast Philby as 'vain, spiteful, and murderous', more driven to react against his overbearing father than by ideology. Greene, in the *Observer*, challenged this 'vulgar and untrue' depiction, and likened le Carré to E. Phillips Oppenheim, author of popular spy thrillers.

TO GRAHAM GREENE

Tregiffian
St Buryan
Penzance
Cornwall

12 November 1974

Dear Graham Greene,
Thank you very much for your letter, which gave me great joy. I hope to go back to Phnom Penh in the new year, & by then, I hope, the museum will be open. It was closed because a Khmer Rouge rocket fell very close, and everyone had become extrèmement serieux, & no wonder. The new Saigon is absolutely unvisitable, the present régime is even more frightful than one would suppose, but above all the charm is dead. You are an extraordinarily cherished absentee there, a reminder of times lost. 'He sat here, he sat there' at the Continental. Richard West has just done a book, extinguished by legislation, on Saigon now.[3] Not very good, but the only one.

Yours ever
David Cornwell

For all this warm exchange, Greene described le Carré's novels after 1968 as too long, writes his biographer Richard Greene, and showed little interest in renewing a personal connection.

~

---

3. The veteran foreign correspondent Richard West. His book *Victory in Vietnam*, published in 1974, was a personal narrative about the life and culture of the country, but its launch was threatened by a libel suit (that ultimately failed).

TO JOHN MARGETSON

Chalet Chamois
3823 Wengen
Switzerland

5 January 1975

My dear John,

Thanks so much for your letter and card – it was good to hear from you and to know that, well, things weren't going too badly. I think Foreign Office life must get harder & harder privately, & increasingly attractive professionally.[4] What a tug o'war. One buys a lovely house or two, makes a pattern, shoots roots, renews friendships and bingo, it's back to the Min of Works hiring and the Harrods task. But for work those changes are just the job: new challenges, great gollups of ignorance to cover up fast, new people, fresh air, power always closer. As the showbiz boys would say these days, it's about sexism and the Great Seesaw, etc.

I'm glad you noticed the success of Tinker Tailor Soldier Spy – despite some bloody English reviews – & you'll be amazed to hear that London Weekend TV are doing a 7 (or 13) x 1½ hour presentation of the novel some time this 'Fall' (whatever the hell that is) and otherwise next Spring.[5] Sorry you'll miss it but I expect it will be very lousy. I had film offers but they stank. We've just had/are having but it's nearly over i.e. a very good holiday here with Timo & Stephen & [. . .] Chris, Timo's friend – good snow, perfect sun, long bouts of happiness all round & me less neurotic than before – and now they're sizing

---

4. Margetson served in Saigon from 1968 to 1970 during the Vietnam War; he was now in Brussels, as head of chancery in the UK delegation to NATO. In 1978, three years after Vietnam's reunification, he was posted back there in his first ambassadorship. He later became ambassador to the United Nations and the Netherlands.

5. It became a seven-part BBC series.

up to go home to Coxley[6] (about to fold/close) and school. 63 Cloudesley Road is now a gem of a little house, thanks to Jane & N. MacFadyean, I like it <u>very</u> much.[7] The wing at Tregiffian is done – 2 bedrooms, bathroom, kitchen, study, storeroom, etc. – and so the schlosses are complete & ready to be blown up. Stevie will come to us for weekends and we'll take them to Tregiffian for half terms & parts of the hols.

Wengen has been brightened this time round by our meeting with one Ambassador (h.c.) Paul Jolles,[8] who seems to be the Swiss plenipotentiary on trade negotiations & effective head of the Board of Trade to boot. Very foxy, interesting bird [. . .] & a chalet here that cost a couple of hundred thou. <u>Sharp</u>, though, and mercifully a fan. So we talk, not long enough for him to see through me, & he also drinks vodka, which never did me any harm. We're supposed to dine tonight. The S.E.A. book is gelling nicely & I go back to H K in April to watch the Swatow fleet round some boring small island where a <u>great scene</u> plays,[9] on their way to Canton. The Thais sent word that if I ever go back they'll put me inside for consorting with hoodlums in the Golden Triangle and conspiring with Shan State generals. The Burmese, apparently, are also sharpening their knives: isn't it rum to be <u>wanted</u>?

I feel very lucky these days, and dreadfully lonely, which is nothing anyone can cure. Jane is in marvellous shape (but has a ricked back) and Stevie tends her like a knight. They're just

---

6. Le Carré's first wife, Ann, had remarried: Roger Martin was a diplomat, and living at Coxley House.

7. Likely the London architect Neil Macfadyen, who died in 2017. Cloudesley Road was the first London home le Carré and Jane bought together.

8. The imperturbable Swiss diplomat, art collector, and future Nestlé Group chairman. Paul Jolles was secretary to the Swiss delegation that negotiated the handover of Nazi gold and German assets after the Second World War. The Jolles family became winter friends of the Cornwells, and with the family of le Carré's friend David Greenway, also regular visitors to Wengen.

9. The finale of *The Honourable Schoolboy*.

back from shopping. Simon got a scholarship to Wadham in physics – what the hell <u>are</u> physics? – and is tonight arriving at Biggin Hill to be interviewed by the RAF for a 4 month commission! I don't understand any of my children, but I have an uncomfortable feeling they understand me. Nicholas is about six feet tall.

> I miss you.
> best
> David

~

TO JANE CORNWELL AND 'A'

Room 1714
The Mandarin
Hong Kong

[n.d. but likely April 1975]

Dearest O, and A, [10]
Start was sticky. Lufthansa rather 2nd rate, no better than BOAC, not as good as Swissair or SAS – no Lowenbräu or Schnapps, short rations on booze but empty so I slept. DC 10. When I didn't sleep I read & finished the Indian Mutiny book 'The Sound of Fury' by Collier – c<u>d</u> you order it? And c<u>d</u> you ask Samurai Smith[11] whether he's sent Fowles The Politics of Opium in SE Asia? The Collier is good – do read it – a bit by Macauley out of Morris West but good.[12]

---

10. 'O' is for Oysters, Jane's nickname. 'A' is currently unidentified.

11. John Saumarez Smith, manager of Heywood Hill bookshop in Mayfair.

12. Writing unclear; Fowles or Joules. *The Sound of Fury: An Account of the Indian Mutiny* by Richard Collier was published in 1963. Morris West is presumably the Australian author.

Got here & <u>Stafford</u>[13] saw me to my suite, my dear, all terrifically discreet. Slept 14 hours and lunched with Laurence who was useful. Wrote bits, mooned, collected stuff, phoned Simms who's arriving on Monday, negotiated a boat for Po Toi (difficult & expensive) bought a document carrier, wrote, dined with one of those Chinese millionaire boys the Browns[14] laid on but not much help. Simms frosty on the phone because I hadn't acknowledged receipt of his stuff. Sod him. Today woke late again and set the 1st ch. to get us straight into the story. Feel a bit odd – useless writing in the hotel but not much I can do. I think it's quite good. My plan is to do as many scenes from the start sketchily getting in the places & atmosphere & little details even if the drama isn't right so that I don't simply run out of ammunition.

Tomorrow thanks to Stafford I go to the races with the organiser, a general, and on Sunday dinner with the Kinlochs[15] who had another daughter – do you remember them? Last night late went to Kadoori's, he's a millionaire playboy & he was showing films of himself skiing in St Moritz.[16] Weather very white & hot. Saigon almost unapproachable now, PP [Phnom Penh] finished, noone here gives a damn, or even thinks of it. Notes going well on the side. Had one bad night (the first) before I fell asleep determined to return next day. But it passed & I think I'm doing the right thing.

If you feel strong enough w<u>d</u> you try to slice up the notes into subjects/places, etc., so that they are more coordinated & indexed?

---

13. Australian Peter Stafford was general manager of the Mandarin, a legendary figure at a legendary hotel.

14. Charles Brown, an architect, and his wife Rosamund Brown, an artist, well known in Hong Kong. Le Carré used their home, the Pink House, for a scene in *The Honourable Schoolboy*.

15. Currently unidentified.

16. Michael Kadoori, now a billionaire Hong Kong businessman.

My new notes I'm keeping in separate batches according to subject.

I miss you though, and often turn to tell you something only to find, as so often, that you have inconsiderately bolted.

Love you
D

∾

My father wrote me a long, handwritten letter from Phnom Penh and sent it to my school, describing how seventy rockets were falling on the city a day, which I vividly remember. It is sadly lost, but this later type-written letter survived. After his research trips to South-East Asia I decided to do my entry project for Westminster School on the Vietnam War. He sent copies of Newsweek *and* Time *magazines from the war's key turning points, and soldiers' jacket patches with slogans like 'Kill a Commie for Christ'.*

TO TIMOTHY CORNWELL

63 Cloudesley Road
London, N1

26 September 1975

Dearest Timo,

Here for once is a type-written letter because there are various administrative things to talk about.

Firstly, here is a spare watch for you 'till your own comes back from Harrods. They seem to be taking all the time in the world.

Secondly, I have spoken to Mummy and she tells me that she wants you to have the influenza injection, so I'm afraid you will just have to grin and bear it.

Thirdly, and most important, is the matter of your Westminster project. I have also discussed this with Mummy and she tells me that you really have masses of notes from last holidays as well as lots of printed material which you could use. I may be wrong, but we both feel that if you could settle to it and use the material you have got, you would find it a lot easier than you realise. The important things to remember are that Vietnam has been colonised by so many people in the past and that is where the trouble began; first the Chinese ran it, then the French grabbed it, then the Japanese threw the French out, then with the '39–'45 war ended the British supported the return of the French, rather than giving the Vietnamese the independence they wanted. When colonial powers are in control, it is always the left wing which tends to form the strongest opposition. Just as it was the left wing inside Germany which did most to combat Nazism in the German underground. So you have to think of the growth of communism in Indo-China as a natural result of colonialism. Under Dulles, the American Secretary of State, who effectively determined the American cold war policy, the theory of containment grew up which said that wherever communists threaten a border, they should be contained at all costs. This was how the iron curtain in Europe became such a rigid thing, it was the line along which the Americans contained communism. They thought they could do the same in South East Asia and that was the doctrine which got them there.

Now, once you have got that in your mind I believe that discussion with other masters and the material you have got already will help you along the rest of the way. I am trying to get you some more simple material and I will put it in the post to you as soon as possible. I will also talk to Mr Heazell[17] at length before we see you the weekend after next.

The copy of the letter in my father's archive is unsigned.

---

17. Paddy Heazell, headmaster of Hazlegrove House; my prep school's rolling country drive seemed reminiscent of Thursgood's school in *Tinker Tailor Soldier Spy*.

~

Horace Hale Crosse was le Carré's accountant, who had advised him to stay abroad after the huge earnings from The Spy Who Came in from the Cold. *He had a high-domed head and high 'H's on his signature.*

TO H. HALE CROSSE

63 Cloudesley Road
London, N1

2 October 1975

My dear Hale,

I promised you some while back an explanation of how I had incurred expenses of around £2,500, largely unaccounted for by receipts during my explorations of northern Indo-China for the purposes of my new and as yet unpublished book, of which the working title is THE CHINA TARGET.

Largely, these expenses relate to the period when I was based on Chiang Mai, and from there exploring the illicit growing and refining of opium poppies in the area of the so-called Golden Triangle, which joins Burma, Thailand and Laos. Through the offices of the illegal Shan State Army in Chiang Mai, I succeeded in getting myself escorted along their supply line into the heart of the opium growing area. To do this I was obliged to make a contribution to their fighting fund of $1,000. You probably know that the Thais tolerate the Shans because both groups are opposed to the Rangoon Government. But the Shans are at war with one another, and the group with which I was involved had formed an uneasy truce with the remnants of the Kuo Min Tang Army who supplied the body-guards for the opium caravans. The thousand dollars covered several passages in and out of the Shan states and incidentally secured me a considerable amount of material which I hope to be able to fit into the novel.

The other leg of the same journey took me to Vientiane where I was able to pick up an ex-Air America (CIA) mercenary pilot who had fought all through the secret war in Laos. He was at that time running heroin (from the Shan states) and diamonds to Pailin in Cambodia for onward transmission to Battambang and Phnom Penh. For $500 he allowed me to fly with him as far as Pailin, and I continued with the merchandise in another plane as far as Battambang.

You have already the receipt from a firm called Swiss-Indo accounting for a private charter to operate around these parts, but Royal Air Lao, the airline which flew the last leg over communist territory to Phnom Penh would issue neither tickets nor receipts, and has since – as you may have read – lost its only plane, a DC 8, in mysterious circumstances. You can imagine that I was also obliged, on this rather rackety trail, to pay for information as well as transport, and the only real evidence I can offer of having done so is contained in the as yet unpublished manuscript!

The Washington Post did in fact run an article on my exploits in the north of Thailand and if the Revenue were sufficiently curious, I suppose I could unearth it and offer it as some sort of substantiation. Their correspondent followed a part of my trail.

Yours ever,
David

Sure enough, le Carré's journeys to Battambang and across South-East Asia in the twilight of the Vietnam War were echoed in the travels of Jerry Westerby, journalist and spy, the leading character of The Honourable Schoolboy.

∾

TO JEAN CORNWELL

1 Gayton Crescent
London, NW3 1TT

19 October 1976

Dearest Jeannie,

Today I emerged from my three year tunnel & we carted the 650 page manuscript down to the Xerox artists and tonight it goes to my agent & publisher and suddenly it's all over by yesterday. I leave for the Far East again in a day or two to check out references & locations for the last time – those that survive. I am very proud of the book but it was a bit of a marathon – I've never attempted anything like it before. I'm sorry that our mutual good intentions to meet were not fulfilled but let us do so as soon as I return from this trip – end of Nov. – & before we go to Switzerland for the kids & thence for our own holiday to the sun. The book is called 'The Honourable Schoolboy' and is a sequel of a sort to the last; it will be published late Aug, early Sep, I suppose. We moved to a new (old) schloss up here where growing boys can expand without hitting their heads on the ceiling & by the time I get back it shd be fairly much ready for your inspection. I've seen nobody – Charlotte, Rupert, no friends either really – it just was a long lonely time and Father's death – all the awful people – did somehow turn me into myself, as I think the book will show you.[18]

Ah well. Much love as ever
David

～

---

18. Ronnie Cornwell had died the previous year, on 29 June 1975.

Mrs Ståhl wrote on 19 August 1977 to say that she was preparing a series of articles for the Swedish and Finnish press on the Nobel Prize in Literature. She had asked various poets and writers how the prize should be structured, what writers of the past deserved it, and the names of five or six people who should be candidates.

TO MRS PIRKKO-LIISA STÅHL

> c/o John Farquharson Ltd
> 15 Red Lion Square
> London, WC2A 2JR

> [n.d. but likely August 1977]

Dear Mrs Ståhl,
It is very kind of you to seek my opinion on the Nobel Prize in Literature, but I must tell you honestly that I have never given the subject a moment's thought, except perhaps to reflect that, like the Olympic Games, a great concept has been ruined by political greed.

> Yours sincerely,
> John le Carré

~

'Not that I know a great lot about precious books,' le Carré told an audience at the independent Morrab Library in Penzance, when he was president and patron, in 1997. 'My critics would certainly say I don't write them. I was brought up in a bookless household, and I have a natural sympathy for people who grow up without the example of reading, or come late to it, or never come at all.'

TO PETER RAINSFORD[19]

Tregiffian
St Buryan
Penzance
Cornwall

28 August 1977

Dear Peter,

For a start, how about a decent set of George Eliot, & of D. H. Lawrence, a good volume of The Seven Pillars of Wisdom, together with the biography by T. E.'s brother, and a volume of the unexpurgated version of 'The Mint'. Then an 'Inferno', a set of Aristotle's essays & critical writings & major works, a Dryden, a Swift, a Pope, an Adison, a Coleridge, something of (Adison &) Steel;[20] Keats & Shelley; a nice set of Scott; Josephus' history of the Jews; Motley's Rise of the Dutch Republic; a Plato; a lot of Homer; Burton's Arabian Nights; Frazer's Golden Bough; Wilkie Collins; some early Conan Doyle would be marvellous, preferably Sherlock Holmes & the historical romances – really if you were putting together, over a period, a Catholic library – basically English, but with a wide investment in European & American heritage – imagine that, & you can't go far wrong! I am prepared to spend up to, about, £1,000 p.a., & would like here & there to pick up really good art books, which I love browsing in – & which, on any realistical prediction are bound to appreciate. (The Maillol are now beautiful, incidentally.[21]) And any particular little nuggets that come your way, like an unexpected 1st edition, are always worth discussing. As to the invoicing, the more your bills can look like the sort of bills which are consistent with the compilation of an author's

---

19. Peter Rainsford is an artist and antiquarian bookseller in St Ives.

20. Joseph Addison and Richard Steele.

21. Presumably Aristide Maillol, French sculptor and printmaker.

library the better – (which, as it happens, is the truth, but the hounds can't recognise truth unless it's shoved up their muzzles). If you bill me (or rather Authors Workshop, c/o Black Geoghegan and Till, at Kingsbourne House, 229–231 High Holborn, London WC1V 7DA) in small lots rather than big ones, it's probably best, since the expenditure then looks like a running cost instead of a zonking great capital purchase. I would suggest, never more than £75 a time. Any problems of communication, billing, etc., pl. ring Mr Crosse at that address, he knows all. Anything hot, ring me in London after Sep 6 because of course I've hardly scratched the surface of what I would like to assemble.

I hope all goes well with you, and that you prosper. My new book comes out on Sep 8th.

Best
David

~

On 7 February 1978, le Carré wrote to Gerald Isaaman, long-time editor of the Hampstead & Highgate Express, *who had asked if he wanted to review Graham Greene's new novel,* The Human Factor, *out on 16 March. He wrote a P.S.: Have you heard of Chutzpah?*

TO GERALD ISAAMAN

1 Gayton Crescent
London, NW3 1TT

7 February 1978

<u>Confidential</u>

Dear Gerald,

Thanks very much for your letter of the 6th February: I didn't think that was chutzpah at all – simply very good journalism. I have already received a proof copy of Greene's new novel and declined the opportunity of interviewing him for the <u>New York Times</u>. Or maybe he declined me. And I have several tentative requests to review the book. I think first of all I will just read it before deciding, since I really couldn't bring myself to write a negative review even if, for instance, I found the book as weak as I found 'The Honorary Consul', or as dishonest as I found 'A Sort of Life'. He is a great writer who has, as he says himself, to put up with longevity, and I have a suspicion it's an off book.

But it may very well be that if I can relate to the novel, I will do you a review for The Hampstead and Highgate Express rather than the competition.

Will you please tell me how many words, and when by?

Thanks again for asking, and see you both on the 26th,[22]

Best,
David

---

22. No review by le Carré of *The Human Factor* appeared in the *Ham & High*.

GUINNESS AND SMILEY

Watching him putting on an identity is like watching a man set out on a mission into enemy territory.

– on Alec Guinness, in an eightieth-birthday tribute written in 1993

I'm the worst judge, thanks to Alec Guinness. His voice was so beguiling, on stage, radio or across the fire that it's printed into my head as The One. Which is silly of me, because I secretly thought Gary Oldman was the better Smiley, and Simon RB the better voice, more naturalistic and impassioned.

– by email to Simon Prince, on 5 April 2020, comparing Guinness's television Smiley to Gary Oldman's on film and Simon Russell Beale on radio.

Le Carré's relationship with film and television began in 1965, when the actor Richard Burton demanded a rewrite of his lines in The Spy Who Came in from the Cold, *and ran through to the 2018 BBC television series of* The Little Drummer Girl. *In 1978 the BBC commissioned a major seven-part series of* Tinker Tailor Soldier Spy, *the first television adaptation of le Carré's work.*

TO SIR ALEC GUINNESS

1 Gayton Crescent
London, NW3 1TT

27 February 1978

Dear Sir Alec,

I write to you as an unbounded admirer of your work for many years. The BBC has just acquired television rights in 'Tinker, Tailor, Soldier, Spy', a novel which I wrote a few years back, of which the plot, narrative and heart are all sustained by one character – George Smiley. Arthur Hopcraft[1] is to write the script, and seems willing to let me look over his shoulder now and then. Jonathan Powell is the producer,[2] knows I am writing you this letter and supports its aspiration. Otherwise I have no responsibility in the project, which is as I would wish. But already we are all of us agreed on one thing: that if we were to cry for the moon, we would cry for Guinness as Smiley,[3] and

---

1. The journalist, sports writer, author, and one of the great scriptwriters of his day. Adapting *Tinker Tailor Soldier Spy* was a career high but he turned down the sequel, *Smiley's People*. He scripted *A Perfect Spy* in 1987.

2. Producer of both *Tinker Tailor Soldier Spy* and its sequel *Smiley's People*; later head of BBC drama serials and series, and controller of BBC1.

3. Guinness's many starring roles included James Wormold, vacuum-cleaner salesman-turned-spy, in Graham Greene's *Our Man in Havana* – the acknowledged inspiration of le Carré's *The Tailor of Panama*.

build everything else to fit. They plan to shoot this coming Autumn of seventy-eight. Will you read the book and consider it? Will you let them send you some early script as soon as they are ready to do so? I believe they are thinking of eight or nine hours, and in almost all of them, Smiley is the 'motor', as the Germans say. It is the first time a book of mine has received this sort of treatment, and it would be the first portrayal of Smiley on the screen, except for a sadly inadequate dash at it by Rupert Davies in 'The Spy Who Came in from the Cold' in 1963, and a little comedy piece recently by Arthur Lowe.[4] The truth is that ever since I started writing about Smiley, I dreamed of your playing him one day. That is not just talk, but the reason for my writing to you now, informally.

Please do not bother to reply, but if this 'early warning' makes it easier for you to consider your schedule, and if your schedule were to include 'Tinker, Tailor', that is all the justification I need for appealing to you so early in the day.

And in any case, my sincerest good wishes and continuing admiration.

Yours sincerely,
John le Carré
(David Cornwell)

∾

TO SIR ALEC GUINNESS

3 March 1978

---

4. In the short but memorable dramatisation of the scene in *Call for the Dead* where George Smiley returns home to unwelcome visitors (BBC's *Lively Arts* programme, 1977).

Dear Sir Alec,

How wonderful to have your letter, the contents of which I passed to Jonathan Powell at the BBC this morning. If possible, he was even happier than I was to hear that, in principle, you are enthusiastic to take on Smiley.

Let me go straight to your points. 64 is the ideal age. Smiley can't be less, arithmetically, and I fear that he may be more, though I have deliberately arrested the passage of time in the later books! So nobody is at all worried on that score, and you must not be either. Spry, certainly, and at times in his prime; hardy when he needs to be; all of those things.

No, you are not rotund <u>or</u> double chinned, though I think I have seen you in rôles where you have, almost as an act of will, acquired a sort of cherubic look! Let me answer this question together with your point about Arthur Lowe, because, speaking personally, they enable me to say why I at least see you as the ideal Smiley.

Apart from plumpness, you have all the other physical qualities: a mildness of manner, stretched taut, when you wish it, by an unearthly stillness and an electrifying watchfulness. In the best sense, you are uncomfortable company, as I suspect Smiley is. An audience wishes – when <u>you</u> wish it – to take you into its protection. It feels responsible for you, it worries about you. I don't know what you call that kind of empathy but it is very rare, & Smiley and Guinness have it: when either of you gets his feet wet, I can't help shivering. So it is the double standard – to be unobtrusive, yet to command – which your physique perfectly satisfies. No problem there. And why not Arthur Lowe? (Incidentally, it was an eight-minute playlet he did, in the middle of a long Arts programme, so you mustn't fear that he is already there ahead of you!) I would rather answer the question, once more, 'why Guinness?'

For me, it has to do with depth. Smiley is an Abbey, made up of different periods, fashions and even different religions, not all of them necessarily harmonious. His authority springs from experience, ages of it, compassion, and at root an inconsolable pessimism which gives a certain fatalism to much that he does. If you think about it, Smiley almost <u>invented</u> The Honourable Schoolboy out of his own mind and creative energy; just as he almost invents Tinker Tailor out of his own past.

If I may say so, you communicate to me many of his pains, and the almost <u>archeological</u> authority of so many lives and identities. He is also a guilty man, as all men are who <u>do</u>, who insist on action. To this, you add another, more practical sort of authority terribly important in the several interrogations, in the research, and in the dénoument of Tinker Tailor: the authority of plain <u>intellect</u>. We shall believe Guinness when he tells us things from the past, when he theorises, when he acts in accordance with unstated predictions – because, simply, the intellect is patent, and commanding, yours & Smiley's both.

Some actors can act intelligent. Others <u>are</u> intelligent and come over dull, because of some mannerism which gets in the way. And a very few are intelligent and convey it: in Tinker Tailor, this gift will be pure gold, because it gives such base to the other things – the solitude, the moral concern, the humanity of Smiley – all, because of the intelligence of his perceptions, grow under our eyes and in your care.

About discussing Smiley and his background – yes, of course, as much as you wish, provided I don't in any way overstep Arthur Hopcraft's territory, or that of producer & director.

And lastly the memorising and the problem of getting out the scripts in plenty of time for you. I read this passage to Jonathan Powell verbatim this morning and he felt that there need be no problem there at all: no doubt, however, you will be able to take all that up with them formally very soon. I believe we are all meeting for lunch on March 10th.

But if you would like to meet me before then, or afterwards before I leave for Cornwall, why not let me know?

Forgive this ramble but there are good things in it, & I find I can't think without a pen in my hand! What a wonderful prospect it all is!

Yours
David Cornwell

The American newspaper cartoonist Jeff Danziger (see letter 4 March 1994, p. 348) recalled a different story le Carré told about Guinness's recruitment, on a visit to New York in the mid 2010s. Guinness had begged off the part, saying he was too old, le Carré told the audience at the 92nd Street Y cultural and community centre. The producers arranged a dinner where le Carré implored him to take the role; Guinness said he was flattered but too busy. Finally le Carré, in desperation, said that if Guinness wouldn't take the role, they were going to give it to Donald Sutherland. Guinness paused, then said, 'I'll do it.'

~

TO ARTHUR HOPCRAFT

Tregiffian
St Buryan
Penzance
Cornwall

18 August 1978

Dear Arthur,

I think you've done wonders. Many congratulations! With a good wind now – and it's looking <u>horribly</u> good – I believe we may see something very remarkable indeed. And if it <u>isn't</u> good, I'm sure it won't be the scripts which let it down. I've still some reservations about 1 and 2, as Jonathan has probably told you – particularly 1. I think we can get a lot more electricity out of your structuring of 7 with very little work. I think there are odd stitches here and there which need picking up. I expect I always will, and that's secondary. The main thing is – you've done it, and done it in spades, as we say down here, handsome. So again, from the heart, my sincerest congratulations on a robust intellectual effort, a sensitive artistic arrangement, and beautifully achieved orchestration.

Best,
David

~

TO VIVIAN GREEN

1 Gayton Crescent
London, NW3 ITT

17 December 1978

My dear Vivian,
[. . .]
I've just finished a new book, in rough, and shall work on the revisions through the winter, delivering the m.s. in early April. It went well in the writing & has been quicker in consequence. It puts the Captains & the Kings to bed & leaves me time to start some new things, without, perhaps, the spy theme at the centre.[5] Perhaps something, finally, about my late papa.
[. . .]

Love, as ever
David

~

TO SIR ALEC GUINNESS

1 Gayton Crescent
London, NW3 1TT

27 June 1979

---

5. *Smiley's People* was published in late 1979.

My dear Alec,

Smiley is marvellous. We saw episodes 1–3 on Monday & see the rest tomorrow. You carry it all. What more can I say? Immense range, yet all within the difficult bounds of the character; heart; humour; occasional surprising fury. It's amazing, and I am sure Smiley will be heralded as one of your great parts. The support you get is mainly excellent. Prideaux the only serious disappointment, so far as I'm concerned, Guillam masterly, Control, Toby both fine. Bland too much, Haydon a fraction too foxy too soon, I suspect, but I may be wrong. The direction has great quality, & I saw nothing in the first 3 eps to make me blush, & much to delight me. Lisbon too long away from Lacon's room/house, as you suspected it would be, but not one half as awful, as an 'interlude with screen value', as I had feared. Tarr is really _very_ good, & I think the girl right too. The Czecho sequence weakened by a couple of spy-clichés, which is a pity coming so early, & by the fact that Prideaux can't move very well – his efforts at ageing fail, & the result is camel-like. All the stuff in Lacon's house great, Oxford stunning (Smiley–Connie made Jonathan _and_ Jane weep) the big conference scenes with Control really gripping, Mendel charming & the Islay claustrophobic & unnerving. Lacon excellent.[6] That's the sum of my notes & anyway I've run out of adjectives, and had dinner with Dr Owen, the Death Doctor, last night so I'm not at my sparkling best. Did he find that as Foreign Secretary his performance was affected by jet-lag?

'No.'

Did he miss the Foreign Office?

'I _detest_ bureaucrats,' gnash, gnash. Charm all the way.

We have taken a private cinema in Piccadilly – 200 seats – & are showing the whole thing to my foreign publishers in one

---

6. Michael Jayston's 'masterly' Peter Guillam paved the way for his narration of twenty-one le Carré audiobooks. Scots actor Ian Bannen found no favour with le Carré as Prideaux. Control was played by Alexander Knox, Toby Esterhase by Bernard Hepton, Roy Bland by Terence Rigby, Bill Haydon by Ian Richardson, Ricki Tarr by Hywel Bennett, Oliver Lacon by Anthony Bate and Mendel by George Sewell.

day, starting at 9.30 am & going on till evening. Coffee, lunch, champagne, go home. Hodder & Stoughton & Pan are co-hosts, the date July 27th. If you felt strong enough to come in at champagne time and shake a few hands, that would of course make everyone's day – we are asking all the featured cast, John,[7] Arthur & Jonathan as well – but we would absolutely understand if you preferred your peace! We'll send you an invitation anyway – would you like me to invite Denis[8] to the screening? Would Merula like to come? I guess you yourself would rather see it, if at all, far from anywhere!

The news from the States is really that there is no news, except that we have a couple of offers for the rights, which will have to hold off until the Paramount hurdle is behind us. Paramount have also asked for footage. I know nothing more, except that both offers accepted as self-evident that you w<u>d</u> play Smiley, and that no other Smiley would be considered by ourselves. The noises in N Y about the T T S S series are apparently very positive indeed – George Greenfield came back yesterday & said everybody, but <u>everybody</u>, etc. – but I personally doubt very much, after seeing the stuff, whether the great American public will be permitted such quality, & cerebration, on a major network. My guess is P B S, which is probably better anyway.

You can see from the length of this that the new book goes slowly . . .

Best to you both,
David

P.S. Jonathan mysteriously shifty about everything – not least because they've goofed on the length of episodes; & are having to recut to <u>6</u> episodes to meet US requirements!

~

---

7. *Tinker Tailor Soldier Spy*'s director, John Irvin.

8. Unidentified.

Tina Brown, George Will, Norman Rush and other critics were the objects of le Carré's coruscating scorn, but Clive James occupied a special space on the Cornwell family enemies list. 'Le Carré's new novel is about twice as long as it should be,' James began his review of The Honourable Schoolboy *in the* New York Review of Books *in 1977. Two years later he wrote in the* Observer *of the television series of* Tinker Tailor Soldier Spy: *'The first instalment fully lived up to the standard set by the original novel. Though not quite as incomprehensible, it was equally turgid.'*

TO THE EDITOR, THE *OBSERVER*

> *c/o John Farquharson Ltd*
> *Bell House*
> *Bell Yard*
> *London, WC2A 2JR*

> 6 October 1979

Dear Sir,

It is amusing that Clive James should agonise in public about whether he is conducting a personal vendetta against me, and significant that he does not answer the question. Perhaps I may use your columns to assist him, and incidentally spare him further readers' enquiries. More than a year ago I warned Sir Alec Guinness, Arthur Hopcraft and the assembled producers of TINKER TAILOR SOLDIER SPY that, regardless of the merits of their labours, we could hope for nothing but abuse from James' pen. I even went so far as to scribble down a few of the choicer adjectives we might expect. Clive James did not disappoint. Perhaps people in the debunking business do genuinely forget whom they have had a go at and who still awaits their attentions, but it is only a couple of years or so, after all, while moonlighting in America as a literary critic, that Clive James in a long, sloppy review damned me and my works to eternity. This naturally annoyed me but I consoled myself with the thought that an expatriate Australian television critic from

England who is trying to work his way into a new market has probably to jump about a bit. A few months went by and James took another swipe at me in a British journal – for all I remember, yours. The occasion was the publication of a Graham Greene novel. One did not have to be a student of Jamesian psychology, therefore, to know that he would use the book as a club to beat the television series, and the series as a club to beat the book. For added entertainment there was the opportunity to be thoroughly offensive to our best living actor, and James would be less than flesh if he resisted. Your readers should at least know, therefore, even if Mr James has conveniently forgotten, that his position regarding my work was taken long before the series appeared. What he has given his readers this Sunday by way of explanation is in fact no more than a warmed-up rehash of his review of THE HONOURABLE SCHOOLBOY published in the New York Review of Books. I look forward to reading it again when my new novel appears next February.

Yours faithfully,
John le Carré

~

While he corresponded with the physical embodiment of his fictional spy chief, le Carré was writing to the real-life 'C'. Le Carré's former head of station in Bonn, Dick Franks, had been appointed to the head of the Secret Intelligence Service.

TO SIR DICK AND RACHEL FRANKS

1 Gayton Crescent
London, NW3 1TT

[n.d. but likely early October 1979]

Dear Dickie & Rachel,

How very kind of you, and what a happy evening. For some reason it touched me quite particularly – just time, I suppose, and the changes in all our lives, & the things we leave behind. I was dreadfully tired and fed up when we met – I'd spent a day or two caught in a mucky journalistic crossfire & that always makes me feel grubby and invaded. Your joint calm restored me very quickly, & I felt so grateful for that & everything else. The Stoppard[9] did collapse in the 2nd act, but it was still marvellously entertaining & as Rachel said, very clever at saying what one had always felt.

We got home to hear that the New York Times is running my piece on the Powers book[10] on the front page of its Review on 14 Oct, which pleases me, & I think the piece will please you too. I will send you a copy probably today with a page-proof of the Hodder edn. of Smiley's People.

I decided that the only way I cd write about my father was in a quasi-documentary style, visiting all the places where things happened – his prisons (Exeter, the Scrubs, Zurich Bezirksgefängnis, Djakarta, Hong Kong – not a bad record!) his race tracks where he kept his horses, the constituencies where he ran for Parliament & so on. I think it will be a very long, rather agonised journey, but oh it was funny too! We move for certain on Jan 17th after our skiing holiday: the new London house is really so pretty & quiet, & now we're a bit restless to be in it.

In the long run we'll probably sell Tregiffian & get somewhere nearer & smaller – or maybe nowhere, just be content with Hampstead & Switzerland. But in the long run, as Churchill interrupted some hapless advisor, we'll all be dead.

---

9. Stoppard's *Undiscovered Country*, an adaptation of *Das weite Land* by Austrian playwright Arthur Schnitzler, opened at the National in 1979.

10. Thomas Powers's *The Man Who Kept the Secrets: Richard Helms and the CIA*. Le Carré called it 'a splendid spy-story . . . He tells us as much about the Presidency as he does about the CIA and he leaves me scared stiff of both.'

Let me know if I can ever help. Thanks again, & love to you both –

David

~

Wilmers was co-founder that year of the London Review of Books, *a publication she would go on to edit for twenty-nine years.*

TO MARY-KAY WILMERS, *NEW YORK REVIEW OF BOOKS*[11]

> *1 Gayton Crescent*
> *London, NW3 1TT*
>
> 27 November 1979

Dear Mary-Kay,

It was kind of you to ask me to review the Cheever,[12] and thank you for sending the book. It is a little difficult for me to explain why I have decided not to review it, but I surely owe you an explanation. I don't think very fast on the telephone, but afterwards it occurred to me all too clearly that I had almost by mistake agreed to depart from a firm principle which I made when I first became a full-time novelist – namely, never to get involved in the London reviewing scene, never to confuse the production industry with the service industry. Reviewing for the New York Times is something remote. But reviewing for

---

11. The *LRB* took its title and finance from the *New York Review of Books*, and was folded inside it for the first six months of publication. Le Carré's letter was addressed to the *NYRB*.

12. *The Stories of John Cheever* was published by Jonathan Cape in 1979. It won the Pulitzer Prize for Fiction in the United States that year.

London literary journals immediately involves me in a kind of partisanship which I find very difficult to live with so long as I remain in England. I think Cheever is a magnificent story-teller, but I know that when I say that in the context of a London literary journal, I appear to be making a case for narrative writers like myself to the detriment of more fashionable trends. I think he is better at English prose than anybody practising in this country, but this is a view that takes on a quite disproportionate significance when I say it here.

I suppose what I am saying really is that I find the business of being a successful English novelist living in England hard enough already – there is nothing quite like the flak of home guns – without walking into the minefields of the London literary scene as well. Sorry.

> Best
> David

~

Le Carré's friend Buzz Berger, with his company Titus Productions, had proposed to do a film of Smiley's People. *Berger had produced the Emmy-award-winning series* Holocaust *in 1978.*

TO BUZZ BERGER

> *1 Gayton Crescent*
> *London, NW3 1TT*
>
> 29 November 1979

My dear Buzz,
What a mess!

The explanation, I am afraid, is dishearteningly simple. Guinness, for whatever reasons, was on one hand tremendously pleased with the reception of TINKER, TAILOR ... here and with his treatment by the BBC. On the other hand he was puzzled and wary that we couldn't offer him a movie of SMILEY'S PEOPLE straight away. He had visions of the thing being toted around, he was acutely conscious of the fact that Hollywood did not regard him as star material on his own, and he became increasingly unhappy at the thought that name actors would have to be dragged in in order to shore him up. He has an extremely fine – probably over-fine – instinct for these things, and on top of all that, he feared that the thing would drag out interminably. So perhaps understandably he reached for the safest and nearest solution, and announced that he would rather go back to the BBC with the old team. In the event, neither Irvin nor Hopcraft will be free, so the old team is already beginning to look pretty much like a new team. We offered him the alternative of much more money and an independent production, preferably with Titus. But there again, he feared we would lose what he persistently refers to as the 'distinction' of the first production.

So there it is. I know very well we threw in the game before the first ball had been bowled, but Guinness was not to be persuaded, and even now his agent is making strong statements about 'having to shoot' in November 1980. The truth is, I think, that we are dealing with a great actor of 67 who feels there are not that number of major roles for him to play, and not that number of years in which to play them. He wants, he says, to keep Smiley alive inside himself, and the sooner he can get back to Smiley – or, alternatively, be rid of him – the happier he will be.

One day I hope that you and I shall manage something. In the meantime, please accept my sincere apologies, and please convey them to Herb.[13] For a short while at least it was wonderful to contemplate a partnership with Titus.

---

13. Herbert Brodkin, Buzz Berger's partner in Titus Productions.

Yours ever,
David

~

TO ANTHONY SAMPSON[14]

> *1 Gayton Crescent*
> *London, NW3 1TT*

> [n.d. but *Smiley's People* was published in
> November 1979]

Dear Anthony,

How very kind of you to write – & I'm so glad you warmed to
'Smiley's People'. It made me very sad to write it somehow – the
spiritual death of a marooned Brit administrator, Smiley as a
doomed anachronism, me as another,[15] it all seemed so hopeless. Then somehow it became fun, & somehow Toby[16] helped. I
suppose it's true of anything really – when you get to the top of the
mountain, all you see is pygmies, & miles & miles of bugger all!

Off to foreign parts in early Dec, back late Jan. Do let's meet
& schmooze around then.

Thanks again – love to you both
David

---

14. The journalist and author of *Anatomy of Britain*; shared the publisher Robin
Denniston with le Carré; helped with research on arms dealing for *The Night Manager*.

15. Karla comes over the bridge in the closing scene of *Smiley's People*, 'knowing he
has renounced the absolutism of his creed', le Carré said in the 'Berliner Salon' on 3
March 2020. 'Smiley knows that he has renounced humanism and blackmailed Karla
about his love for his daughter and that for Smiley is a great shame.' Le Carré's unfinished novel on his death included a last meeting between the two.

16. Toby Esterhase, whom le Carré viewed as theatrically fraudulent, with the manners of a middle-European waiter who would sell his own mother; Smiley's suspect in
Tinker Tailor Soldier Spy and a sidekick in *Smiley's People*; a character le Carré relished.
'Toby was a confidence trickster of a sort, a middle European who allocated to himself an elegant Hungarian name and didn't spell it right', 'Berliner Salon', 3 March 2020.

~

TO SIR DICK AND RACHEL FRANKS

Chalet Chamois
3823 Wengen
Switzerland

15 December 1979

Dear Dickie & Rachel,

This is instead of a drawing of drunk squirrels dancing around a holly tree, & is intended to wish you both an extremely happy Christmas & New Year, & to send our love to the family.

[. . .]

We move into our new (old) house in Hampstead on Jan 17[17] – Jane is insisting that she handle the move alone – she has some extraordinary notion I'll get in the way. Then in the next year we plan to phase out Tregiffian, I'm afraid, because we feel we must make our base in London, travel more, and just generally reduce our administrative & financial overheads.[18] One reason for this is my own feeling that I <u>must</u> now write the riskier books which I have put off, & that we can't reckon on big royalties forever. So we want to cut down a bit, so that we can more or less live off our humps if necessary, & not spend so much on houses we don't often occupy. I've been dithering for the last 6 months between the book on my father & a book I w<u>d</u> quite like to do on terrorism, but I finally plumped for the Daddy book & some plays, & put terrorism on the back burner: not least, because when I started to delve around in it, in Amsterdam, Hamburg & so on, I found the whole subject so inexpressibly drab that I really couldn't face two years of it,

---

17. In Gainsborough Gardens, Hampstead.

18. Le Carré periodically announced he would settle in either Hampstead or Cornwall; he kept homes in both places until his death.

at least until I'd done something a little more amusing first! My Tiefpunkt[19] was a queasy little Hamburg lawyer who is or was the bane of Hans Horchem's life,[20] and seems to have handled the defence of several of the Baader–Meinhof star performers: one Groenewold,[21] a weed. Somehow, he was the turning point. Terrorism later, I decided; and Daddy <u>now</u>.

The weather here is rather good – that's to say there's good snow & more forecast, & as I write there are big flakes falling on a village locked in a pre-season quiet. We're going to use the chalet more as a writing place, I think, & as a part-time holiday house for the adult children (!) when they can get to it. The first reviews of 'Smiley's People' are good – from the States, where it is now just appearing – 'Time' & 'Newsweek' review it on Monday, in their editions dated 24th December; the 'Telegraph' colour section is serialising bits of it, so is the 'Evening Standard' – UK pub date Feb 3rd. The TV of TTSS became almost crazy: ITV strike, the Blunt affair as a sort of public sequel to it, not to mention Smiley's dispatch to Ireland.[22] Guinness does 'Smiley's People' this winter, all being well, but the BBC wants to make it Mar 1981 for budget reasons so the big G is saying 'let's do a movie instead'. The idea of <u>ever</u> going back to the Hollywood scene scares me stiff, but one way or another I suppose we'll be shooting in Nov.

All love to you all – & a successful 1980. Let's show off our new schloss to you soon.

Best
David

---

19. Low point.

20. Hans Josef Horchem was responsible for combating terrorism as president of the Office for the Protection of the Constitution in Hamburg. He became an expert on terrorism and the Red Army Faction.

21. Hamburg attorney Kurt Groenewold was convicted and disbarred in the 1970s for representing members of the Baader–Meinhof Group.

22. In November 1979 Prime Minister Margaret Thatcher named Professor Sir Anthony Blunt as a Soviet spy and released details of his case. Smiley's 'dispatch to Ireland' is a mystery.

In the event, the terror novel came first; The Little Drummer Girl *followed* Smiley's People *in 1983, and* A Perfect Spy *followed in 1986.*

~

Vivian Green's letter to le Carré here is lost; but le Carré's response suggests Green had noticed for the first time that he was a model for George Smiley.

TO VIVIAN GREEN

9 Gainsborough Gardens
London, NW3 1BJ

12 February 1980

My dear Vivian,

I was so glad you picked up the references. I felt diffident about them, & it always amused me, secretly, that you didn't seem to notice where so much of Smiley came from – his humanity, at least, his perception of human frailty, & his difficulty about buying clothes![23]

Nobody ever did so much to set me on my feet as you did, and probably nobody gave me the feeling of seeing me so clearly. Yes, it was the Dudley & Skipton building society,[24] & the reason Hatch Beauchamp goes through your mind is that the vicar of Pilton is Hurst-Bannister[25] (or was – he is now Chaplain to London's actors' guild, if you can believe it!)

---

23. Green's loud tweed jackets and leather trousers were noted wryly by Lincoln College students; his *Times* obituary noted his 'daring, even discordant taste in ties and shirts'.

24. Actually the Skipton and Dudley building societies, the two principal lenders to Ronnie Cornwell's web of property companies before his bankruptcy in 1954.

25. The Reverend M. Hurst-Bannister.

Please come & see us soon. The book sells prodigiously –
93,000 so far, plus 125,000 book club – I've never known such
figures in England.

Love
David

*Three years later Green's face was splashed over the tabloids along-
side that of Alec Guinness when the connection became public.
Among Green's papers is a card from le Carré, which apparently
came with caviar and a bottle of vodka, reading: 'With love from
Karla'. In* The Pigeon Tunnel *le Carré described Green as 'my wise
Oxford mentor . . . who gave me by his example the inner life of
George Smiley'.*

∾

TO JEAN CORNWELL

*9 Gainsborough Gardens
London, NW3 1BJ*

[Postmark] 18 February 1980

Dearest Jeannie,

How lovely of you to write. I'm so glad you enjoyed the
book & that it moved you – it made me awfully sad when I
had finished it. We meant to ask you both much sooner, but
I suddenly got deeply tired & depressed – post publicatio
tristis – and couldn't face anyone, particularly myself. I hope
to get down to Cornwall on Tuesday, for a week or so; the <u>new</u>
book is a big awful project & I have to get locked into it firmly.
Stanley Kubrick wants to film SP but I've turned him down
for the Beeb.

love
D

~

From Portsmouth Mrs Betty Quail had written to suggest that Smiley becoming a Roman Catholic 'would be the answer to a lot of his problems', including his marriage.

TO BETTY QUAIL

> *c/o John Farquharson Ltd*
> *Bell House*
> *Bell Yard*
> *London, WC2A 2JU*
>
> 18 March 1980

Dear Mrs Quail,

Thank you very much for your kind and interesting letter. What can I say? I am glad at least that Smiley and all his People have given you such entertainment, and while I cannot see him being embraced either by Ann or the Catholic Church in the near future, I will certainly communicate your hopes to him when we next converse!

Yours sincerely,

John le Carré

THE LITTLE DRUMMER GIRL

There's no consolation. Smiley isn't there to cheer us up and explain things and say we'll carry on another time. When the curtain comes down, as Charlie is warned, in the Theatre of the Real, nobody gets up and goes home. The bodies stay where they are.

– to Melvyn Bragg, *The South Bank Show*, 1983

Le Carré first went to the Middle East in 1977, after *The Honourable Schoolboy* was published, to Israel, Lebanon, Jordan and Syria. His initial plan was to take George Smiley with him, but 'I couldn't find a plot for him there.'[1] After writing *Smiley's People*, he returned in 1980, with an opening inspired by watching his half-sister Charlotte performing in a provincial theatre show. He met with Israeli military and intelligence officials, as well as Yasser Arafat, with several visits to Beirut. The Arab–Israeli conflict 'had long been in my sights, even if it had always scared the wits out of me', he later said.[2]

---

1. *Newsweek*, 7 March 1983.

2. Interview with Douglas Davis, 1 January 1998, *Jewish World Review*.

A first outline of The Little Drummer Girl *to his long-time American lawyer, Mort Leavy.*

to MORTON LEAVY

14 July 1980

<u>PRIVATE & CONFIDENTIAL</u>

My dear Mort,

<u>THE CHARLIE JOSEPH SHOW</u>

I have no better working title yet for my new novel, but below is a summary of the project I have in mind.

My subject is international terrorism and my story concerns the recruitment, training and deployment of a female agent – in this case, an English out-of-work actress named Charlie – who under the influence of her 'handler', Joseph, infiltrates her way through loosely-linked urban guerrilla cells (German, Italian, etc.) until, by proving herself in a series of violent actions, she ends up alongside the target organisation, an extremist group which has recently been perpetrating bomb outrages against overseas Israeli missions, synagogues, schools, etc.[3]

At the head of this organisation stands her quarry, a 'Carlos' figure who sees himself as the latter-day Che Guevara of the urban guerrilla game, and whose mistress, under Joseph's guidance, Charlie finally becomes.

The climax of the action approaches when, having betrayed the group's hideouts and dispositions Charlie is on the run with its leader.

My settings would be West European, Middle Eastern (including South Lebanon and probably Tripoli) with the denouement in England, but I would not care to be too precise

---

3. Joseph recruits Charlie to play the terrorist's part in what he calls the 'Theatre of the Real', a phrase that recurs in *The Little Drummer Girl*.

in advance, because, as you know, I like the freedom to change up to (and I fear sometimes beyond!) the last moment.[4] The story opens in Greece, where Charlie – intelligent, acerbic and not by any means beautiful – is on holiday with her lover of the moment and a bunch of out-of-work English actors and actresses. On the beach at Mykonos she meets the aloof, rather puritanical figure of Joseph, and through a series of 'chance' circumstances finds herself forming a platonic friendship with him. After her boyfriend has been recalled to London to be auditioned for a film part – a most unexpected development – she agrees to go with Joseph on a week's tour of Greek antiquities. The intelligence courtship has begun.

Joseph charms her, plies her with questions, introduces her to his friend Shlomo in a pleasant apartment in Athens, takes her to Delphi, etc., and little by little reveals to her that he knows almost as much about Charlie as she does herself: about her abortion, her middle-class background and private education, and her periodic flirtation with English radical groups such as the Workers' Revolutionary Party – a body much favoured by left-wing actors and actresses.[5] By the time Charlie returns to England, Joseph has performed his fan dance well enough to take her to what the professionals call the first stage of consciousness: she knows that she is in touch with an intelligence service, and that something will later be required of her. She knows – or thinks she knows – that the service is Israeli. Above all, she is under the spell of an intelligent, charming man ten years her senior who treats her with great consideration without

---

4. In this letter the novel's denouement is in England; le Carré finally set it in Germany, with the attempted assassination of a liberal Israeli academic, Professor Hansi Minkel, at the University of Freiburg. In the 2018 television series of *The Little Drummer Girl* the action is moved to London, where the target is Irene Minkel, at the London Polytechnic.

5. Charlotte Cornwell, le Carré's close model for Charlie, was a passionate political activist, involved with Artists Against Apartheid, and the Nicaragua Solidarity Campaign. A vice-chair of the actors' union, Equity, she later tried to establish a free training project for young actors.

ever laying a finger on her, a thing totally new and exciting to her. Their relationship is the lynchpin of the story, and its resolution provides the end. Joseph becomes by turn her mentor, confessor, pimp, Nemesis and ultimately – when he has turned her, among other things, into an international outlaw – her only lifeline.

I'm sure this is enough for 'identification' purposes, and I offer it on the binding understanding that it remains confidential to the parties involved; not only for professional reasons, but because my researches will take me back to several Arab countries as well as to Israel.

Best,
David

In 1982 Mort Leavy introduced le Carré to another of his formidable roster of showbusiness clients, the Academy-award-winning director George Roy Hill, who read The Little Drummer Girl *in manuscript and was eager to direct it. Hill's 1984 film starred Diane Keaton as Charlie, reframed as an American actress working in London, in an unlikely piece of casting. The film, le Carré later told director John Boorman, was 'embarrassing'.*

～

TO SIR DICK FRANKS

Tregiffian
St Buryan
Penzance
Cornwall

4 August 1981

My dear Dickie,
My sources told me yesterday that you had officially retired, which, knowing my sources, probably means you have signed

on for another 10 years without the option. But, taking it for true, I write to send you my most sincere good wishes for a long, very happy & richly deserved retirement, and to thank you, in a way I never quite could when you were still in the saddle, for the kindness & support you managed to show me ever since my life took its own strange course. There were times, I think, when you knew me better than anyone, even when I stretched your tolerance to its limit; at least I always felt so, and shall always feel the deepest gratitude for your loyalty, & generosity of spirit. There. It's said. The occasion provides the opportunity. I wish so much that, in other circumstances, we could have worked together, but probably the truth is, I would have been awful at it – as Graham [Greene] assured me <u>he</u> was – over-imaginative, sloppy about detail, totally impractical.

Mrs T. offered me a CBE a while back, and I can't imagine she took the plunge without you being consulted. I didn't feel I could take it. I don't quite know why: the guilts, a peculiar modesty, a feeling I wanted to stay out of the citadel. Certainly not pique or false pride so far as I know. Secretly, I think, a feeling I hadn't earned it. All a muddle as usual. Anyway, my lunch with the Queen turned me into such an abject monarchist that I didn't think I needed a second bite!

The book (Israelis v. European terrorism) is nearly done. [. . .]

We have gone to earth here till September (our new no. is St Buryan 612) we have a self-contained guest wing and a decent cellar, and if you are loafing round Cornwall ever – this year, next year, whenever – please come & sample us. All my love to Rachel too. By all accounts – and there my sources are blameless – the two of you supplied the best leadership & the best morale anyone can remember for a long time.

Oh, and 'Smiley's People' is shooting now. Guinness is having the vapours as usual – this time it's the director who is too something & not enough something else. Just now I forget what.

Love to you both as ever
David

~

The British historian Hugh Thomas was le Carré's contemporary at Sherborne School; he was on the committee for the Yalta Memorial in South Kensington, commemorating people displaced as a result of the 1945 Yalta Conference.

TO HUGH THOMAS

> 9 Gainsborough Gardens
> London, NW3 1BJ

> 25 January 1982

Dear Hugh,

Thanks for the note about the Yalta memorial. I sent them some money – yes, it was a truly awful thing. I just came back from Beirut after a long session with Arafat. Then to the Deep South – Tyre & Sidon & the busted landscape. In a few years, we'll be building another monument to the Palestinians.

Best to you, du coeur,
David (CORNWELL)

~

Le Carré twice spells 'yoghurt' here with a 'j', in the German manner. Blessings in Disguise, *the first part of Guinness's three-volume autobiography, was published in 1985.*

TO SIR ALEC GUINNESS

9 Gainsborough Gardens
London, NW3 1BJ

27 January 1982

My dear Alec,

I think that really <u>was</u> the best meal ever; and such fun too. Thank you very, very much for that and so many blessings. If you are just easing away from your diet, Jane and I are decisively easing towards one: joghurt & soup and the wagon look like the awful recipe. This morning I got a letter from Svetlana Stalin,[6] delighted to hear we w<u>d</u> be working on a 'philosophical non-fiction' together and signing herself Mrs Peters ('but to my friends new & old I remain Svetlana'). It seems my Swiss agent[7] cunningly misrepresented our mutual interest in one another in order to produce 'a property'. He told S I was mustard to meet her, and me that S was m. to meet <u>me</u>, then dropped into her ear that I might co-write her newest project with her. She then took the bit between her – & so forth. Showbiz publishing . . .

On which note – I <u>do</u> think your plan for <u>not</u> showbiz publishing, but doing your own kind of book, is an excellent one. On second & third thoughts I tend to agree with Merula, though, that the title[8] does not quite do you justice – too reminiscent, now, of Graham's [Greene] miserable 'Sort of Life', as if being a best-selling novelist for fifty years, living in the S. of France, having lots of money & ladies <u>and</u> discovering God into the bargain all added up to very little. Whereas for most people, pains & all, his life is the nearest man can get to

---

6. Svetlana Stalin, born in 1926, was the youngest child of Joseph Stalin. The 'little princess of the Kremlin' defected to the United States in 1967. She published memoirs about her life inside the Soviet Union and her decision to flee, then largely dropped from public sight.

7. Rainer Heumann.

8. Guinness proposed to call it *A Halfway Man*.

perfection. I think one has to remember that somehow. My first US publisher[9] reminded <u>me</u> of it, after I had done a misguided TV interview on the Pains of Being Me, by hauling me down to Grand Central Stn & asking me very sharply whether I would prefer to be <u>them</u>. And since your theme is people who have made life interesting for you, the sense of incompletion in the title (inadvertent) does seem to me a bit too grey. Forgive me for saying this but it haunted me over my joghurt.

We must make an occasion before long – I w<u>d</u> love to produce the fighters for you if it can be done, but in any case, now you've established our taste for it, we can't go too long at a time without caviare . . .

Our love to Merula, & to yourself, and again – thank you.
Ever,
David

∼

On 27 November 1979 le Carré had turned down the request from Mary-Kay Wilmers of the London Review of Books *to review a book by the American writer John Cheever. Three years later Bob Gottlieb, editor at Alfred A. Knopf to both le Carré and Cheever, wrote to le Carré with the news that Cheever was ill.*

TO JOHN CHEEVER

Tregiffian
St Buryan
Penzance
Cornwall

7 April 1982

---

9. Jack Geoghegan.

Dear Maître,

Bob Gottlieb wrote to us that you were ill, and sent us your new book. The book is so perfectly and beautifully healthy that I know Gottlieb is lying as usual; but if you <u>are</u> ill, then the book is surely a most lovely thing to have beside you.

I am glad in one sense that we have not met, because at least I can say things to you that no decent Englishman could say to anybody's face and survive. You have given so much <u>light</u> to our common language, so much dance and melody; you listen so carefully to how you speak – and to how <u>they</u> do. And you dramatise the perception so gracefully. So please take good care of our inheritance, and continue to add to it.

I send you, as ever, my homage and my gratitude, and my urgent good wishes for your recovery.

There is no signature on the draft copy in le Carré's archive. Cheever died of cancer on 18 June 1982.

∼

The Israeli journalist, diplomat and author Yuval Elizur was a correspondent for Haaretz *as well as the* Washington Post *and the* Boston Globe. *He was introduced to le Carré by David Greenway,*[10] *then working for the* Washington Post *in Israel.*

---

10. By the time of this letter, Greenway had moved on to work for the *Boston Globe*. Having travelled with le Carré in South-East Asia, he reunited with him in the Middle East. 'My debt to David Greenway is huge,' le Carré stressed to his biographer, Adam Sisman, in 2015. 'I would never have found the nerve to go to the places & do the things we did, if he hadn't been there to guide & indeed protect me.'

Tregiffian
St Buryan
Cornwall
7 April 82

Dear Maître, ~~Bob John Cheever~~,

Bob Gottlieb

to us
wrote / that you were ill, and
sent us your new book. The
book is so ~~perfectly~~ and beautifully
healthy, ~~and moving beyond~~
~~useful praise;~~ and if you are
ill, ~~The book~~ then ~~the book is a surely~~
a most
lovely thing to have beside you.
~~In a way,~~ I am glad (in one sense that) we have
at least
not met, because / I can say
things to you that no decent
any body's
Englishman could say to ~~any one~~
face + survive. You have given
our common
so much light to ∧ language, so much

that
I know
Gottlieb
is lyric
as usual;
but

dance +
melody; you listen so carefully to how you speak
~~and the do~~ and to how they do.

And ~~you~~ you ~~see so wonderfully, and~~ and ~~painfully,~~

dramatise

~~take off~~ from the perception so

gracefully; ~~that~~ ~~the faculties~~

In short your contribution and the art ~~are not~~ your

~~property alone,~~ ~~and~~ ~~Therefore severely~~

~~you will take good~~ So please take good care of

our inheritance, ~~I have~~ because ~~no doubt~~

~~at all that you are going to~~

and continue to be ~~eat~~ for centuries, ~~so I~~

add to it. ~~I send~~ I send you ~~my~~ as ever, homage

~~Most~~ ~~when~~ my devoted ~~admiration,~~

~~and acknowledgements,~~

and gratitude, and ~~my~~ ~~my~~

~~Most~~ my urgent good wishes

for your every. ~~The~~ Do

~~please write~~ ~~As we may~~ may

~~your~~

~~for writes, so~~

TO YUVAL ELIZUR

> 9 *Gainsborough Gardens*
> *London, NW3 1BJ*

> 3 May 1982

Dear Yuval,

Wonderful to hear that, all being well, you will be free to read my book & discuss it with me. As I told you, I plan to arrive on 14th May, Friday, and stay about five days. If the Gods allow, we should therefore have about three clear days to talk, which must be enough!

I would normally get my lawyer to write you a pompous letter proposing terms, but there isn't really time. What I would suggest is this. I will drop the m.s. on you on Friday evening & leave you in peace till you let me know you have read it.

We then discuss: and, as you will see, the story is very sensitive, in that it really speaks of the irreconcilable nature of the Arab–Israeli conflict. Undoubtedly, at this stage, I will have written things which are inaccurate/inadvertently offensive/unfair, etc. Our job, together, is to get the fictional 'record' as straight as possible. I have a list of things I would like to discuss with you – you will have your own by then, no doubt! The character and origin of 'Joseph', for instance, the disenchanted Israeli special forces man – the plausibility of Kurtz, Litvak and their crew – we have to talk it all through, as writers and you have to enlighten me where my own artistic needs have run ahead of the facts and realities. My ignorance in lots of fields is self-evident, and I shall depend on you to mend the holes. I am in the large content with the shape and feel of the story: within it, all sorts of things are changeable.

I would propose, for the immediate operation, a flat fee of £1,000 (U.K.) for five days' labour: two for reading, three for discussion. If there are things to be checked out after I've gone, follow-up questions & so forth, and if you are still interested in the project, I would suggest we function at the ad-hoc rate of £100 per day, £50 per half day, and of course your expenses – travel, phone, meals on the way. I somehow think we shan't have much of that, but it may happen. If these terms aren't okay, please say.

It is agreed between us, I suggest, that our work should remain confidential between us until either of us releases the other from that agreement, because you may decide you do not wish to be associated with the book, which is quite reasonable. Such a question becomes particularly real when we come to acknowledgements & thanks at the beginning of the book & so forth: in other words, we should respect one another's right to privacy, now or later. I have told Jane obviously, and David, about the planned collaboration, but I am concerned that, if certain people hate the book (& they are sure to) it won't bounce back on you in some unpleasant way.

I look forward enormously to our first talk – and of course there may well be others later in the year. We'll just see how it goes and how much there is to do. If I make changes of any scale, then it might be sensible for you to read them before they go to print.

Sorry to run on – it was good talking to you.
Best
David

P.S. <u>And</u> if there's anything in this you don't care for or wish to discuss, please let me know when I arrive!

∾

то GRAHAM GREENE

9 Gainsborough Gardens
London, NW3 1BJ

6 September 1982

Dear Graham Greene,

I write to you in great embarrassment after reading today's reported interview with myself in 'The Times', in which I appear to claim a far greater and more significant acquaintance with you than was ever the case. The words which the reporter has put into my mouth are, in several instances, the sheerest nonsense, but nowhere more so than where your own name appears. 'The Times' appears to be aware of this for they have already agreed to hold up syndication of the piece; we have been on to your publishers and tried, as yet unsuccessfully, to reach your sister in order to send you my most sincere apologies. The reporter himself has prudently disappeared on holiday, but his superior has already privately admitted to my agent that the piece is full of inaccuracies. I really am so sorry. We both know, I am sure, what rough instruments such 'interviews' can be, but this one really has turned out most unhappily. If you wish, I am sure I can oblige the Times to print a disclaimer or an apology or whatever, but I fear this may simply compound the apparent presumption of my words, and attract interest where probably little has been aroused. Or you may prefer to write to them yourself. But in any case, I am awfully sorry it happened. And I will make sure the passage is removed if ever the wretched piece is to appear elsewhere.

With best wishes,
David Cornwell

The publisher Max Reinhardt had a long association with Graham Greene. He brought Greene into the Bodley Head publishing house as director.

TO MAX REINHARDT

> *9 Gainsborough Gardens*
> *London, NW3 1BJ*
>
> 26 September 1982

<u>PERSONAL</u>

Dear Max Reinhardt,
Thanks for taking care of it all – GG wrote a very super letter. I owe him <u>so</u> much, in spirit, in sheer literary scale, and it made me sick to think that I seemed to be chucking his name around. It makes me fairly sick to be compared with him too; for I am content to <u>know</u> he is an immeasurably greater talent. Period.

Best,
David C

≈

TO SIR DICK FRANKS

> *9 Gainsborough Gardens*
> *London, NW3 1BJ*
>
> 24 January 1983

My dear Dickie,
I thought I'd better let you know that 'Newsweek' are doing a cover story on me, and that in the course of it they have unearthed a fair amount of detail about old associations. It

seems everyone wanted to give them the dirt. Their excursions have included interviews with old members of (both) offices, and such weird Seitensprünge[11] as an interview with A. B.[12] They've also been to see John Bingham, I gather, and got some lurid stories from other ex-members (not John) about my supposed talent for dreaming up cold war operations – I think they have been to 'Nigel West'[13] also, but I'm not sure. All of which amounts, probably, to very little in the long run, but they're very pleased with themselves. Where I could I walked round it, but I don't hold out much hopes. So I expect the gaff will be blown.

Are you well? Have you sold the house, moved into the new one? We have a new phone number here (01) 431 0362 – changed before publication. Warners traipsed round Lebanon with me, Newsweek followed, I got back yesterday. The film is in production, they hope to shoot in September, & I'm putting the arm on them to take Charlotte.[14] I doubt it though. The Israelis have made it clear they loathe my book, I just wish I'd been harder on them, the devastation in Lebanon is <u>awful,</u> but I never saw it so quiet: one bang in eight days of Beirut. Tyre & Sidon devastated, Sabra & Chattila visions of Hades. Please give us a chance to feed you here soon. Love to Rachel.

Best – ever
David

The cover story in Newsweek *came out on 7 March 1983. Reported by Alexis Gelber and Edward Behr, the seasoned foreign and war*

---

11. Extramarital escapades.

12. Name withheld.

13. Nigel West, the pen-name of Rupert Allason, was building his career as a prolific author on espionage.

14. Writing to Franks in 1978, le Carré had described Charlotte's performance in a London production of *As You Like It* as 'unnervingly good'.

*correspondents, in Beirut, it included a remarkably thorough time-
line of le Carré's intelligence career in Bern, Austria, and MI5 and
MI6, including his reports on left-wing groups in Oxford. After*
The Spy Who Came in from the Cold *was published, le Carré
was identified by name as a diplomat serving in Germany, but he
had consistently denied being an intelligence agent. Now the gaff,
as he noted, was truly blown.*

∾

TO MARGARET THATCHER

*9 Gainsborough Gardens
London, NW3 1BJ*

2 March 1983

Dear Prime Minister,
I cannot return to the Middle East tomorrow without first
expressing my gratitude for today's luncheon. It was a great
honour to be invited, and I thank you most sincerely; and
I hope that your talks with the Netherlands Prime Minister
were indeed as cordial and as fruitful as they appeared.
Perhaps 'The Little Drummer Girl' will give you a few hours'
relief from the burdens of office; but then I am sure that the
consensus of all your guests was that relief was the last thing
you needed!
  Thank you again – & what a masterly speech.

  Yours sincerely,
  David Cornwell

*Thatcher hosted the luncheon at 10 Downing Street for Ruud
Lubbers, the Dutch prime minister; le Carré quickly added Lubbers*

to his list of impressions. Thatcher centred her speech on George Downing, for whom Downing Street is named; Downing was chief of the intelligence staff of Oliver Cromwell's forces and then ambassador to The Hague.

Hugh Thomas, recently created Baron Thomas of Swynnerton, first tried to enlist le Carré for a secret literary dinner for Thatcher in 1982. He tried again six months after le Carré's lunch at Downing Street. 'I'm sorry I'm away then. It's just a bad time for me – shy and scared and after-book, & sick to death of my own company. The usual trough,' le Carré wrote on 26 September 1983. 'Please give her my good wishes, if you have a chance. I never thought I could find her admirable, but I do somehow. Even though the immediate consequences, at least, are so wretched. Perhaps because I really _do_ believe she is an honest and extraordinary person.'

≈

Janet Lee Stevens, who was working on a PhD in Egyptian theatre, lived in Cairo and Tunis before moving to Beirut as a freelance journalist, where she covered the Sabra and Shatila massacres. She met le Carré in late 1982 as he researched The Little Drummer Girl. Stevens was killed in the bombing of the US Embassy in Beirut on 18 April 1983. The film of The Little Drummer Girl was dedicated to her; le Carré made the first donation to a memorial fund in Stevens's name.

TO MR [HAZEN] AND MRS [JEAN] STEVENS
AND JO ANNE STEVENS

9 Gainsborough Gardens
London, NW3 1BJ

29 April 1983

Dear Mr and Mrs Stevens and Jo Anne,
You will know that Janet worked with us as guide, interpreter
and irrepressible philosopher while George Roy Hill, Loring
Mandel[15] and myself visited Lebanon to make a preliminary
tour of the locations of our film. At their request, I enclose
their letters to you. Let me try to add a word of my own,
which I pray may ease your grief just a little. It is no convenient, retrospective adjustment of truth to say that we all loved
Janet, and quickly appointed her to be our instructress and –
even more – our moral and compassionate focus for the pain
and devastation which we witnessed. It was only days before
her eye and her heart, and her tremendous courage, became
in some way the window through which we perceived the
landscape she knew so well. It was Janet's sensitivity which
guided us through Sabra and Chatila, the Gaza hospital, and
the camps of the south; Janet's amazing capacity to reach the
poor and bereaved and destitute that made us <u>feel</u> their plight,
and her own unswerving commitment. By the time we left, I
had unhesitatingly asked her to research some stories for me,
and even recommended her to a major American newspaper
as a potential recruit. I told Janet once that, when she was
old, she would acquire the venerability, if not the piety, of a
Mother Theresa, and she laughed pretty loud at me for that.
But she couldn't fool any of us: her dedication to the people
she loved was absolute, and I cannot resist adding that she
was ready to die for them. And in a sense she did: by staying
on, by being there, by refusing to count the risk, or quit, so

---

15. The director and screenwriter of the film of *The Little Drummer Girl*.

long as the others were suffering. Quite simply, she inspired a lot of people with her courage and strength. And we were among them.[16]

Yours sincerely,
John le Carré
(David Cornwell)

---

16. *The Good Spy*, a book by the Pulitzer Prize-winning journalist Kai Bird, on the CIA operative Robert Ames, claims Stevens was due to meet le Carré in Cyprus the day after she was killed. Two days after the blast, the book says, le Carré flew back to Beirut, checked into the Commodore Hotel and went to see the ruined site. The book further claims that the Palestinians gave Janet Lee Stevens the nickname 'the little drummer girl' for her unceasing advocacy of their cause, 'a title le Carré appropriated from Janet's moniker in the refugee camps'. Stevens's niece has questioned Bird's sourcing for this account, and whether Stevens was even nicknamed 'the little drummer girl', before or after the novel; however, it is a claim that has found its way into Wikipedia. Le Carré's friend David Greenway reports that *The Little Drummer Girl* was a title le Carré was contemplating in the late 1970s, before he had finished researching the book and before he met Janet Stevens. He confirmed to Greenway he had his half-sister Charlotte in mind as his model.

A PERFECT SPY

It took me a long while to get on writing terms with Ronnie, conman, fantasist, occasional jailbird, and my father.

– in *The Pigeon Tunnel*, Chapter 33, 'Son of the author's father'

Ronnie's life accomplishments, if unorthodox, were dazzling: a string of bankruptcies spread over nearly 50 years and accounting for several millions of pounds; literally hundreds of companies with grandiose letter paper and scarcely a speck of capital; a host of faithful friends who smiled on his business ventures even when they were themselves the victims of them; four healthy and successful children; seven grandsons; an undimmed faith in his creator; spells of imprisonment on two continents which had left no discernible mark upon everything; spectacular acts of individual charity that would be remembered by the beneficiaries as long as they had breath; and a sexual virility which, as he had assured me only a few months earlier, could still surprise the most optimistic.

– 'Spying on My Father', *Sunday Times*, 6 March 1986

Sons and their dubious fathers found their way into earlier le Carré novels: the character of Cassidy's father in *The Naive and Sentimental Lover*; and in *The Honourable Schoolboy*, Jerry Westerby finds the cupboard bare in his father's complex will. But the semi-autobiographical *A Perfect Spy* centred on a thinly disguised portrait of Ronnie as Rick, the fictional ringmaster of arguably le Carré's greatest work.

TO JOHN AND MIRANDA MARGETSON

Chalet Chamois
3823 Wengen
Switzerland

19 December 1985

Dearest Miranda & John,

[. . .]

I was sorry to be handing you such a scruffy version of the book, printed on cheap blotting paper & half its size. Here at the chalet there were three copies of the final format waiting for me & I wanted to send you one at once. But the final book will be ready in late Jan & I'll have one sent to you then.

Copenhagen passed in a haze, Finland in the dark, but both were lovely. The best thing about Helsinki was the sudden chunks of old Berlin, & the splendid Art Nouveau railway station at night, & watching the Tolstoi Express depart for Leningrad & Moscow – only Anna Karenina was missing. I was thrilled by it. Saunas, I don't know. I stood with a huddled group at the edge of the frozen sea. They had cut a hole in the ice & were preparing to jump in after the sauna. Would I join them? No, I said, because there is only one hole. I need two, I said, one to get into, & one to come out of. Puzzled silence as the Finns slipped one by one into the gloomy chasm of iced sea.

Much love & thanks again,
David

~

Al Alvarez and le Carré were neighbours in Hampstead and close friends for over forty years. Alvarez was a poet, critic, gambler, writer and rock climber, as well as the poetry editor of the Observer *for ten years. His book* Offshore, *about his travels to the oil fields three*

hundred miles off Aberdeen and the Shetlands, was first published in
two parts in the New Yorker *magazine.*

TO AL ALVAREZ

9 Gainsborough Gardens
London, NW3 1BJ

3 May 1986

My dear Al,

I was slightly thrown when you asked me whether I had read
the book because in fact I had read it first in the New Yorker
& for some freak reason of circumstance – travel I suppose –
totally failed to communicate my enthusiasm, which was very,
very considerable. Then H&S dropped a t/s in on me, & it sat
about in an accusing sort of way, but I thought I w<u>d</u> wait till
the book came – & so on. So last night I sat down & read it
through at one whack, rather than one half in Oshkosh & the
other in Toronto, & had myself a marvellous time. (In brackets
first, I do think H&S have made a <u>very</u> attractive book. I haven't
seen margins like that since Dietrich wore suspenders – a really
good page, gentle illustrations, a sense of sober quality borne
out by the text.) But the reason I wanted to write to you, confirmed by this reading, is that I did & do feel that, as with the
poker book, you have discovered an ease of personal narrative
that is at once authoritative and affectionate and sometimes
touching: you really <u>are</u> the reader as well as the writer, and
your measured excitements (as you say, of a chap who's had to
wait 40 years to do something every schoolboy would like to
do) are perfect pitch for read-communication & identification.

As I also said, I love it when you go ashore: the interlude
in the Shetlands, which you make us love, & that whole tender
passage, which actually tells us it's over for them, but they're
going down fighting, is really a classic piece of reporting. And,
like you, the reader is by then pawing the earth to get ashore,

he's had exactly enough of the spooky platforms & is longing for dry land. As to Aberdeen . . .

But it's the humanity, & the voice, that you've found (the artist's attachment absolutely edited out) that I think can take you anywhere you want to go with books like this. I know that the dangerous edge draws you, but I think you are also allowing yourself to report <u>fun</u> in a way that occasionally takes you & the reader pleasantly by surprise. And we romp along with you, with fact tripping over insight, in the most enjoyable way.

Which prompts me to suggest that you would be the most marvellous chronicler of the next Everest climb, as it were (but of a more amusing expedition perhaps) <u>or</u> of the Trans Siberian Railway, <u>or</u> of practically any travelling experience I can think of where the prickle of danger mixes with human encounter. I know that when you're low, you think 'why bother with this writing shit?' But I honestly do think that you are developing a style of involved reporting that gives you & the reader the opportunity to stay young and engaged for a long time to come.

Anyway thanks for the lovely read, forgive my daft disconnection, and thanks also for the book itself, and its lovely inscription.

Love to you both,
David

~

Ronnie Cornwell's sisters Ella and Ruby had taken exception to le Carré's portrayal of his father, Ronnie, in fact and fiction, a decade after his death. Le Carré's article 'Spying on My Father' had just appeared in the Sunday Times.

TO ELLA HAYMES

9 Gainsborough Gardens
London, NW3 1BJ

3 May 1986

Dear Auntie Ella,

Thank you for your letter which was kindly and delicately written. I am of course sorry that you and Auntie Ruby have been upset by my articles and my novel, though I take it that you have not read the latter.

Let me say first that I consulted just about everybody <u>except</u> yourselves before publishing the article. My mother felt that it was a fairy-tale by comparison with the reality. Jeannie admired it greatly, and Joy,[1] on second thoughts, waived her initial objection to it. All Ronnie's children read both the article and the novel before publication and loved both. The same goes for my own children. My brother Tony, who has long wished to write a novel on the same theme, has written his own memoir of Ronnie and has been trying, so far without success, to publish it.

I am sorry in retrospect that I did not include yourself and Auntie Ruby and Auntie Doris among those whom I consulted in advance, but perhaps I knew subconsciously that you would not approve, although I believe that I have written about Ronnie with tolerance and love, both in the article and in the fictionalised portrait of him. I have been a bit harder on myself.

I don't expect a novel of any quality has ever been written which did not offend somebody. If Dickens had held back about the facts of his own childhood, we would have no Dickens. The same goes for writers on subjects as varied as love and war. The justification for what I have done, if one is needed, is surely in the comfort that I have given to people who

---

1. Ronnie's third wife.

are living, or have lived, in the shadow of their own Ronnie – for if my readers' reactions have taught me anything, it is that he was far more of a type than I had ever realised when he was alive.

A theme of the novel is that hypocrisy thrives upon the silence and the goodheartedness of respectable people, and that deceit, when it passes unchallenged, can be bestowed upon one generation by another. If you were to read the novel, I am sure you would recognise, at the most elementary moral level, the value of saying these things instead of sweeping them under the carpet. Like all of us who were obliged to live with Ronnie, to be charmed and ultimately deceived by him, you have surely suffered great pain. In writing as I have done, I believe that I have not only alleviated my own pain, which has been prolonged and crippling, but lightened the burden of others who, in cloistered situations, are enduring similar miseries without being able to share them.

You all gave Ronnie an almost endless amount of love, as your parents did, and as his children did – not to speak of his wives and girlfriends. We probably all love him still. I thought the article suggested that. Certainly there is nothing in your letter that says you disagree with the content of what I wrote, but rather with the fact that I wrote the book at all. But if a writer has any usefulness, it is to say out loud what others perhaps feel and cannot say; and so add – we hope – to the sum of human compassion and understanding. Now that the book is written, and the story is out, my job is done. A televised seven-hour BBC film version of the book is in preparation, for release in September 1987, but I shall have little to do with it and you may have noticed already that I do not give interviews to the British press or television. So the end that you ask for, though long in coming, is in sight. If I have really caused you pain, I am very sorry. But I would have thought it was a Christian wish that we should live with greater truth and frankness among ourselves, and acknowledge the limitless ways in which pain and love can instruct us.

I enclose a copy of Tony's piece, which I feel you ought to look at, if only for its affectionate tone.[2]

As ever,
David

~

In the wake of le Carré's novel A Perfect Spy, *Vivian Green wrote the article 'A Perfect Spy: A Personal Reminiscence' about the book and his recollections of Ronnie and David Cornwell. Interweaving the stories of Ronnie, his chicanery and braggadocio, and the fictional Rick as 'interchangeable personalities', it explored le Carré's ambivalent attitude to Sherborne School and his arrival at Oxford. Green wrote of the two men's walking tour of the Swiss Alps after Ronnie's bankruptcy, of George Smiley as a fictional father figure. It was published in 1988 in* The Quest for le Carré, *a collection of nine essays, edited by Alan Bold. Le Carré often insisted he did not read critical studies of his work.*

TO VIVIAN GREEN

9 Gainsborough Gardens
London, NW3 1BJ

5 November 1986

My dear Vivian,
I have just finished your piece. Nothing I have read about myself or my work has ever touched me so deeply. I was reminded of so much of my own life, and of how you yourself contributed

---

2. After le Carré wrote *A Perfect Spy*, Tony Cornwell wrote an unpublished account of Ronnie, 'My Brother's Father and Mine', describing 'a picaresque, charming, maddening man' who 'copulated for England'.

so much to it; I was reminded of your lovely, Smiley like intelligence and shrewdness – and of your scholarly powers. It's a splendid piece. I would not mind if you came a bit cleaner about the Ox<u>fd</u> communism stuff, but perhaps it would be unwise.[3] My penname is spelt, in fact, with a small 'l' though it is constantly misprinted. I have made some tiny textual changes of spelling. Sorry not to be more coherent – I'm just <u>very</u> moved by the piece.

Yes, yes, thanks for the cheque – I think I finally paid it in. Is there any chance I might slip down to Oxford for a night soon & have an ordinary college dinner with you? I've been wanting to for so long, but I'm terrified of [Burke] Trend & keep thinking he'll arrest me![4]

Thank you again for the brilliant, provocative & touching piece.

Love –

David

≈

Philip Roth had described A Perfect Spy *as 'the best English novel since the war'.*[5]

---

3. The article hinted at le Carré's work for the intelligence services at Oxford; it noted 'considerable difficulty' with Ronnie when he learnt that his son was associating with undergraduates with left-wing political views.

4. Cabinet secretary from 1963 to 1973, he was rector of Lincoln College from 1973 to 1983, a formidable public servant 'of sometimes austere countenance', in Vivian Green's words. He led a review of the allegations of further Soviet penetration of the British secret services.

5. Roth's words appeared in the *Observer*'s 'Books of the Year' on 30 November 1986. Le Carré was right in saying the quote would never go away; it appears routinely in any Google search for *A Perfect Spy*.

TO PHILIP ROTH[6]

> *9 Gainsborough Gardens*
> *London, NW3 1BJ*
>
> 8 December 1986

Dear Philip,

It took a while for the sheer scale of your generosity to sink in. The muffled 'phews' from my English publisher, the unmuffled 'phews' from Gottlieb, the eye-stopping calmness of the statement – too much, all at once. And of course in a way one cannot seriously thank people for their good opinion, however much one struggles to obtain it: they don't hold it for love of you, sometimes they hold it despite their distaste for you, sometimes they like you as a person & think you write crap. But there is a dimension between writers where we can genuinely say 'thanks' – & that, as I say, is generosity: finally it's you who have to have the guts to say what you think, & stand up with it & live with it. Because the quotes never go away. And it's you who will probably have to fight off the derision of your chums, the 'honestly Philip, old boy, you went over the top a bit there, didn't you?' And with a literary reputation as august as yours to protect, you did make a stunningly generous gesture, & I do feel deeply grateful to you, & can't let any more time go by without saying it: for all time, thanks from the heart for the best quote at the best time from the best source, ever. And that's the last thing I have to say. From almost anyone else, the same words would have been a normal peak in the valley-peak-valley landscape that we cross as we continue to read about ourselves. From you, dear Philip, as you must have long known, this is praise from a unique quarter, since I cannot

---

6. American novelist and short-story writer, author of *Portnoy's Complaint*, 'who explored lust, Jewish life, and America', in the words of the *New York Times*. Roth lived part time in London in the late 1970s with the actress Claire Bloom, co-star of *The Spy Who Came in from the Cold*; Al Alvarez was a close mutual friend.

conceal from you that I think you are one of the three or four best writers of English in the world, & arguably the very best: & <u>certainly</u> the best living humourist, & certainly the most elusive, truthful – oh shit, I rest on my oars.

About dinner & Wednesday: my problem is my mother, who hovers all the time at the end of life, is bed ridden & is to have a hip operation on Wednesday, after we have taken her out for a car-ride. J & I just felt we were going to be too fucked up when we got back, & that we w<u>d</u> take you up on your suggestion that we make it a calmer affair in the New Year instead of racing back to cook. Maybe by the time you get this, we'll have fixed a day.

I don't usually write such long letters or such bad ones. But it would be hard for me at any time to escape a tasteless expression of affection after your golden, courageous words.

Best
David

~

TO JANE CORNWELL

634 Charles River Street
Needham
Nr Boston

13 March 1987

My darling you,
It must be a hundred years since I wrote you a love letter. Usually they were dreary, evasive letters loosening vows at the same time they renewed them, qualified, haunted, the reverse of reassuring. But in the last year or so I have felt things for you that I don't think I have ever felt before: a reliance on your love and goodness and humbling unselfishness, an immense gratitude for your secret understanding of me, and for your

endless forgiveness of my inconstancies of mind & behaviour as I tried to get to the centre of myself, often at some cost to us both; and – you as Nicholas' mother – I have loved very particularly, because, as you know, sometimes your love for us both is like a single love, and it embraces the child in me just as it embraces him, and it is the source of our collective strength. And I love you too because you have managed, without intruding, to become the familiar to my writing self, the provoker and supplier of good things, the rounder & extender of ideas, now practical, now abstract, in short my indispensable literary partner & editor-of-first-instance, totally unsung to anyone outside our smallest circle; but essential to me in this as in so many ways. It was thus, dearest love, that you achieved my revival, & survival, & finally my present celebration, as a novelist; & I know that without you it would not have happened.

So this letter is to express, and thank you, for all that & more, and to renew my vows to you without qualification & to point to greater happiness in the future, & a growing love, filling & defining the spirit, a growing spirituality too, &, I believe, an intensifying harmony & mutual appreciation.

Is that a love letter? Does it say enough thank yous? Does it say enough that I am constantly lonely without you, even when I know I must go alone? That I want you? And wish to revive & intensify our love life too, to make more love & more journeys together? I hope it says all those things. And that I love you. And that, contrary to many bad signals in the past, I am pledged to you in love & constancy for always.

David

THE RUSSIA HOUSE

Each novel I have written has been a complete life. The novels that I wrote about Russia were lives that you enabled me to lead . . .

– to Vladimir Stabnikov, by email, 4 March 2016

John le Carré's fascination with Russia was such that in the 1970s, flying to the Far East, he flew via Copenhagen so as to touch down in Tashkent, where he could 'whiff the fumes of Russian petrol on the hot tarmac' and see the lamplit faces of the tribesmen.[1] At the same time he turned down any official invitation from the Union of Soviet Writers while it publicly approved the imprisonment of its members. The Moscow Centre spy chief Karla was George Smiley's ultimate protagonist, but le Carré made no visit there to his home.

A year after the publication of *A Perfect Spy*, however, le Carré's focus shifted squarely from his father to Mikhail Gorbachev's Russia. Russia, the Russians and the Russian region would provide le Carré's material for several major books: *The Russia House*, which 'introduced glasnost into espionage',[2] *Our Game*, *Single & Single*, *Our Kind of Traitor* and *A Most Wanted Man*.

For each book le Carré found his guides to show the way to others' lives. Vladimir Stabnikov was official host on le Carré's first visit to Moscow in 1987, as he researched *The Russia House*; Stabnikov translated *The Looking-Glass War* into Russian, and in 1994, as head of Russian PEN, he helped le Carré with research on *Our Game*.

John Roberts, for twenty years director of the Great Britain–USSR Association, acted as le Carré's guide and translator in 1987; while Federico Varese, a specialist on the Russian mafia, advised on both *Our Game* and *Our Kind of Traitor*.

In 1987 le Carré made two visits to Russia of about two weeks each, in May and September. Visiting Moscow Centre, the Soviet espionage headquarters, he found Russian students reading his pirated novels on word-processing machines.[3]

1. 'Le Carré and the Cheque that Came in from the Cold . .', *Sunday Times*, 10 November 1985.

2. 'Why I Came in from the Cold', *New York Times*, 29 September 1989.

3. 'Russians Warm to le Carré', Craig R. Whitney, *New York Times*, 22 May 1989.

'My secret life and my writing put together make a heady and irresistible mix for the Russian mentality, in Soviet times as now,' he wrote years later to Graham Greene's biographer Richard Greene, by email, on 28 July 2019. 'It's too easy for me to forget that in the Russian tradition, writers enjoy infinitely more esteem than we can imagine in our own western societies. Writers in the Russian tradition encourage revolutions, frustrate them, shape the minds of friends and enemies. They are to be praised to the skies, reviled, shot or exiled, or all four. To obtain us, to obtain our western favour, is for a Russian almost a national duty. And if we possess the additional mystique of the (despite all the cockups in the world) revered and feared British Secret Service, our allure is absolute.'

TO JOHN ROBERTS

9 Gainsborough Gardens
London, NW3 1BJ

12 May 1987

Dear John,

[. . .]

I do not want to meet Philby on this trip & an answer to any such suggestion should be a straight 'no thanks'. I feel sure that to do otherwise would be to embarrass you, the Association, the Ambassador and, as a matter of fact, myself. As I told you, I'd like to meet him for zoological reasons, but not at anyone's expense. And on this trip, absolutely no, not on any pretext, in any circumstances.[4]

My only other concern is that [British Ambassador] Bryan Cartledge knows for certain that we are coming – I'm sure you've told him – & that we dumped the Press Conference idea, which I am sure in the circumstance was the wise thing to do. But I have not told him that we have dumped it. Will you be in touch with him, or would you care for me to phone him?

And finally we talked about your own expenses in so kindly coming – for which I am extremely grateful – & you said that at some point you might allow me the opportunity to contribute, a thing I would most gladly do.

Best – David

~

4. Thirty years later le Carré told Philippe Sands at the Hay Festival that it was a lasting regret. 'I must have been a fool. I think it would have been quite extraordinary to have spent a few days with Philby, but it was more than I could swallow at the time and I refused.'

Stabnikov, a former official of the Union of Soviet Writers, became the first director of Russian PEN Centre in 1989. He escorted le Carré to Moscow and Leningrad in 1987 as his official host, and later to Kazakhstan and Kyrgyzstan. He co-translated The Looking-Glass War *into Russian, and later twice visited Cornwall. He called le Carré an 'adornment of humankind'.*

TO VLADIMIR STABNIKOV

> 9 Gainsborough Gardens
> London, NW3 1BJ

> 12 June 1987

Dear Vladimir,

What more can I say? It was wonderful, full of information, illumination, heart. The caviar tasted a little wistful in Switzerland, I had no sense of relief on departing, and an odd sense of sadness as I landed. Perhaps it wd have been different if I had flown straight home.

And you did all things so well – even the weekend of translating when you could have been looking after your family! I felt your support and your sovereignty equally, & was grateful for both, and still am. Please make every effort to come here soon. There is so much to make you laugh, though I cannot guarantee royalist taxi drivers.

Thank you again. I am sending you some books care of the Embassy.

My very best –
David

~

John Margetson was in his last diplomatic post as Britain's ambas-
sador to the Netherlands, where his predecessor had been assassinated
by the IRA. He was knighted in 1986.

TO SIR JOHN MARGETSON

9 Gainsborough Gardens
London, NW3 1BJ

24 September 1987

My dear John,
Back at last from the Algarve (Gerrards-Cross-sur-mer)
Moscow (2nd trip to top up the book) Leningrad (to see
Sakharov & Bonner who were weekending there)[5] Capri (to
collect an Italian lit prize & schmooze in the smog) and Zurich,
for reasons I barely remember – & now Jane reminds me of
your warm, kind invitation to us to visit you before your tour
ends, and you take up an honest profession at last. And we
would love to say 'yes' but, honestly John, I don't think we can
or should, because it is time for me to pull down the shutters
& write my long delayed oeuvre, and we have cancelled everything, even Christmas in Wengen, till I have a complete first
draft behind me.

Will you forgive us? I find that the Russian stuff simply evap-
orates once I am away from the place, unless I really hide myself
away & stare at blank walls: particularly the extraordinary, sad

---

5. At the time of his death in 2020 le Carré's photograph of himself meeting the
Soviet dissidents Yelena Bonner and Andrei Sakharov in 1987 remained on the wall
of his writing studio in Cornwall. In a 4 October 2017 letter to William Waldegrave,
provost of Eton College, le Carré relayed Bonner's story that when the couple came
out of six years in internal exile, Sakharov had memorised all of Shakespeare's
plays, 'but had no way of knowing how they were pronounced'. In an interview with
Philippe Sands at the Hay Festival in 2013, le Carré named Sakharov as his greatest
hero: the father of the Soviet hydrogen bomb, who 'realised he'd given the bomb to
a bunch of gangsters'.

compassion that I find sloshing around in me as I survey those misled, misgoverned, jolly people and their huge brick forests. My best moment was being offered a chance to meet Philby,[6] which I declined. Genrikh Borovik, an old hood who is writing P's 'biography' and has 17 hrs of tape recording with him, told me what a nice guy Kim was, and what a great patriot. I said I fully agreed. He was just like Penkovsky, I said: fun, and straight as a dye. Just a pity poor old Oleg[7] wasn't in London, I said, for me to introduce him to Genrikh. Genrikh nearly popped his garters & said the cases were <u>quite</u> different. I said they both wanted to screw their superiors & Genrikh said prissily that we c<u>d</u> continue the discussion at the Brit Ambassador's reception tomorrow night. I agreed, but warned him that we'd have to be very careful of the microphones. For a lovely moment, he gave a sage nod, & the complicity was absolute. Then to his credit he let out a wild whoop of laughter, remembering too late that they were his mikes . . .[8]

Love to you both/all, & do please forgive us,
David

∽

Letters came to le Carré from all manner of people fascinated by spying: from former spies to would-be spies, to those who felt they

---

6. In 2012, twenty-four years after Kim Philby's death, a *Russia Today* TV crew visited his widow, Rufina, at the Philbys' apartment. All le Carré's novels were on Philby's shelves, they reported to le Carré's agent Curtis Brown, and Rufina said, 'He used to read all these novels before he went to sleep.'

7. Oleg Penkovsky, a colonel in Soviet military intelligence who spied for the West, was executed in 1963.

8. When Borovik offered the chance to meet Philby, le Carré recalled in 2019 to Richard Greene, Graham Greene's biographer, 'I replied rather pompously that since I was about to dine with the Queen's ambassador, I did not feel able to square that with dining with the Queen's traitor. Borovik was angry, and that was that, except that when I departed from Leningrad airport, I was subjected to a full body search.'

were spied upon, and everything in between. Nicholas Greaves, aged ten, wrote asking how to be a spy.

TO NICHOLAS GREAVES (AGED TEN)

> *9 Gainsborough Gardens*
> *London, NW3 1BJ*

> 31 January 1988

Dear Nicholas,

Thank you very much for your letter. To be a spy, you need first to know what you think about the world, whom you would like to help, whom to frustrate. This, I am afraid, takes time. Also, you have to decide how much you are prepared to do by dishonest means. You are very young to decide to be dishonest. My guess is, you want excitement and a great cause. But I think and hope that if you ever find the great cause, the excitement will come naturally from the pleasure of serving it, & then you won't need to deceive anybody, you will have found what you are looking for. You will be more than a spy then. You will be a good, happy man.

All good wishes,
John le Carré

~

David Greenway had guided le Carré through South-East Asia, where he reported the Vietnam War over seven years for Time *magazine and the* Washington Post. *Le Carré now turned to Greenway and his wife, J. B., as he researched the US characters in* The Russia House.

to DAVID AND J. B. GREENWAY

9 Gainsborough Gardens
London, NW3 1BJ

11 August 1988

Dear David and JB,

Nico rang this morning and his voice was crammed with pleasure. It is a wonderful thing that his first solo flight should have been, by his own choice, to yourselves, and I am sure that he will have learnt all sorts of marvellous, unforgettable tastes & flavours & lifelong memories; he will certainly have derived enormous satisfaction from seeing you all in your two habitats, Needham & Maine. We look forward so much to collecting him tomorrow & hearing all his news, which will probably emerge partially & incidentally over several weeks. I hope he was a good guest; he meant to be, but we can always goof.

As to ourselves, myself, the book has taken a sudden leap forward & I find myself with a 350pp manuscript & the end in sight. North Haven has a key part, so has the Bishop.[9] My dilemma – or pleasant choice – is now whether to complete the whole book first, in one way or another, and <u>then</u> do the research, or whether to do the Boston North Haven stuff next, & afterwards complete the book. I think that on balance, because/although [*'because' is laid above 'although' in the manuscript*] the research is always <u>far</u> more fun than the writing, I sh<u>d</u> complete the m.s. & then bring it warts & all to America for the crucial revision. I need so <u>much</u> stuff from America

---

9. Davis Pike, a 'forceful and merry' friend of the Greenways. The island of North Haven, where the Greenways kept a summer home, lies off the coast of Maine. In *The Russia House*, Barley Blair's fictional debriefing by the 'Cousins' of the CIA takes place on a Maine island. Le Carré wanted to use North Haven as a location for the subsequent film, but Canada was substituted, because Sean Connery could not film in the US for tax reasons. The disappointed North Haveners forgave Connery, it is said, because in the closing scenes of *The Hunt for Red October* he sails his submarine into Maine's Penobscot River.

now, from how lie detectors work (or don't) to the true flavour of the Cousins, that I think I'm really best off establishing from beginning to end all my key scenes & characters, then working within that matrix. Like Truman Capote, I have decided I am not a writer at all, but a rewriter. But the alternative is chaotic.

So what I have planned to do is resolve all my story as best I can from my own ignorant state – I guess I have 2–3 months more original writing to do – and then propose myself to you, if I may, and you will then say whether or not it's convenient. It may even be that I will dump a 'finished' typescript on you in Wengen & propose myself in the New Year if that were acceptable. It matters very much to me that this time I should get my American stuff <u>very</u> right, & very amusing. Even, Lord help us, fair . . .

England is extraordinary now. I thought you'd be amused to hear that Gottlieb (Topsecret this) has offered me the Moscow bureau of the <u>New Yorker</u> and is waiting anxiously for my decision.[10] Whereas me, I can't wait never to have to write about the Russians again. It's a bit like being invited to stay behind in Hong Kong after writing 'Schoolboy'.

Had lunch at Willie's Dad's with Thatcher & Dennis, & the Powells (Principle Private Dessicated Ex F.O. Secretary & wild Italian wife)[11] and I suddenly realised: we're a one-party state, & it really isn't her fault that there isn't anyone else around who can hold a candle to her when it comes either to forensic argument or Tamany (?) Hall barnstorming. Her views quite interesting too: there are three men in the world who are at the turning point of their political destiny & must either deliver or leave the stage: Peres, Gorbachev and (oh glory) Bush, to whom she sends frequent stiffening letters. The Little Drummer Girl

---

10. Bob Gottlieb, le Carré's editor at Alfred A. Knopf, had been made editor of the *New Yorker*.

11. With William Shawcross's father, Hartley Shawcross, who was lead British prosecutor at the Nuremberg Trials of the International Military Tribunal. Margaret Thatcher's private secretary Charles Powell was married to the Italian-born socialite Carla Bonardi.

a GOOD book (hammer-blows on all adjectives) because it showed terrorists as they were <u>and</u> proved that the M.E. was near-insoluble. She was interested that I'd met Dukakis – 'I hear he's very drab'. She said how grim it was to have to see the families of the hostages every six months, but both she & the families knew it must be done. 'And I say to them every time: probably we could make <u>enough</u> concessions to buy them out. But we mustn't do that, because it simply means a <u>new</u> lot of people, & more of them will be <u>taken</u>. Reagan had a moment of weakness & look where it got <u>him</u>.' And on Reagan himself: 'People misunderstand him. He has about three great convictions, things that he feels extremely deeply about. If you attach everything to them, he'll talk straight to you, & understand you, & stick by you. He's a much greater man than is generally understood.' Well golly, what are they? we wanted to ask, but Willy's father had forgotten to supply a knife for the salmon en croûte, so she'd decided to tear it apart with two forks. For a moment, it looked as though she'd killed it too.

Dennis is far tougher than you'd suppose. Drinks more than the rumours say, brays golf-club aphorisms at you, has a set of values that would wow them at the Rotarians' (Bears?) Annual Dinner, [. . .] and at 72 keeps referring to Mrs T as the future widow Thatcher. Reads. Likes Archer, likes me: 'Why don't you bring Smiley back?' Says Archer has become 'a big friend actually'. Really, between them, they need their Kapuczinski.[12]

Thanks again for giving Nico what I'm sure will have been a glorious time. I'm writing this now because I suspect the Portuguese post in high season – & anyway, it's fun waiting for him to come back. On Monday, can you believe it, the Inland Revenue withdrew the vast majority of its claims against me & in a weirdly human letter admitted that their interpretation of

---

12. Polish journalist Ryszard Kapuściński wrote *The Emperor*, about the downfall of Haile Selassie, and *Shah of Shahs*, about the final years of the last Shah of Iran.

my affairs had been misplaced. That doesn't mean it's over, but maybe it's going a bit our way.[13]

Love to you all,
David

~

While le Carré had addressed his father's ghost in *A Perfect Spy*, his mother, Olive, was still alive, though ailing, in 1988.

Olive Moore Cornwell, later Hill, left le Carré and his brother, Tony, when le Carré was aged five, and he did not see her again until he was twenty-one.[14] 'My mother had left us when my father finished his second spell in prison and had got through his second or third bankruptcy,' was how le Carré described it to the psychiatrist Dr Bockner.[15]

In those first meetings his mother described how Ronnie had given her venereal disease and how he beat her up – the latter no surprise to le Carré, who had seen the same behaviour meted out to his stepmother. After seeing her three times, he told Bockner in 1968: 'I declined to see her any more . . . I have not seen her since those rather gruesome meetings; and really find her awfully hard to tolerate at all.'

---

13. The Inland Revenue launched an inquiry into le Carré's tax affairs in 1987, particularly into Authors Workshop, the Swiss-based company that owned his copyrights and paid him a salary. The Revenue threatened to assess le Carré for twenty years of taxes; the Swiss authorities offered le Carré Swiss nationality, a bargaining chip in negotiations, but he would have to stay outside the UK for five years. Authors Workshop was wound up, and he became a self-employed UK taxpayer. The case was settled in 1989.

14. Ann's recollection suggested he was twenty-two. See note on p. 44.

15. On 24 June 1968 le Carré was prevented by a rail strike from travelling to meet Dr Bockner, a London psychiatrist. He wrote a seventy-page account of 'some of the things I would have told you', ranging across his marriage, his father, his writing and his relationship with the Kennaways.

Writing in *The Pigeon Tunnel* in 2016, le Carré recalled: 'I ran her to earth when I was twenty-one, and thereafter broadly attended to her needs, not always with good grace.

'In the nursing home where she stayed during her last years, we spent much of our time deploring or laughing at my father's misdeeds. As my visits continued, I came to realize that she had created for herself – and for me – an idyllic mother–son relationship that had flowed uninterrupted from my birth till now.'

The only letters that appear to survive from le Carré to his mother were written in 1988 and 1989, and faxed to her, sometimes via her daughter, his half-sister Alex. They seem emotionally anodyne; le Carré stays on safe ground, writing comfortingly as Olive goes through an operation on her back and then returns to her care home, with enthusiastic family news and bucolic descriptions of Cornwall and Switzerland, as he moves between there and London. There is no probing of their relationship, or what might have been. They have the character of letters sent home from school.

TO OLIVE HILL

By fax

London

11 July 1988

Dearest Mother,

Good evening! We had a safe journey back, slightly piano, and forgot to turn on the air conditioning. But with the car telephone, we could make sure that the tea was waiting! Here's another example of the modern age.

There will never be another generation like yours. When you were born, not a plane in the sky, and the sky all the better for it. Radio a miracle and no anaesthetics. Now we've got the National Health Service, bloody telly, and you coming back from the doghouse with a hole in your back. Where's progress? we ask ourselves. As they say in Russia, 'is all illusion'.

It was lovely to see you today, you were marvellous. I'll always think of you popping back the smokers and watching the swifts. Sometimes Paradise is so close to home. And thank Heaven they love you there. They really do.

Take care, and let's have another lovely meeting soon.

Much love,
David

∽

TO OLIVE HILL
Fax for Alexandra Williams please to pass to her mum

By fax

Cornwall

4 August 1988
1 o'clock

Dearest Muvver,

I've been scribbling since early morning and have only this minute lifted my head from the paper to wish you a much happier time in the nick than you had before, a very <u>brief</u> wait for the much needed equipment, and endurance and good heart when the pain won't go to sleep.

My book is going a treat now, the weather has been dreamy, the air off the Atlantic is making us both feel 10 years younger and the bloody builders are turning the playroom into a couple of bedrooms because we have now moved the playroom out of doors. The dogs very smelly from eating too much rabbit. Just spoke to Nico who is sailing in Maine & loving it. This by fax from both of us with all our love & good wishes. Alex says flowers wouldn't be a lot of use at the moment but we'll telepathise them anyway!

XX
David

~

In August, le Carré wrote of being in the 'last stages of my new novel now – about 100 to go'. The book was The Russia House.

TO OLIVE HILL

By fax

Chalet Chamois
3823 Wengen
Switzerland

8 September 1988

DEAR LOVELY ALL,
FIRST OF SIX PAGES FOR OLIVE HILL, PLEASE
Best, David C

My dearest Mother,
Jane just phoned <u>me</u> that Alex had faxed <u>her</u> that you were back
in Howard House, to our great relief, and that you were half if
not completely mended, and that if I sent you a fax we could beat
the postman's strike, always a pleasure. I arrived here yesterday
from Portugal, where Jane & Nico & I had an amazing holiday
because:

1) It shone all the time, we swam & fooled around & had a
   pleasantly empty time.
2) To everyone's astonishment except Nick's, he scored 7 <u>A</u>s
   and 1 <u>C</u> in his GCSE papers and looks like getting an 8th
   A for his design work.
3) I finished my book, put the final full stop. And although
   I have a mass of stuff to do within it, that's an enormous
   relief to me and Jane & all the publishers. I also think it's
   rather good, or could be. So sod them. Baby will eat.[16]

[. . .]

We really had a happy holiday. So many men fantasize
about marrying their secretaries, and I, in the very best sense,
did, because Jane is secretary, editor, and above all friend to me,
and it's fun when we can share the work & it pays off. Plus, as
they say these days, love.

[. . .]

Other news – picture me. In the Alps, this is a lovely Indian
summer, no people, flowers you want to eat, and a low sun on
the hayfields that smells of cricket fields the moment you enter
the shade. Damp, Christmassy evenings already, wood fires
necessary after sunset. My work room overlooks the whole

16. 'Baby will eat tonight' was a repeated catchphrase of le Carré's after he landed a
lucrative publishing deal.

village, and the Lauterbrunnen valley, and this is the odd evening hour when a grimy mist rolls off the mountains & turns the
sunbeams into gunsmoke. In an hour it will be clear again, and
dusk. Huge searchlight sunrays over the peaks, shooting down
into the valley. And the bloody birds talking their heads off, no
respect. You can't trust anyone these days.

Dearest Mother, I hope you feel wonderful that you have
returned to the slammer, where you are known & loved. We
will come & see you very soon after my return.

Love again,
David

~

TO BRUCE HUNTER

*Bruce Hunter became le Carré's agent in 1985, working with him for
more than twenty years.*

By fax

London

27 January 1989

Dear Bruce,
Thank you for the OUP 'Oxford Bookworms' proposal.[17] I
think we sh<u>d</u> ask OUP to abandon their search. It is not that
I object to the truncation of the book so much as the selection, & the expression, of the information that the adaptor
has retained. (Even though he is an old Shirburnian, a school
which I attended, & hold in particular loathing.)

---

17. Three months earlier le Carré had told Hunter OUP's 'awful' simplified version
of *The Spy Who Came in from the Cold* made it read like Enid Blyton.

I feel that the story has been 'infantilised' in a way that is not necessary or attractive to young people. They like the head left on, & the teeth left in. He's taken them off, & the balls too.

So, if you agree, let's say 'no thanks'.

Best,
David

~

In December, le Carré reports to Olive 'much enthusiasm for my new book, The Russia House*', promising a proof early in the New Year.*

TO OLIVE HILL

By fax

Cornwall

24 March 1989

My dearest Mother,

I arrived here two days ago after an endless drive in the Mercedes jeep with the whippets, starting at 4.15am, and then breakfast with an antique-dealer friend in Wells,[18] then on, and on, and on, in very windy weather, which the jeep, being tall, took very seriously.

Then I spent the time before Jane arrived finishing Stephen's film script,[19] which annoyed the dogs hugely, since it is their conviction that writing interferes with rabbiting, which is what all sane people come to Cornwall for. And that rabbits don't get caught just by <u>sitting</u> there.

---

18. Eddie Nowell.

19. *Schüss*, a film script about post-war skiing, which le Carré wrote for Stephen Cornwell.

Last night I had some old and dear friends to dinner[20] and cooked them a chicken with bacon & sausages, and we admired the new gateposts that I bought when I was last here, great 11 ft granite things from a chapel in Hayle, and now looking very manorial, but not too much so, I hope.

And today Jane & Nico arrived, having also left at crack of dawn and wrestled with the Bank Holiday traffic, and Jane has wisely crashed to bed, & Nico is setting up his computer, and the dogs are muttering to each other about supper, which isn't due yet, and the fog horn is going, which is always a bore but on still days worse than on stormy ones, & this day began stormy and has decided to be still after all.

I gather from Jill that the daffodils & narcissi & Scilly Whites arrived, and so I expect your room smells like a tart's parlour, but they're straight off the cliff, with our love for Easter. We'll be here for three weeks, then back in London, at which point we'll come & see you. Meanwhile, I'll keep in fax-touch.

Much love,
David

Olive Hill died on 17 April 1989. Le Carré was with her in the hours before, missing the moment of her death by a few minutes. The faxes to her include a last, long letter from le Carré's brother, Tony, full of family news, then describing the patriarch of an American Republican family, aged ninety-nine, who had a live-in lover forty years younger. He 'evokes to me, perhaps unjustly, what Ronnie might have been', Tony wrote.

∼

---

20. Almost certainly John Miller and Michael Truscott.

TO VLADIMIR STABNIKOV

9 Gainsborough Gardens
London, NW3 1BJ

9 March 1989

Dear Volodia,

As you know, I can't type . . . I tried once or twice to ring you, then decided that writing was better anyway, because it gives you a fairer chance to think straight before you reply.

And you must reply exactly as you wish, because it will not send me into a towering rage if you simply say you would rather not accede to my request.

Which is this. My publishers both here & in the United States – and I am sure elsewhere when I consult them – are laudably enthusiastic about 'The Russia House' and would like to promote it as a cross-border book, the first of its kind to appear in the West since the <u>perestroika</u> began – as a book of uncharacteristic optimism, an anti-spy novel, and above all as a novel that could be – and we hope will be – as useful in the Soviet Union as in the West, in the way of opening up the prejudices of readers, and confusing the traditional margins of thought that have been, on both sides, our curse.

What they would therefore like, ideally, is quotes and opinions from people in the Soviet Union that they could use in presenting the book to the Western public. For example, from a prominent Soviet magazine editor (Novy Mir?). For example, from a Professor of English literature at a Soviet university (Moscow State?). For example, from a Soviet publisher, or even from the desk of the distinguished Volodia Stabnikov . . . But only if such people are willing to be quoted publicly, of course. If not, our purpose is defeated, but we would far rather fail in our purpose than occasion the embarrassment of Soviet friends.

And a secondary, obvious condition would be, that the reader's English was good enough for him to read the proof.

(We shall have printed presentation proofs in 3 weeks). If there were any hope of getting what we want, I could send you a dozen or so copies of the proof by way of the Barry Martin courier by about April 5th – maybe earlier. Really, we would like about six quotes, but three would do.

Would you think about this for a little while, & then I will ring you? I expect, in about a week from now, once I am certain you have had this letter. And if it's a hopeless quest, you have only to tell me. If it's not, we would have to have the quotes by May 5th in order to make timely use of them.

I suspect that US & UK press & TV would also like to cover the story at the Soviet end, if we gave them a chance. But let me have your reactions first.

Love to you all –
as ever,
David

P.S. We had Misha Grebnev[21] to lunch & will be taking him to the theatre. D

Stabnikov compiled a group of Soviet comments. 'John le Carré, always a virtuoso and a subtle ironist, is at his best,' wrote the leading Soviet poet Andrei Voznesensky. 'The Russia House is the world's first spy novel whose plot unfolds in Peredelkino [a village of colourful dachas] near Moscow, against the background of the cottage and grave of Boris Pasternak. I live in Peredelkino myself, and now the sound of the local church bells and the squeal of car brakes makes me look around with uneasiness, lest it be someone out of The Russia House. *It seems that every kamaz [heavy] lorry passing is driven by a comely CIA agent.'*

∾

---

21. Mikhail (Misha) Grebnev, university classmate of Vladimir Stabnikov and co-translator of *The Looking-Glass War*.

Le Carré's letter to William J. Weatherby, a Guardian *columnist and feature writer, was published in the* Guardian *in January 1990.*

In November 2012 The Times *reported that after 'one of the most public feuds in modern literature', le Carré and Sir Salman Rushdie had buried the hatchet. After Rushdie told an audience at* The Times *Cheltenham Literature Festival that 'I wished we hadn't done it', le Carré responded that 'I too regret the dispute.'*

On 14 February 1989 Iran's Ayatollah Khomeini had issued a fatwa against Rushdie ordering Muslims to execute the author and anyone else involved in the publication of his novel The Satanic Verses. *While Rushdie went into hiding, twelve people died in a riot in India, London bookshops were firebombed and the book's Norwegian publisher was shot three times outside his home. In 1991 the Japanese translator Hitoshi Igarashi was stabbed to death, and the Italian translator also stabbed.*

Le Carré questioned publicly why Rushdie had not withdrawn The Satanic Verses. *A coruscating review by Rushdie of* The Russia House *gave a personal animus to the dispute, which flared up a second time in a biting exchange of letters in 1997.*

TO W. J. WEATHERBY, *MANCHESTER GUARDIAN*

c/o David Higham Associates
5–8 Lower John Street
Golden Square
London, W1R 4HA

11 October 1989

Dear Mr Weatherby,

Rushdie is a victim, but in my book no hero. I am sorry for him and I respect his courage, but I don't understand him. In the first place, anybody who is familiar with Muslims, even if he has not had the advantage of Rushdie's background, knows that, even among the most relaxed, you make light of the Book at your peril. I don't think there is anything to deplore in religious fervour. American presidents profess to it almost as a ritual, we respect it in Christians and Jews. What we are speaking of in Rushdie's case is incompatible concepts of freedom. For long periods of Christian history, freedom was limited by what was sacred. That is still the case in Islam today. Therefore while I despise the self-serving antics of the Ayatollah and his mullahs, I am not surprised by them nor particularly shocked. I am also unclear about the extent to which Rushdie, perhaps inadvertently, provoked his own misfortune. His open letter to the Indian government seemed to me to be of an almost colonialist arrogance.

Absolute free speech is not a God-given right in any country. It is curtailed by prejudice, by perceptions of morality and by perceptions of decency. Nobody has a God-given right to insult a great religion and be published with impunity.

But all of this is academic, perhaps, beside the human mystery that Rushdie continues to present to me. How can a man whose novel, for whatever twisted reasons, has already been the cause of so much bloodshed, insist on risking more? Anybody who wanted to read this book has had ample opportunity to do so in the countries where it has been published. A great many more people who will never manage to read it have already bought it out of some sense that they are furthering a great cause. Yet we are being invited to believe that paperback publication of SATANIC VERSES is somehow more important to us than, for instance, the lives of innocent young men and women who work at the outer fringes of publishing – in the mail-rooms and stock-rooms of Rushdie's publishers – in bookshops and in public postal services. At this point, my judgment becomes totally subjective. I could not live with the thought that, by continuing to insist that my book be published, I would be inviting further bloodshed. And that is where Rushdie leaves me completely. Again and again, it has been within his power to save the faces of his publishers and, with dignity, withdraw his book until a calmer time has come. It seems to me that he has nothing more to prove except his own insensitivity.

A peculiar justification used by Rushdie's most vociferous defenders is that his novel has great literary merit – some insist it is a masterpiece. I see this as a most dangerous argument, and a self-defeating one. Would the same people have leapt to the defence of a Ludlum or an Archer? Or are we to believe that those who write literature have a greater right to free speech than those who write pulp? Such elitism does not help Rushdie's cause, whatever that cause has now become.

Yours sincerely,
John le Carré

~

TO SIR ALEC AND LADY GUINNESS

Chalet Chamois
3823 Wengen
Switzerland

7 December 1989

Dear Alec & Merula,

Lord knows how long the post will take, but here in good time, I hope, my love to you both for Christmas & the New Year. Jane & Nico come out for Christmas, so will the usual indispensable crowd of celebrants, and this year will be so different from the last God knows how many as to be quite, quite extraordinary. One has to be in Europe now. Eastern Europe obviously, but Western Europe more subtly – I mean continental Europe. The West Germans, having begged so long for the Great Light, are already blinded by it: 'they will pollute our roads, air, prosperity, they haven't earned their place, they have –' this the most noisy complaint – 'they have absolutely NO IDEA OF WORK.' In other words, the good ex-Sozis[22] come to W. Germany and

---

22. In common usage, a 'Sozi' refers to a member of Germany's Social Democratic Party, or SPD. However, given the year and the context, le Carré appears to mean ex-socialists, or former citizens of the German Democratic Republic.

knock off at 5 & go home! They have too little respect for <u>money</u> <u>& order</u> – because of course the poor buggers did their day's work, then hurried home to shop, fiddle, cajole, brew their hooch and fix their lives. Now in W. Germany their lives are pre-fixed, but their work is DISTINCTLY SHABBY. They are learning the other kind of slavery.

And the Frogs, of course, are <u>extremely</u> jumpy. And all along the old lines of hostility, that which was held down by Big Brother is now popping out of the ice: like the Poles saying fuck the Germans, & the Germans saying all Poles are Germans anyway; & the Serbs looking around for the Croats & the Slovenes; and the Czechs wanting to put one over the Magyars; and the old fissures opening up, everywhere.

For my new book, I don't know where to put the knife in, but what I <u>can</u> be sure of is, it will hit a bone. If that's the expression.*

Meanwhile, if life & politics ever give a chance to celebrate, which they don't, we really should. Because, for all our faults, WE were right, & for all their proclaimed ideals, THEY were a bunch of corrupt, foul-minded piglets. Which is a calumny against piglets. So please read, swine.

Very happy Christmas, and New Year, & much love to you both, all.

Ever,
David

[*in margin*] *And the Hungarians offering seriously thousands of US dollars of advance for my books, & the Czechs saying, please may we do them for nothing? And the Poles saying, please will you pay for publication?

~

1. (*Back row*) Olive and Ronnie Cornwell, with Ronnie's parents, Elizabeth (Bessie) and Frank. (*Front row*) David and elder brother, Tony, with Frank's parents. Eighty years later le Carré claimed his Irish citizenship through Bessie. *Circa* 1935/6.

2. Ronnie, Olive, David and Tony Cornwell. A short-lived vision of a happy family: Olive left the family when David was five, and they did not meet again until he was twenty-one. *Circa* 1935.

3. Ronnie basks in close proximity to Princess Elizabeth's husband, as the Albany Sports Society Committee presents a cheque for £10,000 to the Duke of Edinburgh for the National Playing Fields Association. 1950.

4. David and Tony Cornwell.

5. Jeannie Cornwell. Jeannie, then aged twenty-seven, married Ronnie in 1944; she read coded messages to the Resistance as a wartime announcer for the BBC, and *The Wind in the Willows* to David.

6. David in the Sherborne School Junior Hockey Team, 1947. David is in the back row, second from right. He also captained the Westcott House Junior Cricket Team and won the school poetry prize, but made his escape at age sixteen.

7. Reginald Stanley Thompson by Elliott & Fry. 'Thomper', as he was known, for sixteen years housemaster of Westcott House at Sherborne, was a man of strong convictions and profound Christian faith. 1952.

8. Top hat and furs: Ronnie, Jeannie, David and Tony Cornwell.

9. David as downhill ski racer – 'I took part in the Lauberhorn Race when I was an English bloody fool and nearly killed myself.'

10. David, in ceremonial uniform, and Ann at a dance. They met when he was eighteen and she seventeen.

11. David and his half-sister Charlotte, Jeannie Cornwell's daughter, seventeen years his junior.

12. Vivian Green, chaplain and tutor at Sherborne School and Lincoln College, Oxford – the model for Smiley's humanity, his perception of human frailty and his difficulty in buying clothes.

13. David's drawing of Ann. She cherished his early ambition to be a commercial artist.

14. John and Miranda Margetson at their wedding on 11 May 1963. Miranda's sister Juliet and le Carré, who was best man, stand behind.

15. Sir Victor Gollancz. In 1960 he paid an advance of £100 for *Call for the Dead*, by 'a gifted new crime novelist', John le Carré. He later agreed to 'stretch a point' and pay £175 for *The Spy Who Came in from the Cold*.

Best Seller List

August 2	August 9	August 16	This Week	An analysis, based on reports from more than 125 bookstores in 64 communities throughout the United States, showing the sales rating of the leading fiction and general titles. Sales through outlets other than bookstores are not included, and figures which are shown in the right-hand column do not necessarily represent consecutive weeks appearance on the list.	Weeks on List
				Fiction	
1	1	1	1	The Spy Who Came in From the Cold. *Le Carré*	32
2	2	2	2	Armageddon. *Uris*	10
6	5	5	3	The Rector of Justin. *Auchincloss*	4
5	3	3	4	Julian. *Vidal*	10
3	4	4	5	Candy. *Southern and Hoffenberg*	13
4	6	6	6	Convention. *Knebel and Bailey*	22
9	7	7	7	The 480. *Burdick*	7
10	9	10	8	The Group. *McCarthy*	51
			9	This Rough Magic. *Stewart*	1
7	8	9	10	The Night in Lisbon. *Remarque*	19

16. *The Spy Who Came in from the Cold* atop the *New York Times* bestseller list for its thirty-second week.

17. Graham Greene. He endorsed *The Spy Who Came in from the Cold* as 'the best spy story I have ever read'.

18. The Cornwell family left Germany for Greece in 1964 after le Carré resigned from the Foreign Office, travelling to Crete and Spetses.

19. Pipe and pen in hand, le Carré draws with young Simon and Stephen.

20. Richard Burton and le Carré in 1965 making the film of *The Spy Who Came in from the Cold*.

21. Susan Kennaway, later Susan Vereker. She was married to the writer James Kennaway, until his early death in a car accident. Le Carré admitted their affair to Ann in 1965.

22. Director Sydney Pollack, around the time of *They Shoot Horses, Don't They?*, released in 1969. His proposed film projects with le Carré ran from *A Small Town in Germany* to *The Night Manager*.

24. A legendary figure in American publishing, Robert Gottlieb was editor-in-chief of Simon & Schuster and Alfred A. Knopf, and editor of the *New Yorker*. For le Carré 'the greatest of them all'.

23. Valerie Jane Eustace became Jane Cornwell on her marriage to le Carré in 1972. 'I find her compassionate, understanding, and remarkably intelligent,' he wrote, after they met at a literary event in Birmingham.

25. Le Carré and Jane working on *Tinker Tailor Soldier Spy* in his Tregiffian office in 1974.

The Russia House *in June 1989 was dedicated 'For Bob Gottlieb, a great editor and long-suffering friend'. Gottlieb, a pre-eminent figure in American publishing, and le Carré's editor at Alfred A. Knopf, sensed 'a gesture meant to smooth the way for him to move on'.*[23] *Gottlieb first edited* The Naive and Sentimental Lover, *then did substantial work on* Tinker Tailor Soldier Spy, *where he prompted le Carré to expand the character of Connie Sachs, and suggested the title for* A Perfect Spy. *In 1987 he was appointed editor of the* New Yorker, *but continued to work on Knopf titles.*

TO BOB GOTTLIEB

9 Gainsborough Gardens
London, NW3 1BJ

25 September 1989

Dear Bob,

A lovely evening – happy times! It was very moving to see you all in such glowing form & I have lost my heart to Nicholas[24] – but then who hasn't? Thank you both so much for making us at home.

Bob, I think the time has come for us to recognise that the forces of life have brought us to the end of our editorial relationship – at least in the formal sense. I wanted to talk to you about this, but it certainly wasn't the evening to do so. But I find there is something unnatural & a little tense about being edited outside the house, even by you, even after all these glorious years. Somewhere between Sonny [Mehta][25] & Bill Loverd,[26]

---

23. Gottlieb, *Avid Reader* (2016), 'Working: Knopf Redux', p. 238.

24. Gottlieb's son Nicholas.

25. President and editor-in-chief at Knopf; hand-picked by Robert Gottlieb as his successor.

26. Director of publicity at Knopf for nearly forty years.

I have to have a kindred soul inside the house who is not in conference, not under siege, or trying to get me on television, & I'm prepared to give Elizabeth Sifton[27] a try, because I find her very bright.

I had thought at first I would postpone this decision till I had a new novel, but somehow with your departure, & Lynn's,[28] the reconstruction requires that figure now. And I really can't address myself to you on house matters, and only occasionally to Sonny, and – outside promotional stuff – not to Bill.

Perhaps I couldn't have taken this decision if our collaboration had not given me the confidence for it – the master-classes will never be the same, I know, and the fun will be missing, or different. But for me to be at ease with my publishers, I know that the time has come where I must pitch my tent within their walls, for better or worse. If really worse – well, then I'll have to move. But I want to give it a whirl.

Do write & tell me you understand – or that you don't – and thank you again, I wish I could say it better, for all the magic of the last 15 years.

As ever,
David

Gottlieb wrote in his memoir Avid Reader *that le Carré was right, in this 'charming letter of regret', to seek a direct connection to the heart of his American publishing house.*

∾

The Secret Pilgrim was dedicated: 'For Alec Guinness, with affection and thanks'. Gottlieb, no longer editing, declared it 'the weakest of all

27. Book editor and then executive vice-president of Knopf.

28. In 1989 Lynn Nesbitt, le Carré's agent, left International Creative Management to start her own agency, Janklow & Nesbitt Associates, with Morton Janklow.

his novels and could think of nothing I might have suggested to salvage it.[29]

TO SIR ALEC GUINNESS

9 Gainsborough Gardens
London, NW3 1BJ

7 June 1990

My dear Alec,

A long overdue letter, but my tardiness has its reasons. I set to work on Smiley's speech to the passing-out class at Sarratt, and it ran away with me and became a novel. Smiley presides over it, as you will see, and I am sending you a copy today. I am actually rather pleased with it – it has an odd, loose form, and seems quite relevant to what's happening now.

I have also – pending your approval, of course – taken the liberty of dedicating it to you, because of Smiley, because of the mood of it, because of anything. But if you find this uncomfortable for some reason, I am sure you know me well enough to tell me, and I will at once take the appropriate action!

There are obvious possibilities for the material in film/TV terms: another series, a collection of TV plays, or even theatre. At this stage, I simply haven't put my mind to them, and much would depend on how <u>you</u> felt. We have plenty of time. Personally, I think we might best fish out one or two episodes and make quite separate pieces of them. But all that – if at all – for later.

Nico is in the middle of A-levels, the film of 'The Russia House' is largely pretty good, with the usual maddening idiocies in it, but [Michelle] Pfeiffer is extraordinary in her Slav persona, & Connery has a feral strength that is disconcerting

---

29. Gottlieb, *Avid Reader*, p. 238.

& for once very well applied. It just might be <u>very</u> good. My eye is too beady.

Please give our love to Merula, and let us give you a meal soon; we would love to see you both.

As ever,
David

~

Nicholas Shakespeare was literary editor of the Telegraph *until 1991, when he left to concentrate on his second novel, with le Carré's encouragement.*

TO NICHOLAS SHAKESPEARE

9 Gainsborough Gardens
London, NW3 1BJ

19 April 1991

Dear Nicholas,

I got back from Cornwall to your letter last night, & thank you for it very sincerely. First to Graham: yes, it's a big gap, the General is dead, and he won.[30] He won his war, if not all his battles; he left imperishable work and the self-perpetuating memory of a very large man with all sorts of fascinating smallnesses – a lot of them sprang from boredom, from too much ease with his talent, but a lot of them were diligently tended by himself in order to keep the child in him alive. I think that was why he was such a writer's writer: he was all of

---

30. Graham Greene died on 3 April 1991. Kingsley Amis, whose review of *The Comedians* saw le Carré commiserate with Greene in 1966, said: 'He will be missed all over the world. He was our greatest living novelist.'

us, but more so. To write to you this way is already to pray to him: he woke the agnostic in all of us! – and put it to work.

But you're alive, & therefore more important, & you have his imprint, & your talent, which is now to have its head. And it was time. If you fail, which you won't, it was still time. And if you doubt, & get the blacks, & wonder why on earth we bother with fiction when the facts of our time are so monstrous, you will only be following Graham's path; & it will still have been the right step at the right time. So in a humble way, I am pleased if I gave you a little extra shove, and I wish you from the heart the fulfilment of your art, and all the pleasure & magic of the journey. I hope you will not be pulled too often by the quick fixes of journalism, but you'll work out a balance between the sprint & the marathon. I hope you get the right woman to write with, and to. And I hope you keep your generosity of spirit when they (the hacks & worst of all the fellow novelists) go for you, because your writing has great humanity, & so have you. My hardest duty to myself was to keep the bitterness at bay – if I let off steam, it's supposed to be a cleansing, not a vengeance. I love it all far too much to let them fuck it up for me. I won't write to you like this again, I promise, but your appearance in my life touched me, & so did your letter.

And there is Cornwall. To borrow when I'm not there, and to share occasionally if I am, borrow a car & meet in the evenings & write in the day. I want to settle down there for good soon, & add a chunk to the house first, so that it's two houses, one for us, one for the occasional guest & his or her guest, where guests can also be sovereign, & cook their own meals when they want, & join in when it suits us all. I'm very much hoping you'll use it as a place of escape when you feel like it – we're there very little at present. Anyway, see.

We are off next week to Italy, then the States, back early June. I'm marrying off a son in Boston, then researching in Washington, Northern Quebec & maybe the Gulf of Mexico.

Here's a deal for you: let's never have a professional relationship again. You'll never interview me or write about me while I'm alive; I'll keep some kind of safe house for you if you ever need one, though I doubt you will! That way, I would feel I might be of some distant use to you, and you wouldn't feel you owed. I'd be more comfortable like that. I still haven't called your parents, but I will when we return. If you're talking to them, will you please say I did a duck dive into my book? And that we look forward greatly to playing together in the summer? Forgive this long scrawl.

Best,
David

The two men formed a close friendship. Le Carré knew Shakespeare's father, John, modern linguist and diplomat, at Oxford; he was one of the few friends le Carré invited to his first wedding, and he later suggested that le Carré should take over his teaching job at Eton. Nicholas Shakespeare made repeated visits to le Carré's Cornish home; he went on to write The Dancer Upstairs *(a title suggested by le Carré) and other novels, as well as his biography of Bruce Chatwin.*

'As a young writer, I looked up at Greene as a role model, and nothing in my writing life has made me happier than the supremely generous support he gave to my early work,' le Carré wrote in an article on the day of Greene's death. 'As a diplomat in Bonn, I blushed for him when he stood on the Eastern side of the Berlin Wall and made some unhappy comment about preferring it there. I thought his anti-Americanism too much. I thought him daft about the possible marriage of Communism and Christianity, and dafter still in his defence of Kim Philby.' Even when they quarrelled over Philby in print, he said, Greene typically 'sent me kindly messages through intermediaries'. While the 'British literary bureaucracy' tried to shake him off his pedestal, Greene had 'wit and grace and character and story, and a transcendent, universal compassion that places him for all time in the ranks of world literature'.

In print and broadcast interviews, from the New Yorker *to the* BBC, *le Carré later routinely quoted Greene's 'dictum' that childhood is the bank balance of the writer. As he told Philippe Sands at the Hay Festival in 2013, 'I always quote Graham Greene, that the credit balance of the writer is his childhood, and by those standards I was a millionaire.' However, neither Greene's biographer, Richard Greene, nor his bibliographers can identify the source of the phrase, or trace a record of it in Greene's interviews, outside of le Carré's own use of it. The aphorism now appears commonly on the internet, attributed to Greene.*[31]

A month before his death in 2020, le Carré was reading Richard Greene's biography. 'I knew him only slightly, but he still spooks me,' he told the writer Ben Macintyre.

∽

After his sixtieth birthday, le Carré recalled his days with John Margetson as a fellow trainee at MI6 with four other new recruits, thirty years before.

TO SIR JOHN AND LADY MARGETSON

> *Tregiffian*
> *St Buryan*
> *Penzance*
> *Cornwall*

> 24 October 1991

Best beloved John and Miranda,
What a perfectly beautiful piece of George II silver, what a lovely thing, and how very, very generous of you both. Really

---

31. In 2009 Joseph Finder wrote to le Carré saying he'd love to source this quote for a friend for the *Yale Book of Quotations.* 'I am very sorry to tell you that I am not able to place the quote in Greene's canon, and have no way of tracking it down,' le Carré replied. 'I surely have read it somewhere as coming from Greene and certainly it bears out the odd remark he dropped in conversation about his early life. But I'm afraid I can't pin it down.'

it is <u>so</u> sumptuous. And thank you too for coming to the Savoy, and adding your own lustre and kindness to the party – &, John, thank you for the elegant & affectionate speech. It's too precious and too funny to publicise how we met (as well as a breach of the OSA [Official Secrets Act], but who's counting these days?) but I was tempted, as I rose to my feet, to recount the despair of Rod Wells as he opened the box of stones; or the rage of the photographic section staff when we threw together the all-in-one developing cocktail for your quick negative response; or the day the tearful [Robin] Hooper confided to us that we should put the chairs on the tables and go home until normal service could be resumed . . .[32]

But I abstained, I abstained. But I would love to have told them how John was at my elbow when the news came through the electric cables (via Room 9) that 'Call for the Dead' had been accepted for publication by Gollancz – if only VG had known where we were at the time, what a scoop! And what a giggle.

So as I scoop my thoughtful piece of marrow from its recesses, I shall have a lot of secret memories to bring a smile to the ageing chops – mine, not the bone's – and a lot of friendship to remember, & great loyalty, to my children as well as to me.

Please come & stay in our new cottage at the end of the field (or in the palatial west wing with its unhampered views over traditional Cornish surroundings and traditional bath en suite) and please let us enjoy each other in this fascinating time. I feel <u>wonderful</u> – you both <u>look</u> wonderful – aren't we lucky?

Jane sends love, as I do.

Ever,
David

---

32. Adventures of spies in training. Rod Wells, another MI6 trainee, who had been brutally tortured in a Japanese camp after building a secret radio, found an airdrop of promised equipment contained nothing but stones. In a rush to develop photographs before getting away for the weekend, Margetson ignored the careful instructions and poured all the chemicals into the mix. Robin Hooper, head of training, tearfully broke the news to the new recruits that George Blake was a Soviet spy.

THE NIGHT MANAGER

I know that this is my best time. I'm pushing 62. It's not going to be long. But I know I'm best now. I know that if I want to do something I can play all the instruments in the orchestra. Whether I make good music is another matter but I feel I'm completely in charge of my craft.

– to the American television journalist Charlie Rose, PBS, 1983

Le Carré's research for the 1993 novel would end in tortuous failed efforts to create a film; even as he researched the book, he imagined Daniel Day-Lewis and Julia Roberts in the lead roles.[1] He later embraced the 2015 television series, produced by his sons Simon and Stephen, as the most successful production of his work since Sir Alec Guinness played Smiley.

1. Jeff Leen, 'My Dinners with le Carré', *Washington Post*, 30 December 2020.

As he began to craft Jonathan Pine's character in The Night Manager, *le Carré turned to his old friend the Hollywood studio boss John Calley. Calley had literally worked his way up from the bottom, a fact that delighted le Carré. He started out in the mailroom at the NBC network and rose to become production chief at Warner Bros in the 1970s, where he green-lit films such as* A Clockwork Orange, The Towering Inferno, The Exorcist, Dog Day Afternoon *and* Dirty Harry. *Calley's endless supply of industry gossip and his real love and understanding of film made him wonderful company. He would earn an Oscar nomination for* The Remains of the Day *in 1993.*

TO JOHN CALLEY

By fax

Cornwall

[n.d.]

Dear John,

Not going up to London till tomorrow now, but I expect we'll talk today anyway. Dare I ask your help on something else? My character is now travelling on a Canadian passport, he is a 38 year old hotelier/chef/fixer figure, personable and smart-looking. He wants to break into the yachting, island-resort scene, either as a cook or a head waiter or under-manager type. (He's white, I should add.) Is there an agency he might turn to in New York who looks these people over & supplies them to yachts & hotels? I've put it badly, but the scam is he wants to end up as maître d', or factotum, on the large luxury yacht of my Mister Big, and is prepared to earn his stripes around the place first in order to do so. I dream of a seedy office on the fringes of Manhattan run by two stern-jawed gays in button-down collars who supply under managers at short notice to the Paradise Island Hotel, for instance, or Caneel Bay, or Ivana Trump's yacht if she's got one, or send a maître d' to Grenada – or whatever. If you can lay your long finger on some such outfit, I cd go & see them in NY or Miami or wherever they hang out. But if not, please don't worry, because I can simply ask around on Paradise Island and get my nose broken.

Anyway, please give it a think & we'll talk! Love to Sandy. Greatly looking forward to seeing you.

David

In 1991 John Calley put le Carré in touch with Jim Webster, a Florida yacht broker whose clients included Tim Landon, who had helped to stage a British-backed coup in Oman. Webster – who still runs Florida boat charters – met le Carré in Miami, and they talked about his ideas for The Night Manager *and the Landon connection. They spent a day on a large yacht owned by a billionaire family to see guest and crew interactions. 'David all the time had his notebooks going. His charming ways always got a lot of good information,' Webster recalled. When le Carré drew up an escape plan for Stephen Fry (see p. 407), he gave him Webster's phone number.*

∾

The director of They Shoot Horses, Don't They *and later* Out of Africa, *Sydney Pollack worked at length with le Carré on a screenplay based on* A Small Town in Germany *in 1969 (distracted, le Carré would relate, by Pollack's new-found passion for the Swiss ski slopes around his chalet in Wengen). That project went nowhere. In 1991 Pollack had returned to acting, in Woody Allen's couples comedy-drama* Husbands and Wives, *and as an ER doctor in* Death Becomes Her.

TO SYDNEY POLLACK

By fax

Cornwall

16 December 1991

Dear Sydney,

Thanks for your letter. I should have answered earlier but I have been struck down by a hellish 'flu bug, and had no spirit for a few days, and how can I write to you without spirit? Now I have moved to the vodka and anti-biotic stage, and am a little dopey, and rather blessedly drunk, and as a matter of fact I can't help wondering whether – since I have almost never been ill – illness is not the only way in which the likes of you and me can relax. It is thick mist here, & the foghorn is going all the time, and we are trying to shoo the builders out before Christmas, but they are so happy – really so happy, & there is so little work – that it is hard to persuade them they shd go back to being unemployed. So we dig great trenches, & erect great granite fortifications against our common mysterious enemies, and in this poor place I rate as the last of the great crazy spenders.

I am thrilled to think of you acting again, and of course very envious. I also think you are very wise, cher auteur, to work, and do the trades, and be unpredictable in your attachments – you really don't have to be Zeus all the time (as I tell myself repeatedly). You can also have some fun, explore, be part of someone else's fuckup, instead of being in the hot seat all the time. I wish I cd follow in your footsteps. But then I see Harold Pinter act & think: nothing can be this painful, please go back to the typewriter. On which subject: are you going to do Remains of the Day? I'm quite in love with the book (American quite) and I don't think I agree with you that no one would see it. But I think it needs the discipline of a small budget, no up-front greed, a perfect script and a gentle, loving director-ial eye. What [director Jack] Clayton did to poor Gatsby, an unthinking American director could do to [Kazuo] Ishiguro – and I don't mean you in any sense: quite the reverse, I think you would have a marvellous time with it, if you could give yourself the space, and the time, and use the English stable of actors, and perhaps make it here entirely. The political stuff is tiny – the aristocratic fascists, the Mosley movement, you can shake that out of your sleeve any time – the rest is about the great bitch goddess of non communication & failure: would they really have been happy if they had got together? Ask Ish.[2] The point is, they knew that the servant classes have no right to love. Oh Sydney.

<u>Lovely</u> to hear from you. I persevere. Maybe by June/July, something. It's like a year's shoot, and scarcely remembering what's in the early reels, and the repeated loss of faith is impressive.

All the best with your acting – have fun – Happy Christmas.
Best as ever,
David

~

Michael Attenborough was the great-grandson of Matthew Hodder, founder of Hodder & Stoughton, and the group's publishing director. Settling on a book jacket design or illustration that satisfied le Carré was a particular challenge for his publishers. The Russian dolls on the original cover of Tinker Tailor Soldier Spy, *and the pinstripe effect for* A Perfect Spy, *were quick matches – others not. 'Time and again we were encouraged to find the illustration of the man carrying his horse up a hill – George Smiley against the world at large, perhaps – but we and our researchers failed,' Attenborough recalled. With* The Night Manager, *Hodder & Stoughton sent a synopsis of the plot to a design school asking its students for ideas.*

---

2. While le Carré and Kazuo Ishiguro met, in Hampstead and once for breakfast in a Boston hotel when they crossed paths on US book tours, they never corresponded.

TO MICHAEL ATTENBOROUGH

By fax

London

24 January 1992

Dear Michael,

I went to bed last night convinced we were on the right lines with the cover, and woke up this morning equally convinced that we were not. I think the only one we are discussing from the batch you brought is the all-black cover with the close observer's eyes. My first feeling, already expressed to you yesterday, is that black to me suggests le Carré gloom and doom or, worse still, Stephen King horror. The pair of eyes struck me as ethnically ambivalent, violent and spooky. I think it is a strong cover, but not for this book.

We have talked about going for midnight blue, and doing something different with the face. I have no quarrel with the lettering at all.

But as we go back to the drawing-board, can I please state what I think was the gap between the design you showed me and the book you are publishing? The book, it seems to me, is brightly painted, with the gold of sunlight and huge money, remote landscapes and Caribbean places. It has exotica and beautiful women, and a great air of luxury. The symbols that come to mind when I think of it are Rolls-Royces, jewellery, Egyptian temples, tropical paradises, luxury hotels and yachts – and beside them, in violent contrast, guns, murder, torture, corruption and perpetual world mayhem. I do not think it would be difficult to catch something of this dichotomy in our design. But if we can't, and remain with something very simple indeed, I think the book should still have a lush quality, not an austere one. The concept that we discussed yesterday is seriously short on the book's pleasures, and that is surely something we all want to avoid when we are trying to appeal to a holiday public!

I know we have little time but I have to say also that yesterday was my first shot at your ideas. I am fairly free, in the early part of this week, to drop into Bedford Square if that would be any help, but I guess this letter pretty much covers what I feel.

Yours,
David

P.S. We spoke last night and said all this to each other, but here's the letter anyway.

Eventually the first-edition cover of The Night Manager *carried a single mounted knight, driving his spear downwards, like St George attacking the dragon.*

∿

In the New York Post's *'Between the Covers' column, Matthew Flamm reported that Random House had made a deal with the 'one-time East German spymaster' and former head of the Stasi, Markus Wolf, for a tell-all book. Associate publisher Peter Osnos was to edit it. The column stated that John le Carré had used Wolf as the model for Karla.*

TO PETER OSNOS, RANDOM HOUSE, NEW YORK

By fax

London

26 January 1992

Dear Peter,
I chanced to read a piece in the New York Post dated January 20th in which you announce your plans for publishing a book

by Markus Wolf. The article states – and one suspects that Random House endorses the suggestion – that Markus Wolf was the model for Karla in the Smiley/Karla books. Since this is utter nonsense, I thought I had better let you know this in case you and your sales force see it as a selling point.

Ever since his fortunes changed for the worse, Wolf has been trying to link his name with mine. If I have received one request to appear with him in public, I have received a hundred, let alone the stream of press-cuttings I have read which claim my literary paternity. I can only imagine that Wolf sees me as part of his overall defence, and wishes to portray himself as a rugged humanitarian who did his duty but played a clean game while he did it. I would no more have chosen Wolf as the model for Karla than I would have chosen Caligula as the model for Smiley. Wolf served a disgusting regime in disgusting ways and knew exactly what he was doing. In my book, he deserves everything that the Federal Prosecutor's office in Karlsruhe is trying to throw at him.

You may wonder that I have not denied a link with Wolf already. But experience has taught me that, as far as the media is concerned, denials are ignored if they are inconvenient, or else taken as confirmation.

I have no doubt Wolf has already proposed that he and I should appear together on American television. If he has not, he very shortly will. The answer to all of it is no. Forgive this broadside, but the man has been a total pain-in-the-arse and I have to tell you that it would be more than I could stomach to see this stuff being put out by the Group to which Knopf belongs.

Yours,
David

~

Derek and Jeannie Tangye had lived the simple life on Cornish cliffs since the 1950s, relating the story of their lives in a series of books called 'The Minack Chronicles'. Derek, le Carré's closest neighbour on the coast path, had worked for MI5 in the war. His wife, Jeannie, had died four years before this fax from Panama.

TO DEREK TANGYE

By fax

Hotel Continental
Panama

23 February 1992

My dear old friend,
I was sorry to be away when Jeannie's anniversary came round, but when Jane reminded me, the same old lump came up in my throat, and the same sense of deprival, as if I had just heard the news for the first time. I send you all love and sympathy, and my sense of companionship even from so far away. A small drink in mid-March is particularly inviting.

Bless you Derek – God bless.
David

≈

Ronnie Cornwell was determined that his eldest son should be called to the bar – but Tony Cornwell made his own flight from his father. He took a scholarship to Bowdoin College in the United States, and later settled there. As a young man he dreamt of becoming a novelist, and was still pursuing that ambition late in his sixties. On 19 April 1992 Tony wrote le Carré 'a love letter, sort of' to say that he had irrevocably committed himself to 'the identity, the will, the failure, the epiphany and inevitability of writing'.

TO TONY CORNWELL

Tregiffian
St Buryan
Penzance
Cornwall

24 April 1992

Dearest To,

What can I say but 'thanks' – & thanks again, for discovering the cost of living like this! It isn't a way of life, is it, it's just life. It isn't an activity, or a pursuit, or an amusement, it's an enormous, consuming, scaring swing through all one's feelings all the time, and through one's reactions to those feelings also: exultation, when you suddenly fight free & it's sitting up in front of you & talking to you; total bewilderment, resentment & despair when it won't take a blind bit of notice, doesn't care about you, doesn't respect you, would prefer to be spoken for by someone more talented – or simply, talented.

I'm not sure you should worry about beginning late – there isn't time. And in a whole lot of ways, you will organise your thoughts more economically & get there faster. It isn't as if you've been wasting your time or not doing IT – you've probably been stalking it, & foxing around it, & preparing yourself in all sorts of ways you are now discovering. And you saw a lot of life, but most of all you lived it, & you have self knowledge. I don't think it's bad – I rather envy you your freshness!

Thank you for writing so very, very generously. It was – it really was – awfully hard to be that person in your life. I never meant to be the person who did the things you were so keen on doing, or Mr Successful, or Mr Literature, or anything else much. I just wanted to improve my game, & since you can't disown success, having trodden over bodies to get it, I tried to enjoy it too! But I never enjoyed shoving it up your chuff – I hope you know that, I really hope that terribly, for I have always loved you. And though I have often been a right little cutthroat, on my way up, I've also been an insecure softie, and I took some awful knocks, and learned the very hard way that there is no such thing as an 'established' writer. Right now, I'm about as disestablished as you can get – 350 pages written, the story barely told, far too many characters, no focus, the whole catastrophe, and this after 2 years at it! But it was never different. You just have to show up in the gym next morning, & behave as if nobody knocked you cold the day before. And there isn't anyone watching, or listening, not really. There's a sympathetic ear – but <u>my</u> ear's sympathetic too! Yesterday in despair I bought Jane a new desk & a primitive painting of a cow. I thought it might do the trick, and this evening I have a hunch it did: things look a little rosier. So it goes, dear old love. And I'm full of fondness for you, and I can imagine, just, what you may be going through every hour.

Love,
D

Two years after this letter, le Carré pressed Tony's book 'Born of the Sun', also titled 'Too Close to the Sun', on Sonny Mehta, the head of Knopf, with no success.

∾

Don Chapman, cultural development officer for the City of Marion, South Australia, wrote to le Carré to ask for a tie for a community exhibition and auction. 'In particular, we are looking for a tie that you never wanted, or were too embarrassed to wear, or an outrageous, silly, party, business or even arty tie.'

TO DON CHAPMAN

9 Gainsborough Gardens
London, NW3 1BJ

20 August 1992

Dear Don Chapman,

This tie was given to me by my wife when I went to lunch with Mrs Thatcher. Its colours were aptly chosen: the deep blue of Mrs Thatcher's convictions, shot with the intermittent red of my own frail socialism, and an insipid yellowish colour which I am afraid says much about my moral courage. In the end, I selected a quite different tie, an equally awful confection of blue upon blue. Mrs Thatcher is one of those politicians who are even more unreal than their waxworks. The eyeballs are straighter, the perfect vowels are prerecorded, each sentence makes a deadly point and jokes are out of place unless they are hers. Although I never wore this tie, it conjures up for me a moment in British history comparable with the great stagnation of Soviet Russia, when Brezhnev sold his country's silver, plundered its resources, and the pigs-in-clover boys had a really good time. May this stupid little tie remind the lucky buyer that there are some things about the recession which are worth keeping.

Yours sincerely,
John le Carré

～

TO SIR JOHN MARGETSON

9 Gainsborough Gardens
London, NW3 1BJ

8 October 1992

Dear John,

I at last finished my long novel, provisionally entitled 'The Night Manager' in its first draft, and my loony secretary is sending you a copy – sh<u>d</u> be with you on Wednesday or Thursday next week. May I enlist your help? The book is slightly surrealistic, & contains a number of passages about Whitehall, W'minster & the spies. And since I have very little knowledge of real W'minster committees & so forth, I have tried to be as unspecific as I can. Nonetheless, I'm obliged to give ranks here & there, & want to be sure I haven't made an ass of myself. Could you run your eye over it from the point of view of plausibility? (Authenticity is a dead duck – we're into political neo sci-fi.) There are lots of other bits I have to check – container ships, freight lore, company structures, etc. – but the UK political stuff (since it is the least easy to write perhaps) causes me the most grief. Do please share the book with Miranda if you wish – I think she may enjoy it. Just to fill your cup, I'm afraid it is 755 pp of manuscript . . .

We are very well, as I hope you are, and just leaving for Zurich & then NY in order to watch over the negotiations for the book. <u>Nobody</u> has yet read it, except Jane, which makes it more exciting.

Had a <u>foul</u> wet workaholic summer, and we are now reckoning on a three-month break. Where, remains to be seen. And the bloody dogs as ever rule.

Shall we all have a meal together in early Nov? We w<u>d</u> <u>love</u> to take you back to the Connaught – or w<u>d</u> Miranda's social conscience prefer the simple homespun atmosphere of 'Nico at 90' – not bad either? Or right downmarket, if you don't mind the people, is the Gavroche . . . We'd love to do one with you, anyway, if you were game.

Love to you both,
David

P.S. Did they ever show the G. Greene? Did you tape it? We missed it anyway, in the last rush of the book, if it did even appear. D.[3]

~

Philip Roth's Operation Shylock *was published in 1993. He won the Pulitzer Prize in 1997.*

TO PHILIP ROTH

By fax

London

11 October 1992

Dear Philip,
Congratulations! What else can I say? What other use can I be, than to tell you what you know – that you have moved, embarrassed, entertained and maddened me, driven me through a city of lights at dead of night at breakneck speed, perplexed me, summoned my anti-semitic self from his contented grave, and given me a great time? McSmilesburger salutes you![4] I don't know how you want me to help otherwise – I was no use to Joyce on Ulysses, fucked up completely when Kafka needed

---

3. The BBC's *Arena* programme *The Graham Greene Trilogy* aired in January 1993, two years after Greene's death. It included interviews with le Carré, reflecting sympathetically on Greene's career, their differences on Philby and how Greene was 'dotty about the possibilities of reconciling Catholicism with communism, especially in southern America'.

4. 'There are powerful, self-excoriating passages about anti-Semitism in history and in literature throughout the book,' wrote *New York Times* reviewer D. M. Thomas of *Shylock*. Smilesburger is a Mossad agent who recruits Roth to infiltrate a group of Jews with ties to the Palestinian Liberation Organisation.

me, all I could suggest to Nabokov was 'couldn't you just maybe give her a couple more years?' but he wouldn't listen. You are so far from form by the end that this old formalist can only shake his formal white locks and say – 'well, if he can do it, and he can, why undo it?'[5] It's brilliant, perplexing, suicidal and great. If I can offer one formal suggestion: when he meets his other self, I need a thousand violins and you don't give them to me until the following chapter. It works okay as you have it, but I would favour a prolonged examination (you give it later but I say give it earlier) BEFORE you make the recognition of 'Christ, it's me.' I really wanted to eat, drink, and fuck that moment, before you give me the solution. The chapter break at that moment robs me of my satisfaction.

Anyway, I promise to keep it all fresh in my head till we meet. Oh – and pissy small – why not Brodsky among the Jewish Nobel prize winners?[6]

No more picking the flyshit out of the pepper. A huge, grand, tragic thing, & insoluble. Thanks.

Love to you both,
David

∿

In 1986 le Carré's friend the journalist and author William Shawcross wrote to the Observer *calling Anthony Burgess's review of* A Perfect Spy *'a triumph of spite and incomprehension'. In 1992 the journalist Francis Wheen wrote a review of* Murdoch, *Shawcross's biography*

---

5. Shylock's bewilderingly complex plot sees Philip Roth, the narrator of his own novel, learning of a man impersonating Philip Roth in Jerusalem, preaching 'Diasporism', the idea that the Jews should leave Israel and resettle in Europe, a sort of Zionism in reverse.

6. A passage in the book lists Jewish winners of the Nobel Prize, including Elie Wiesel, Isaac Bashevis Singer and Saul Bellow. It does not mention Joseph Brodsky, who was with le Carré when he heard he'd won the 1987 Nobel Prize for Literature.

of Rupert Murdoch, questioning how Shawcross could write such 'a remarkably sympathetic study of the much-vilified media baron'. Wheen had already slated the book in the Literary Review *in London.*

TO TINA BROWN, EDITOR, THE *NEW YORKER*

By fax

London

12 October 1992

Madam,

The issue of the <u>New Yorker</u> dated 12th October contains one of the ugliest pieces of partisan journalism that I have witnessed in a long life of writing. That the article is inaccurate is incidental to the larger point: namely that, in one of your first assays to live up to the noble standards of your new magazine, you have used your columns to strike a blow in defence of your own husband, without revealing to your readers that the Editor-in-Chief at Random House, Mr Harold Evans, is your husband, that he was formerly editor of the British <u>Sunday Times</u> and fell foul of Rupert Murdoch in circumstances that are still disputed, and that, although your husband's name is disingenuously withheld from the article in question (entitled 'Seduction' and written by yet another Englishman named Francis Wheen), he is at the very focus of it, and has recently been in furious correspondence – to the tune of 27 pages of telefax – with the author whom the article just happens to disparage.

Let me declare my interest – a thing you somehow omitted to do. I am a friend of William Shawcross. I have known him for many years, and throughout the four years during which, with great bravery, he struggled to present an objective portrait of Rupert Murdoch that would be untainted by the easy anti-Murdoch hysteria that the dreadful British press wheels out whenever it wants to show that it has an ethical conscience.

The convenient suggestion, peddled in your article, that in Shawcross Murdoch has found his <u>Boswell</u>, that Shawcross became his <u>hagiographer</u>, was <u>beguiled</u> by him, was <u>wooed and flattered and given every kind of assistance</u> and that <u>in return</u> (*sic*) Shawcross wrote <u>a remarkably sympathetic</u> study of his subject, whom Wheen calls <u>the enemy</u> – all this, for anyone who knows the score as well as you do, has just one shabby purpose: to rubbish the author and his judgments in advance of the book's publication in America, and to assure your readers that the unflattering portrait of Harold Evans provided in the book is mere Murdoch propaganda, fed into Shawcross's servile ear.

To reinforce this shameful picture of a brilliant journalist who has sold himself to the devil, your Mr Wheen – who as you must know has already paraded the same distorted views in the London literary press – has the vulgarity to drag in both Mr Shawcross's parentage and his lovelife, suggesting that his <u>turnabout</u> is <u>genetically programmed</u> by his father's actions in the fifties, and by the influence of <u>an heiress who sits on the Westminster City Council as a Conservative and is a friend of Mrs Thatcher</u>, namely Mrs Olga Polizzi.

Perhaps, when you pen the apology that Mr Shawcross so richly deserves, you will let us know whether the influence of your own father has recently affected your judgment, or whether – as your readers are now entitled to enquire – it is your lovelife that is really to blame.

God protect the <u>New Yorker</u> from the English. It is not the press barons who are responsible for the decline of our journalistic standards, but the press itself.

Yours faithfully,
John le Carré

P.S. All the underlined passages are direct quotes from Mr Wheen's article as it appeared in the <u>New Yorker</u>.

Tina Brown called le Carré's charge that she was acting for her husband 'extraordinarily sexist', and wrote that the New Yorker *only published letters of one short paragraph. That would pack more punch, she suggested to him, than sounding 'like a choleric Colonel in Angmering-on-Sea'. Le Carré faxed the correspondence to Joe Lelyveld, who had interviewed him for the* New York Times, *signing himself 'Lt Col. Retired', and to his friend David Greenway at the* Boston Globe. *Extensive coverage of the row followed in the UK and US press.*

∾

TO MICHAEL ATTENBOROUGH

By fax

Cornwall

3 November 1992

Dear Michael,

Titles. The favourite at the moment is A WOMAN OF CAIRO, which I suggested, and is based on my intention to raise Sophie's importance through the book by means of flash-backs, right up to the end. Let me know what you think.

Best
David

∾

Weiss's article in Esquire *magazine, in January 1993, was titled 'The Martyr'. 'Salman Rushdie has made his most public appeal yet for sympathy' ran the sub-headline. 'Why is nobody listening?'*

to PHILIP WEISS

By fax

23 January 1993

<u>PRIVATE AND CONFIDENTIAL</u>

Dear Philip,

I don't think it appropriate, having given you a lengthy interview and featured in your article, that I should now come to your aid because the going has got rough. I believe you should take the high ground and stop being nervous or apologetic.

You knew by the time we spoke that you were taking on the Rushdie Thought Police. In fact, your article struck me as extraordinarily restrained. If the cause of Salman Rushdie is really to do with free speech, his supporters should damn well allow you yours. It seems to me that what is lacking at this moment is not a letter from me but the courage of your editor and yourself. A bold editorial and a brave stand would do wonders for your readers, and your magazine, and the Fourth Estate.

Journalists always overreact to a negative press. They want to hand it out, not take it. You wrote a good article for a good magazine. You wanted to stir it, and you've stirred it. Stick to your guns.

Yours,
David

~

Eric Abraham is a South African/British film producer. He produced le Carré's A Murder of Quality, *starring Denholm Elliott, in 1991.*

TO ERIC ABRAHAM

By fax

London

3 March 1993

Dear Eric,

Thanks for your fax of 20.2. from Berlin. I've sorted out my affairs a little – and successfully sued a would-be biographer & emerged fairly unscathed[7] – and am therefore better able to decide how to respond to your kind proposal for 'Darkness at Noon.' It's this way. I'm pretty sure that, one way or another, I have to script 'The Night Manager'. I also have a new novel that is buzzing ever-louder in my ear, and for which I shall begin the research in May. I am doing everything I can to escape the distractions of publication in July – like going to earth in Rekjavik or somewhere equally conspicuous. I think I would go nuts, if I saddled myself with a second screenplay, and an adaptation of something not my own at that, with the inevitable & entirely justified rewrites that always follow the first draft. It's just, I'm afraid, too much stuff for one year, when my greatest wish is to fight free & get into fresh ground. I thought I should say this at once, so that I don't keep you waiting.[8]

As to the chances that we might work together on a European production of The Night Manager, I would like to think that, as you so generously suggest, we can keep these open. I'm sorry that, having waxed so lyrical about 'Darkness'

---

7. Graham Lord, the *Sunday Express* literary editor, novelist and biographer, promised in his outline to expose le Carré's 'weird' relationship with the Kennaways, among other things. Le Carré issued a writ for libel, and the book was stopped.

8. Abraham had commissioned a screenplay of Arthur Koestler's *Darkness at Noon* but felt the writer had been strait-jacketed by the novel. 'If you are still serious about writing a screenplay I would like to take you up on it,' he wrote to le Carré, who asked for a month to decide before this response.

over your splendid hospitality at the Connaught, I should let you down on the script, and I would be only too happy, when I return the compliment, to share with you my unpolished notions of how the film might be done, such as they are: but I think there are a lot of original scenes & devices that have to be worked out (his women, not only his secretary; his previous experience of prison; his intellectual roots & so on) and I could see myself with 6 months' hard labour, no problem.

I wish you, as ever, great success & look forward to talking soon.

Best,
David

~

To SYDNEY POLLACK

By fax

Cornwall

28 July 1993

Dear Sydney,
As Paramount and myself lumber towards agreement, I have been searching my soul about the kind of film I believe you could make. And although this will be totally different from the film you do make – as it should be – I thought nevertheless it would be worth trying to indicate some of my thoughts to you.

The first is also the last. It seems to me to be the one creative imperative we cannot escape. As with The Spy Who Came in from the Cold, so with The Night Manager, the story is nothing if it does not have moral anger. This is not to be expressed in noble lines, but in some kind of pulse that beats from the first to the last frame. You had it in They Shoot Horses, and you knew where it came from. It was not an intellectualised or perceived anger, but one that you managed to feel on your own body. Somehow, for all the structural problems we are sure to face, you have to feel it again for this movie.

Where does it come from? In Jonathan, there is some kind of terrible wall around his life that he is trying to scale. He espouses convention, dresses for it, behaves for it. We meet him when he is a servant of luxury, yet he loathes luxury as he loathes waste and wasted lives. He is at heart a monk, a mountain climber, a solitary soldier, a watcher, and a person of determined solitude and self-sufficiency, even though he longs to connect. And before you start to place other constructions on Jonathan – you were already doing this in New York – I think it would be wise to pause a while and find out what is there, rather than decide that he must be fleshed out.

The other sources of anger are much easier to grasp: Burr's rage with a man like Roper, born to all the advantages, who sets about screwing up society rather than going to its protection. Strelski's rage which derives from knowing almost from the start that the fix between politicians and the crooks is permanent and unbreakable; and Goodhew's anger when his reforming zeal strikes the realities of corrupt government.

And Sophie's anger that the wretched of the earth are obliged again and again to pay for the fantasies of the rich, and for the war-games of tyrants and arms dealers.

My second point expresses a very real concern that I have for the film: that in our haste to give the story universality, we shall abandon its Englishness, and consequently the theatre of manners which is so crucial to portraying the anger of those in search of truth. I am not clinging to Englishness for its own sake or out of some cock-eyed sense of pride. I am using its persiflage, its class prejudices and its infuriating assumptions of superiority in order to choreograph the very universality that we aspire to. When Chariots of Fire took off, the posturing of English dons and the English sporting establishment acquired a universality that was as well-respected in Central

Thailand as it was in London. We can produce the same kind of frustration in our own film. So again I am suggesting that instead of looking for different ways to address the gradations of London bureaucracy, we espouse them lovingly, and that our shafts be accurate as well as lethal.

I could go on a lot, but my last point should take me back to the first. How should the audience feel when it leaves our film? I asked myself the same question repeatedly as I approached the end of the novel. And the ending that I finally gave the book reflected exactly – rightly or wrongly – my intentions. I wanted to give the reader the satisfaction of knowing that at some simple level personal courage and personal humanity had triumphed. I wanted him also to feel a sense of outrage at the way the world was going to the devil, seemingly unchecked by the very forces appointed to control it. I think if we can get that over, we will make – that is, of course, you will make – the film you saw when you first read the book.[9] And that, I am convinced, is the film we should be making.

Best,
David

Le Carré should have been wary of Pollack's 'glorious but short-lived bursts of enthusiasm', he wrote in The Pigeon Tunnel, *after the experience with* A Small Town in Germany. *Instead, when Pollack announced his plan to film* The Night Manager, *'I dropped everything and caught the first available flight to New York.' Paramount agreed to buy the rights, and the two men had a first brain-storming session in California.*

∾

9. In 1993 Pollack told le Carré's friend, the studio boss John Calley, that *The Night Manager* was le Carré's 'best and most cinematic work'.

Stephen Fry first wrote to le Carré in 1991 after finishing The Secret
Pilgrim *at 3 a.m. 'The English dam can withstand the pressure of
fifteen years of admiration and affection no longer,' he said, apologising for 'schoolboy gushing'. 'The only writer I've ever written to apart
from yourself was P. G. Wodehouse, when I was twelve.' In 1993, after
reading* The Night Manager, *he wrote a lengthy rave for the 'feeling
of wonder' for the story-telling, the writing and 'the actual milieu, the
ghastly world, the dreadful trade'.*

TO STEPHEN FRY [10]

> *Tregiffian*
> *St Buryan*
> *Penzance*
> *Cornwall*

> 13 September 1993

Dear Stephen,
Just got back from bloody Russia to your wonderful letter,
for which I thank you very much. Russia is a kind of Czarist
Wild West, but tortured by guilt, religion, laziness, and its own
unbelievable waste of talent. I never went anywhere that gave
me such an appalling sense of anarchy got up as change. If we
ever doubted that the world had altered after the Cold War, a
couple of days in Moscow would put us out of our misery. I took
my twenty-year-old son with me and he is still walking around
like a zombie. I crossed Red Square and walked into the old
Gumm [GUM] building. It now houses Estée Lauder, Galerie
Lafayette and half the brand names of Bond Street. They don't
rely on the Western tourists – understandably, since everything
is 50% more expensive than in the West. Their customers are

---

10. From 1991 to 1993 the richly talented British actor, writer and comedian Stephen
Fry played Jeeves opposite Hugh Laurie, future star of *The Night Manager*, in the
Jeeves and Wooster series for ITV.

the new Moscow millionaires, of whom there are so many that Rolls Royce and Mercedes report that they sell more of their top models in Russia than in the rest of Europe put together.

I don't quite know why, but I had a lousy year, and I am delighted that its end is in sight. Being published in England has become an act of wanton masochism, and since it is my one window upon British industry, I assume that the whole country is equally incompetent, vicious and loony.

Sydney Pollack is supposed to be directing the movie of THE NIGHT MANAGER and I would be enormously tickled if you were to find a place in it. For my money, I would ask you to play Corkoran tomorrow but we are dealing with minds, if that is the word, that function on other planes, so they will probably give it to Dicky Attenborough.

We all root for you here, and love your work. Thanks again for writing.

As ever,
David

～

Early in Tinker Tailor Soldier Spy, *on page 30 of the Pan Books edition, George Smiley returns to his home in Bywater Street. He checks before opening his front door that two splinters of wood, which he had placed below and above the lock, are still in place. Stepping inside, however, he finds an unfamiliar umbrella in the stand in the hall; and realises 'its owner had known about the wedges and known how to put them back once he was inside the house.' Sure enough Peter Guillam awaits Smiley in the drawing room. 'Please Mr le Carré,' asked J. E. C. Kuitenbrouwer, 'how did Peter Guillam put them back?'*

to J. E. C. KUITENBROUWER, A FAN FROM
THE NETHERLANDS

Tregiffian
St Buryan
Penzance
Cornwall

21 October 1993

Dear Mr Kuitenbrouwer,
Thank you very much for your amusing letter of September
10th. Do you know, I never quite knew the answer myself? I
imagine him balancing the wedges on top of the door, then
drawing the door slowly towards him, and giving it a last hard
pull as he closes it.

But I don't really know, and perhaps it's impossible. It was
just one of those little bits of mystique with which I wanted
to adorn the story. But I was most touched, and so was my
wife, by your terrible question. And since I notice that you
have TINKER TAILOR SOLDIER SPY in paperback, perhaps you will accept the house prize for attentive proof reading,
which I enclose.

Yours sincerely,
John le Carré

～

Isaaman was the long-time editor of the Hampstead & Highgate
Express.

to GERALD ISAAMAN

By fax

London

[n.d. but likely mid 1990s]

Dear Gerald,

It went:

Male stranger in adjoining seat on Swissair flight bound for Zurich: 'Is that his new one?'

Me, sitting on stationary plane correcting Hodders' bound proof: 'Yes.'

Stranger: 'Is it any good?'

Me, pissed off by delay caused by snow in Zurich, and fearful of missing meeting with movie mogul: 'I don't know. I wrote it.'

Stranger: 'I thought so.'

Soon after that, recognising that the meeting was not going to be possible, I left the plane.

Best,

David

P.S. Off to France, no forwarding address.

∼

Nicholas Elliott was an MI6 officer and long-time friend of Kim Philby, whose partial confession he heard in Beirut before Philby fled to Moscow. Le Carré dreamt of turning the relationship into a play.[11]

11. See letter to John Keegan, 28 April 1994, p. 356.

TO NICHOLAS ELLIOTT

> *Tregiffian*
> *St Buryan*
> *Penzance*
> *Cornwall*

> 9 November 1993

Dear Nicholas,

Forgive this typed letter, but I am caught midway between a new novel and the film of the last one, and the days are whizzing by too fast.

I cannot at the moment say when we shall be next in London – we come so seldom. But we are going to the West Indies and United States in late November, and it is very possible that we will stay in London on our return in early December, in which case I will give you a buzz.

I am delighted to hear that you have a new book coming out. If you can give me an early peek of it, I would welcome the chance to give it a puff.

I still hanker after our plan to do a Philby play, and I think the time is coming round again where it might be an attractive project commercially. My trouble is, that for as long as the novels really pull me, I find them totally satisfying, and of course, financially they are much more rewarding. And at the moment, the present novel pulls me very hard indeed.

I love your father's view of foreigners. A few more like him and we would never have got into this mess with the Common Market![12]

All the best to you both from both of us, and let's try and do it soon.

---

12. Sir Claude Aurelius Elliott, headmaster at Eton College from 1933 to 1949, where he was known as 'The Emperor'. He was still provost of Eton when le Carré was a master there.

Oh, by the way, as you may have read, I had a fairly odious meeting with General Oleg Kalugin, lately of the KGB, in Moscow. He boasted of how he had provided the umbrella and the poisoned dart for the assassination of Georgi Markov.[13] I was sufficiently irritated by this to mention it to Sir Rodric Braithwaite,[14] and perhaps my protests, along with several other people's, contributed to his arrest at London Airport last week. Unfortunately, the Director of Public Prosecutions determined that there was insufficient evidence of Kalugin's complicity in the affair. In that case the law is, once again, an ass, for both my son Nicholas and myself would happily have gone into the witness box to repeat what Kalugin[15] had told us in the comfort of his apartment in Moscow.

Yours sincerely,
David Cornwell

Le Carré's fascination with Philby and Elliott's relationship convinced his friend the author and journalist Ben Macintyre to write A Spy among Friends: Kim Philby and the Great Betrayal. *Le Carré wrote an afterword for the book. Le Carré's play never progressed, but the dramatic potential of the friendship produced a BBC drama-documentary and recently a mini-series of Macintyre's book, starring Guy Pearce as Philby and Damian Lewis as Elliott.*

∾

13. The Bulgarian dissident Georgi Markov was murdered in 1978, when he was injected with a poisoned pellet in a London street.

14. Sir Rodric Braithwaite was the UK ambassador in Moscow during the critical perestroika years from 1988 to 1992. He was later John Major's foreign policy adviser and chairman of the Joint Intelligence Committee.

15. Oleg Kalugin ran the Soviet Union's counter-intelligence operations from 1973 to 1980. Now a US citizen, in 2002 he was convicted in absentia by a Russian court for treason regarding disclosures in his 1994 autobiography, *The First Chief Directorate: My Thirty-two Years in Intelligence and Espionage against the West*. He downplayed his role in the Markov killing in the book.

In 1989 Mikhail Lyubimov wrote to le Carré for the first time, enclosing his play, a 'farce on espionage'. He introduced himself as a graduate of the Moscow School of International Relations who had worked in the Soviet diplomatic service in London from 1961 to 1965 and as a counsellor at the embassy in Denmark. He proposed the two men work together on a 'literary translation' of his script, 'perhaps a musical'. Le Carré wrote back saying, 'Surely you should try Alan Bennett or Michael Frayn?'[16]

In 1992 Christopher Robbins, the journalist and screenwriter, wrote to le Carré, enclosing another letter from Lyubimov. Robbins – who would become a close friend of le Carré – explained that Lyubimov was a KGB officer and Anglophile who had been expelled from Britain in 1965 for trying to recruit a cipher clerk. The head of station in London and Cophenhagen, he ran the KGB's British desk in Moscow until he was sacked in 1980. Robbins was seeking to get Lyubimov's 'persona non grata' status lifted so that he could bring him to the UK to make a film.

'This is to remind you of a KGB colonel whom you helped to find a hope for a play,' Lyubimov wrote to le Carré. He explained that his own novel, The Life and Adventures of Alex Wilkie, Spy, *inspired by* A Perfect Spy, *about a KGB illegal living in Hampstead, had since become a hit in Russia.*

Le Carré promised to 'do what little I can to assist your early return to England in your new disguise as a novelist'. He met Lyubimov in Moscow in 1993, as well as Oleg Kalugin, and in May 1994 Lyubimov travelled to le Carré's home in Cornwall – after promising 'to work and not to appear drunk and naked in a colonel's uniform'.

Their correspondence remained warm and funny. Le Carré wrote about Lyubimov in 'Smiley Mike', a short chapter designed for The Pigeon Tunnel, *for which he invited Lyubimov to contribute his own piece, but which he excluded from the published version.*

Lyubimov wrote to le Carré saying how he had read The Night Manager *twice for its 'blissful aroma', a book that was 'very burning for Russia where Ropers are acquiring more and more power'.*

---

16. According to Lyubimov, le Carré sent on Lyubimov's play to Frayn, who responded with a tactful refusal.

TO MIKHAIL LYUBIMOV

Tregiffian
St Buryan
Penzance
Cornwall

15 November 1993

Dear Michael,

That was indeed a wonderful letter. I have just read your joke to Jane over the intercom between my workroom and her study, and she cracked up.

I really enjoyed our meeting in Moscow, and would relish talking to you more about what is going on in Russia now, and less about spying, which to be truthful, is a subject that increasingly bores me. But I hasten to say that my novel is going fine . . .

I hope you were as amused as I was that Oleg Kalugin was arrested at London Airport on his arrival in the United Kingdom, and interrogated about his part in the murder of Markov. I did rather have a feeling, as we sat listening to him, that he was pushing his luck a little bit. Lord Bethel went for him in the House of Lords, and I believe that Markov's relations have also fixed their sights on him, and I don't think it by any means impossible that, particularly if he goes on shooting his mouth off, he will end up behind Western bars. The Markov affair is still very alive in people's memories, and it didn't go down at all well here.

Kalugin called me from his room at the Hilton Hotel in London, but I could only speak to a Mr Reid in his hotel room, and the hotel had no Kalugin on its books. This is extremely funny, because it seems that Kalugin was in the room, but hiding behind Reid's name – Reid being his publisher or agent, I don't know who. Anyway, we missed each other. Maybe another time.

As to your good self, I hope you come in December, but it is going to be difficult for me, because we are going to the West

Indies and perhaps America on the 28th November, and I am not yet sure when we will return. Maybe Jane will come back ahead of me. Or maybe neither of us will go to America. But I have a notion that you should come down here sometime, and spend long enough for it to be worthwhile. We have an entirely separate cottage for guests, and we like them best when they bring work and are self-sufficient during the day. The ideal would be, if you brought a manuscript to revise, or a novel to write, and we could play in the evenings. And if you wished to bring a Significant Other of either sex, there is plenty of room in the cottage for them too.

And thank you for enjoying THE NIGHT MANAGER. I loved what you wrote to me about it. You mention also that you wrote something in the Literary Gazette. Now here's a strange thing. The Independent newspaper here published a pretty unsympathetic piece about me recently, drawing on an article by someone called Lvov, said to have appeared in the Literary Gazette, and said to accuse me of harbouring romantic notions about the KGB. The Independent did a kind of retrospective Macarthyite smear, suggesting that my real philosophy was 'anti-anti-Communist'.

I am used to the smear, but did you see the Lvov piece? And if so, would you be kind enough to tell me what it contained, or perhaps send me a copy which I can have translated. I almost never reply to attacks in the press, but I might feel obliged to defend myself in this case.

I shall send this letter express in the hope that it will encourage some drunken Muscovite postman to move his legs a little faster. Or do I mean his drunken Cornish colleague? I send you much affection, and, if we miss each other this time, all good wishes for Christmas. But let's catch up soon.

Yours ever,
David Cornwell

Lyubimov replied that, after his inquiries, 'one possible Lvov is detected', an expatriate living in America, who 'writes mostly bad prose and nobody apart from critics knows him'.

~

Le Carré returned to the Kalugin affair in early 1995 with a lengthy article, first carried in the book-review section of the New York Times *under the title 'My New Friends in the New Russia: In Search of a Few Good Crooks, Cops and Former Agents', and later in the* Observer *in London. In it le Carré detailed Kalugin's confession of his role in arranging the 'disgusting, vindictive murder' of Markov, 'a brave man, and greatly loved'.*

Alice Mary Dilke's daughter Annabel was Georgi Markov's widow. Mrs Dilke wrote to thank le Carré for his words. There had been 'an orchestrated attempt to blacken Georgi's name', she said, including claims he was a KGB double-agent. 'Your portrayal of Georgi has been very heartening.'

то ALICE MARY DILKE

Tregiffian
St Buryan
Penzance
Cornwall

4 March 1995

Dear Mrs Dilke,

Thank you so much for your letter of 26 Feb, which I read as soon as we returned from a holiday in the Bahamas. I'm glad I was able to do something for Georgi's reputation. Alas, I never met him, but those who did spoke of him with great admiration.

Thank you for taking the trouble to write. I'm not sure how welcome I shall be at the Kalugins in future, but I don't think that bothers me.

All good wishes –
David Cornwell

Mrs Dilke gave le Carré's letter to her granddaughter, Markov's daughter Sasha, to keep. She still has it.

~

In April 1995 the New York Times *published a lengthy response to le Carré's article by Oleg Kalugin, who was 'upset and somewhat perplexed, though still a fan'. He challenged le Carré's description of his home and what was said about Markov. 'In his wording, it looks as if I condoned the murder of this man and have no remorse over what happened . . . I did not participate in the planning, discussion or execution of the plot. I did not train either Russians or Bulgarians, nor did I hand over to them the lethal weapon.' He noted that le Carré had left warm inscriptions in five or six of his books in Kalugin's library, and said he had 'not one nice word' to say about Russia's people.*

to THE EDITOR, THE *NEW YORK TIMES*

[22 March 1995, for 2 April publication]

Sir,

There were two other witnesses to my meeting with Major General Kalugin, apart from my son: Mikhail Lyubimov, the writer and former KGB Colonel in charge of the London residency, and Vladimir Stabnikov, at that time administrative head of Moscow PEN. Is the General really denying that he said what I have reported him saying? He would be hard put to do it. I do not believe I have erred in any material point: neither in my account of what he said of his own part in the murder of Markov, nor of how he said it. I have no recollection of the broad philosophical discussion he refers to. Rather I remember a monologue, singularly free of the remorse that he now claims is his.

He asks, where is my compassion for the plight of modern Russia? It is everywhere. I am quite as distressed as he is, I believe, by the sight of a country that can't face its past, its present or its future without a shudder. And I am sorry for the many decent Russian people who grew up as Communists in good faith, and must now accept that their faith was misplaced.

And I am sorrier still, not for Communism's winners, among whom I count the General, but its losers. For which reason, the General will perhaps allow me a little compassion for the surviving family of Georgi Markov whom his former service murdered, and who even in death is being hounded by the Bulgarian regime which now cynically and untruthfully brands him a former KGB double agent. And when the General speaks of my venom, I would prefer him to call it plain anger at the notion of a former KGB luminary making a party piece out of his involvement in the murder of a brave opponent of a disgusting regime, however much he now wishes to explain it away.

And of course I wrote a lavish inscription in his book. To my shame, I was courtesy itself, as my piece was at pains to point out. When the General complains that I have abused his hospitality, I am embarrassed. He has my full apology. Perhaps one day he will apologise to Mrs Markov.

Yours, etc.,
John le Carré

⁓

TO JACK BURKHARDT

Tregiffian
St Buryan
Penzance
Cornwall

19 November 1993

Dear Mr Burkhardt,

Thank you for your letter. I am sorry that the ending of THE NIGHT MANAGER disappointed you. I cannot share your disappointment, although I confess that the ending went through many stages. The trick was to make the bad guys win, which in this case they surely do, while at the same time giving some kind of redemption to Jonathan, because I felt he needed it. In other words, I wanted humanity to prevail against evil, because in the end, it should.

So I allowed myself the conceit of a Shakespearian comedy, and after portraying the folly of the world, I put the lovers together after all, tying a sweet bow around them, and gave them some kind of afterlife. So of course there were lots of loose ends, and I am sorry if they bothered you. I could easily have ended the book, as at first I did, with Jed and Jonathan in the dinghy in the water, and left the reader to decide what became of them. Or I could have had Jonathan blow up the boat and himself with it.

But in the end I did what I did, and I must live with it.

Thanks for writing.

Yours sincerely,
John le Carré

⁓

Le Carré wrote to Nick Cornwell, his fourth son, on his twenty-first birthday. He was in his final year at Cambridge University.

TO NICHOLAS CORNWELL

> *9 Gainsborough Gardens*
> *London, NW3 1BJ*
>
> 26 November 1993

My dearest Nick,

I have had this little candlestick in my workroom for the last twenty-five years, from the last years of my first marriage and all through my second till today. It acquired a corny but real symbolism for me, and in bad times I would shove a candle into it & light it as some kind of affirmation of belief in myself, my talent, my survival. For this reason, I wish you to have it now, with my love, as an antidote to occasional despair.

I hope it will remind you that you are a good man when you need reminding; and your own man and noone else's; and that you have one life only, and no candle ever got longer; and that you have a great spirit, and a lot to do.

With all my love,
David

Nick Cornwell, writing as Nick Harkaway, published his first novel, The Gone Away World, *in 2008. He edited le Carré's novel* Silverview, *published after le Carré's death, in 2021.*

∽

In 1994 a cartoon by Jeff Danziger in the Christian Science Monitor *showed le Carré raising his arms heavenward in grateful thanks when CIA officer Aldrich Ames was exposed as a Russian spy. Le Carré kept it framed on his wall.*

TO JEFF DANZIGER

Tregiffian
St Buryan
Penzance
Cornwall

4 March 1994

Maestro,

I am not alone in regarding you as one of the great modern cartoonists, and I greatly admire the accuracy of your work, particularly when it portrays me as slim, sensitive, over-worked and God-fearing.

However, genius has its price, and I am therefore forcing upon you one of the five novels I have written which have nothing whatever to do with the Cold War, and have not done too badly. The others are A MURDER OF QUALITY, THE NAIVE AND SENTIMENTAL LOVER, A SMALL TOWN IN GERMANY and THE LITTLE DRUMMER GIRL

I don't mean that I didn't enjoy your cartoon, and I don't mean I can't take the heat. But as an artist you will appreciate that it's a little weird, when one is at the very best time in one's life, to be reading one's creative obituary.

Many congratulations on your splendid work, thank you for including me in it, and I wish you all good things for a continued and triumphant career.

Yours sincerely,
John le Carré

Mr. John Le Carré rescued from writer's block

TO ERIC ABRAHAM[17]

Tregiffian
St Buryan
Penzance
Cornwall

29 March 1994

Dear Eric,

[. . .]

I greatly look forward to seeing the film, and if I possibly can I will come to the opening, wherever it is. I think of you a great deal as the preparations for Sydney Pollack's version of THE NIGHT MANAGER lumber along. Bob Towne[18] is scripting, and against all expectations, appears to be working moderately fast, and not wandering off on other crazed projects of his own. Pollack still seems unable to decide whether to do another film before ours, but as the weeks slip by I suspect he will reconcile himself to sitting out the writing time and going straight to THE NIGHT MANAGER. But I already begin to feel the terrible Hollywooden hand settling on the project. Everything from the casting discussions onwards is becoming predictable and a little depressing. But perhaps that's just me. What I do believe is that you and I might have a serious chance to make a non-American film with the next book, which, incidentally, contains no American characters, and would not, I suspect, appeal naturally to the Hollywegians.

I have not yet managed to read the Ogonyok[19] piece and the other material you have sent me, but I will.

---

17. *The Life and Extraordinary Adventures of Private Ivan Chonkin*, produced by Eric Abraham, had its London preview in October 1994.

18. Screenwriter of *Chinatown* and a Hollywood legend.

19. Until recently, a popular weekly Russian magazine. It serialised *The Russia House*.

Jane and I will remain down here pretty much all this year, except for a holiday in Northern Spain in May, and a projected trip that I must make to the Caucasus before the winter snows.

Thanks again for thinking of us.

As ever,
David

～

Le Carré set out to entertain Margetson after he was hospitalised with a subdural haematoma.

TO SIR JOHN MARGETSON

By fax

Cornwall

9 April 1994

TO THE ADMINISTRATION OFFICE,
ADDENBROOKES HOSPITAL, CAMBRIDGE

Dear Madam/Sir,
Please would you very kindly pass the following fax to my close friend Sir John Margetson, an in-patient at your hospital.

Many thanks, and may you win on the Grand National.

Yours sincerely,
David Cornwell

FOR SIR JOHN MARGETSON (in-patient)

My dear John,

We were extremely sorry to hear your news, but at once delighted again that you had been in the hands of such a splendid surgeon, and that by all accounts you are making a sterling recovery. I'd love to come and see you, either in Cambridge or Ipswich, and will discuss best times and places with Miranda, who called Jane last night.

We have been stuck down here all winter, and stuck in most senses: huge storms, on and on, rain, running fog, then huge storms again. I don't think we've seen a decent spell of warm sun since June. The result is, I've written ¾ of a very muddy, fog-laden book, very introverted and strange, but I'm rather pleased with it, at least so far. The last 100 pages play in the Central Caucasus mountains, where I hope to go this summer, under the aegis of the Ingush, who are on edgy terms with the Osetians, who are on edgy terms with the Chechen, who hate the Georgians, the Abkhazians, the Azerbaijanis and, one suspects, themselves. Apparently the airport is <u>always</u> in someone's hands, but if you go by train you risk having your earrings torn off by bearded men with carbines.

The moral: take an absolute <u>minimum</u> of jewelry.

[. . .]

We go to London a week on Monday, but I would come up earlier to visit you in the nick: I'll talk to Miranda and for safety's sake send her this letter also, after I've faxed it.

Timo didn't get a staff job with the Obs, but a fail-wait, & he continues writing for them hard. Read Clare's piece in the Grauniad on Rome – very impressive. Steve is oiling round Hollywood trying to get his movie together, & seems to be ahead. Simon has bought a <u>huge</u> house in Primrose Hill, Victorian semi with an 80' back garden, 20' front, and so much space they'll have to have quads. I'm delighted. At present they're in the chalet having a spring ski.

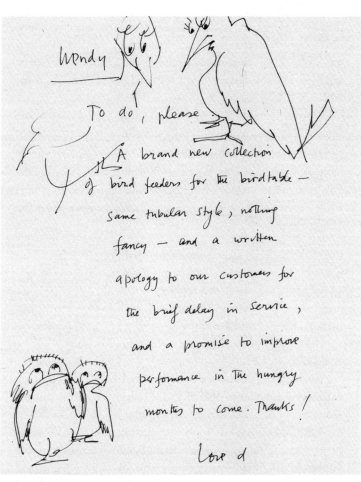

Wendy

To do, please:

A brand new collection of bird feeders for the bird table — same tubular style, nothing fancy — and a written apology to our customers for the brief delay in service, and a promise to improve performance in the hungry months to come. Thanks!

Love d

An undated note to Wendy Le Grice, housekeeper and Tregiffian's first archivist, on keeping the birds fed.

Dear John, pay close attention to your recovery, live forever, your friends insist on it, and let's meet soon.

The wind is howling in my workroom windows again, black cloud, northern menace, bloody cold. Spring is upon us.

Love,
David

~

Martina Wiegandt, then a student at the Technical University Berlin, wrote to le Carré noting some striking inconsistencies in The Spy Who Came in from the Cold: *in the dates of Leamas's career, that Mundt 'doesn't seem to age', and in Mundt's and Fielder's ranks. Jane marked the letter with a note to their secretary: 'pl. bring forward when David is feeling strong!'*

TO MARTINA WIEGANDT

Tregiffian
St Buryan
Penzance
Cornwall

15 April 1994

Dear Ms Wiegandt,

I was charmed by your letter of 9th March which reached me this week, pointing out some – but not all – of the inconsistencies in <u>The Spy Who Came in from the Cold</u>. The book, as you rightly perceive, is riddled with inaccuracies. It was written mostly in the small hours of the morning in the few weeks after I had made my first experience of the Berlin Wall. The book was always a rough instrument and underwent none of the fine editorial tuning to which I and my publishers have subjected my more recent work.

Like many novelists, I am far more interested in plausibility than in authenticity, and in <u>The Spy</u> you have a fine example of me in my primitive state!

It was always open to me to correct the inaccuracies and fix the story in later editions. But I came to the conclusion that this was unfair on the reader, and in an odd way unfair upon myself. And it amuses me very much that, out of the many millions of people who have now read the book, only a distinguished handful – of whom you are one – have discovered the shifting grounds on which it was built.

It is no defence, and I wish for none, to remind you that much greater novels than mine do not bear the test of factual analysis. Dickens, to my delight, falls over himself at the end of his novels in an effort to collect the threads that he has woven into the earliest chapters. Scott Fitzgerald mired himself in plots he could not handle, and I watch him with collegial sympathy trying to fight his way out.

And don't forget to marvel, next time you watch that great Hollywood costume epic, when the errant jeep moves slowly across the background.

I thank you again for writing but as the Germans say, you are running through open doors. I wish you great success with your studies.

Yours sincerely,
John le Carré

The 'distinguished few' who spotted errors in the novel also included an S. L. Hourmouzios, who wrote in January 1965 to point out two 'silly mistakes': that Alec Leamas flew to The Hague, and took a tube from Ludgate Hill, when neither airport nor station existed.

≈

*The English military historian and journalist John Keegan inter-
viewed le Carré for a cover article in the* Telegraph *magazine in June
1993. 'I am a card carrying le Carré devotee, who knows some of the
books almost by heart,' he wrote to Jane. Le Carré wrote afterwards
proposing – as he did to the former* Telegraph *literary editor Nicholas
Shakespeare – 'that we will henceforth not write about one another,
and simply enjoy one another's company instead?'*

TO JOHN KEEGAN

As from: Tregiffian
St Buryan
Penzance
Cornwall

28 April 1994

Dear John,

Thanks for your lovely cards. I have always dreamed of
writing a two-hander for the stage, just called Elliott, docu-
menting the interviews he had with Philby right up to P's
confession. E says they ran over 13 years, frequently ended
with both men inert with drink and E having to load P into
a taxi & pre-pay the fare, usually with an extra £5 in case P
was incontinent during the journey! But can you imagine that
Wodehousian character – son of Claud, Provost of Eton, pillar
of the climbing-scholar establishment – matched against the
appallingly devious son of St John Philby, one of the biggest
shits of the 20th century?[20]

One day, says an old song probably, I'll have a go at it. It's
beautiful to chart because E was convinced for <u>years</u> that P was
innocent; in that time P concealed from E his Communism, his

---

20. Le Carré was fascinated when Nicholas Elliott, the MI6 veteran and 'Philby's
most loyal friend, confident and devoted brother-in-arms', poured out the story of
Philby's betrayal and flight over several evenings in le Carré's Hampstead home. It
became a chapter of *The Pigeon Tunnel*.

espionage activities, his secret homosexuality <u>and</u> the depth of his momentous relationship with Litzi Friedmann. E thought he'd just slipped somewhere & had something to get off his chest.

But here's a nice sub-plot. <u>E</u> played <u>me</u> for years, telling me I was the one he wanted to write the story, etc., and I got quite close to downing tools & doing a deal with him because the deal (& the notoriety) were what he wanted. Now I find that half the novelists/playwrights in London were kept on similar strings, each independently of the other, each believing that they had sole access to the old boy. He was quite as much as a poseur, in his way, as Philby – just a lot nicer!

Good to hear from you. I am hull down in what I hope is a good novel – we're going to sneak 2 weeks in Spain, then I'll come back & finish it.

Best to you both –
David

~

The Hamburg-born Horst Gerkens, long a US resident, wrote about his own attempts at espionage fiction and said that 'my own Germanness sometimes severely hampers my writing, even my reading.'

TO HORST GERKENS

Tregiffian
St Buryan
Penzance
Cornwall

29 April 1994

Dear Mr Gerkens,

[. . .]

You asked me for a comment, but I think what you really want is encouragement. I think a combination of the German and English mentality, which seems to be something we share, can be a wonderful thing for someone writing in either language. I would suggest that if you are uncertain which to choose, you should choose English, since its variety is vastly greater than that of German, and it is not beset by what Goethe calls the rats tails of prepositions and word-order.

If you wish for inspiration, turn, perhaps, to Joseph Conrad, who never spoke English properly, whose mother tongues were Polish and German, and yet he endowed the written English language with a majesty it didn't quite achieve before. And finally, do remember what Dickens said about storytelling: it is facts, and facts. Facts are all they want. He didn't mean that we should all write like Clancy, but he meant we should stick to the <u>Sache</u>.[21]

Best wishes,
Yours sincerely,
John le Carré

~

Mark Wilcocks, aged eleven, was given Tinker Tailor Soldier Spy *for Christmas. He wrote: 'I wanted to ask you where you got your inspiration, ideas and information from to write your books; if you like reading and when did you start writing books?' He added a P.S.: 'Please could you reply.'*

---

21. Thing, point, subject.

TO MARK WILCOCKS

Tregiffian
St Buryan
Penzance
Cornwall

1 July 1994

Dear Mark,
Thank you for your letter.

[...]

If I were to answer all your questions I would never get down to writing any more books. I don't think anybody can say where they get inspiration from, no more than a musician can tell you where he gets his musical ear from, or an athlete his physical skills. We have the gift, and the trick is to work on it and respect it and stretch it and make it do its best work for us. I started writing very early and wrote poetry at school which now embarrasses me, but at the time I thought was the best poetry in the world. I didn't start writing books until I was twenty-nine, after I had done a lot of other things. The only advice I give to my sons when they tell me they want to write is to leave it as late as they decently can, so that they have experience of other jobs and relationships, good and bad, before they start trying to describe human characters and situations. TINKER TAILOR, as you will have found, was an enormously complicated artefact at one level, but what makes it work, if it does, is the human variety and the bitter compassion of George Smiley. In the end, it is character that drives plot.

It was kind of you to write. I shall not write to you again, but I wish you luck if you ever take up writing.

Yours sincerely,
John le Carré

OUR GAME:
WAR IN THE CAUCASUS,
AND A BOOK JACKET

I too keep hearing rumours of great unrest in the air in the North Caucasus and the prospect of bad things in the autumn. We shall see.

– to Vladimir Stabnikov, who had helped him with research on *Our Game*, on 3 August 1994

Le Carré made his first research trip to Moscow for *Our Game* in 1993. In 1994 he cancelled a planned visit to Russia and the Caucasus to avoid interrupting his work on the novel; he then failed to get to Ingushetia itself before it was published. Later le Carré called *Our Game* a 'bum novel',[1] but the outbreak of war in Chechnya in December 1994 made its publication seem prophetic.

1. Letter to Tony Cornwell, 15 May 2007.

Pusya, or Ruslan, Jopua, was an Abkhazian sportsman and wealthy businessman, a wrestler with a physique likened to that of Dima in Our Kind of Traitor.

TO PUSYA JOPUA

By fax

Cornwall

15 November 1993

PRIVATE & CONFIDENTIAL

Dear Pusya,

I was extremely touched by your beautiful letter. Nick and I so much enjoyed your company on our trip, and greatly wished we could have had the privilege of getting to know you a little better. If Nick was sometimes flippant or inattentive, I think that was because his batteries sometimes over-charged, and he needed to behave like a boy again. Both of us returned to England so full of memories and impressions that it took us weeks to come to terms with them. We learned so much that it was like looking at the map of one's experience for the first time, and identifying the unexplored places.

Much of what you had to tell, and much of what you represented, about the Abkhazian struggle, was new to me, and of course, we read and followed the news with great absorption. I have been looking, for the purposes of my present novel, for a struggle in the Caucasus that would appeal to the romantic desperation of a British man who in a sense has been exhausted by the causes of the West. I want him to make a quixotic gesture on behalf of a people he barely knows, in the interest of some absolute notion of justice. The Abkhazian cause struck me as suitable, but ironically it's a lot less suitable now that it's been, at least partly, won. My mind, therefore, turns a little in the direction of the Ingush, whose cause seems to me to be just and unwinnable. Or is this an unfair description?

Sometime in the spring I want to come to the Caucasus and if I knew by then which of the various ethnic minorities would most attract my character, and would best impress my reader with the justice of their cause, and with the injustices done against them, this would be an immense advantage.

I find it very hard to speak of books not yet written, but if you think of a much compromised and dissolute Englishman looking for virtue – let's say a figure like Barley in THE RUSSIA HOUSE – and imagine him deciding to throw his life away for a just but lost cause, you have the picture.

Dear Pusya, I write you this in some confidence, because I have absolute trust in your discretion. I get a little embarrassed sometimes when I have put out an enquiry of this sort, but read of my work in progress in the newspaper! I am sure Volodya [Stabnikov] would translate this for you, and then we would have no fear of compromise. Therefore I am faxing this letter to him in English, and asking him to pass it on to you in Russian.

Does the coat still fit? Are the shadows leaving your face now that your cause has been recognised? Will the fighting soon stop? Nick was also thrilled by your letter, a copy of which I sent to him in Cambridge. He asks me to send you his best greetings, and his thanks for so many happy memories.

Yours sincerely,
David Cornwell

∾

TO PROFESSOR GEORGE HEWITT

Tregiffian
St Buryan
Penzance
Cornwall

4 May 1994

Dear Professor,

Our mutual friend Pusya Jopua gave me your name, and I am taking the liberty of writing to ask whether you could possibly spare me an hour of your time, perhaps over lunch, either in Doncaster or London. I am a novelist, and write under the name of John le Carré. I am presently working on a novel which touches upon the Ossetian–Ingushi conflict, and speculates about whether it might lead to open warfare. The book ends in the Caucasus, where I have yet to go, but so has my leading character, so we shall both arrive as novices! I set great store by catching the right note when I plunge into these things, and I would be extremely grateful for the opportunity to sit at your feet.

I am sending this letter to both your addresses – and by fax to Doncaster.

All good wishes,
David Cornwell

~

A prelude to le Carré cancelling his planned research trip to the Caucasus for Our Game.

TO VLADIMIR STABNIKOV

Tregiffian
St Buryan
Penzance
Cornwall

11 July 1994

Dear Vladimir,

Decisions, decisions. I spent the weekend revising my writing plans. I have decided that I cannot continue with the book for a month and then interrupt the flow in order to fit in the Russian trip. And that my best course must be to go right through to the end, even if I am short of research material, and complete the book in terms of resolving the plot and characters, even if I have to go back over the last hundred odd pages and alter them on the strength of subsequent research.

What I am saying, therefore, is really this: I don't wish to appoint another date until I have completed the first draft of the novel. If I am lucky and the book continues to the end at a good speed, this could still mean the same sort of dates that we have been discussing. But it could also mean that I would not be coming to Russia for six or eight weeks, or even more. I know that we may then run into difficulties with the seasons in the North Caucasus, since by October the weather is likely to be bad, and travel more difficult. But I still think that the decision I have taken must be the right one, even if I end up going to the Caucasus in the spring, and re-writing the last hundred pages in proof.

So while I would like to keep the dialogue with Kostoev[2] going, and to collect images and information about Ingushetia, I do not wish to attach myself to any firm dates at this stage. I will, of course, keep in close touch with you in the meantime.

All good wishes, and love to you all.
David

∾

2. Issa Kostoev, the Ingush police officer who, as head of Russia's Department of Crimes of Special Importance, cracked the case of serial killer Andrei Chikatilo, executed for the mutilation and murder of fifty-six women and children. He had offered to escort le Carré to Ingushetia, as related in *The Pigeon Tunnel*.

TO MARIANNE SCHINDLER, SWITZERLAND

Tregiffian
St Buryan
Penzance
Cornwall

11 July 1994

Dear Ms. Schindler,

Thank you for your letter of June 28th. I was touched by the point you made, but I do not see the problem quite as literally as you do. I have written much about men who are not able to relate to women, because in the male oriented world from which I draw my experience – and indeed, my upbringing – the gap you deplore is, unfortunately, all too common. So I beg you to believe me when I tell you that I share your respect for the qualities and sufferings of women, whose company and talents I indeed greatly prefer to those of men.

Yours sincerely,
John le Carré

~

The journalist Edward Behr wrote to le Carré about a convoluted article in the New York Times *magazine by Ron Rosenbaum, suggesting that on his deathbed Graham Greene was wrestling with the question of whether Kim Philby had actually been a Western agent.*

TO EDWARD BEHR

By fax

Cornwall

1 August 1994

Dear Ed,

Thanks for your fax. It would be madness for me to let you anywhere near me at the moment. I am in the last throes of a very long and intricate novel. I also have no time to get into a pissing-match about the perfectly ludicrous article in the New York Times Magazine about Philby, which was faxed to me from elsewhere. Unattributably, it is simply not possible that any intelligence service, let alone the British one during that shaming period of its existence, could take upon itself the persistent public humiliation of a high profile triple-agent operation which, at the public relations level alone, practically destroyed it. The article was otherwise so crowded with inaccuracies (one of them relating to the origin of one of my characters, and another, if I am correct, referring to Dancy as the chief of SIS[3]) that I for one would not know how to address it without cutting it to pieces.

Both Philby and Blake effectively crippled SIS liaison and field operations at the middle levels for years and years. No secret service is strong enough to break its own rice bowl like this, and maintain its clout in the corridors of power. What we saw was what we got: a nasty little establishment traitor with a revolting father, a fake stammer and an anguished sexuality who spent his life getting his own back on the England that made him.

But that's all for your own deep background, and you know it anyway. Meanwhile, I will get back to my moutons and wish

3. The dapper Claude Dansey, 'Colonel Z', assistant chief of SIS in the Second World War, set up the Z Organisation to develop intelligence sources in Italy and Germany.

you luck. We would love to see you down here, but not until this war is won!

As ever,
David

[*handwritten addition to typed letter*]
P.S. And for mother's sake – if it <u>was</u> a triple, what was the dividend?

~

Susan D. Anderson is History Curator and Program Manager at the California African American Museum in Los Angeles, and a member of the editorial board of the California History *journal. She first wrote to John le Carré in September 1993, and he sent a brief typed reply, but was quickly moved by her responses to a less formal tone. Amid the Cornish storms in December 1993, he wrote: 'Everyone's dying . . . If you're 62, as I am, that happens a bit more often . . . I can't be morbid about anything until the 4am screams begin, and we've all had them since 30 . . . And the art of it all is to go on being fine for as long as you can.' In February 1994 a Rubicon was crossed. He had been to Los Angeles on a flying visit but not contacted her: 'I fretted and thought I might embarrass you . . . maybe writing is what we like better, and six other reasons.' Having then no knowledge of her physical appearance – 'whether you are sixty or thirty or long or short or white or black' – he invited her to write to him through John Miller and Michael Truscott, noting in a postscript: 'yours was a <u>very</u> sexy letter.' More exchanges followed: 'I kiss your eyelids, and your erudition, and I send you the rush of the Atlantic storm on the windows of my work room, and I relish you as the most beautiful woman in the world.' The correspondence continued until the beginning of 1997.*

to SUSAN D. ANDERSON

Tregiffian
St Buryan
Penzance
Cornwall

[Postmark] 24 August 1994

Darling,

Got your marvellous, long, funny, interesting letter, and I love you shedding the shoe on the way up to the restaurant, & if anyone had been even half a man they'd have filled it with champagne for you and – I'm sorry it's a rough time for you, and a muddled one, but be assured it is here too – but we'll prevail.

Here's the state of play this end. When they barred me I sat down with all the material I cd assemble, and a young Chechen guy from St Anthony's, Oxford who came & stayed here, & I dug out all my own notes on Khirgizi where I went in '87 & Moscow where I was last summer, & the Palestinians when I stayed in S. Lebanon, & I faked the last 100 pp of the book – i.e., faked the wallpaper – & to my huge pleasure resolved the internal, real novel very well. I went to Paris & saw some Ingush there also, & watched endless videos of the region and, to be honest, I don't think I can much improve on what I've done – but that's not the point at all. So I'm now arranging to make, in effect, an unheralded entry via Turkey & Grozniy (which being Chechnya is independent of Russian restrictions, being notionally a separate country for however long it takes for Yeltsin to loose his temper & march in) – and for this I'll take a Chechen–Ingush interpreter and <u>not</u> a Russian (taking a Russian is about as helpful as taking a member of the Knesset to the occupied territories). I can't set this up before October which makes me doubly, trebly grateful for your letter, and your bigness of spirit, and the generosity with which you write – my guess is that we'll still make it this year somehow somewhere, but I have you, & you have me, and the wonder of you is, you let me breathe & write and fly first, and you're still you afterwards, & thanks. Everyone sent me the NYT piece which was really unspeakable nonsense: pure fantasy, as you say, shamefully uninformed on points of fact, & ludicrous as speculation. There is not an Int. Service in the world that is strong enough & cool enough to appear to be in pieces on the floor when it isn't. The hateful barons of the business wd fall on their swords rather than be seen as incompetents. And even if such an amazing decision were taken – what, please, was the dividend? Names & addresses of his minders in Moscow? Give me, as my American granddaughter has it, a break. [. . .] As to the games that Graham Greene played, knowing Graham they were as perverse & feeble as his awful practical jokes, exercises in self dramatisation rather than spying. The CIA, by the way, has been amusing itself by sniping at me in a completely barmy way in its ('privately' circulated) house magazine. A couple of months back a stuffy 'appraisal' of my work & now a vitriolic attack on my ignorance (which, they're right, is total) of signals interception! Isn't it beautiful? These really are the guys who wd treat 'Lady Chatterley's Lover' as a handbook on employer-staff relationships, or how to handle your gamekeeper . . .

On which subject, oh rose-open one, I expect you to be fully & effectively dressed when we meet, jewels, your longest fingernails & at least a ruby in your naval, which I shall remove with my teeth.

Thank you, thank you, for the wonderful onward and upward letter; I haven't thanked you either for being my secret sharer through the last half of the book, which in all but the final impulse is finished and, dare I say it, wonderful. Or it seems so still, & today, even today, I shall send it to my US, UK & European agents &, after 10 days or so, the mainstream publishers. But I won't send you a copy too early – I only want you ever to see one version, so you'll have it a little later.

Last night I lay with you at last in the dark, and felt safe, & we talked ourselves to sleep. If your 1st chapter doesn't read right, you've either read it too often, or it's self conscious because you wrote it without the benefit of the rest. But probably it's the first; and if it's the second, probably your agent or publisher sh<u>d</u> tell you. Shall I ever get to read it?

This is a morning letter. I actually have no more writing to do on the novel till I have broken the code & got myself in & out of the Caucasus. I'll keep writing to you, & tell you when it will be unless it happens at v. short notice. Sorry about the long silence but I just hurled myself at the book in anger, & now I've got a twitch in my right eyelid, I feel as fat as a puppy from too little walking, I'm <u>sure</u> I'm impotent, but I suspect you can repair that, and I feel very protective of you at this minute, & just want to give you a great big hug.

D.

~

After Knopf bought Our Game, *le Carré set to work rewriting the central character, Tim Cranmer.*

TO SONNY MEHTA

By fax

Cornwall

19 September 1994

Dear Sonny,
Lynn tells me you are likely to be tied up today, but I'll try and call you anyway, just to say hullo.

I'm delighted by the deal and hope you are. It seems sane and fair. So hooray, and let's enjoy it. I'm about to launch on a pretty extensive re-write, the goals of which are so far mainly of my own choosing, but do definitely embrace your own point that – if I have you right – we need more <u>heart</u> from Tim, <u>more information about his own personal life</u>, and more <u>to like about him</u>, in the early pages, than is presently on offer. I have no difficulty with that. Along the way I have a mass of stuff of my own to add to that – as Tim is 'tenderised' and shaping, that will help Emma along too. I have a wad of stuff from my Caucasus expert, my wine maker, and so forth. I am considering giving Tim some more stuff in Moscow.

So what I am asking – as I am asking also of Hodders – is that you get me your thoughts as best you can by fax, as soon as you can, so that I can throw everything into the pot and get to work. Don't worry too much about suggesting remedies at this stage, though if any occur to you they're welcome – just give me the diagnoses and let me anguish over them, because now is often the time when I do my best work.

There's no point in my rabbiting on about what more I intend to do – best you look at it when it's done, and see how it fits. I'll call you about 10am today your time.

Best,
David

~

In 1992 Gottlieb, now in his sixties, returned as an editor at Knopf and 'remarried' with le Carré for The Night Manager. *He 'had a hand' in* Our Game, *with a late look at* The Tailor of Panama, *according to his memoir* Avid Reader. *Le Carré appears to dispense with Gottlieb's services for a second time in this letter. However, in 1999 he wrote to Frances Gertler of* The Good Book Guide *that: 'It is true that a large part of my editing has been done in the United States where for more than twenty years I had the privilege of being edited by the greatest of them all, Robert Gottlieb.'*

TO BOB GOTTLIEB

By fax

Cornwall

22 September 1994

Dear Bob,

I don't know whether word has reached you, but I have finished the first version of a new novel, & Sonny likes it, & has bought it. He doesn't like the title, which was The Passion of his Time. Till now, it has no other name.

And of course the question immediately arose of who should edit it, and although I tried to make this Sonny's decision rather than mine, I will not insult you by pretending that it wasn't mine in the end, and that the decision wasn't extremely painful to me, or taken after long reflection and thinking aloud with Jane.

In the end, two factors weighed heaviest. The first was quite simply our mutual familiarity, which I began to feel last time round was having a soporiphic effect on my performance. It was as if we both know I cd only jump a certain height or run at a certain speed. I began to want something a little more knockabout & challenging, even if, at first glance, I couldn't agree with all of it. And since Sonny already had a clear view of what he wanted done to the book, that seemed an interesting way to go.

The second factor is probably inescapable from the first: I felt in some way outside my own publishing house & cut off from its voice and energy. It was like being edited in secret somehow, rather than out in the open. After all, for a couple of years I flog away with no consultation with anyone except Jane, and by the end of them I really come to look forward to some shortlived institutional correction. But I didn't have it, or didn't feel I had it; I seemed to be in a bit of a no man's land, and not even sure that what I was doing had the backing of those who were taking the publishing decisions.

None of this is easy to say, & I'm sure it's no easier to read, and I've no doubt there are going to be times when I miss your wisdom and support enormously. But I suppose the truth is that, as we get older, the affirmation of younger people becomes some sort of reassurance that we aren't dancing to music that nobody else can hear, which is what I fear the most. Of the rest – of my fondness for you and my profound gratitude for all your skills and input and support – well, you know all that, but I'll say it again anyway.

As ever,
David

~

TO JOHN CALLEY

By fax

Cornwall

30 September 1994

Dear John,
Just to tell you I have nearly completed my usual mammoth rewrite. We also have a new title, which all the publishers like very much. It is OUR GAME. There is also now a reference inside the text to the obscure form of football played by Winchester schoolboys, which is known in the jargon as 'Our Game'.

Here for another week.
All love,
David

~

26. Le Carré with Nicholas, Jane and Stephen Cornwell in the kitchen of their Cornwall home. 1974.

27. Le Carré and Alec Guinness, likely on Hampstead Heath, where critical scenes of *Smiley's People* played out. 'If we were to cry for the moon, we would cry for Guinness as Smiley.'

28. Yvette Pierpaoli, 'who lived and died giving a damn,' according to her dedication in *The Constant Gardener*.

29. Le Carré with David Greenway on Corfu, where their two families holidayed together in the 1970s. Greenway covered the Vietnam War for *Time* magazine and the *Washington Post* from 1967 to 1975. He helped le Carré navigate South-East Asia for *The Honourable Schoolboy* and the Middle East for *The Little Drummer Girl*.

30. Le Carré and Al Alvarez. 'The moment Al and I got within six feet of each other, we started laughing.'

31. Le Carré with Mach, his whippet, on Hampstead Heath – where Smiley retrieves a vital clue to Vladimir's murder on a tree-lined avenue.

32. Charlotte Cornwell when she was working with the Royal Shakespeare Company, soon after the second series of *Rock Follies* in 1977; her roles included Joan la Pucelle in *Henry VI* and Rosalind in *As You Like It*.

33. Le Carré and Vladimir Stabnikov, translator and le Carré's official host from the Writers' Union on his first visit to the Soviet Union in 1987. 'A real friendship formed,' le Carré wrote.

34. Le Carré and Jane with Anatoly Adamishin and his wife, when they visited Tregiffian and were treated to a day at the races.

36. Le Carré on an anti-war march with writer and campaigner Anthony Barnett in 2003. In interviews for *Our Game*, le Carré called for Tony Blair's resignation, and recognition that the UK had been led to war on misleading intelligence confected in Downing Street.

35. Sonny Mehta, editor-in-chief at Alfred A. Knopf, le Carré's American publisher for thirty years.

37. Le Carré with Ralph Fiennes, who starred as Justin in Fernando Meirelles's film of *The Constant Gardener*. 'Nothing in my life has compared with the movie, and its aftermath,' le Carré wrote in 2006.

38. Le Carré on the set of the 2014 film of *A Most Wanted Man* with Philip Seymour Hoffman; le Carré sported a beard for his cameo role in a seedy bar.

39. Le Carré and the cast of the 2011 film of *Tinker Tailor Soldier Spy*: Roger Lloyd-Pack, John Hurt, Benedict Cumberbatch, Colin Firth, Gary Oldman and director Tomas Alfredson.

40. Le Carré and the journalist and author Ben Macintyre. Le Carré gave Macintyre a glowing endorsement for his first book on an espionage theme, *Agent Zigzag*, and directly inspired the writing of *A Spy Among Friends*, three books later.

41. August Hanning, Germany's former head of both foreign and domestic intelligence, with Tim Garton-Ash, le Carré and Prince Albrecht Ernst of Oettingen-Spielberg.

42. Simon Cornwell, left, co-founder of the Ink Factory production company, with le Carré and *The Night Manager*'s cast, including Hugh Laurie, Tom Hollander, director Susanne Bier, Tom Hiddleston and Elizabeth Debicki.

43. Le Carré with sons Simon and Stephen Cornwell, film producers; Nicholas Cornwell, novelist; and Tim Cornwell, arts journalist.

44. Le Carré with Yassin Musharbash – a journalist with the German weekly *Die Zeit* and an expert in jihadist ideologies and terrorism – helped le Carré fine-tune characters in *A Most Wanted Man*.

45. Le Carré and his agent Jonny Geller, CEO of Curtis Brown, at le Carré's birthday and launch party in London, 2019. 'We know each other pretty well by now, and I trust your advice,' he wrote.

46. On an anti-Brexit march in 2019, against 'an act of economic suicide mounted by charlatans'.

47. Draped in the Irish flag for his birthday, 19 October 2020, with Jane, celebrating his Irish citizenship.

Yvette Pierpaoli (1938–1999) was an aid worker, refugee activist and firebrand, and a family friend. There was a considerable body of correspondence between le Carré and Pierpaoli, almost all of which is lost (see p. xxi). Le Carré supported and deeply respected her charity work; if she was also, as seems quite likely, one of his lovers, it was an affair in a different mode. Her picture still hangs on the wall in Jane Cornwell's study.

TO YVETTE PIERPAOLI

By fax

Cornwall

19 December 1994

Dearest Yvette,

To wish you all a very, very happy Christmas and '95. Will you all be together? At the moment we are 2. Then Nick comes, then Charlotte with her daughter. Then Charlotte's mother. We had hoped that we would have our indoor swimming pool by now but it has no roof & no water and the crane to lift the roof into position is stuck in a ditch, blocking entry & exit from Tregiffian. So no pool.

Yesterday I received an invitation from Mort Abramovitz[4] asking me to join a Carnegie trust committee that will solve the problems of the world. I was so pleased to hear that someone had finally decided to do this, for I had observed that certain things were not as they should be. But I think you have done more for the world than all the wise committees put together.

---

4. Morton Abramowitz (b. 1933) was head of the oldest civilian intelligence agency in the US – the small but formidable Bureau of Intelligence and Research – from 1985 to 1989, then US ambassador to Turkey until 1991, when he retired and became president of the Carnegie Endowment for International Peace until 1997.

So I hope the world will be good to you over Christmas and make you all happy with one another, as you deserve.

With very much love –
David

~

The US jacket design for Our Game *became a tussle between the ever vigilant le Carré and Sonny Mehta, the head of the country's biggest publishing house – even as the growing tension in Chechnya, leading to open conflict in December, grimly underlined the timeliness of the book. The design of a proposed watchtower on the cover was a sticking point. 'Too much an obelisk. Too Egyptian. Windows?' le Carré scribbled on a note from Mehta, and tracked down some illustrations of watchtowers which he sent. Later, two faxes winged their way to the president and editor-in-chief of Alfred A. Knopf on one day, one handwritten, the second typed.*

TO SONNY MEHTA

By fax

21 November 1994

Dear Sonny,
I put the design up on the wall and have been living with it these past few hours, and I have to say that, pistol or whatever, it really doesn't work for me at all. At a distance, it's obscurely phallic and rather gloomy. Close to, it's a mystery that doesn't resolve itself. What do you think? Please let's talk.

Best,
David

By fax

21 November 1994

Dear Sonny,

I was disconcerted to receive the reworked versions of the cover design because I thought I had told you that, ingenious as the design is, I really don't like guns on the jacket.

That said, if time and the house opinion are emphatically against me, I will live with it.

My other problem is the perennial one. Almost all the fan letters I get from America address me as leCarré written as one word – even those from publishing houses and newspapers. I know the le is a beastly little rat's tail for a design to accommodate but I wish it could somehow be separated from the Carré.

Of the three, I agree with you: the one with the full name is best.

Sorry to be a pain in the arse, but I really thought you were looking for quite a different design by now.

Yours,
David

∾

In a column on President Boris Yeltsin's decision to send armed forces to re-establish Russian rule in Chechnya, US commentator William Safire said the US understood the need for Moscow to defend its sovereignty, but should support 'an accommodation' between the Kremlin and the 'fierce, often crooked secessionist Chechens'. An opinion piece by le Carré on the crisis – published in the New York Times *as 'The Shame of the West' – ran worldwide.*

TO SONNY MEHTA

By fax

Cornwall

20 December 1994

Dear Sonny,

Thanks for sending me the Safire piece, which runs in today's Guardian. I think it's fine as it is, and I don't want to get any deeper into the politics of the novel by taking issue with him. I think my job is to tiptoe quietly from the stage and wait for the book to come out.

But it is important, I think, that the reps should understand that the North Caucasus is almost certainly going to be Boris Yeltsin's grave. And that we are very likely to watch his downfall while the book is running at its height.

If we don't communicate again before the holiday, we wish you all the best for 1995, and a great celebration.

Best,
David

Boris Yeltsin survived as president until 1999, but his reputation in the West suffered badly from the invasion of Chechnya.

RUSSIA, CORNWALL
AND A RACEHORSE

Being my father's son at times was extraordinary. He had race horses. But because he hadn't paid the bookmakers he did not dare go to the race course. So he would give me a bunch of money and I – a boy! – would arrive at the race course and go from one bookmaker to another, betting on his horse.

– in an interview carried by South Africa's News24,
24 October 2011

When Colin McColl became the SIS chief in 1989, he felt that le Carré had become estranged from his former service, and asked Alan Judd, a former-soldier-and-diplomat-turned-novelist, to write to him. Le Carré responded warmly to Judd, who had written about his own encounter with Graham Greene; le Carré eventually went to meet the heads of MI6 and give a speech to the MI6 spouses.

In 2003, after the invasion of Iraq, his relationship with SIS cooled; le Carré maintained that Richard Dearlove, chief from 1999 to 2004, was instrumental in causing 'raw, single-source, unchecked intelligence' being passed to Tony Blair. But he continued his connections with MI5, where he visited for lunch and gave a talk.

TO ALAN JUDD[1]

> *Tregiffian*
> *St Buryan*
> *Penzance*
> *Cornwall*

> 24 June 1995

Dear Alan,

Thank you so much for the book, & yr letter. I sort of woke to your distinction later – lunch was such an event for me that I couldn't sort everything out at once! But I greatly enjoyed meeting you, & this weekend, as soon as our guests have left, I shall dive into the novel. Of course I knew of it, and knew of your reputation, but to my shame I haven't read you, & shall

---

1. The novels of the award-winning writer Alan Judd include his series on the intelligence officer Charles Thoroughgood, who rises from a junior army officer in Northern Ireland (in *A Breed of Heroes*, published in 1981) to chief of MI6 (in *The Accidental Agent* in 2019).

now repair that. I ordered the 'doorstopper'[2] from Blackwell's already, & shall surely greatly enjoy it – I read one biography of poor Ford, but didn't get the heart out of it that I wanted. How odd that you visited Graham [Greene] in the Antibes. I never did. We met in Paris & Vienna &, very briefly, in London. And of course, like most people who met him in like circumstances, I had surges of fondness for him, and surges of revulsion. Which I expect would have suited him well enough, though I never knew anyone who tended his image more carefully than Graham – enraged letters to editors at the drop of a hat, huge charm beamed on worthless hacks, backing into the limelight at every opportunity. Anthony Powell, who loathed him, told me he was the most professional 'career-novelist' he had ever known. But what's Anthony? you ask yourself.

I too hope we'll meet again. I come to London very seldom these days, but a lunch wd be 3 star Michelin, worth the journey. It's very hard to explain what it meant to me, the invitation to the office. I hadn't realised, until it happened, that it cd mean so much. Anyway, we can talk about that, and about your writing, which after a furtive peek, already fascinates me. Do you ever come this way? It's so beautiful, & we have a guest cottage where writing friends roost & work; and a heated indoor pool where they can work out!

All good wishes – & thanks again for the book –
David

~

In 1996 the Cornwells were preparing for a visit by the Russian ambassador. One of the entertainments in Cornwall was a day at the races near Launceston, in which Tinstreamer Johnny was running for the first time. Jane had bought le Carré a half share in the four-year-old horse

---

2. Judd's biography of Ford Madox Ford.

in 1995. Owning a racehorse brought wry echoes of Ronnie's days at the racetrack, when he named his horses for his children: Dato, for David and Tony, Prince Rupert for Rupert, Rose Sang for Charlotte's red hair.

TO ANATOLY ADAMISHIN, AMBASSADOR OF THE RUSSIAN FEDERATION

Tregiffian
St Buryan
Penzance
Cornwall

6 February 1996

Dear Anatoly,

I am writing with pleasure to confirm our invitation to yourself and your wife to stay with us over the weekend of 24th and 25th February. You will see from the enclosed map that we live at the end of the earth. The most pleasant way to travel here, in my opinion, is by train, as you simply get on at Paddington and go as far as the train goes, to Penzance. I don't know whether this appeals to you, or when you will be able to travel, but on the assumption that your commitments will keep you in London until Friday night, I could recommend the night sleeper to Penzance, which leaves around midnight and arrives at Penzance at half-past eight in the morning or so. We would collect you from the train. There is also a night sleeper on the Sunday, but you may prefer a day train on the Monday.

If on the other hand you are coming by car, you would have to allow a good seven hours for the journey from Kensington.

As I told you, we have a guest cottage here, situated about 300 metres inland from the main house, and fully equipped. What we normally do is suggest to our guests that they rise at their leisure and cook themselves their own breakfast. If you come by train and would like the use of a car, we have a spare small car here, which we can park at the cottage for the duration of your stay.

Now the 24th is a very important day in our lives at the moment, because on my last birthday my wife, Jane, made me a present of a young racehorse, which is taking part in its first race on that day. He is a steeplechaser, and the races at this stage in his career are all country events and very typical of the old life that is led down here. The race on the 24th takes place near the town of Bodmin, about one-and-a-half hours' drive from here. The meet starts at 12.00 noon, and we don't yet know at what time our horse will be running. There are usually some eight races between twelve and five, and our horse will run in one of them.

So there is another possibility, which is this: that you catch a Saturday morning train that will take you to Bodmin, which lies on the direct route to Penzance, and we would meet you at Bodmin and take you straight to the races. We would stay long enough to see our horse run, and drive down to the house in the early evening, in time for you to take a bath and change for dinner. We would be providing a picnic lunch at the races, and nobody down here wears any formal clothes at any time, so please feel entirely comfortable. If we go to the races, it can be bitterly cold, but you will not be strangers to that problem. Warm hats, heavy coats and boots are essential. I shall probably wear my fur hat . . .

We also have in mind to take you to St Michael's Mount, an ancient Benedictine monastery situated on an island in the bay at Penzance, and now occupied as a private house by Lord and Lady St Levan. I think the best time to do this would be Sunday morning, and I am writing to the St Levans to ask them if they will have us for a drink. There is no finer view of the area, and the house itself is extraordinary.

I will write to you with other suggestions a little nearer the time, and if you have any wishes of your own, please let us know. Please also tell us if you have any particular likes or dislikes as regards food and drink – for instance, the local lobster is wonderful if the sea is calm enough to catch them, and so is the local fish, but you may not care for them.

We greatly look forward to your visit, and to hearing how and when you will be arriving and leaving, so that we can make plans accordingly.

With all good wishes from us both, to you both.
Yours sincerely,
David Cornwell

~

In several letters to Judd, le Carré took the tone of someone reporting back to his former employers. He wrote to Judd in enigmatic terms on the same day as he wrote to the Russian ambassador.

TO ALAN JUDD

Tregiffian
St Buryan
Penzance
Cornwall

6 February 1996

Dear Alan,
I expect you will not be surprised to hear that the gentleman named in the accompanying letter has invited himself down here for the w/end of 24/25 Feb, with his wife. He wants me to call him by his first name, speaks to me already as a blood brother (we are the same age, he says) but I have never met him. His predecessor used to ring me too, and I suspect the present man's insistence is, so to speak, conferred. Incidentally, I never met his predecessor.

I don't know whether there is some other angle to this, or whether one will emerge, or whether he just wants a treat, but if there's anything I can usefully do, let me know. We are giving him the same accommodation that you had yourselves.

Best –
David

[*on a single page sent separately to Alan Judd*]
The Russian Ambassador to the Court of St James and his wife.

～

Le Carré wrote to Lord St Levan on St Michael's Mount, initially asking whether they would receive the ambassador and his wife for a drink. After Lord St Levan invited them for lunch, le Carré warned that 'past experience has taught me that Russians are terrific cancellers.'

TO ANATOLY ADAMISHIN, AMBASSADOR OF THE RUSSIAN FEDERATION

By fax

Cornwall

21 February 1996

Dear Anatoly,
Here is a provisional programme for you and Olga to look at while you ride on the train. First of all, Jane and I are quite delighted that you are coming, and we think we can offer you plenty of amusement. The household is completely informal, and nobody dresses for anything. However, I shall probably wear a suit to go to the St Levans', or a sports coat and grey flannels at least. You and Olga will have a cottage, which lies 300

metres inland from the house. The house itself stands on the cliff directly facing the Atlantic. The weather in the last couple of weeks has varied from arctic winds and ferocious sea storms to calm spring days like today. The forecast for the weekend is equally unpredictable.

Friday 23rd February

8.15pm – You arrive at Penzance Station and I will meet you. I shall have a grey Mercedes car, I am 6 feet tall, white haired and senile. I shall bring you directly to the main house, then Jane will take you up to the cottage with your luggage and install you there. There will be a small Volvo car parked there at your disposal.

Light dinner that evening with one other guest: Timothy Garton Ash, who will certainly be known to your Information Department as the most acute observer of the post-Cold War European scene.[3] His most recent book was on the role of Germany at the end of this century, and it might be worth dipping into it. Tim is here on other business, and it is understood among us all that all discussions are totally off the record.

After dinner we will return you to your cottage.

Saturday 24th February

It is my invariable practice to write for the first hours of each day, so we ask our guests to take breakfast in their cottage, and you will find everything there that you can need. You will also find newspapers on your doorstep. And of course, if you wish to explore the region, the car is at your disposal.

11.00am – We will ring you at the cottage and if you are feeling like a walk before we leave for the races, we would be delighted to accompany you.

---

3. The historian and journalist Timothy Garton Ash made several visits to Cornwall in the 1990s – 'Versailles-sur-mer', as he teasingly called it. He wrote a perceptive profile of le Carré, Ronnie Cornwell and spying for the *New Yorker* in 1999. It noted a 'tortured' sixteen-page letter le Carré wrote him on the morality of spying, for now untraceable.

12.00 noon – We depart for Bodmin to attend the races. The Secretary of the local hunt has been told privately that you are coming, and has invited me to bring you around to his tent during the meeting so that you can shake his hand and meet the Master of the Hunt. I have asked that your presence not be publicised in any other way, but it is possible that they will take you to some particular vantage point to watch the great sporting event of the weekend, namely the participation of my horse in a beginners' race.

<u>Sunday 25th February</u>
Morning free.

12.00 noon – We depart for Marazion, where at 12.30pm Lord St Levan's amphicraft will be on the beach at the slipway in front of the car park to transport us to the Mount for lunch. Also in the lunch party and waiting for the amphicraft will be Piers St Aubyn, who is Lord St Levan's brother, and Stuart Money (who learnt Russian in the army), with his wife Kay.

After lunch, we will take you back to Penzance Station in time to catch the train at 3.45pm.

I have not mentioned swimming, because the pool is always at your disposal, and we would be happy to show you how everything works and provide you with a key. Jane and I swim in the early morning as a private ritual, and we leave our guests to swim at any other time in the day.

We much look forward to seeing you on Friday.

Yours sincerely,
David

TO ALAN JUDD

Tregiffian
St Buryan
Penzance
Cornwall

27 February 1996

Dear Alan,

So they came, on Friday night, and left on Sunday afternoon. Tim Garton Ash was here for Friday dinner. On Saturday we took them to a point-to-point, dined them à quatre at home, on Sunday we lunched with Lord & Lady St Levan on St Michael's Mount. Plenty of talk between, quite a lot of booze, all very pleasant, no fuss, more fun than we expected, <u>better</u> than we expected & still a bit <u>odd</u>. Specifically, the only earnest moment was when he took me aside & asked me whether I had a solution to the Chechnya problem, & specifically what I thought of the idea of mustering a commission of outside Muslim states to address the problem of Chechen claims, as a way of buying time while tempers cooled. I replied that there were enough Muslim states and other states <u>within</u> Russia not to have to go outside the country, since I would suppose that any proposal that smacked of foreign arbitration over a 'Russian' problem would be a dead duck politically. He said it was all terribly difficult. Nobody in Moscow was doing anything, suggesting anything, it was a really prickly issue & getting steadily worse. Any proposal from himself, he said, would have to be most tactfully introduced, probably by a third party. I said, not me, I wasn't qualified, & so on. But I had a feeling he thought he might appoint me some kind of informal emissary; I just don't know.

He writes, & wants to produce more books. Apparently he published one or two already, including one work of fiction, and w<u>d</u> like to do more fiction. He talked quite a lot about Gromyko,[4] with whom he worked for 25 (!) years, he says. His

---

4. Andrei Gromyko, Soviet foreign minister, 1957 to 1985.

wife, who enthuses a great deal, is some kind of art historian. They brought a book they had 'written' together – it's all
photographs – of the ambassadorial villa in Italy. Both are privately totally dispairing about Russia, she in particular regrets
the passing of the old guard, facetiously, on the grounds that
at least in those days you knew who the crooks were. Most of
all, they share a loss of national pride which feels quite genuine & touching. In his speech at the St Levan luncheon he
urged us to support Russia as the only available counterweight
to American hegemony. As if Europe scarcely counted. It was
very old fashioned. Now and then, I had the feeling he wanted
to approach me in some other matter and either didn't dare or
changed his mind. We are showered with invitations to visit
their dacha in Kent etc., and perhaps we will, for fun. What I do
feel, immodestly, is that he has a high regard for me, and that I
somehow satisfied his expectation – met it – in a way that made
him very pleased with himself. He is <u>very</u> mischievous, quite
witty after a drink or two, and perfectly likeable thus far. I also
think he's pretty smart. Smarter than I am certainly!

Anyway, that's all I can really come up with!

Best,
David

P.S. <u>She</u> says writing would help him put up with the pain of
what's going on in Russia.

*Adamishin wrote on 25 February 1996, thanking the Cornwells for
a splendid weekend and 'genuine Penzancenian hospitality'. 'We
hope that your young horse will be lucky to win next races.'*

~

*The artist Karl Weschke and his wife, Petronilla, joined the group for
race day. While the Russian ambassador enjoyed himself in Barbour
and wellingtons, she recalled, the horse 'disgraced himself by running*

*the wrong way round the racetrack and then had to be rescued from
the road'. Tinstreamer Johnny had a habit of kicking himself at the first
fence, and developed a bronchial infection; the* Racing Post *records
that, of thirteen races, the horse once came third. 'I don't dare hope
anything about TJ,' Jane wrote to the stables in 1997. Le Carré wrote to
his Israeli friends Yuval and Judy Elizur, in 1998: 'We own a Cornish
racehorse that has not yet completed a race, let alone won one. So he
has never actually <u>seen</u> the last straight!' Three years later the bills
were running at about five hundred pounds a month.*

TO STEPHEN LONG[5]

14 December 1999

Dear Steve,

Thank you for your letter. Like you, we have been wondering
what should be done with Tinstreamer Jonny, and until your
letter came we had pretty much decided, as we thought you
had, that he was not cut out for racing, and the most important thing was to find him a good life. I believe you talked about
the possibility that he might be a good horse for eventing, but
we know that even that puts a considerable strain on the liga-
ments and tendons.

The problem is, I think that is still our view. We didn't enjoy
the feeling that we were pressing TJ into racing – however will-
ingly he went – when his physique simply didn't measure up. I
am afraid, therefore, that we have come to the conclusion that
we should not be financing his racing training, since we would
really rather find him a less hazardous and less competitive
occupation.

We quite understand that this raises serious questions about
his future, and how we resolve the financial side of it, and perhaps the best thing would be for you to have a good think after

5. Stephen Long, racehorse trainer, owner of the other half of Tinstreamer Johnny.

reading this letter, and to suggest to us the course of action you consider most appropriate. It simply doesn't seem right to us that we should be carrying the quite heavy cost of preparing him for the race course when, in our hearts, we don't feel he should be there.

We send, as ever, all good wishes and affection to you and your family for a great Christmas and new year.

With love from us both,
David & Jane

THE TAILOR OF PANAMA

I went to Panama seven or eight years ago just to write one passage for *The Night Manager*. There was a drug dealer in that book who was buying arms . . . What I saw was a Casablanca without heroes, and I thought I had to come back . . . And the whole farce of the last American colony being handed over – we colonial Brits know what that means.

– interviewed by George Plimpton for the *Paris Review*, 1996

While work on the film of *The Night Manager* 'lumbered along', le Carré began his research for *The Tailor of Panama*.

The novelist and journalist Richard Koster was to become le Carré's friend and fixer in Panama. For le Carré's first trip he offered the help of his bilingual nephew, Reyin Teijeira, who came equipped with an air-conditioned Korean Jeep and a girlfriend who was a member of the Panamanian bar. Koster said he had put an 'inexorable mobilization plan', similar to von Moltke's of August 1914, into action to secure le Carré's hotel reservation.

TO DICK KOSTER

By fax

3 April 1995

Dear Dick,

Thanks so much for the von Moltke assault! Ayscough Travel have booked me in the El Panama from 8 May–21st May, a 'superior' suite at $165 a night. I don't know whether this clashes with anything you have kindly done, but I shall try to get written confirmation out of them, and I shall passionately reconfirm myself as the day approaches, and I promise not to use you as a travel agent any more. I'll be flying Boston–Panama on the 8th, & will let you know my flight in due course. If it's any help to your nephew, my interests are as usual arcane. If an English tailor had set up a high-quality custom tailoring business for the élite of Panama & surrounding countries, where would it be sited, how would he live, where – he's married with children – what would his social life be (he aspires, and she does quite particularly, to the 'quality' of Panama) and what competitive pressures would he live under? – protection money, visa problems, work permits, etc.

That's just the beginning and of course it's topsecret. I want to make his whole life in Panama. Oh, and he's half a Catholic, half a Jew, and he was in trouble with the police before he came to Panama (I mean the UK police) and he's a pechvogel – a bad luck sort of guy always being kicked around. So who would do the kicking?

There's much more, but these are the kind of things we w<u>d</u> be exploring together, your nephew & I, treating fantasy as non-fiction & researching it on the ground, if that w<u>d</u> amuse him.

Thanks again – much look forward to seeing you –

Best,
David

~

The English Book Club of Novosibirsk was led by Helen Goldfield, an American woman who had lived in Siberia for thirty years, and who had survived the Siege of Leningrad. The club had hosted Graham Greene and devoted several sessions to his work; now they were considering the novels of John le Carré, and had dramatised several scenes from his books for English speakers at the regional library. In an earlier letter to Goldfield in 1994, le Carré observed: 'It always surprises me when I hear how willing Graham Greene was to make public appearances.'

TO HELEN GOLDFIELD

10 April 1995

Dear Helen Goldfield,

Thank you for your letter, not dated, in which you tell me of all your activities associated with my work. I am most flattered! You ask for a letter – here is a brief one.

My new novel 'Our Game' came out in America to a mixed reception, but largely a good one, though several critics found it 'politically incorrect', which I consider a compliment, and even anti-Christian, whereas I merely consider it humanist. Anyway, it attracted much argument in which I did not take part, and sold a lot of copies, in which I did! It also had the peculiar timeliness of being partly set in Ingushetia at the time of an attack by Moscow, so I was considered a great prophet, which I am not; merely lucky.

I also wrote several articles attacking Yeltsin for his invasion of Chechnya, and the West for sitting idly by and letting him do it; and I asked what we had fought the Cold War for, if not for the dignity and protection of minorities and small nations in the face of totalitarian action? After all, I pointed out, even the map is questionable. If Communism had ended while Stalin was still alive, neither Chechnya nor Ingushetia would have existed at all: he had them removed from the map. So why do we accept the maps bequeathed to us by Communist cartographers? Why refuse to contemplate the sovereignty of small nations merely because the Communists did? These provocative ideas were not at all well received by those whom they indirectly criticized, and Mr [Eduard] Shevardnadze,[1] on a visit to England, referred to the 'misleading opinions' of 'an English detective writer', in his speech at Chatham House. I found all this very pleasing, for it is occasionally nice to discover that one is heard after all! I also believe it is a most useful discussion. Why are we so scared of diversity? Are we so afraid of chaos? The chaos of great nations strikes me as far greater than the chaos of small ones. And I hate bullies.

> All good wishes for Easter –
> Yours,
> John le Carré

~

---

1. Georgian leader and the Soviet Union's last foreign minister under Mikhail Gorbachev. He spoke at Chatham House, the Royal Institute of International Affairs, on 16 February 1995.

In the spring of 1995, Fry wrote again to le Carré with 'a long and dreadful story of escape' to Germany. He had walked out of the West End show Cell Mates, *and gone to ground in Europe.*

TO STEPHEN FRY

Tregiffian
St Buryan
Penzance
Cornwall

4 May 1995

Dear Stephen,

Got back from the Bahamas yesterday. Now, if you're in the escaping business, here's what you do: you call Jim Webster, boat broker, in Fort Lauderdale, you charter a small motor yacht with crew out of Nassau, and you cruise the remote islands of the Exumas for 2 weeks at unbelievable cost, and you will have escaped as never before. You take friends if you need them, speak or don't speak to the crew, anchor in empty bays rather than marinas, & you escape all mankind. (Most of the islands are empty.) Webster's no is [. . .] and he is the soul of absolute discretion, particularly if you tell him to be. Mention my name. He loves to serve . . . The next thing about escape, speaking as sth of an artist in this field, if a failed one, is that Germany isn't, in the long run, funny enough. There may be a few laughs in Osnabrück but I never heard them. Husum, also low on laughs; Oldenburg a frost. But I do think you c̱d make a life in Munich (though you'd be too visible) or you could do worse than Wolfenbüttel, where the Herzog Albrecht Bibliothek[2] would surely give you a reader's ticket or

---

2. Actually the Herzog August Bibliothek. The research library, founded in 1572, is a treasure house of European cultural history in a building styled on the model of an Italian palazzo.

whatever, & the library is the nearest thing to heaven you'll get. The people, however, I'm not sure. But they seemed to be nice & loony. Or there's Freiburg im Breisgau – nice dotty families hidden in the hills.

Stephen, I have a pile of fatuous letters before me but they are all junk beside yours. For once in my life I feel I could even be useful. I know something about acquiring huge audiences I don't want, and about being spoken for by arseholes, and about being good at everything, and never hitting the mark. (And I detest old farts who tell me they went through it in their day.) I think you're a polymath, école Coward, with the same gravitas and the same rhythms of engagement, challenge and escape. (See Goethe.) I completely relate to your duckdive & it fascinates me that the German muse sang to you at that moment, and I am instinctively fond & protective of you and neben mir ist das Grab a chatterbox,[3] as my old Jewish agent in Zurich used to say. I escaped from Sherborne to Berne (at 16), dived into a monastery in an effort to escape marriage, escaped to the spooks, escaped the spooks to writing, nearly at times escaped writing for the ultimate escape, and now I'm 63 so who gives a fuck anyway? Five years ago I got Swiss residence because I really didn't think I could stand being English for another day, or in England. But I couldn't do without it – the barbs, the language, the laughs. I once asked [Simon] Wiesenthal why he lived in anti-Semitic Vienna. Answer: 'If you're studying the disease, you've got to live in the swamp.' So I never became a Swisser & the accountants had to un-screw the screw-up. Cornwall is my feeble substitute for exile. Finally, I have the advantage of knowing very little about you, & having nothing left to prove to myself except the grim suspicion that I'll never write my Ur-buch (though A Perfect Spy had its moments), and I'll be in Zurich at the Dolder Grand March 17th–19th or so and could meet you somewhere in Europa if you wished it:

3. 'Next to me the grave is a chatterbox' – a saying of le Carré's friend and agent Rainer Heumann, it appears, meaning 'I am more discreet than the grave.'

if you haven't lunched at the Kronenhalle in Zurich it's high time you did. I'm going to copy this letter & send it to likely places. All it says really is – with Fontaine – 'alles in allen, es ist nicht viel',[4] but let's meet somewhere & have a couple of meals if that would amuse you; and if it is not a timely suggestion, then please accept this letter as a token of my concern for you, my sense of kinship, and of course my thanks for what you say about 'Our Game'. But let's meet if it suits you. Have suitcase, will travel. Let me know here or in Zurich.

Best,
David

P.S. Fuck them all. D.

'Your letter made me laugh, bounce, and cheer,' Fry replied. In Cell Mates *Fry played the British spy George Blake – whose treachery had so scarred le Carré's MI6 training. Fry was subsequently diagnosed with bipolar disorder; amid his sensational disappearance, le Carré tried to help book him into the Dolder Hotel under an assumed name. A caricature of Fry, playing Jeeves, by Michael Cummings, was on the wall of le Carré's library at his death.*

∼

TO JANE CORNWELL

By fax

Hotel Panama

10 May 1995

---

4. 'All in all – it wasn't much.' A slight variation on the aphorism from the last line of Theodor Fontane's poem 'Summa Summarum': '*Alles in allem – es war nicht viel*' (not *alles in allen*).

Dearest O.,

Don't bother to send the stuff; I'm flooded out. Research goes frantically well – wood is visible despite trees. [Dick] Koster a prince. Many bizarre people & places, and a burgeoning plot. No doubt that the baby is conceived. I am very glad the S Times has me at One. Did it also review me with respect? I guess not, or you wd have said. So it go. Sod 'em. It rain, it glow, it rain. The hotel very suite but no one fax me except in terse phrases. No Sieglafaxes, fax all, no Stevienews,[5] where everybody? Today went West to a rice farm in which Pendel has an interest and it's in trouble. Please send me more news. How Fox?[6] How You? How Grünwegstay?[7] Much love your unfaxed One.

~

The American academic Matthew J. Bruccoli was called 'the Dean of Fitzgerald Studies' in the United States; his 1981 biography, Some Sort of Epic Grandeur: The Life of F. Scott Fitzgerald, *was said by many to be definitive, and he wrote more than fifty publications over his lifetime.[8] He edited* Conversations with John le Carré, *a collection of reprinted interviews, in 2004.*

TO MATTHEW BRUCCOLI

By fax

Cornwall

19 October 1995

---

5. i.e., from Michael Siegel, representing le Carré at the Creative Artists Agency, and le Carré's son Stephen.

6. Le Carré's nickname for his son Nicholas.

7. David Greenway's nickname was 'Grünweg', but he has no record of having been in London that spring.

8. William Grimes, *New York Times*, 6 June 2008.

Dear Mr Bruccoli,

Thank you for your letter of 9th October. Fitzgerald is the writer's ultimate writer. You know the trick, you watch him perform it, and all of a sudden you don't know how it's done any more. How did he get there from here? How does he keep the light on in the dark? Why do I know that when he never told me? How does he make a rainbow out of black and white? I go back to him when I want to be revived. Or better perhaps, reassured that words can be made to do anything in the right hands.

Best wishes,
John le Carré

(faxed – this to follow by post.)

~

TO DOUGLAS HAYWARD, TAILOR

Tregiffian
St Buryan
Penzance
Cornwall

2 February 1996

Dear Doug,
Just back from California and I've gone to ground in Cornwall. I am afraid the corduroys suffer from the same problem as the grey flannels had: they simply don't give me enough sitting space, and I think I must have expanded, because they are a bit tight around the waist, particularly when I sit. Could you kindly loosen them a bit around the waist and in the seat and around the thighs? I am asking the man who looks after our house in London to drop them in to you this afternoon or tomorrow.

My tailor flourishes wonderfully, and I will dump a whole manuscript on you in a few months. We hope to stay here until the book is finished in its first draft.

Yours sincerely,
David Cornwell

In the acknowledgements of The Tailor of Panama, *le Carré thanked 'Doug Hayward of Mount Street W, who allowed me my first misty glimpse of Harry Pendel the tailor.' He thanked 'another great tailor', Dennis Wilkinson, of L. G. Wilkinson, St George Street, who supplied le Carré with suits, cardigans, waistcoats and braces; Wilkinson inspired Pendel's love of classic cars and Mozart, and worked in counter-intelligence with the Allied occupying forces in Germany. Le Carré's description of Harry Pendel – 'unexpectedly physical . . . broad as well as tall' – was read at Doug Hayward's funeral in 2008. Hayward's roster of celebrity clients included Roger Moore and Michael Parkinson.*

≈

By the time of this 1996 letter, Pollack had spent more than two years with The Night Manager, *employing the famed screenwriter Robert Towne and then the novelist and Tufts University professor Jay Cantor to write the script. He had faxed le Carré that day to tell him he wanted to hire another writer, but also wanted Anthony Minghella to direct the film.*

TO SYDNEY POLLACK

By fax

Cornwall

13 June 1996

This is supposed
to be me &
actually it's
VERY like
me indeed ...

John le Carré

31 May '97
On a fairly
bad day in
Cornwall, about
a hundred pages into
a new novel &
doubting it.

Dear Sydney,

I simply waited for your fax and it came exactly as I expected it to, and had expected it to for the better part of two years. You will never make 'The Night Manager', and that was clear long ago. So if I have any say left, this is it: for Heaven's sake, leave the project for good, and say you are doing so, and let someone else have a go at it. Just let yourself stop, and give it up, which in reality you did long ago. And please let's never talk about it again.

Best,
David

The relationship with Sydney Pollack was one of the great unfulfilled film collaborations of le Carré's life. Seven years later, on 2 April 2003, Pollack would write to le Carré: 'I think of you often and am sorry I made you angry not getting The Night Manager *solved. I so wished, still wish, I knew how to do it.' The letter was marked only: 'File'. A month later Pollack would add, in a handwritten note: 'I still think about* The Night Manager *every day – and poke around in the ashes looking for a way to push it to the finish line.'*

∼

The correspondence with Susan Anderson was exposed at the end of 1996. The event prompted le Carré to ask himself what he most valued. This letter is undated – and indeed unsigned – but was received by Anderson on 20 December 1996.

TO SUSAN D. ANDERSON

[Postmark] *Wengen*

[n.d.]

Your letter arrived, sent on to me in Switzerland, having caused its share of embarrassment. I sat on it for three days before replying, while I was blown in different directions by its conflicting messages. Now it's the fourth day and I am no different, except that I find that my confusion matches yours at certain points. You are angry; so am I. You are brave, I'm a coward, except that you too, presumably, live a life of concessions, since you refer to <u>our</u> 'wardens'. Nevertheless, the preponderance of courage is yours; I'm the weakling, you the martyr, except that both of us are martyrs to life: we have to conform, to accept 2nd or 3rd or 4th best, meet life's obligations however dreary. Above all, I am the traitor – we had it made, & I walked away from it. And though I am usually able to see the force of any argument directed against me, I found this portrait of our relationship unjust, and of myself selective, to say the least. I was greatly & truthfully moved by you & remain so. We did indeed have much to share, much in common that was profound, fascinating & exciting. Our meeting left me, as it left you, fragmented & amazed: our one meeting. It was all very new to me & alarming too. But as the weeks went by I became increasingly certain that the intensity was for me unsustainable, & that to continue was to risk more than I was prepared to give up: the tranquility in which to write, the privacy of my inner life, & the love of those around me. At 65, I reckoned, the concessions were the norm; everyone makes them; the structures of survival, & the promises that must be kept, were more important to me than anything else, even if the anything else was unique. And if I had been carried away by feelings that surprised me, I knew also that I could not sustain them in the face of the unhappiness I risked around me. If that is despicable, it is also the path that I believe right. That we touched something very rare is beyond doubt. But that is not a reason to visit misery & solitude on the people round us. Or it isn't for me.

I am sorry that I disappeared, but my friends at Sancreed sold their house & left the area, and believe it or not there is nobody else I know or trust well enough. I care very much about your writing, & had hopes for the novel you sent me – I still believe it shd be published, & that it reveals a real writing talent. I believe in your goodness & humanity as I did from the moment we began writing to each other. I have the strongest memories of our meeting & they will be with me always; I love all the crazy and funny things that happen to you, and your courage and goodness, again, & your humour. But I have promised myself certain things too: a few more novels before I'm done, the continuity of the painfully constructed life around me, and the resolution, somehow, of all the wrong turnings I have taken. Here's an address in London that works, would work, though my visits there are not regular: please address the outer envelope to:

[. . .]

and the inner envelope to me, marked personal.

∾

'As one of your many fans', wrote Jack Carley, executive vice-president of Avis Inc., he was delighted to find in The Tailor of Panama *that Andy Osnard was an Avis customer. 'In that respect I write to make certain that we at Avis are doing all we can to retain the continued loyalty of all your future creations who may need to rent a car.'*

TO JACK CARLEY

Tregiffian
St Buryan
Penzance
Cornwall

12 March 1997

Dear Mr Carley,

Thank you for your kind letter of 17th January, which has only just reached me from New York. I have taken your letter to heart, and shall give my characters every opportunity to rent Avis cars. If they are particularly unsavoury characters, I may divert them to Hertz, which I must confess crossed my mind in the case of Osnard. But it was Osnard's nature to exploit the trusting and virtuous, so I allowed him to make use of Avis instead, knowing of course that 'they try harder'.

Thanks for brightening my day.

Yours sincerely,

The copy in the le Carré archive is unsigned.

∾

TO JANE CORNWELL

27 April 1998
for 28 April 1998

My dearest one,

These absurd cards & inadequate gifts cannot express a part of my gratitude for the gift of the best of your life. We shall be very happy for the rest of it, and we have done wonderful things together. Nobody will ever know how deep is my gratitude or how constant – even at the worst times – was my love, and how constant it remains.

This is not my most elegant piece of prose, but it is written with all my heart.

David

Jane had turned sixty.

⁓

In le Carré's Single & Single, *the character Oliver Single turns inform-
ant on his father, Tiger Single, a Ronnie-style figure.*

TO SIR JOHN MARGETSON

Tregiffian
St Buryan
Penzance
Cornwall

19 August 1998

Dear John,

Thanks so much for your letter. Yes, to me too it's a companion volume to 'A Perfect Spy' but, as you suggest, nobody will
bother with that except the ordinary reader. The 'Times' will
give it to their thriller man, the 'Observer' will trash it because
I've been le Carré for too long, & the Guardian will as usual
refuse to treat it as a novel at all, and – see last time – give it to
one of their political-investigative reporters who moves his lips
when he reads anything but his own prose. On the other hand,
I'll have my book, & they'll have their yellowing opinions!

And it was <u>such</u> fun to write. I went back to Georgia a
month ago just to check out places, ditto Turkey & Zurich.
And I really enjoyed re-reading the book as I went along. I'm
so glad you enjoyed it too. I've taken abt 15 pages out – tiny,
useful cuts – & written in some new short scenes – I'll send
you the final version.

Thank you for inviting us to stay. We are a bit oversub-
scribed just for the next few months as we are remodelling
part of the house & adding a library, and I am supposed to go
to Hollywood on 28th Sep, after receiving my new US publisher & editor here on 26/27th. The Hollywood trip is always

at the whim of the idiots who make the films, but anyway I'll keep you up to date.

[. . .]

I <u>love</u> the Clinton scandal,[9] don't you? It reminds one, if a reminder were needed, that the world is governed from Ruislip – will the au pair tell all? And when she <u>does</u> tell all, what do we discover? Il Presidente doesn't even bonk.

Ah well. Much love to you both/all, as always. Do let's meet soon, somehow, & thanks so much for the lovely letter.

As ever,
David

~

TO JOHN CALLEY

By fax

Cornwall

7 September 1998

Dear John,

Just to let you know we're moving to London to escape the builders, & will be there from Wednesday evening on.

If there's any movement on 'Tailor' I'd love to hear of it, when you have a moment. Meanwhile I bought a Mercedes SL, kept it 10 weeks, & returned it to the garage. One of us was the wrong age.

Love to you both –
David

~

9. After seven months of denials, Bill Clinton admitted in a televised address on 17 August his relationship with intern Monica Lewinsky was 'not appropriate'.

TO TONY CORNWELL

9 Gainsborough Gardens
London, NW3 1BJ

13 December 1998

Dearest To,

Thanks so much for your letter, and for the <u>amazing</u> desktop printing at its head: tomorrow the world! Thanks also for your generous response to Single & S – I just fell to wondering what c<u>d</u> have happened to either of us if Ronnie had been smoother, smarter, shorter even than he was, and sufficiently honest to be successful, which he assuredly <u>never</u> was. And it grew from there . . .

[. . .]

I have publication here in Feb, & in the States soon after, so there's plenty to do – also the movie of 'Tailor of P' is in preproduction, so I'm off to Panama in mid-January with the director Tony Scott – also 'The Night Manager' is to be filmed in 1999 & they want my input fairly soon – so I wouldn't be getting much real time in Cornwall anyway. All the same, it pisses me off: I was never an urban child, & now I'm a positive hayseed. Above all, I want to get going on a new book, but the whole apparatus of mod. publishing makes that a no-no. A novel – or non-fiction for that matter – has such a short time in the public eye that the only way to get the word out fast enough (that it exists) is put the poor bloody writer into bat, on the most demeaning programmes possible – or so they say. Since largely I refuse to do that – haven't given an interview in the UK for going on 10 years – they are now lining me up to do public readings, which I don't mind so much – personal questions from brain-dead journalists being my total worst nightmare. So I may head for Seattle in March – apparently there's some highbrow audience that I'm to gull into buying a few copies. <u>And I've agreed</u>. Why? Do I need the folding stuff? No. Do I think it makes one tart's kiss worth of difference to the ultimate fate of the book? Do I hell. Do I get my rocks off imitating C. Dickens' public readings? One rock. The other one sinks in my stomach. The biggest reason for doing it is weakness, closely followed by the sheer boredom of hanging around waiting to start writing again. It's like going out & bearding the publicity machine in its lair. We start here, I gather, with the Festival Hall, proceed to the Theatre Royal Bath and thus process through the chattering classes of middle England, not omitting our cousins Ireland & Scotland en route . . . In April, it's all over, the house is ready & I'm going to get a dog called Poppy. I want a dog, Jane wants a bitch, so Poppy can be a transvestite & we'll all be happy.

The best remark about Clinton was made by Warren Harding's minders when they were trying to laugh off his libido: 'We're not running this horse as a gelding.' If McCurry had had the balls (forgive me) to say this 10 years ago, if he was around, we'd all be silent or still laughing.[10]

Very happy Christmas to you both – all – and our love to you, & let's hope for a jar in March.

All love,
D

~

Le Carré met Tom Stoppard in 1989, when Stoppard was hired as the screenwriter for the film of The Russia House. *'I found Stoppard enchanting and extremely intelligent,' he told Alec Guinness. A late friendship developed.*

---

10. President Bill Clinton's press secretary Mike McCurry left the job in October 1998 after months of fielding constant and often graphic questions about the Monica Lewinsky scandal.

TO SIR TOM STOPPARD

9 Gainsborough Gardens
London, NW3 1BJ

4 February 1999

Dear Tom,
I <u>loved</u> 'Shakespeare in Love', & loved you for writing it. It will
last & last, my children & grandchildren <u>already</u> love it, it's one
of those perfect, lighthearted, profound works of art that actually increase the public's awareness of its own cultural heritage.
Very pompous of me, but true. And at the personal level, it
was like a kind of doting Stoppard soliloquy on a balmy summer's afternoon, all wit & affection & musing. I identified most
naturally with Webster, of course, who was surely one of your
most delicious conceits. Just wonderful. All, all wonderful –
Ever,
David

In a scene in Shakespeare in Love *a young John Webster, future*
writer of The Duchess of Malfi, *avers his love for gory theatre and*
then feeds a live mouse to a cat.

❧

The film of The Tailor of Panama *continued a wild ride. When the*
book was first published, everyone from the Coen Brothers to Sir Ian
McKellen showed interest. In 1998 le Carré reported to Alec Guinness
that Sir Anthony Hopkins had twice turned down the role of the tailor,
Pendel; Dustin Hoffman and Robin Williams were pursuing the part,
and Kevin Kline was then slated to star opposite Jamie Lee Curtis. The
role finally went to Geoffrey Rush. In Kenya, le Carré began research
on The Constant Gardener.

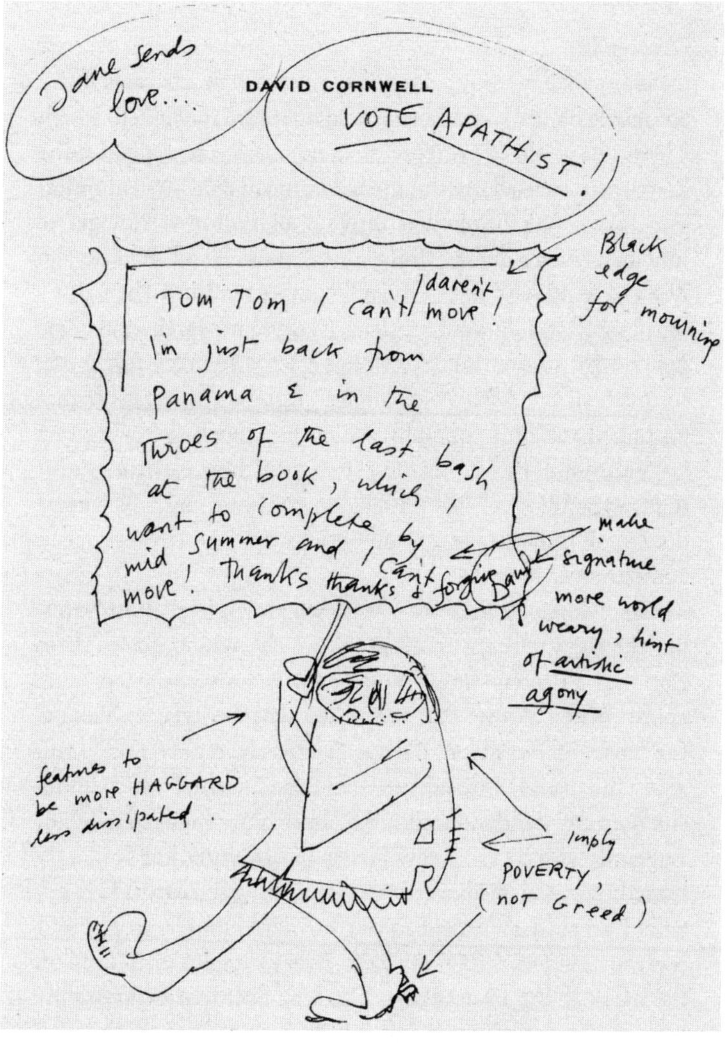
Jane sends love...
DAVID CORNWELL
VOTE APATHIST!
Black edge for mourning
TOM TOM I can't/daren't move! I'm just back from Panama & in the throes of the last bash at the book, which I want to complete by mid summer and I can't move! Thanks thanks & forgive Dav
make signature more world weary, hint of artistic agony
features to be more HAGGARD less dissipated.
imply POVERTY, (not Greed)

to TONY CORNWELL

30 May 1999

Dearest To,

I was appalled, on returning today from North Africa, to find a second, splendid letter from you so hot upon the first, to which I had, out of sheer pressure of events, failed to reply. I don't know even now all the things that happened or in what order: Tony Scott was dumped as director of 'Tailor of Panama' & John Boorman signed. ('Deliverance', 'Point Blank', etc., etc.) So I had to bond with him. I did a few more readings, then gloriously signed off, & went to Africa (Kenya) in search of my new novel, which now, thank God, has started to talk back to me, so much so that I have been able confidently to put aside that unlonged-for autobiography, which I so much fear will put a knife through my writing life – '<u>before</u> it, then, oh dear, <u>the bit that's left after it</u> . . .' But I'll have to do it one day, and when I do, I shall indeed take you up on your very generous offer to compare memories.

Englishness & the box – well, we are <u>all</u> born into boxes, but the Brits perhaps more so than most, which makes them (for me) so interesting – and quaintly universal – to write about. When Wiesenthal was asked why he lived in Vienna, the most anti-Semitic of European cities, he replied that 'if you study the disease, you gotta live in the schwamp,' which about sums up my dependence on the sheer bloodiness of much of England, with its too many boxes, but overarching humanity nonetheless – or so I have forced my writing self to think. Every time I go abroad (except to our former colonies, as a rule) I feel the boulders roll off my back. Every time I return, I put on the harness. But I know myself so well now that I can use the burden as a constructive force, in my writing if nothing else.

Jane & I had a glorious 10 days in Morocco, in an oasis hotel run by a psychopath who claims to have been some kind of top hitman or runner for Secret England. I thought he was a total fantasist, which accounts for the excellent (escapist) qualities of his hotel. We were happier together than perhaps we've ever been, a condition that I hope may continue, despite my little ways!

Good of you to read 'Our Game', which was an odd book, not bad, but too driven by its unacknowledged German models of the education of the senses. It is at least credited, though, with predicting the outbreak of hostilities in Ingushetia & Chechnya, & appeared almost to the day as war broke out.

I return to Kenya on June 14th & hope that by mid July I shall be able to begin a big ambitious novel that will no doubt fall on its arse. We think & talk of you both often – thanks, please, to Nettie for the tape, & renewed apologies for my churlish silence, which was unpardonable, if human. And thank you again for all your generous thoughts & words about my writing. The Frogs are making a film about me for the millennium, which makes me 1000 years old, I suppose, but at least I don't have to take part in it.

Read Tom Wolfe's 'Man in Full' & thought it overwritten & pointless. Very sad. Read McEwan's 'Amsterdam' – piss awful. Read Japrisot's 'A Very Long Engagement' & urge you to read it. Glorious.

Jane joins me in her greetings.

Love,
David

Somewhat contradictorily, on 27 October 1998 le Carré had written furiously to the Observer *protesting Peter Conrad's early review of Tom Wolfe's novel as 'vicious, ignorant and disgraceful. Vicious because it is so patently prejudiced against the one great journalist and novelist of our time who can decently claim Balzac's mantle.' He added, 'Wolfe's novel, I am assured by many people I respect, is even finer than its predecessor.'* A Man in Full *was Wolfe's first major novel since* The Bonfire of the Vanities.

≈

to JOHN CALLEY

By fax

London

27 September 1999

Dear John,

Just to let you know: we saw 'Eyes Wide Shut' last night and
found it just awful: not bad taste, not bad acting or bad script,
just bad like boring bad, and profoundly dismaying to those
who loved him and his work. So in that sense only, I'm glad
he didn't survive it. At least we can write it off as the mistaken
work of a great director at the end of his life, & leave it at that.

Love to you both from us both.

D

*Stanley Kubrick's erotic drama, starring Tom Cruise and Nicole
Kidman and featuring Sydney Pollack, was based on Arthur
Schnitzler's* Traumnovelle (Dream Story)*; early on Kubrick had
asked le Carré to adapt it. He had first rights on a film of* The
Night Manager; *'there was Kubrick; then there were the others', le
Carré wrote to him when the deal fell through.*

∾

Le Carré's letters to John Calley about The Tailor of Panama *reflected
tension over Sony–Columbia's approach to the film.*

to JOHN CALLEY

By fax

17 February 2000

Dear John,

Thanks very much for sending me the draft press releases. The first point to make, please, is that my pen name is spelt with a small 'l'.

The repeated description of the movie as a 'contemporary spy thriller' confuses, since the way we have it now, it is set in the recent future.

At the ego level, I am distressed to see myself described as 'the greatest spy novelist of the Cold War era'. This is unhelpful since our story has nothing to do with the Cold War. More particularly, it puts me in the past, and I would suggest, immodestly, a phrase like 'the acknowledged master of the spy novel' or some such crap. Or we could use a quote, e.g., from 'Time' magazine, which in its mealy-mouthed way described me as 'the greatest spywriter of his time – perhaps of all time'.

Presumably you have taken some kind of policy decision on how you describe the picture. I would have thought comedy thriller would be a safer description than plain thriller. Comedy spy thriller, also possible.

I don't expect you want grace-notes in these hand-outs but, if you do, let me know!

As ever,
David

～

In Single & Single, *Oliver and Tiger have a father–son dinner of 'chopped veal and Rösti and house red' at the Kronenhalle in Zurich. This prompted Stephen James Joyce, Joyce's grandson, to pen a protest from France. 'Your prose is generally characterised by factual exactitude, in so far as this is possible,' he wrote to le Carré. 'I am most disappointed and even irate as a result of the first paragraph of chapter fourteen . . . While freely admitting that to talk about Swiss gastronomy, with certain rare exceptions, is to skate on very thin ice, your "chopped veal" simply sticks in my craw.'*

The dish, Geschnetzeltes Kalbfleisch Zürcher Art, *or* Émincé de veau à la zurichoise, *was not some 'banal McDonald burger' but an authentic delicacy, he continued. 'Would you call "boeuf Stroganoff" chopped beef?'*

Joyce had been a customer of the Kronenhalle, famous for its collection of twentieth-century paintings, Zaaff Wappen *(coats of arms) and dark wood panelling, for close to sixty years. His grandfather was among the artists and writers who had gathered there.*

TO STEPHEN JAMES JOYCE

Tregiffian
St Buryan
Penzance
Cornwall

3 March 2000

Dear Stephen James Joyce,

Thank you for your splendid letter of 17th February. And I am delighted to be able to count you among my readers. Let me state my credentials on the matter of G'schnetzeltes. I was partly educated in Switzerland, studied at Bern University, and consider that I have something of a Swiss soul in me somewhere. Certainly I yield to none in my admiration for G'schnetzeltes mit Rösti, which I have eaten even more times than I have had birthdays. And indeed frequently at the Kronenhalle, where it is my pleasure to wheedle a corner table out of the great Santo and admire both the Wappen and paintings, including the forbidding portrait of Frau Zumstegg[11] herself.

So I can't claim ignorance of my subject, quite the reverse. What's at issue here is translation and style. I do not care to strain my average reader's eyes with a mouthful of unintelligible

11. Hulda Zumsteg shaped the Kronenhalle's history for sixty years from 1921. Santo Maraia joined as a young waiter in 1974 and retired in 2015.

Swiss. It infuriates me when this is done to me in books. I recently read a novel which included long passages of demotic Greek and Spanish, and it threw me into a rage. So I refuse to throw words at my reader that he can't even find in a dictionary. So I had to find a translation. My wife now tells me – too late, but such are wives – that I should have said 'sliced' instead of 'chopped'. And for this I surely apologise to you, to the Kronenhalle, and to the Swiss at large.

But I am delighted that you care so much about such important matters, and that we share a taste for one of nature's finest dishes, and that I may count your august name among my readers. Thank you again for writing and please do not be irate with me any more. Perhaps, who knows, we shall one day meet at the Kronenhalle. You will find me in Santo's corner, tucking into G'schnetzeltes.

All good wishes,
David

~

Pierce Brosnan, James Bond for four films of the franchise, took the anti-role in The Tailor of Panama *as the MI6 agent and sleazy chancer Andy Osnard, between* The World is Not Enough *and* Die Another Day.

TO PIERCE BROSNAN

By fax

Cornwall

5 March 2000

Dear Pierce,
Just a line to send you my sincere good wishes for your Osnard odysee,* and to thank you sincerely for playing him. After our day in Ojai I was certain that the casting was inspired, and I believe the world will see a PB they hadn't dreamed of!

All good things, have a ball, and my love to you & yours,
David

[*in left-hand margin*] * My German ancestry got into the spelling

In September, after watching early edits of the film, le Carré told director John Boorman that 'Pierce's excellent acting & range do make it his movie. It's Pierce's hare to Geoffrey's tortoise and they're both wonderful', but he found himself living more in Osnard's part.

Sue Lawley first approached le Carré to appear on Desert Island Discs *in 1997. Three years later he finally agreed, but then withdrew from the show. 'Loath as I am to admit it and disappointed as I am to accept it, I suspect you're right,' she responded. 'More, I know you're right.'*

TO SUE LAWLEY

> *As from: Tregiffian*
> *St Buryan*
> *Penzance*
> *Cornwall*
>
> *9 July 2000*

Dear Sue Lawley,
I'm having serious second thoughts about the projected interview for 'Desert Island Discs' and wonder whether it would

not be better for me to withdraw now, when you have time to repair the gap. The reason is very simple. Seen from this side of the table, you will be bound to ask me about a series of subjects that I don't want to discuss. These are childhood, fathers, spying, Salman Rushdie, Stella Rimington's book, and – probably – why I don't give interviews, to which the answer is incidentally contained in this letter: I've had enough of all the stock questions.[12] Oh, and the other one is, 'what have you got to write about now the Cold War's over?' which drives me to near dementia. So I don't really think I'm your man. Do you? I have great admiration for your programme and it seems to get along fine without me. But I have reached an age where I would pay good money never again to have to talk my way through a sanitised version of my life, so I don't think there's the smallest chance of either of us having a good time. Which means disappointed listeners too.

Yours sincerely,
David Cornwell

[*a note is filed with the letter, typed with additions in Jane's handwriting*]

David's provisional choices are:
Crazy Gang – Underneath the Arches (Ronnie and all that)
Noel Coward – Mrs Wentworth-Brewster ('A bar on the Piccola Marina')
Alec Guinness reading 'Four Quartets' – studious period
Fischer-Dieskau – Schubert songs? the trout? (Alfred Deller – folk songs) [*bracketed and replaced in Jane's handwriting with*] Purcell's Sound the Trumpet
Sibelius – PINE FOREST
Alfie Brendel on the joanna – I hear it as dialogue . . . conversation . . . Beethoven

---

12. Stella Rimington, former director-general of MI5.

Geoffrey Burgon's Nunc Dimittis from Tinker Tailor

Other: a burst of zither music from *The Third Man* – at the risk of being banal
Über allen Gipfeln ist Ruh, etc. – Goethe

'Underneath the Arches', sung by Bud Flanagan and Chesney Allen, part of the Crazy Gang, was used in the television series of A Perfect Spy *for the scene in which Magnus Pym and his father, Rick, run under arches. Alec Guinness recorded T. S. Eliot's* The Four Quartets *in 1971. Dietrich Fischer-Dieskau, the German baritone, sang* The Trout Quintet *(Forellenquintett) by Franz Schubert. The 'pine forest' may have referred to Sibelius's popular* Tree Cycle, *which includes 'The Solitary Fir' (sometimes translated as 'The Solitary Pine'). Pianist Alfred Brendel was a Hampstead friend of le Carré and Jane. 'Über allen Gipfeln ist Ruh' is one of two poems in* The Wanderer's Nightsong *(Wandrers Nachtlied) by Goethe, also sung by Fischer-Dieskau in settings by Schubert and Lizst.*

THE CONSTANT GARDENER

I seem to have written what the Germans would call a Bildungsroman – a novel of education. And the recipient of that education, and ultimately its victim, is Justin Quayle, where in some earlier books it might have been George Smiley.

– writing on *The Constant Gardener*, in November 2000

Le Carré found a new adversary, the pharmaceutical industry, and a new audience with the publication of *The Constant Gardener* and the subsequent film by Fernando Meirelles. 'The pharmaceutical world, once I entered it, got me by the throat and wouldn't let me go,' he wrote.

He dedicated the book to the international relief worker Yvette Pierpaoli, 'who lived and died giving a damn'. Pierpaoli was killed on 18 April 1999, when her car ran off a mountain road in Albania, travelling to visit newly arrived refugees from Kosovo; le Carré was in Kenya, researching the novel. Four days before her death, Yvette had faxed him to call off a planned meeting in early May; 'reason is Kosovo', she said.

Writing in the *Guardian* in February 2001, le Carré recalled how he had met Pierpaoli in the besieged city of Phnom Penh in about 1974. 'She had all the wiles. She could spread her elbows and upbraid you like a bargee. She could tip you a smile to melt your heart, cajole, flatter, and win you in any way you needed to be won,' he wrote. Even before her own death her character was shaping the character of Tessa, Justin's murdered wife.

'And though by age, occupation, nationality, and birth my Tessa was far removed from Yvette, Tessa's commitment to the poor of Africa, particularly its women, her contempt for protocol, and her unswerving, often maddening determination to have her way stemmed quite consciously so far as I was concerned, from Yvette's example.'

In one of three surviving letters to Pierpaoli held in his archive, le Carré told Yvette on 19 December 1994 (see p. 379) that he had been asked to join a Carnegie Trust committee 'that will solve the problems of the world. I was so pleased to hear that someone had finally decided to do this, for I had observed that certain things were not as they should be. But I think you have done more for the world than all the wise committees put together.'

The character of Lara Emrich was partly modelled on Dr Nancy Olivieri, the Canadian medical researcher and campaigner whom le Carré tapped as a source for his research. A phrase used by the diplomatic spouse Gloria in the novel – 'well, here we all are' – was borrowed from Dick Franks's wife, Rachel.

Le Carré met Olivieri in the summer of 2000 in Canada. In the mid 1990s Olivieri raised concerns over clinical trials of the drug deferiprone, funded by the Canadian pharmaceutical giant Apotex, which warned her over breaching confidentiality agreements. Years of controversy followed in 'the Olivieri affair'; it was fertile fictional territory, with one scientist exposed for writing 'poison pen' letters through the saliva on stamps. Deferiprone is now approved for use in the UK and in more than fifty other countries, but not in Canada. 'He created a story,' Olivieri wrote of le Carré, 'that brilliantly succeeded in helping the public to understand the murky business of prescription-drug research.'[1]

TO DR NANCY OLIVIERI, TORONTO, CANADA

By email

22 May 2000

Dear Nancy,

I won't drool on about our conversations. They were extremely fruitful and informative for me, and I hope that you will eventually feel that I have not wasted your time, or too much traduced your story.

My attention was drawn recently to an article in The London Sunday Times of 14th May in which the German firm of Bayer is shown to have suppressed negative information from clinical trials and thus caused the death of at least one patient. I have asked Julia to give you a web site address for the article. If you have any problem locating it, let us know and we will fax it to you.

Let me know also if there is some way in which I can help you. I don't want to get into journalism at the moment – I don't really want to do anything that takes me away from the novel, which I hope to have in draft form by the late Summer. I keep

---

1. Nancy Olivieri to Tim Cornwell, 29 January 2022.

thinking that there must be institutions that should be providing you with encouragement and financial support, and I wish I knew what they were. In that regard, perhaps BUKO[2] would have an idea – they are certainly worth a shot. And if you are putting together a fighting fund for your own legal actions, I hope you will send me the literature and give me a chance to contribute.

What sticks in my mind above everything else – what I find shameful and utterly unforgivable – is the extent to which your own academic and professional colleagues have connived in the suppression of debate. I cannot believe that the matter should be allowed to rest there. I hope I can do justice to that element of your story when I come to write it.

Thank you again for agreeing to see me and for being so frank and patient with me. We should love to see you in London or in Cornwall when you are next over here – but I am in purdah until September.

All the very best.
As ever
David Cornwell

~

TO DR NANCY OLIVIERI

Tregiffian
St Buryan
Penzance
Cornwall

18 July 2000

<u>Personal and Confidential</u>

---

2. The German-based BUKO organisation campaigning on 'big pharma'.

Dear Nancy,

This is very much a first draft. It has yet to be submitted to publishers, and there are all sorts of research matters to be completed. Nevertheless I thought it might amuse you to see it at this stage, and particularly the two chapters 18 and 19, which seek to capture the ironies of your predicament as you told it to me, though I have invested it in a totally different character and called her Lara. The text is wide open and I can add and subtract as I wish. Have I got the heart of it? How do you feel about it? If you haven't the time to read the whole book maybe you could just look at those two chapters (18 and 19).

There is no great hurry. I look forward to hearing from you and wish you all the best.

As ever,
David

P.S. This is a <u>very</u> confidential document – e.g. Penguin Canada won't get a sight of it for weeks, & certainly not in this form, so please keep it under yr hat –

David

The character of Lara featured in the script for the 2005 film of The Constant Gardener, *but ended up on the cutting-room floor.*

≈

TO JANET BERGER

By fax

8 August 2000

Very dear Janet,

Despite my total conversing with computers, as evidenced in the book, I have decided to give the old machine a rest and use my neglected pen. Thank you so much for your generous words about poor Justin. I'm <u>so glad</u> you both enjoyed the book, and its fauna, and its themes. I loved writing it, and now all I can do is rewrite it, which is driving my publishers nuts, never bad.

I want to rewrite Lorbeer[3] and take him out of vernacular – his shift is better au clair (fr.) and I can make those scenes more dramatic.

Alec died in one hospital while Merula was in another (his wife). What a sadness.

Love to you both, and renewed thanks,
David

Alec and Merula: Sir Alec and Lady Guinness. In 1994 le Carré was a contributor to a book secretly compiled for Guinness's eightieth birthday; Guinness wrote to say that only one piece in it 'was perceptive and new and interesting, and that was yours'. Guinness chose the piece as the preface to his last memoir, My Name Escapes Me: The Diary of a Retiring Actor.

∾

TO J. R. JAMES ESQ., CMG [LATER SIR JEFFREY JAMES], BRITISH HIGH COMMISSIONER, NAIROBI

By fax

London

11 September 2000

Dear High Commissioner,
We once shared a ginger beer on the verandah of the Norfolk Hotel, & I mentioned that I was setting a novel in Kenya. This, to some extent, I have now done – the title is The Constant

---

3. Markus Lorbeer, instrumental in marketing Dypraxa in *The Constant Gardener*.

Gardener, & it will appear in the US & UK simultaneously just in time for Christmas. Some of the story takes place inside the High Commission – a building I have never entered – and there are several characters who are members of the HC staff, but only in fiction, since again I have barely met one apart from yourself.

[. . .]

Most of the fictional characters – including the High Commissioner – are aimiable enough characters, but there's one absolutely awful chap – the Head of Chancery – to whom I have given the name of Sandy Woodrow. So really I am writing to make sure that I have not by accident chosen names that cd give unintended embarrassment or offence to any member of your staff, and of course if I have inadvertently sinned, I can still change them . . . here is the whole cast list anyway. Even an approximation can upset people, so please don't hesitate to object.

As soon as I have a proof copy of the book, I'll send it to you.

With all good wishes
David C

～

John Boorman, director of The Tailor of Panama, *had faxed asking what the office of Luxmore, Osnard's London MI6 boss, should look like. This description of his office followed le Carré's speaking engagements at MI6 in the 1990s.*

to JOHN BOORMAN

By fax

Cornwall

22 September 2000

Dear John,

Luxmore's office would be quite expansive and sparse. Spooks have an infuriating habit of slipping papers from desks into drawers as you enter. He could certainly have a map of his region on the wall, but any markers on it would have to be codified and removable because of the cleaners who come during the night. He would have big picture windows looking across the river towards Millbank and The Palace of Westminster. The windows from the outside would look like dull copper, and from the inside have a smoky quality. The glass would be armour-plated. All this to prevent long range photography and sniper bullets, courtesy of the IRA. He would have three telephones: one for internal use only, which would not be connected to any outside exchange, one ordinary telephone for receiving direct calls over open lines, e.g. from his terrifying wife. The third telephone would be an encryption telephone. When last seen, this was a cumbersome affair sitting on a green stippled box of tricks. It would obviously be useful to make it the twin of the encryption system in Osnard's office in the embassy in Panama.

Walls would be white 'broken with the colour of his choice'. He might well have family photographs on his desk or on the wall, and prestige photographs of him shaking hands with e.g. The Spanish Prime Minister, The President of Argentina, or some illustrious general from the Pentagon. On the shelves, very little, maybe a few handbooks on countries, guides to Central and South America and foreign telephone directories.

In terms of rank, Luxmore is one of six or seven regional directors, even if his region is a relatively humble one. He would rate an assistant and an ante-room if you wish, but this is not necessary. He would have at least one computer on his desk. Secretaries may wear jeans these days, but Luxmore would wear a suit five days a week. Other mementos in the room would include a graduation shield from e.g. The Special Warfare Department of Washington State University and another shield anointing him an honorary member of The Society of Codebreakers.

In haste –
Best,
David

$\approx$

Le Carré had spied on his left-wing friend Stanley Mitchell at Oxford, where they were both at Lincoln College. Decades later they corresponded and then met for a meal. Two letters to Stanley Mitchell stand out; this is the first, quite different in tone from the later 2006 letter (see p. 475).

TO STANLEY MITCHELL

> *Tregiffian*
> *St Buryan*
> *Penzance*
> *Cornwall*

6 January 2001

Dear Stanley,

I was very moved by our meeting and I suppose I came away with exactly the same sentiment: 'well, I <u>did</u> betray our friendship'. But I have several excuses I make to myself, though as you would know if only you were a spy, anyone with more than one excuse is almost certainly a liar. The first is that I was approached only <u>after</u> our friendship had begun. The second is that I was a nasty, vengeful little orphan with a psychopathic liar for a father and a boy-scout self-image as an antidote, and the third is that awful reality that I was later able to confirm objectively: real 'fellow travellers' were recruited by the Sov intelligence services, were deluded, misused and often had their lives wrecked in consequence, let alone what they were supposed to have done or not done in the way of 'damage to national security', a sacred cow I have long ago learned to treat with the deepest suspicion. But quand-même. The thing is, in retrospect, that radical socialism simply got into the wrong hands, just as God did, and just as the God Profit is doing now, to the despair of all decent people.

Anyway, about now, rather than then. Here's some more speciousness for you. If I hadn't greatly valued our friendship, I would not have had anything to betray. If you read 'A Perfect Spy' you will find this sentiment – & perhaps a whiff of our relationship – reflected in the relationship between Axel & Magnus. (On the principle that Judas was a shit not so much because he betrayed Christ but because he loved him).

I greatly enjoyed our friendship & learned from it and, in my head, could never let it go – partly for shame, partly for honest admiration & affection. I don't think that paradox is beyond you! And when we met again, I was delighted to discover you just as stimulating & honourable as I recall you, and I was ridiculously happy that Jane immediately took to you also. And I truly believe that, by the weirdest of separate journeys, we have arrived at very much the same larger vision of mankind & its failures. My own, anyway, runs from black to dark black. I also am impertinent enough to believe that a renewal of our acquaintance/friendship would do us both nothing but good, not least because neither of us shows any sign of giving in to age. To despair perhaps, to anger and frustration. But the lusts & love of life still beat in us, somewhere, and I think we c<u>d</u> share some good times. This place, if you like countryside still, is a dream, & there's a comfortable guest cottage & an indoor pool & all the toys. Best there are the cliffs for walking. And if you can bring a Sig. Other, a friend or relation, or more than one, so much the better – the cottage sleeps six with comfort, or more accurately 3 couples. And we're in London for you when you're feeling like it – <u>and perhaps more importantly when</u>

<u>you're not</u>. Write to me about all this – when you feel like it. And let's hope to see you on the 15th, details to follow.

As ever –
David

∾

TO JOHN CALLEY

By fax

Cornwall

6 January 2001

Dear John,
Down here in Tregiffian in the usual publishing purdah, waiting for it all to blow over, trying to work out, like you, what to do next. We sent you some truffles from Wengen (to Canada) and I fear that if they ever arrived they were squidged mousse. Anyway John Miller's were, but he & Mike ate them with spoons. [. . .]

Other stuff. The Constant Gardener got a huge reception here, sold 104,000 by publication & has now run out of print. Nobody quite expected the reception. In the US the reception has been weird – Time & Newsweek say they will never run their reviews because Bush hogged all the space. Which is a pity because apparently Time, by Paul Gray, is an aria. The NYT, daily & Sunday, were both apparently sniffy though I haven't seen them; raves in Boston, San Francisco, etc., But publishing just before Christmas has its price. All the same, Scribners say it's selling like crazy & they've just gone back for a reprint. We'll see. On the movie front, the outing of a very big deal, Euro-financed, so I'm pleased. European publishing prospects extraordinary. Pharma-bashing looks like being the new sport – did you see the Wash. Post articles on pharma stuff in the 3rd World? Makes mine look like kids' play. Much love to you all – and thanks again for the offer.

As ever,
David

~

As editor and publisher, Roland Philipps worked on seven of le Carré's books, including The Constant Gardener and A Most Wanted Man; they remained friends after le Carré left Hodder & Stoughton for Viking Penguin in 2009.

The film producer Simon Channing Williams – rotund, energetic and quietly brilliant – had made a work approach to le Carré in Cornwall and rapidly become a fixture. He was adept at handling the writer's occasional stormy responses to the film-making process and sensitive to the creative imperatives behind le Carré's work; the professional relationship evolved into a deep friendship. He produced The Constant Gardener (2005).

TO ROLAND PHILIPPS

Tregiffian
St Buryan
Penzance
Cornwall

19 January 2001

Dear Roland,
Thanks! I think I'm actually relieved & excited to have the movie to play with. I unfolded my plan for it to Simon Channing Williams (Channers in the household) & he was very excited. I'm committed to one draft & one set of revisions, & as much or as little coproduction as I want. I have awesome controls

that I shall never exercise. He wants Daniel Day L. for Justin at the moment. But everything will change when we have a director. He persuaded me that we didn't need one yet & I've come round to his way of thinking; a director on one's back so early, not good. I've done it before (Pollack twice, Jack Clayton, Karel Reisz) & it's never worked. I do have a new novel, but not yet, if you know what I mean, & I can't write small any more. Single & Single cd never have followed TCG – it had to be this way round.

You write kindly about the speed with which I got down to TCG. I don't know (but then I never know in retrospect) how it happened: Yvette's death, a bit of rage, and hitting a fluid pattern of writing, all at the same time. But you leave out your own ever-supportive self, and the sure touches of reassurance and discreet counsel along the way. For which I am, & shall remain, deeply grateful.

The movie will be something to hang on to in Australia, and it will stop me, I hope, from treating every encounter as potential material for a novel I'll never write. It will go quickly once I get back, and I think it will provide – as we Americans say – a necessary closure to the book.

[. . .]

The time drags awfully when I'm not working. The main event of the day is a 2.30 pm telephone interview with a woman in South Africa who likes to keep her radio programme light-hearted. If I lived in South Africa, so would I. Boorman is in foul dispute with Sony Columbia about the poster for the film. His last email read (addressed to some luckless underling) 'I have consultation. Being presented with a fait accompli is not consultation.' So it goes.

As ever,
David

∾

Green had written to le Carré with passages of R. S. Thompson's 1952 reference letter sent to Lincoln College, Oxford. In it, le Carré's old Sherborne housemaster recommended the college give him a place, but make him wait until 1953, because 'the Cornwells tend to assume that what they want they get.' Fifty years later it still rankled.

TO VIVIAN GREEN

> *Tregiffian*
> *St Buryan*
> *Penzance*
> *Cornwall*

25 January 2001

My dear Vivian,

Thank you for your wonderful letter, and for taking the trouble to copy out Thomper-to-Keith-Murray. I found his letter very sad – a sense of personal failure turning suddenly outward into a rather pitiful and petty suggestion[4] that I be made to cool my heels for a year to teach us Cornwells that we can't always have our way! Yes, we must both keep writing, keep creating, it's the only weapon against death. When I'm writing properly I still feel 23. When I'm not, I can hardly sleep for dispair: such an awful life in so many ways, and looks so terribly impressive from the outside. But the inside has been such a ferment of buried anger and lovelessness from childhood that it was sometimes almost uncontainable.

And yes, I remember our Swiss adventures with the same pleasure & the same gratitude, and the same rapture about the

---

4. The children of R. S. Thompson, who kindly gave permission for the use of extracts of his letter, asked to stress that Thompson 'did his level best for every single boy in his house at Sherborne'; that he took his life's vocation as a teacher seriously and would never have made a recommendation out of petty-minded pique.

landscape, as you describe. You once told me that landscape was your path to God and I feel exactly the same.

To practical matters. July looks much better for your visit here than March, because we're not sure how long we shall stay in Australia. (I wd give anything not to go, but it's too late to back out. People are determined to turn me into an instant expert on the pharmaceutical industry, and it scares me.) Might we pencil in some days when we cd reserve the cottage for you here? We would enjoy it hugely, & if we can book you in soon, we can fit the children round the dates so that there's no clash. I shall be writing the screenplay of The Constant Gardener, but only in the mornings, and Jane has become a marvellous cook. We also want to take you to the Seafood Restaurant at Padstow & the Tresanton Hotel at St Mawes.

Jane has been my extraordinarily loyal and ever-decent support for 30 years now. I sometimes feel I shd get on a soapbox & proclaim my gratitude to her, but it sounds so hollow. But I'm sure you know. And you, dear Vivian, even in the times when we barely communicated, have been one of those life-long secret sharers to whom I also owe a debt I can never repay.

Please come in July, & perhaps we shall be able to squeeze in another meal before then, e.g. when 'The Tailor of Panama' has its London première.

As ever, my love & Jane's,
David

~

On 10 April 2001 Andreas Seiter, the head of stakeholder relations for the pharmaceutical giant Novartis, and Katharina Amacker, president of its Employee Representation Council, wrote to le Carré in the wake of the publication of The Constant Gardener. *They invited him to Basel for a face-to-face discussion with employees and/or managers of Novartis.*

'It is not the book which has triggered this request – readers found it well written, thrilling and entertaining,' they wrote. 'What is actually creating an increasing level of unease, if not outrage, is a series of interviews Mr Cornwell is currently giving to media in the US and Europe . . . he is quoted as portraying our industry as a bunch of greedy criminals who ignore basic human rights in order to maximise profits.

'We know there are issues our industry has been slow in addressing,' they wrote. 'However, we are asking ourselves whether Mr Cornwell is in a very strong moral position to attack us in public, when at the same time he has a clear commercial interest to boost the sales of his book. We would also like to know whether he has got the courage to repeat his challenge in front of our employees or managers.'

TO ANDREAS SEITER AND KATHARINA AMACKER, NOVARTIS PHARMA AG

c/o David Higham Associates
5/8 Lower John Street
Golden Square
London, W1F 9HA

11 April 2001

Dear Mr Seiter, dear Ms Amacker,
Thank you for your e-mail of 10th April to Bruce Hunter, my agent. Its ingredients would surely confuse the most skilled analyst. You extend an invitation to me, and in the same breath question my moral position since I have 'a clear commercial interest in boosting the sales of my book'. Coming from writers employed by a company with annual declared profits of however many billion US dollars, that is an inappropriate anxiety.

You extend an invitation to me, but question in the same breath whether I have the courage to accept it. It is true that I do not have the courage that is conferred by membership of an over-mighty industry that has the power of life and death over a large part of the world. But my goodness, whatever do you intend to do with me? I prefer to ask myself whether your employees and managers have the courage to question the nostrums that prompt you to invite me in the first place.

It is not I who should be frightened. My business is not facts and figures and formulae. It is not, despite your unpleasant insinuation, the god profit, whom I have not worshipped for many years. I am not employed by an industry accused, by the most sober critics, of amassing excessive wealth at the expense of the wretched of the earth. I am what used to be called in German a free writer. Nobody buys my opinions. In your world, that is unusual and perhaps unsettling.

When I ask myself what you might be hoping to achieve by your invitation, one answer presents itself ahead of others. You wish to paint me, I fear, as a romantic ignoramus, a high-profile example of the pseudo-liberal, anti-scientific culture that dares to speak ill of a sacred industry. And perhaps you imagine that my public biodegradation will prove to your employees and managers the supremacy of your corporate culture, and leave me gasping on the floor.

And maybe you're right at that. Maybe it would. I know nothing of your business except what I have seen and heard of its effect on people in less fortunate parts of the globe than Basel. My job as a novelist is to approach the heart of the matter, not the statistics: I can't speak with the authority of the <u>Washington Post</u>, for instance, which devoted ten months of last year to an investigation of your industry's activities in the Third World, and found them disgraceful, a conclusion that I had by my own route already reached. Perhaps you missed those articles. They were a lot more destructive than my interviews, and a lot better informed. Perhaps you also missed the articles published two months ago in the <u>Guardian</u> newspaper of London, which in some ways were even more devastating than those of the <u>Washington Post</u>. I think you must have missed them, for otherwise you would be aware of the mounting and informed public outcry against the practices of an industry that persists in regarding itself as a gift to mankind.

I have a suggestion for you that comes from your own world. It is that I am only a symptom. I am not the disease. By treating me as you would like to, you will not remove the root causes of your anger, which I suspect are insecurity and borrowed shame.

If you had sent me a civilised invitation instead of an abusive one; if you had proposed a forum which included informed critics of your industry from the responsible press; concerned aid workers; medical doctors, academics, researchers and editors of medical journals, who have suffered the long reach of your industry's terrible power; if you had included articulate representatives of the world's thirty-five million AIDS sufferers and the eighty percent of the world's population with no access to your industry's products; then I might have agreed to be part of that forum.

But you didn't do that. You proposed to put me on trial. So no. If you had really wanted me to come, you could scarcely have written a sillier letter. But I doubt whether you did want me to come. I think I struck a nerve, and made you angry. Which, believe it or not, is one of the most useful functions that a free writer can perform in an era of insufferable corporate arrogance.

Yours faithfully,
David Cornwell

~

to JOHN CALLEY

By fax

London

11 June 2001

Dear John,

Thanks for all the info about the release of 'Tailor' in UK. My own enquiries paint a rather different picture. Your man speaks of 'medium' reviews, but the Observer and Time Out alone would have supplied <u>superb</u> quote-ads, and so would many other of the more popular papers. We had a few pans, a few maybes, but some great reviews in places where it matters, upscale and downscale.

In the event, there was not a single quote-ad, or so I'm told. The film opened splendidly in the first week and might have continued that way if it had had the necessary help. I don't know who decreed that it was an 'over 35s' film, but Nick and his friends (aged 25) raved about it, and it has become something of a cult among all sorts of people – provided they got a chance to see it, or managed to find out that it was around.

Sorry, but I don't think SC[5] has anything to congratulate itself about its UK performance on this movie. I believe they missed a great chance.

As ever,
David

~

TO DAVID'S SONS AND JANE

9 Gainsborough Gardens
London, NW3 1BJ

11 June 2001

(To my sons – & Jane, who gets a separate letter too.)

Here's what to do on my death. If I die abroad & it is more convenient to cremate me abroad, do it. Bring my ashes to

---

5. Sony–Columbia.

Tregiffian and bury them at the folly gate, next to the seaward gate post.*

Jane, when it's her turn, gets the other gatepost.

At this ceremony, let each of my sons say something good about me, then have a good happy party with as many of the grandchildren as can make it. Jane sh<u>d</u> never be expected to speak unless she wants to. May you all continue to be as good hearted & considerate to her as you have been in the past, for I believe she loves you almost as much as I do.

Please take comfort from this: I had an amazing life, against the odds. I turned from a bad man to a much better one. I detest the mumbo-jumbo of organised religion, love the glory of creation and believe in some kind of triumph of that glory. Through my children and their children, I was taught to love. Jane's loyalty and love, and her love for all of you, have been my mainstay. That she prevailed against my infidelities & bad moods, that she preserved her own integrity, that she made our marriage work through thick & thin, became the source of our happiness. Nobody could have been a better partner and friend, nobody could have helped me better to fulfil what talent I possessed, than Jane. Therefore in witness of this I would like her to choose the music that gives her most comfort at my cremation, and at my memorial service, if she decides to have one, in consultation with yourselves. It should also be her pleasure to decide what readings, speeches etc., if any, take place. And if she wants none of the above, that's all right too. I want it to be her day, as well as yours, because her pain & her loneliness will be the greatest. You are <u>all</u> my favourite sons. I regret more than I can ever say the failure of my first marriage and the pain it inflicted on you all. But I knew nothing of life in those days, I had no learning in parental love, no trust in women, no identity beyond a terrible need to escape my vile childhood & be acknowledged in some way. Sometimes I can forgive myself, often not. Perhaps by now you can. Please try, for it will add to your happiness.

David

[*written in left margin*] *This is superceded by my following letter
dated 13 ii '02.

London

13 February 2002

Re my remains. Alternatives are – the churchyard off Church
Row in Hampstead, which I always found pretty, but with a
<u>minimum</u> of religious input – or scatter them at sea off the
Cornish coast – but be guided in this as in all things by Jane,
because we sh<u>d</u> somehow be reunited symbolically when she
dies too.

My love again and again to you all –
D

≈

TO AL AND ANNE ALVAREZ

Tregiffian
St Buryan
Penzance
Cornwall

4 August 2001

Dear lovely Als,

As you may remember, the Hodder [& Stoughton] bash is at
the Ivy on Oct 15th, about 50 people, 25 mine. The Hoddisti are
sweet enough but you know what it's going to be like by the
time you pull up at the door. That's how these parties have to
be, which is why you very wisely didn't have one.

On the other hand, there's this. My kids are organising
a kind of Familien-und-Freundefest in Siena, with apartments in a converted castle, and other rooms & apartments

in neighbouring villages, all just a few miles from Siena. Some people are coming for a week, some just the night of the 19th Oct, when there's a kinderfreundlich party with music, magic, dance* (*no live sex shows. My orders.) (if the boys can get it together) thereafter my age ceases to be a subject & they're organising tours to the surrounding area: Pisa, Florence, etc. – which you've seen till you're sick of it all, but for the kids it's culture & activity & a romp, & for me it gives them something to do other than whisper in small groups about who's going to get the silver cow-creamer.[6] You have a firm invitation to the Ivy. But wd̲ you like to trade it for the Siena option, were that to fit in with yr̲ other plans?

Myself, I intend to commandeer a corner table & the best red, eat pasta & schmooze with friends & family, or not. I've no idea who, if anyone, we like, will rise to the bait. I've asked a few, am asking a few more, but I may end up sitting at my table alone, which needn't necessarily be all that bad either.

Please don't see this letter as anything but a tentative & to- tally declinable enquiry. Have you been to any good funerals lately? I did my oration for Dave and it acquired nightmare proportions as his weeping children pressed more and more poems on me to read aloud in front of his coffin. At a certain point (very easily, in my case) the curtains close on the com- passion & hatred kicks in – in this case for Gerard Manley Hopkins for the worst punctuated piece of (unseen) crap I've ever been confronted with, quickly followed by Walt Whitman's 'Assurances', which was easier to read but even harder to agree with.[7] You wait, Al. I'll want the worst of Ezra Pound and some

---

6. Skulduggery around a silver cow-creamer drives the plot of P. G. Wodehouse's *The Code of the Woosters*.

7. 'I need no assurances, I am a man who is pre-occupied of his own soul' (from *Leaves of Grass*). Le Carré's friend Dave Humphries wrote scripts for *London's Burning* and *Dempsey and Makepeace*.

of the sweetest of Christopher Robin, without the laughs. Let me know – en principe –

Love to you both,
David

~

Le Carré here records the death of the man he called his best friend, the artist John Miller.

TO JOHN BOORMAN

By fax

London

2 October 2002

Dear John,

<u>Particularly</u> good to hear from you. We're in London at the moment, in Cornwall from next Tuesday till 25th Oct, loafing again in London through November & probably December.

We marched for peace last Saturday, and found ourselves surrounded by the Ossie Bin Laden Supporters' Club, the latterday Trotzkyists and about six elderly prep school masters among the remaining 250,000 assorted minorities. But it was fun when we stopped outside No. 10 and a huge boo went up. Like being back at school.

I haven't seen Stoppsie's new opus, I'm afraid. I sort of get the bends when every time I set off.[8]

---

8. *The Coast of Utopia*, Stoppard's nine-hour trilogy of plays about six nineteenth-century Russian writers and activists.

Saw 'Lantana' & loved it, 'Talk to Her' & nearly loved it, 'Road to Perdition' & didn't love it at all, just admired it, which doesn't do. Mainly I've been floundering with a novel that keeps tripping me up & the rule is, you have to start again at the beginning. But I'm getting there, wherever there is.

Yes, I did see about the Bushbaby & his daddy, and I loved the extension of the quote, to the effect that this war was therefore 'personal to America'. If anybody had killed my Daddy, or even tried to, I'd have given him my favourite conker.

So glad you re-read LDG [*The Little Drummer Girl*]. Calley & Mike Nichols were going to do a remake a couple of years back but – surprise, surprise – they sort of forgot. The George Hill version was embarrassing.

Do let's meet if we can, it would be a joy. Tell us your dates when you know them. We can't ask you to Cornwall at the moment, because we've got so much family floating about, but next year, if you're game.

Our love to you both. Mike Newell is supposed to be directing 'The Constant Gardener', starting in March, but he's dreadfully evasive. We have an excellent script and the finance, so I expect it will never be made.

Yes, I'm doing an aria for Alec.[9] My best friend died a few months ago & I read my valedictory oration to him and we fine-tuned the grammar, cleaned up the jokes & took out the split infinitives. He asked me how on earth I thought I'd get through it without blubbing, & I told him it was none of his business. I never thought I could miss a friend so much.

More love from us both, Grüss to Isabella also, and the nippers, David

---

9. Alec Guinness died in 2000. The National Film Theatre held a retrospective of his work in October and November 2002.

ABSOLUTE FRIENDS

I have a new novel coming out at Christmas. It's called *Absolute Friends* and it will make people hopping mad . . . next week we go to London so that I can read the book for *Book at Bedtime*, although if I was going to bed, it's about the last thing I'd like to hear . . .

– to his aunt Ruby Hayman, Ronnie's sister, 8 November 2003

I think we both got a bit weary of the clamour over the book, the bouquets as well as the brickbats. (So of course the only thing to do is start another one . . .)

– to Vivian Green, 16 February 2004

In January 2003 le Carré published his widely read essay against the march to war in Iraq called 'The United States of America Has Gone Mad'. He joined the march against the war in Iraq in March. *Absolute Friends*, published in December that year, was received as 'a work of fist-shaking, Orwellian outrage' in *Time* magazine, and as 'an angry disquisition on contemporary geopolitics' in the *Guardian*. After he called for Tony Blair to resign on the *Today* show, le Carré told his brother, Tony, 'the right-wing press popped its garters'.

Le Carré returned to a German setting with *Absolute Friends*, and again with *A Most Wanted Man*, published in 2008 and set in Hamburg, where he once worked in the British consulate. Both books postulated American intervention in Germany amid the war on terror. Between them came *The Mission Song*, centred on the part-Congolese interpreter Salvo, which le Carré wrote in draft before travelling to the Congo. 'It was the strangest journey of my life and it always will be,' he wrote. 'The reality of the place is so overwhelming that stories about it seem almost an irrelevance.'[1] After his Congo journey, le Carré kept the settings of his stories to Britain and Western Europe. Feeling his age in the context of difficult terrain – both geographical and human – he curtailed the challenging research trips that had been a feature of his writing since *The Honourable Schoolboy*.

---

1. *Nation*, 2 October 2006.

In the wake of The Constant Gardener, *le Carré struggled with the writing of* Absolute Friends.

TO SIR JOHN AND LADY MARGETSON

9 Gainsborough Gardens
London, NW3 1BJ

17 November 2002

Dear Miranda and John,

I'm sorry we are so elusive about accepting your hospitality: do forgive us. I have had a very uphill struggle with the new novel, & much frustration, & at last things are beginning to look right. Endless under-painting, scraping off & beginning again some-where else on the canvas, standards getting ever higher, time & energy diminishing in inverse proportion – but the will, thank Heaven, unbowed so far. The problem is always continuity: not stealing 'a few hours' but getting a sustained run of weeks & months in the same place without the delightful diversions – persons from Porlock[2] – that send one scurrying back to the beginning in order to get inside the cage again.

[. . .]

I was pleased to see that Freud recently failed to attend the opening of his own exhibition in Paris because he was too busy painting: that really is the logic of an obsessive, so I'm not the only loony in the world after all.

[. . .]

Jane & I marched against the war last month & hope we'll get a chance to do it again before the world ends. How we ever got from Osama to Saddam is a mystery not even that arch-sophist Blair will explain. Or can. I do hope somebody decides to inspect our weapons of mass destruction soon. Then maybe

---

2. Samuel Taylor Coleridge was interrupted in the writing of 'Kubla Khan' by a 'person on business from Porlock'.

Israel's & America's. But of course we mustn't think that way, must we? I realise now that the Cold War was a Christian war: Western Christendom versus the Eastern Orthodoxy. But what we've got now is far better: we can <u>really</u> smite the heathen at last. Right wing Christianity & right wing Zionism are a heady mix, but we'll deal with that next time round. Ah well.

Love to you both, & thanks again,
David

∾

TO JANE CORNWELL

21 February 2003

My love, my darling love,
You gave me my life. You taught me the only kind of love that matters. I have grown so close to you in my heart in these recent years that I cannot believe we shall ever be divided. No number of 'sorry's' can wipe away my disloyalties; no amount of 'thank you's' can express my thanks. But the love you have taught me is indestructible, and in the face of it, everything else is diminished. We did a good job with our lives by the end. We were decent people. My darling, I love you, & I always, always shall.

Yours – David

∾

The writer and campaigner Anthony Barnett is the founding editor-in-chief of the media platform openDemocracy. Le Carré and Jane supported the organisation through their charitable trust.

to ANTHONY BARNETT

Tregiffian
St Buryan
Penzance
Cornwall

1 January 2004

Dear Anthony,

Again – sorry about dinner, and happy new year to you both.

It's good of you to suggest we do sth about 'Abs. Friends' and the 'anguished' English reviews, but I can't be part of the debate any more. There's no sillier fellow than the writer complaining about his critics, & I can't be another. If the debate needs to take place, it must do so without me. I have said nothing more radical than, for instance, the late Hugo Young: that it was wrong, immoral & gross political folly to commit Britain to the U.S. war machine unequivocally, and that Blair, by withholding the truth that he had committed us in advance, was lying to the British public. If I'd written a play about it, it w<u>d</u> have been acceptable. A few weeks at the Royal Court & goodnight. My sin was/is to have performed in the heartland: in the Times, in the Today Programme, and as a popular middle class novelist. That I succeeded in awakening minds that would have preferred to remain comfortably dormant is evidenced by the response. I am content with that, and more or less expected it. I wrote what I wrote, & retract nothing. Merde.

But I can't write that for you. Maybe someone else can. And maybe not. In all circumstances, the book will continue to live its own life for a while, I hope, after the clamour has died down.

Love to you both, & renewed New Year's wishes.

Ever,

David

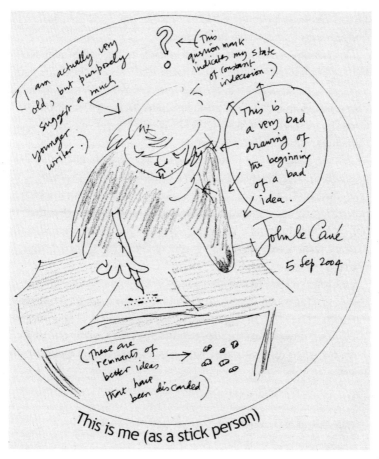

An American fund-raising charity project called 21st Century Leaders asked le Carré and other celebrities to send 'a stick person of themselves'. Le Carré opted for something more ambitious.

Dr August Hanning, president of the Bundesnachrichtendienst, or BND – the foreign intelligence service of the Federal Republic of Germany – first met le Carré at a party to mark the closing of the British Embassy in Bonn. Le Carré visited the BND headquarters, and Hanning came to stay in Cornwall.

Dr Hanning wrote to David and Jane on 21 December 2005 to say that, after an election result in Germany that 'has left the entire political class somewhat clueless', the new minister of the interior had asked him to serve as secretary of state for 'inner security' – as Germany's domestic security chief, with broad responsibility for the police, intelligence services and terrorist threats.

'This presents a few problems, since Germany is not really prepared for serious terrorist and other kinds of threats,' he wrote. 'This is in addition to a general distrust of intelligence work which is nourished by the reporting about actual and alleged practices of the CIA.' Because most Germans rejected the US approach to the 'war on terror', they were losing sight of the original threat from Al Qaeda.

Le Carré's letters to Hanning are markedly sober and considered; copies of Hanning's letters, in German, and le Carré's in English, between 2004 and 2016 were kept carefully filed. The two men tried to arrange a posthumous exhibition for le Carré's friend Karl Weschke, the German artist who had moved to Cornwall in the 1950s.

TO DR AND MRS AUGUST HANNING

Tregiffian
St Buryan
Penzance
Cornwall

28 December 2005

Personal

Dear Ruth and August,

First, our warmest New Year wishes to you both, & to all the family. Our son Nicholas & his fiancée were with us for Christmas and are, at this minute, exploring churches in the neighbourhood, trying to decide which one shd marry them! So we had a great Christmas, as I hope you did, and are secretly relieved that they are disappearing to London for New Year, leaving us free to celebrate the moment at Delhi time rather than U.K. time!

Your news is of course momentous. In the first place, so painful to be leaving the service you built up, the colleagues you have worked with, the wives & families and – here & there, I'm sure – the crazy times as well as the critical ones that you have shared. On the other hand, if I look at my own pygmy-sized experience of the two services that had me, it was actually the domestic one that seemed ultimately more reward-ing, more obviously necessary, more vocational. But from all I read & hear, it's often virtually impossible these days to distin-guish between the functions of the two outfits, particularly in the field of terror. The ethical and actual aspects of the present security situation strike me as quite extraordinary; and that, I am sure, will challenge & fascinate. The War on Terror was/is in so many ways a rhetorical concept, a Scheinkrieg[3] exactly as the Cold War was by the time I left it. Right & wrong lay in one place, the battle-lines in another.

But the objective truth is not the issue. The issue is the public perception of the truth as corrupted & manipulated by our masters, whether here or in the US. There's the extraordin-ary looking-glass effect. A politician tells a lie to a journalist, who prints it. The politician then reads it & believes it. The lie becomes the 'reality', and if the services aren't terribly care-ful, they become its creatures. Which, curiously enough, must

---

3. A mock or make-believe war.

surely make your new job even more worthwhile than the old one: it exists for you to speak truth to power.

And what, for me, would be magical, is the role of Germany at this moment in the defining of Europe's response to the American crusade. Germany must surely be at the brink of predominance in Europe. The graph is turning sharply upward. In matters of civil rights, human rights, & constitutional propriety, your stance has been, publicly at least, the most honourable of all major European nations. We really <u>need</u> you!

Have, again, a great New Year, & all power to your elbow. Jane joins me –

As ever,
David

~

TO DR NANCY OLIVIERI

Tregiffian
St Buryan
Penzance
Cornwall

17 February 2006

Dear Nancy,
I am so glad you enjoyed the film as much as I did.[4] Next time you're in London, <u>please</u> give us a word of warning [. . .] and let us feed & water & entertain you. And if Ralph Fiennes is around & wants to play, we'll haul him along. Nothing in my life has compared with the movie, and its aftermath. The Lara figure, as I told you, I think, in my last letter, ended very soon in her career on the cutting room floor – but mercifully so, because her scenes were poor, it was the first bit of shooting

---

4. *The Constant Gardener.*

anyone did, and she became suddenly very missable: all we had to do was beef up Birgit[5] in Germany, & the job was done. The movie had weaknesses – when did a movie not? Lorbeer never quite came off, at least for me, I was queasy from the start about the memorial service,[6] but none of that mattered in the thrust of it all, in the passion Fernando M brought to the subject, to Africa, to Big Pharma, and given the dedication of Rachel W and Ralph F, which has endured splendidly and most movingly.[7] The Constant Gardener Charity, believe it or not, is now decently funded, registered in Kenya & the UK, has as its trustees the great & good Gethongo,[8] ex-Kenyan minister for anti-corruption (sacked for overzealousness, but bounced back as a whistleblower to huge effect) the former UK High Commissioner in Nairobi (they wouldn't even have me inside the place when I was writing the book) and Ralph, self and Rachel are patrons. While the unit was in place, the lads decided that Kibera slum[9] could do with a leg up, & built a bridge, a drainage system & other mod cons. In Loyangalani on Lake Turkana we have now built a school, loos (plus someone to teach kids how to use them) and far from being a showbiz one-night stand, the projects are flourishing. On March 12th we give yet another charity showing and hold an auction afterwards. Rachel recently was awarded a £30,000 diamond by some ugly group of industrialists as 'Woman of the Year' & promptly handed it over for us to flog. The production company has turned itself into our HQ and sends its staff whizzing

---

5. Birgit was played by Anneke Kim Sarnau. The character of Lara drew on Olivieri's experience.

6. The film's denouement, where Sir Bernard Pellegrin, played by Bill Nighy, is exposed at Justin's memorial service.

7. Director Fernando Meirelles, whose previous film was *City of God*; stars Rachel Weisz and Ralph Fiennes.

8. John Githongo, Kenya's former permanent secretary for governance and ethics.

9. *The Constant Gardener* was filmed on location in Kibera and Loiyangalani.

over to Nairobi & Loy. to remain hands on about details that no big aid agency seems to bother with. I've done a special edition of the paperback where all proceeds go into the pot, and our extraordinary producer Simon Channing-Williams gets on stage whenever he can & simply says 'when we saw what we saw, we decided we couldn't leave it alone, and we never will.' When the movie opens in Nairobi any day now, the High Commission is hosting the bash, charging $100 a plate, & turning over all proceeds to the charity. (Kenya banned the book under Moi, & since the present govt is quite as corrupt, the film still plays nicely in that respect too.)

Your own story runs and runs. It was always extraordinary how much vile behaviour you attracted, & I never for the life of me understood why: too bright, too right and too beautiful, and a woman to boot, you can't win.

[. . .]

We would <u>love</u> to do sth with you next time you surface here. Just give us notice if you can. I have a new novel coming out in September, called 'The Mission Song', I quite like it, but feel flat & useless now it's done.

[. . .]

Dear Nancy, I send, as ever, my admiration, & participation, & affection. Thanks for writing.

love
David

～

In March 2006 Stanley Mitchell, whom le Carré had spied on at Oxford, wrote with a vehement defence of his role in the British Communist Party. He felt 'sick and angry' over le Carré's behaviour, he said, because 'in all innocence I befriended you only to be betrayed, to have my Party betrayed, by you.' With no reply he followed with a terse note in April: 'This is probably the last letter I shall write to you . . . I just want to say that it might stand you in good stead at the pearly gates, if you were to *apologize, not to me but to your better self, for one of the worst things a human being can do and that is to betray a friend.'*

Before and after this letter, le Carré and Mitchell were working towards a reconciliation. A letter from le Carré to Mitchell's family was read aloud at his funeral.

TO STANLEY MITCHELL

9 Gainsborough Gardens
London, NW3 1BJ

19 April 2006

Dear Stanley,

It's hard to respond to hate-mail, & I don't expect you to listen much to what I have to say. When we renewed our acquaintance of fifty years ago, I had hopes that we might be able [to] look back with some detachment and compassion on who we were, where we had come from, and why we did – however mistakenly – the things we did, and why we believed in our respective false gods. I have written about mine, and I thought you might even be able to understand the distance I had come & the ways in which I had changed. It puzzled me, I will admit, that you seemed to display less concern than I might have expected for the fact that you had submitted your life and excellent intellect to the cause of world communism, which even in those days, to those who had half an eye, was responsible for some of the most brutal, conspiratorial, murderous and unprincipled régimes the world has seen. But you were at the soft, kind heart of it, and whatever blemishes you spotted were nothing beside the heady cameraderie fine ideals & intellectual superiority of your élite band. Even if the world was wrong, you were right.

For my own journey, for the world I sprang from, and the world I adopted as my family as you adopted your comrades as yours, you seem to have no understanding, no compassion, no moderate feelings at all, despite the fact that I have spent much of my writing life alternately describing, lampooning and occasionally condemning its elusive nature. To the contrary, it gradually became clear to me that in our revived relationship you saw yourself as the innocent, highminded victim waiting to find it in him to forgive me my trespasses. And it's true – I remember now – I never met an old Communist, whether in Britain or Russia, who didn't see himself as a martyr.

You have called me a lot of things that I am, but others that I am not. You haven't taken even half a step towards the middle ground of reconciliation. Your recent letters have been vile, and of course I didn't reply to them, and this is certainly the last you will hear from me, because the pursuit of reconciliation with you is a dead cause. I betrayed you, you say. What did I know to betray? What did you know or do that was betrayable? We were looking for secret communists and potential traitors. We felt they shouldn't have access to secrets they might betray. Secrets that, in the event of war, would help destroy our own kind. We were in combat with ruthless, insidious people who used British communists and sympathisers as their hunting ground. So we did what any sensible country does: we kept watch, and spread a net, and tried to protect ourselves. Looking back, I don't see anything wrong with that, & I shall be happy to argue the point at the Day of Judgement of which you & Tony Blair make such heavy play. What did I tell my 'masters'? That you were a good man, I expect. I forget, and so I am sure did they.

Best –
David

~

Hugh Thomas had just reread The Spy Who Came in from the Cold. *'I knew Brian Montgomery, who I think was chief of security in MI6 for a bit,' he wrote to le Carré on May Day 2006. 'He told me that he had recommended you to be charged under the Official Secrets Act.'*

TO HUGH THOMAS

Tregiffian
St Buryan
Penzance
Cornwall

10 May 2006

Dear Hugh,

Thanks for your kind letter. Yes, it would be fun to meet. I hope to heaven I had a beautiful girl on my arm when you saw me in the rue Jacob. But perhaps you did & I didn't. There must be a reason why you didn't bellow 'Hoy.'[10]

Just got back from Congo. Not recommended, food awful. We'll be in London in late May for a couple of weeks. I'd love to have lunch with you. [. . .] Poor Monty – for so he was known – was convinced I had lifted the plot of 'The Spy . . .' from an arcane case of double-cross of which I had never heard, & to which I could never have had access. He was talked down by his illustrious peers, one of whom later told me that 'The Spy Who . . .' was 'the only bloody double-agent operation that ever worked.'[11]

Thanks again for writing –
Best,
David

~

10. A typically Wodehousian form of address.

11. Le Carré elsewhere ascribed this remark to the chief of the Secret Intelligence Service. Sir Dick White served as 'C' at the time; he had laughed off attempts to prosecute Graham Greene over *Our Man in Havana*. Le Carré later recalled waiting about four weeks after submitting *The Spy Who Came in from the Cold* to MI6 for approval. 'I still don't know to this day what I would have done if they had said you can't publish it.'

TO CHARLOTTE CORNWELL

By email

17 May 2006

Subject: breathtaking newsflash from yr brother david

dearest sis, this is my day to become an emailist. I have just finished a new novel . . . not a work of genius, but not all lousy either.[12] I'll let you have a proof in a month or so. Are you coming to the wedding? Everyone hopes so.[13] [. . .]

I went to the Eastern Congo a few weeks back to do some last research for my novel and it was fascinating and heartbreaking. Drove to the border from Kigali, Rwanda, and stopped off at a couple of genocide sites. They've pickled the bodies somehow and left them on show, lest anybody should take it into his head to say it never happened. Thousands of bodies, mostly kids, a lot of them chopped to pieces. See 'Shooting Dogs' if you can. Better than 'Hotel Rwanda'. Two town riots in five nights, and a colonel of the MaiMai told me that his best warriors were eleven or twelve years old. Also that he and his lads could turn bullets into water, which gave them the edge in a firefight. When I asked him for the formula he said it wouldn't work on me.

Everyone's ill, and I'm seeing the Rear Admiral[14] next week. [. . .]

Did you get my letter in reply to yours? I was very touched . . .

Much love, David

~

---

12. *The Mission Song.*

13. Nicholas Cornwell married the solicitor Clare Algar on 15 July 2006.

14. Le Carré's nickname for his urologist.

TO RALPH DE BUTLER

Chalet Chamois
3823 Wengen
Switzerland

14 September 2006

Dear Mr de Butler,
Thanks for your letter & your kind words. No, I'm afraid I have long rejected the historical novel as a vehicle for my own writing, although the Nutmeg Wars[15] have always amused me, and the early days of Portuguese slavery have always horrified me.

Best wishes,
John le Carré

∾

Le Carré had met Murat Kurnaz, who would be an inspiration for Issa in A Most Wanted Man.

TO NICHOLAS SHAKESPEARE

9 Gainsborough Gardens
London, NW3 1BJ

14 November 2006

Dear Nicholas,
Well golly how <u>wonderful</u> to hear from you: thought you were still in Tasmania, & here you are with <u>2 sons</u> – zütt! or however it's spelt – & living in Wiltshire. How the Englanders do come home in the end – like the Russians, kicking & screaming, but

---

15. The Dutch and the British went to war in the seventeenth century over the nutmeg trade from the Spice Islands in Indonesia.

there's nowhere else that fucks you up quite as well as the old country. Look at Blair! How did we spawn the mendacious little show-off? This child, playing grown-up games, & fucking up the world in his Noddy car. And today, this very day, proposing 'a new approach to the Middle East'! Like what? Like draining the Red Sea? Blocking the Canal? [Tom] Bower – he's remark-able. Every time I need to know someone really bad, he knows him intimately. He's helped me to people in the City, in Africa & the press. And here & there, I've helped him back. [. . .]

I just today came from Hamburg. In Bremen I spent 2 days interviewing a former Guantanamo detainee, the poor bugger was head-hunted in Pakistan, bought by the CIA for $3000, tortured in Kandahar (electric shock & waterboard-ing), flown to Guantanamo & kept there 4½ years, sprung last August. He's now conducting useless lawsuits against the Germans, US & Turks. Nobody suggests he was ever guilty of being anything remotely like a terrorist. But, my hat, there's a grown-up! Hungerstruck for 20 days, fed through the nose, beaten to a pulp repeatedly, did 'isolation' for 5 weeks as punish-ment, woken every 2 hours & shifted to another cage so that he never slept. Couldn't move his feet more than manacle-distance when he was returned to the Germans who'd set him up.

It wd be lovely to see you all. Let's fix sth. I'm going for a new novel, but it's a labour. Just no autobiog, I pray, & I'm not yet ready to get a dog. Love to Gillian,[16] whose lovely little draw-ings adorn the office, love to all your family, & to you too, dear man –

Best,
David

∼

---

16. Shakespeare's wife, Gillian Johnson, writer and illustrator.

TO BERNHARD DOCKE[17]

By email

9 February 2007

Dear Dr Docke,

I bring greetings to you from Clive Stafford Smith[18] who is a friend of mine. My daughter-in-law actually worked with him on civil rights cases in New Orleans.

I write under the name of John le Carré and am trying to set a novel around the fortunes of a young Chechen Muslim who finds himself in Hamburg, and comes to grief there. I would love the opportunity of a background briefing from you concerning the Muslim community in Bremen and in Hamburg, and the application of German asylum laws in the case of foreign nationals resident in Germany. I have, incidentally, had two prolonged meetings with Murat Kurnaz in Bremen and have followed Murat's case with great interest. I know, of course, that he owes you a very great debt.

I wondered, therefore, whether I might persuade you to have lunch with me, either in Bremen or in Hamburg or, if that is not possible, if I might come to see you in your office? I will be staying at the Hotel Atlantic Kempinski in Hamburg from 23rd February for at least a week, and would, of course, be happy to come to Bremen. Alternatively, if your travels take you to Berlin, I would be happy to meet you there.

With my very best wishes.
Yours sincerely,
David Cornwell

～

17. The prize-winning German human-rights lawyer who represented Murat Kurnaz.

18. Lawyer representing death-penalty defendants in the US as well as Guantánamo Bay prisoners, founder of the legal-action NGO Reprieve.

There was a startling intimacy in le Carré's later letters to his brother, Tony.

TO TONY CORNWELL

> *9 Gainsborough Gardens*
> *London, NW3 1BJ*

> 15 May 2007

Dearest To,

Well, thanks a million for your lovely long letter and all the kind & wise things you say about us, the universe, & the whole catastrophe, as Zorba w<u>d</u> have it. Yes, we have indissoluble and incomparable bonds. Sometimes, with age, one's childhood is the only bit one imagines one sees clearly. But probably what really happens is, we peck everything we know onto its back, & it becomes the lodebearer for all of it. We were frozen children, & will always remain so. The chip of ice that G. Greene said every writer sh<u>d</u> have in his heart was spread over our entire bodies from an early age.[19] Kids who are brought up without the experience of heterosexual love are basically screwed: forget all the smart talk, the 'tolerance' of other orientations which isn't tolerance at all. When you hit the bottom line, it's 'what did you have around you when it mattered?' The only poetry we remember is the stuff we learned as kids, & it's not much different with love. You chase after it, act it, imitate it, and eventually, if you're old & lucky, you believe in it, but it comes hard, it's flawed, & we fake it a lot, like religion, in the hope that one day we'll have it for real. So we loved each other, because actually that's all we had, & we reacted off each other, towards & against each other, & we lived in each other's skins, & revolted against

---

19. 'There is a splinter of ice in the heart of a writer,' Greene wrote in his autobiography *A Sort of Life*. Le Carré also cited Greene's 'chip of ice' in his speech accepting the Olof Palme Prize on 31 January 2020.

the captivity, & the emptiness of the rest of our lives, and we learned sex too late like everything else, and we went our different ways, but probably they were ultimately very similar ways, which is another serious annoyance. Our father was a mad genes-bank, a truly wild card, and in my memory disgusting – still. I never mourned him, never missed him, I rejoiced at his death. Is that so awful? I don't think so. Writing about him, I tried to make him sweeter, but it didn't work. When I was faithless, I blamed him, when I promised love all over town, it was his fault, when I met our mother I thought her spooky & unreal, & I was never able to understand – I still can't even begin to – how you walk out on two sons in the middle of the night, then take the high moral ground. But she was just a poor woman at her wits' end, I expect. We'll never know. Perhaps they were both much more ordinary than we give them credit for – just not for us. Either way, they fucked us up rotten. If we'd been street kids, we'd have been better off by far. But we were locked into the dreadful middle air of sterilised English Bürgertum where you don't even know how to use a screwdriver, can't do a manual day's work, mend a pipe or change a wheel. We were nowhere, and obliged to hang there till someone cut us down. It's a much mistaken fantasy of yours that I 'conformed,' as if somehow by crossing the Atlantic you didn't. The bodies I worked for were so way out in so many ways that they were a kind of nirvana of anti-orthodoxy put to orthodox ends. We were rebels in suits, and much of it – though probably useless – was positively anarchic in its creative thinking. Today it would run, 'Well, suppose we set up our own branch of Al Quaeda . . .' So yes, in the end, the aims were societal. But the means were Ronnie's.

My news? Well, it's rich. Three movies in preparation – TTSS, to be adapted by Peter Morgan for feature film, 'Our Game', a bum novel, to be adapted by a Russian-American, and 'The Mission Song', script due in July. I'm deep in a novel I love, writing well, and the Bodleian Library is taking all my papers, correspondence, mss, the whole crap, which solves

484

a lot of problems, particularly for my kids. I'm off to Berlin tomorrow to do some more research. My sources are Chechen, some ex Guantanamo detainees, their lawyers, & so on. A truly absorbing world, horrific, with a kind of Cancer Ward normality about it which is infectious.

Son Nick, out of the blue, has written a superb 600 page novel, if you can believe it, & people are saying he's a genius, which as a matter of fact I suspect the little bastard is. His war scenes are magnificent & he's never had a whiff of grapeshot, & he's got a lovely, quietly witty style that I think people are going to love. A huge canvas, and I never knew he had it in him. So much for fathers. His book goes out on submission by the best lit agent in London next week. 'Is any of this in the family?' he asked Nick nervously. Nick: 'Well, actually my father is J le C.' Agent: 'Ah. Well, I think we'll keep that quiet for the time being.' Not bad.

Dearest To, I too love you, dearly. Life joined us at the hip, so severance was inevitable. My friends are going down like flies, but we're immortal so it's all right. I'm so glad you've found happiness in Nettie, & joy in her family. Hollanders are a rum bunch in my experience. Like the Englanders. Alexander? Only the good worry about whether they were wrong. No good being a flagellant. We're at the peak of life, not at the bottom of the hill, & bloody lucky to be there.

Take care.
David

～

The veteran journalist Douglas Jackson, an assistant editor at the Scotsman, sent le Carré his first book, Caligula, about a young slave who becomes elephant-keeper to the famously mad emperor.

TO DOUGLAS JACKSON

9 Gainsborough Gardens
London, NW3 1BJ

23 April 2008

Dear Doug Jackson,

Thank you for your letter of 16th, and for 'Caligula', on which I sincerely congratulate you. Tim tells me this is your first novel, and I don't need to tell you that to have <u>completed</u> the damned thing, & then see it placed with a reputable, mainstream publisher is, in these dog days, a miracle in itself. But you have more than that to congratulate yourself on, which is what makes it easy for me to respond to you: you can write. You know how to make a paragraph sit up, you have an ear for the rhythm of what you are saying, and the reader (or certainly this one) is grateful, & appreciates the authority, and reads on. And I can tell you that, if you saw some of the stuff that's sent to me, that already sets you apart from the many.

That said, I'm afraid I don't feel able to supply your publishers with a quote. I give quotes very sparingly, normally for non-fiction, and your material is way outside my sphere. It occurred to me – as it has no doubt occurred to you & your publishers – that Robert Harris w<u>d</u> be the ideal voice. I hope this does not discourage you, for the purpose of my writing to you is the opposite. I believe you have skills & understanding that will carry you forward to justified success. So good luck!

Yours sincerely,
David Cornwell
(John le Carré)

Caligula *was published by the Bantam Press. Fifteen novels followed, mostly set in Ancient Rome, and they were translated into twelve languages, with sales of about half a million books worldwide.*

~

The dramatist Robert Forrest adapted five le Carré books for BBC Radio, starring Simon Russell Beale as Smiley. The first was Call for the Dead. *Forrest had just adapted* The Weir of Hermiston *by Robert Louis Stevenson.*

TO ROBERT FORREST

> *Tregiffian*
> *St Buryan*
> *Penzance*
> *Cornwall*

> 16 June 2008

Dear Robert,

Thanks so much for yours. Like you, I am very excited by the project, and I love radio. To be honest, I've always secretly believed that my work best lends itself to radio adaptation, & I think we may give a lot of pleasure & food for thought to a lot of people. And yes, please do have a lot of fun, which is surely a measure of engagement also. I do find that when I write something scary, I'm scared myself & when I've brought off something comic, I crack up laughing. Always so odd that the Master himself, PG (master of plot as well as humour) never was held to be amusing company. Yes, Stevenson is <u>truly</u> great – never quite accepted by the lit bureaucracy because he's so compelling as a story-teller. So it goes. Thanks so much for writing. Don't be daunted, tell Shaun[20] not to be either, just – yet again – enjoy it!

Best wishes,

David

---

20. The writer Shaun McKenna adapted four Smiley novels in the radio series 'The Complete Smiley'.

~

Dr Hanning, Germany's domestic security chief, wrote to thank le Carré for sending a copy of A Most Wanted Man. *The novel invoked a power struggle between German and US intelligence agencies over an anti-terror operation; it centred on the fate of Issa Karpov, a Muslim refugee from Chechnya, living illegally in Hamburg, where le Carré had his last Foreign Office posting.*

Dr Hanning said le Carré had created a 'literary monument' for Hamburg as he had for Bonn with A Small Town in Germany. *He wrote of the Russian–Chechen conflict and recalled visiting Beslan, the scene of a school hostage-taking by Chechen fighters where more than three hundred people, including many children, died.*

TO DR AUGUST HANNING

By fax

Cornwall

24 December 2008

Dear August,
First, a most happy and peaceful Christmas to you and all your family.

Second, thank you most warmly for your letter, which I was relieved to receive, and which I read with great interest & sympathy. It is my fortune and misfortune to live in an imaginary parallel universe to the realities of your profession: to twist it and shape it until it does the work of the wider world in which the reader can find himself. In consequence, I take my criticism and compliments from two fronts: those who know the real world, and are incensed that I have misrepresented it; and those who take my parallel universe at face value. In the interviews and public debates in which I was involved, nonetheless,

I had the feeling that, however crudely, I had raised some useful issues: the US–German relationship as defined by the so-called war on terror; the danger that, at the lower levels, the security services in your country, as in mine, increasingly if unconsciously, contribute to the demonisation of Islam generally rather than Islamism particularly; and that the mushroom growth of intelligence services since 9/11 has not occurred without a loss of quality, or a widening of the margins of error. In many of these questions, the Germany of my novel inevitably served as the whipping boy for what has already happened in my own country, where draconian laws and excessive powers, and a near-slavish submission to American demands, have taken us over the brink. In Germany, so far as I can read the situation, your much stronger constitution, and greater awareness of the negative alternatives to democracy, have imposed far greater (and admirable) restraints on the deployment & powers of the security authorities. It is not in my view derogatory, rather the reverse, of the Neue Zuricher Zeitung to describe the German intelligence structure (& security structure in particular) as eine ewige Baustelle.[21] Better, in my excessively liberal view, chaos in the world of security, than perfection.

Of Chechnya we have different, but very comparable, experiences. Through the good offices of Issa Kostoyev, an Ingush deputy of the Duma and a celebrated police officer, now dead, I spent quite some time, in Moscow, with Chechen and Ingush groups, and learned what it felt like to be an Untermensch in Russian eyes. Their stories of persecution, bereavement, and mass torture by the Russians occupying their homeland are as indelible in my memory as are yours of the horrified widows & mothers of Beslan. I was also in the Palestinian refugee camps of South Lebanon during Israeli bombardments, and in Chatila shortly after the massacre of Palestinians by Lebanese Christians under Israeli control. There is a poem that covers our dual experience, by WH Auden:

21. An eternal construction site.

> I and the public know
> What all schoolchildren learn
> Those to whom evil is done
> Do evil in return.

But I believe we agree on more than we realise, concerning the real world; and above all, that there is no longterm solution to terrorism on either side (whatever the 'sides' are) without radical political & cultural rethinking and negotiation. If that is what Obama is bringing to your table, then the next four years may not be as bad as the economists predict!

Dear August, again my heartfelt greetings to you all, in which Jane joins me. It was a great compliment that you managed to spend time on my novel. I can only imagine the strains of your life, & only admire the strength & dedication with which you support them.

As ever,
David

P.S. The Baader–Meinhof film in the end sadly disappointed me – I think on the issue of motive, and the political mood of the day.[22]

~

In a letter to le Carré on 11 January 2009, Dr Hanning looked back over the European immigration and integration of Muslims in the previous thirty years. He noted the mixed feelings towards Muslim emigrants to Germany: 'since the times of the Crusades [there has been] a dull sense of a Muslim threat to the "Christian world". 'German majority society is today registering an ever larger number of Muslim communities that are growing more and more self-confident,' he wrote. 'This evokes fear . . .'

---

22. *The Baader Meinhof Complex*, released in 2008, nominated for Best Foreign Language Film at the Academy Awards.

Dr Hanning admitted that with Germany's intelligence services operating across sixteen German federal states, 'our system is not easily understandable from the outside and does have shortcomings.' But in practice it worked well, he said.

TO DR AUGUST HANNING

By fax

London

18 January 2009

Dear August,

Thank you so much for your long and most interesting letter of 11th January, and let me begin by offering you a word of humorous consolation that found no favour when I offered it to a friend in my former service: in a healthy democracy it is probably not desirable that the intelligence services be wholly efficient, or wholly admired. The 'ewige Baustelle' has so many architects, and the clients vary their requirements from day to day. And the eternal conflict between what is expedient and what is ethically tolerable never ceases, nor should it: these are the very principles on which our democracies are established and – as I said before, I think – Germany has thus far clung to them much more faithfully than Britain.

I entirely follow and respect your portrait of the position of Muslims in Germany today, and the historical and cultural attitudes that attach to it. The differences between our two countries in this respect are perhaps two-fold:

1. Christianity as it is practiced in Germany is no longer a concept in Britain. Public church attendance is minimal, we have an Anglican church which is hugely top-heavy (more bishops than communicants, and the Queen personally the Church's presiding figure) and a Catholic church that attends

mostly to immigrants from Ireland (and a minority of mainly upper-class survivors from Henry VIII . . .) As a social-political force, therefore, Christianity here is far less effective than in Germany.

2. Our (largely shameful) colonial past has given us a traditional, if distorted, acquaintance with 'people of colour' from our old possessions, and immigration also has a longer history and a clearer reason. As of today, <u>one in ten Britons</u> is racially mixed, and the dilution of cultural borders is gradually following. So the desired assimilation that you spoke of in Oettingen looks like happening, if at a snail's pace, here. In this respect, the election of Obama will have, is having, a hugely beneficial effect on traditional social prejudices.

But the causes of Islamist militancy and anger, in the case of Britain, go much further back than in the case of Germany, surely. We are the originators of so much of the present discord: we promised Palestine in both directions, we agreed to, and assisted in, the partition of India and the creation of Pakistan & Bangladesh, we conspired in the ousting of Mossadeq and the installation of the Shah, we made fools of ourselves in Suez and again in Iraq; and in the very creation of Iraq, in collusion with the French, we made a time-bomb. The winners forget, but the victims have terribly long memories, and we have paid for that, & <u>will</u> pay for it – just as in Ireland. [. . .]

So there are, from a British perspective, very strong reasons, historically, why we should be hated. Reasons, but not excuses, for the stuff we are all rightly afraid of. What I think we both absolutely agree about – & I don't think actually we disagree at all – is that we can't deal with the symptoms without attacking the disease itself; not by decimating Gazans, but by creative and determined negotiation.

Thanks so much for writing so thoughtfully, and please also forgive this overlong letter. By the way, I met Peer Steinbrück[23] in Hamburg and sat up listening to him till the early hours.

23. Peer Steinbrück was Germany's federal minister of finance from 2005 to 2009.

I didn't come away feeling very relieved about the economic situation!

Dear August, I send you as ever my most sincere good wishes.

Yours,
David

OUR KIND OF TRAITOR

The last I heard of Dima in real life was that he was trying to explain to the Moscow police why he had a couple of business-men chained together in his cellar. He's disappeared from my life. But he kind of hung around as a character to be written about and developed one day.

– in a 2010 interview with NPR's Robert Siegel

Our Kind of Traitor was published in September 2010; it was the first le Carré novel with his new publisher, Viking Penguin. Over the following eight years le Carré's entire backlist would be reissued in the Penguin Modern Classics series. More than ever before le Carré's life would see a spate of intersecting novels and film projects, galvanised by the production company established by his sons Simon and Stephen, the Ink Factory. A phenomenal work-rate was established as he entered his eighties.

In 1993, in his research for Our Game, *le Carré had met a Russian crime boss, Dima, in his Moscow nightclub, who had shot his mother's lover at fourteen and 'who looked ridiculously like Kojak'. Sixteen years later Dima muscled his way into* Our Kind of Traitor, *as a money-launderer for the Russian mafia seeking to defect. Le Carré was sending drafts of the novel to Federico Varese, Oxford criminologist and author of* The Russian Mafia, *to pin down the characterisation.*

TO FEDERICO VARESE

> *9 Gainsborough Gardens*
> *London, NW3 1BJ*

21 April 2009

Dear Federico,

Here are the first hundred pages or so. You will very quickly see the areas where I need your advice: the precise biographies and origin of Anna & Dima, accuracy about Dima's childhood – could he really have elected to remain in the Gulag at his mother's side? I doubt it, so we need a different construct, as we do for his induction into a Brotherhood – let's decide which Brotherhood, make it plausible. Then Dima's first brother: I see him as the Russian vor[1] in Rome you described to me, & I am imagining that Dima & his first brother (my own phrase – is it OK?) have been syphoning off receipts, & fallen foul of the top people – alternatively that the top people have been doing the syphoning, & Dima & his first brother have found out.

Now to the larger picture: The map is a money-laundering & Mafia-operations map showing how funds from all the illicit trades (arms/nuclear?/drugs/people trafficking/extortion/ laundering etc.) are being funnelled towards a central bank, and this bank (though we shall not yet tell Perry this) is in

---

1. Vory, the brotherhood of the Russian criminal underworld, from *vory v zakone*, 'thieves in law'; *vor*, a made man.

London (or will be when it is licenced), where it has the support of 'respectable' establishment figures who will be on the board or otherwise salaried. The licence I am giving myself – and again I shall need your advice, or Lander's – is in ascribing criminal practises to oligarchs – e.g. is there a fictional oligarch in Britain who is helping to push the banking licence through?

Enough food for thought at the moment. You will see how much I have already drawn on your information, & I look fwd very much to our meeting, as soon as you have managed to read the material. Everything is changeable, nothing is set in stone.

Hope Brussels was rewarding. Have you been to wicked King Leopold's African museum? A horror story in disguise.

Best to you all –
David

P.S. I keep copies of these letters, of course!

Le Carré and Varese met to discuss the drafts in person, but in an email on 28 April 2009 Varese observed: 'The general theme of the Russian mafia slowly merging with the state is both correct factually and true to the novel (and it mirrors what David will say about this country). Old Mafiosi either accept to become the subordinates of state interests in Russia, or they are pushed out.' He suggested that Dima could have become infatuated with Anna after she came to work at a private clinic he owned.

∽

Le Carré's first wife, Ann, married to Roger Martin, died on 2 June, aged seventy-six. Ann and Roger had visited Cornwall for the solar eclipse in August 1999, and for Nicholas Cornwell's wedding, among other events involving the extended family.

TO ROGER MARTIN

9 Gainsborough Gardens
London, NW3 1BJ

3 June 2009

Dear Roger,

Nobody could have been a more loyal, honourable and caring husband to Ann, in sickness & in health, or a more steadfast friend and support for her/our children, your stepchildren. We all of us know with what forbearance and soldierly fortitude you attended to her in these last difficult, painful years, and I believe that all of us would want to thank you from our hearts; Jane & I for starters. So I send you my most particular, and dare I say fraternal, commiseration, and thanks, and appreciation.

I'm not sure that in some ways it wasn't for the best. Ann had shown courage beyond courage, exactly as we would expect of her, but the pain of repeated operations & the accumulation of so many drugs, and the sheer spiritual cost of triumphing over so much misfortune, were noticeably taking their toll in these last months, it seemed to us. And in all of it, you were at her side, brushing away the approaching shadows, her most loyal man. That she was reconciled with all of us, and proud of it; that she had found it in her heart, nearly I think, to forgive me my defection and enjoy the friendship that the four of us brokered & built upon so successfully; was a satisfaction to her, as it will remain for all of us. We became what she most wished: a genuine, almost model, extended family, joined by good hearts & pragmatic needs. That actually became rather magical for her, and surprising: the presence of love in new forms, expressing itself over time, and deepening rather than wavering. In all of that your own contribution remains inestimable. And in that spirit, my unstinted gratitude & affection, & shared grief.

As ever,
David

≈

TO JEAN CORNWELL

9 Gainsborough Gardens
London, NW3 1BJ

4 June 2009

Dear Jeannie,

You will have heard the sad news of Ann, and you can certainly imagine the turmoil that has followed: four married sons, fourteen grandchildren [. . .]

It's a jolly-odd thing, being an ex-husband in mourning, & not an easy part to play well, and I suppose equally odd to be the second wife of the first husband, or indeed the second husband of the deceased wife receiving such a motley of mourners, but there we go. The thing about me is, I seem to mourn and giggle at the same time. Do you know the feeling? One's actual emotions are so remote from the ceremonial expression of them that there's always a sort of humour-gap into which the weakly-anchored fall . . .

The mystery is about who one was <u>then</u>, not who one is now. What is certain, though, is that the boys are knocked sideways with grief, and determined to make a fitting affair of it, and that I, as their Dad, wish them to achieve it. And, in a way, I am similarly knocked sideways, even if I defected from the relationship about two hundred years ago, and have been keeping it together for the sake of family, good sense, and old affection.

Our own news is, by contrast, disgracefully good, in that I have a new novel going well, we have no known signs of ill-health, Brad Pitt has just bought 'The Night Manager', an early novel of mine, to produce & star in, which of course is a lottery; three other books are headed for production as films, one starting quite soon, and the BBC 4 (radio) stuff seems to be going down well, & will run – can you believe it? – until May next year.

Tomorrow we leave for Bern, where I am to make a speech in German in the Cathedral to commemorate the foundation of the University. They gave me a doctorate recently for being the most useless student they ever had, for ten months . . . then we go to Paris for the Men's Final of the French Tennis Open, because I have a scene set there in my new novel. Then (next Thursday) we return, and will come & visit you soon thereafter. I'm sorry we've been lax, but we were buried in Cornwall while I scribbled.

Tony surfaced to express his regrets. He's 80 in August. Blimey.

Forgive this long scribe, but sometimes letters are more fun. We think of you often, & send love.

David

~

TO FEDERICO VARESE

By email

3 July 2009

Subject: Manuscript

Dear Federico,
We will be sending to you on Monday the first 170-odd pages of my novel, much revised and restructured. I would be very grateful if you could wade through the whole of it again. You will see that I have compressed and re-ordered the story in order to achieve greater narrative power and I hope that this has not happened at the expense of credibility in areas where you are king. If so, you have but to tell me.

Every novel has its watershed chapter. In this novel, the watershed is Chapter 6.[2] In creative terms, the writing is all downhill from here: Paris, Bern, bureaucratic intrigues back in London, grim resolution.

The coming chapters will also contain negotiations with Dima on his return from Moscow, and I shall again be turning to you. In the meantime, I greatly look forward to your response.

[. . .]

With our love to you and your family.

All the best,
David

~

Ralph Fiennes starred in The Constant Gardener, *released in 2005, critically and commercially one of the most successful film productions of le Carré's work. Le Carré bought a map of East Africa for Fiennes after filming finished, from Bryars & Bryars in Cecil Court, where he was a regular visitor. He had just turned in* Our Kind of Traitor.

TO RALPH FIENNES

> *Tregiffian*
> *St Buryan*
> *Penzance*
> *Cornwall*
>
> 7 October 2009

---

2. In Chapter 6 of *Our Kind of Traitor*, Perry Makepiece describes his meeting with the Russian, Dima, to the British intelligence official Hector Meredith.

Dear Ralph,

I should have thanked you long ago for your very funny letter from Switzerland – the Swiss are <u>so</u> rum. I never knew a country where so many of its citizens conform with their national stereotypes. They were wonderfully depicted in a series of satirical 19th Century novellen by Gottfried Keller – 'The People of Seldwyla' I think they're called, & worth a serious peek because none of the jokes are out of date.

Our own news is good, & explains my silence. I just turned in a novel that I quite like – all done down here for once, with zero social life & going to bed at half past nine, so not a natural recipe for inspiration, but something developed along the way. The last book I wrote without any research, travel or unscripted emotional entanglement, was 'Tinker Tailor . . .' & I took the first 300 pp up to the top of the cliff and burned them in my frustration: a typical author's 'pity-me' lie, because Jane had a copy. Anyway, once it's in proof I'll send you a copy for fun, & I fear that's all, because for once I don't think there's a part that would draw you, whereas in most other books there are about three in which I could see you!

'My movie projects' is the next heading of this letter and as ever they border on the farcical. Peter Morgan did a script for the feature film of TTSS which nobody took to, myself least of all. The general response from directors seems to have been, 'why mess with Alec's stuff, & how can we do it better?' – & they can't. Now Morgan seems to have left the scene and a vampire-director from Sweden (?) called Alfredson ('Let the Right One In') has been signed to work with new writers. (This is all Working Title – Universal.) I saw his movie, & it will be really interesting to see how he handles over-14s.

'The Mission Song' is out on offer – Curtis & Wade?[3] – & I'm not sure whether anyone's bitten. 'A Most Wanted Man',

---

3. Neal Purvis and Robert Wade, screenwriters who co-wrote seven Bond films, produced an adaptation of *The Mission Song*, still unmade. Le Carré was prone to misremembering names; he notoriously came off a call with Working Title bemused

which I really care about, is being scripted by Ronan Bennett, but as yet no egg has been laid. And Brad Pitt has exhumed 'The Night Manager' which would have been <u>perfect</u> for you – still would be – from the contractual morass it was in, and the last I heard was that it would be due on Labour Day, but I still don't know when Labour Day is: maybe if we knew when it was conceived we'd have a clearer idea.

We come to London at the weekend for total immersion in agents, publishers, Tim Bevan, Swedish vampires, family birthdays and – at last – a decent restaurant or two. We see Annie CW[4] when we can, by the way, she's still fighting awful grief & loneliness. Lord, how I miss him too, as I'm sure you do.

If you're around & in the mood, maybe a meal? We cook for you very happily or out somewhere. I've no idea what you're up to professionally, so if you're in far flung places & can't get this, I shan't fret!

Best as ever, love from us both,
David

≈

TO AL ALVAREZ

By email

26 October 2009

Al. Thought this might amuse you. My enlistment papers for Penguin worldwide. d

---

that everyone should be so excited to have secured Barry Goldman – an actor of whom he'd never heard – to play George Smiley in *Tinker Tailor Soldier Spy*.

4. *The Constant Gardener* producer Simon Channing Williams had died in April. Channing Williams, who lived in Cornwall, had entered le Carré's life shortly before the death of his close friend John Miller.

A USER'S MANUAL
(A helpful guide to the Care & Maintenance of an old writing instrument.)

Please don't offer me:
– launch parties for my books, or for anyone else's book
– birthday and Christmas presents
– memorial volumes to surprise me on my 80th birthday in two years' time
– celebratory occasions, grand dinners, etc.
– lunches with influential editors or literary journalists
– propositions over the telephone to which I invariably say 'yes', leaving Jane with the unenviable task of saying 'no'

Writing, reading, publicity and communication generally:
– I write all my books by hand. I barely type, but can do one-finger email. Jane and no one else re-types my handwriting endlessly for me, and is my companion in all literary and pro-fessional matters. Her word is my word, and usually she's better at it than I am. So when you get Jane, you are not getting second best, you are getting The One.
– I read extremely slowly and am probably a late onset dyslexic. Over a single year, I complete the reading of very few books, most of them are either classics or non-fiction. I haven't read a thriller for decades, and know next to nothing of my contem-porary writers, or their work. I have a distaste for the 'literary scene'.
– I never submit my books for literary prizes (e.g., The Booker) and don't intend to start now.
– In matters of editing, you will find me excessively responsive and we must find ways to control this. I suggest that all editor-ial points – wherever they come from in the House, and from whichever side of the world – be channelled through a single editor in London. There will be differences of comprehension and language between the US and the UK and, for as long as the differences are of that kind, I can handle a separate editorial

correspondence with New York. But any bearing on narrative values, aesthetics, character, construction, etc. – e.g., 'I lost my way between pages 83 and 208' – should please come to me by way of the London editor and not directly from the States. The best editor for me is the one who diagnoses freely but never suggests remedies or comes up with alternative wordings.

– I find a multiplicity of contacts within a publishing house muddling. If a draft blurb comes to me from one person, a draft jacket design from a second, and a request for an interview from a third, I am left wondering who knows what, and who is in charge of the project.

– I am a compulsive re-writer. It's how my books develop, and it is a process that doesn't cease until the novel has been through many drafts, followed by at least two proof stages.

– The ideal publishing relationship was the one I enjoyed for twenty-five years with Bob Gottlieb of Knopf, through whom, at his own request, everything was channelled. I care deeply about jacket design, I fuss over layout, the opacity and durability of the paper, and the way a book is spoken for. Bob did too, so we had no problem.

– Given the chance, therefore, I'm a pain in the neck about these things, but my agent is there to hold the ring.

<u>Publicity anywhere in the world:</u>

– Here I suggest we work exclusively through my agent. I am not publicity-shy, simply publicity-exhausted. If I could live henceforth in an interview-free world, I would be a happier writer. I detest appearing on television, I have nothing to say that I haven't said – and probably contradicted – a hundred times over. I don't share the view that public exposure is synonymous with sales, and I am so depressed by the state of the world that, given half a chance, I provide dismal copy.

– The hardest patch for me these days is America, where I am cast as anti-American, anti-Semitic, anti-God and anti pretty-well-everyone-else. Defending that image is about as productive as saying 'No, I am not a paedophile.'

– Better to let the books speak for themselves.

– At 78, I seem to have hit a writing streak. It can't last for ever. If the next twelve months have to be devoted to a book I have written, rather than to the one I should be writing, that would be a pity for us all.

Reviews:

– Half a century of being reviewed has taught me that there is nothing new under the critical sun. In my new novel, the white hats will find all they need to love, and the black hats all they need to revile. As time passes, there are more defectors than converts.

– Jane reads the main reviews and gives me the gist. I tuck into them when the time comes to compile quotes for the paperback.

The Future:

– Please don't ask me what the next book's about. My answer is always GOLF – a game I neither play nor aspire to.

And most important of all:

– My pen-name, properly spelt, defies French grammatical convention by having a small 'l'. This small 'l' has become, for Freudian reasons, an obsession for me in age. Please indulge it, and please ask your correspondents to do the same.

I am very happy to be with Penguin.

∼

Le Carré, nearly eighty, cherished his role as grand-paterfamilias.

to JEAN CORNWELL

9 Gainsborough Gardens
London, NW3 1BJ

13 January 2010

Dearest Jeannie,

We went to Cambodia, stayed in a grand hotel in Siem Reap, near Angkor Wat where the splendid temples are, took Nick & Clare with us, and after 5 days there, flew back to Bangkok, then up to Chiang Mai, where Simon & Mimi have built a beautiful (and _very_ big) traditional Thai house of redwood, with one mercifully air-conditioned, very Western annex. Nick & Clare stayed in the guest room – a kind of tiny house of its own in the courtyard – and Jane & I stayed a few miles up the road in another tiny, very comfortable house in the grounds of a big, empty, very ugly hotel devoted to Buddhist contemplation, but we never saw anyone contemplating anything except breakfast.

We rode elephants, toured remote temples, visited a cave full of Buddhist shrines, and ate ourselves into the ground on superb Thai food. But best of all was the enchantment of a completely happy family Christmas feast taken out of doors by candlelight and moonlight, with Simon cooking a turkey from New Zealand, and serving his own home-made Christmas pudding brought from London, and sweet, shy servants helping, and Mimi in her Thai persona, presiding beautifully over everything, & their two sons bonding with Nick & Clare, and Jane & me pretty well mute with the magic of it all.

Now amazing things are happening with all the family. Next Sunday we celebrate the 18th birthday of Danny, the younger son of Simon & Mimi. Tim and Alice will fly down from Edinburgh, Stephen is over here from California for reasons shortly to be explained, and Nick & Clare will also be in attendance, which means all my four sons will be present for the first time since Ann's funeral. We've taken two big round tables at a brasserie in Camden, but Danny doesn't get a cake because his real birthday is a couple of days later, & Mimi wants to bake him one.

And Stephen is here to co-produce, with Simon, the film of my new novel, not to be published till October, under the title Our Kind of Traitor, and the film of my last novel, and several projects of their own that they believe they can get off the ground. They are calling their company 'White Hare',[5] because that's the name of the ski-slope in Wengen where they first decided to work together as producers. Simon will meanwhile keep his partnership with his venture capital outfit, but he will scale down his work there as the productions take off. He's experienced, of course, at raising finance, & doing all the business side of companies, but he has kept his creativity well & truly alive; Stephen's screenwriting has also started to bear real fruit as well as providing him with a living: he has a film shooting now in Berlin with Liam Neeson in the lead & an all-star cast. Together, the two of them will bit by bit take over all my unfilmed titles – & even some that have been filmed but are remake-able – and I hope that Tim will in due course contribute his own talents to their endeavours. All the augurs are good – & they are all very pleased with themselves!

Nick, meanwhile, has completed his new novel & is in the process of editing it before his agent submits it. His agent thinks highly of it. Clare, Nick's wife, is a very visible campaigner for civil rights these days, and runs Reprieve with notable skill.

So, in short, we're in great shape, with very strong lines of positive communication between all the boys, which pleases me very much.

Charlotte was lovely to see, just before she left. She seems to have her life mapped out, but I think she may have trouble trying to leave her university, where she has become a high-profile asset in the arts department, and a central part of their public relations. My guess is, when she hands in her cards, they're going to make her an offer she can't refuse! – perhaps

---

5. White Hare became the Ink Factory.

raising her status, and giving her more time to act and visit the UK. Only a hunch, but we'll see. Either way, she's made a huge success of her job there, & you must be very proud of her, as we all are.[6]

And lastly – thought I'd tell you in confidence – at the end of March, I get an award from, of all awful rags, the Sunday Times, for 'literary excellence'. But it's a big deal, & I accept it in the Sheldonian Theatre in Oxford, ahead of a dinner co-sponsored by the Bodleian Library, who are taking all my papers & manuscripts. Their list of previous winners was irresistible. No announcement, though, till mid-March. So there we all are.

Jane & I will come & visit you when Stephen has returned to California at the end of this month. In the meantime, since I know you like a letter, here's one, with much love.

Jane joins me – and happy new year too! And to us all.
Love,
David

Jean Cornwell died in 2013, aged ninety-six. David, Charlotte and Rupert Cornwell spoke at her memorial. 'I often thought of Mother as a living summary of twentieth-century history,' Rupert said. Born just before the Battle of the Somme ended, and having lived through the Great Depression, she visited him in the Soviet Union in the waning days of the Cold War. He called her 'a spirited, loving, fiercely loyal, protective, and sometimes cantankerous English lady of an unmistakable type'.

~

---

6. Charlotte was on the teaching staff at the University of Southern California's School of Dramatic Arts, where she was instrumental in creating their MFA in Acting.

Le Carré's agent since 2008, and CEO of the Curtis Brown Group.
Penguin were to publish a fiftieth-anniversary edition of The Spy
Who Came in from the Cold *in 2013.*

TO JONNY GELLER

> *9 Gainsborough Gardens*
> *London, NW3 1BJ*
>
> 31 March 2010

Dear Jonny,
<u>Introduction to SPY WHO . . .</u>

I have thought about this a lot, and you know I am not work-
shy. But I increasingly come to the conclusion that further
introducings from myself are not the way to make Penguin's
publication more interesting, or even, more commercial. I
try to imagine picking up a copy today, as a younger person,
or even an older one. What would I want to read about? Not
the author's agonisings, or his account of how the book came
to be written – specious, for sure – but something about the
historical context, about Communist subversion, & western
counter-subversion, fifty years ago: about Kennedy's humiliation in Vienna in the run-up to the Wall; about the tensions of
the hours of critical confrontation in Berlin that informed the
book. This is far better done by a decent contemporary historian than by me: a Roberts, a Garton Ash, or whoever Adam[7] is
selecting as his 'Third Party' writer. In short, I think the publication needs more thought & debate than is reaching me: even
the question of whether stuff should be run as epilogue rather
than prologue is worth some thought. But my gut feeling is:
phase the author <u>out</u>, and phase <u>in</u> a good voice with some

---

7. Adam Freudenheim, Penguin Classics, Modern Classics and Reference Publisher.

historical authority to set the book in period for a new generation of readers.

You heard my Oxf̲d speech: of course, I could cut in passages of that – being in Bonn, going to Nuremberg, all that – even the Roger Hollis stuff[8] – but more & more, I think it's time that someone interesting did the talking for me. Do we <u>really</u> pick up a Graham Greene because it has a 'new introduction by the author'? I don't, I'm sure. But a critical appraisal by V S Pritchett – & I might.

I'm well aware that Adam feels he sh̲d be getting more for his money – but I'm not sure it's <u>me</u> he really needs here. But over to you, & I'll listen carefully.

Best, as ever,
David

Le Carré's afterword to the anniversary edition, 'Fifty Years Later',
was carried at the back of the book. 'I wrote The Spy Who Came
in from the Cold *at the age of thirty under intense, unshared, personal stress, and in extreme privacy,' he wrote. 'As an intelligence*
officer in the guise of a junior diplomat at the British Embassy in
Bonn, I was a secret to my colleagues, and much of the time to
myself.' The book, he said, 'was the work of a wayward imagination brought to the end of its tether by political disgust and
personal confusion'.

∽

---

8. Le Carré told two familiar stories at the Sheldonian in Oxford. The first was how, as a young diplomat at a German Socialist Party rally in Nuremberg in 1961, he had picked up warnings about events unfolding in Berlin (see note, p. 115). Secondly, how in the mid 1960s Sir Roger Hollis, former director-general of MI5, took shelter at le Carré's Somerset house, simply sitting and reading the newspaper, between hostile interrogations over suspicions he was a Soviet spy.

TO TONY CORNWELL

9 Gainsborough Gardens
London, NW3 1BJ

18 May 2010

Dearest To,

You will no doubt remember the old story of the public school headmaster's circular to parents, regretting that fees would have to rise by £500 anally. A parent wrote back saying he would rather pay through the nose as usual. Now I'm not suggesting that this has anything to do with the way they're feeding you, but I do puzzle a bit, in my unmedical way, about how on earth they get a decent meal into you by way of your stomach. I see a whole industry at work: the roast beef carvers, the suppliers of spring vegetables, the Yorkshire pudding makers, the plum-duff specialists, all taking their turn at the Moulinex in order to make their presence felt, then the long slow dripping process – 'oh shit, did we forget the horse-radish?' – 'no, here it is, and let's pop in a bit of Coleman's mustard while we're about it', and bit by bit our Tony gets his feed.

We got back from Scotland by night-sleeper at crack of dawn this morning and are now waiting for the assault of all the Aliens: film makers, publishers, publicists and the whole mercenary army of distractors who want to make sure I do nothing fruitful till mid September when the new book appears here. I really think that, if I promised to go on the circuit publicising this book for the rest of my life, and not writing anything more, they wd be perfectly content. Publishers – the whole industry indeed – lives only in order to eat tonight. Which brings me back to the purpose of this letter, which is to wish you true grit as you go to war, and send you love, both, and urge you to raise hell if the roast beef is overdone.

All love,
D

~

In 2010 Al Alvarez was awarded the Benson Medal by the Royal Society of Literature.

TO AL ALVAREZ

> *9 Gainsborough Gardens,*
> *London, NW3 1BJ*
>
> Sonntag, late May 2010

Dear Al,

My spies have told me that the RLS has decided to bestow a most coveted honour on you, and I am therefore writing in haste to commiserate. Honours suck. Flattery sucks. Recognition is for the birds. On the other hand, it's nice to be fancied, and nicer still to be fancied by people who, by & large, know their poetic arses from their literary elbows. And it's nice for one's chums, who are sick of saying nice things about one in vain, to let the other buggers say it for them.

Love,
David

~

The writer and biographer Adam Sisman won the National Book Critics Circle Award for Biography in 2001 for Boswell's Presumptuous Task: The Making of the Life of Dr Johnson. *His biography of the historian Hugh Trevor-Roper appeared in 2010.*

то ADAM SISMAN

9 Gainsborough Gardens
London, NW3 1BJ

15 July 2010

Dear Mr Sisman,

Let me say first that I was on the point of going up to Waterstone's in Hampstead to buy your book on H T-R when your letter arrived: so thank you for it, and for what you kindly say about my work. I am, as you may suppose, very divided about how to respond – flattered by your interest, & consoled by it, since I have had similar letters from biographers whom I do not rate highly – and I think, as you say, it would be best to meet, & explore the possibilities. There are huge hindrances: my own messy private life, the demise of so many people I worked with or otherwise knew, and my habitual reluctance to discuss my very limited & unspectacular career in intelligence. I see you finding disenchantment everywhere, and your readers doing the same, and I worry, of course, about my children & grand-children, probably quite unnecessarily. Anyway, do let's meet and talk, if only that I may give you the longer version of my relationship with H T-R, from which I emerge an even bigger fool than the one he describes.[9]

I haven't read your 'Hugh' from beginning to end, just dipped, but let me in passing congratulate you on its splendid reception, and thank you again for writing. Like H T-R, I would wish you to write without restraints – perhaps that's the problem!

With best wishes,
David Cornwell

---

9. Hugh Trevor-Roper had described le Carré's preface to a book about Kim Philby by the *Sunday Times* Insight team as 'vapid and vulgar . . . an exercise in pretentious, rhetorical class-hatred which nowhere touches any point of fact'.

P.S. [. . .] We expect to be in London for most of the summer – we're there now – but I have a new novel coming out in Sep., & 5 of my books are supposedly in preparation for film, one shooting in October already, so we're hopping about. I wd be very happy to give you lunch if you're coming up. Best D.

~

TO SIR JOHN MARGETSON

Tregiffian
St Buryan
Penzance
Cornwall

3 August 2010

Dear John,

[. . .]

News. One Adam Sisman, who has just written an excellent & much-lauded biography of Hugh Trevor Roper, is going to write mine, and reckons it will take him four years. I'm staying as far away from it as I can [. . .] and inviting my rabbits, friends & relations to make their own decisions about whether to talk to him, & in what terms. But I like him, and welcome his endeavour, however painful & embarrassing in the short term. He's already spent 10 hours with Charlotte, & visited Jeannie, Charlotte's mother, in her care home, & contacted my elder brother Tony in Seattle, planning to visit him in October if Tony survives his present cancer treatment. If you & Miranda feel like talking to him, that would be a bonus, as I have few friends, & even fewer have survived as long as you!

We have Nick & Clare with us at present; Tim came back from the US yesterday; Simon will return from Thailand next week; Steve may come in September for the films that they are producing. I do hope so.

So glad you met Jessie.[10] She's quite a star. Working in Catalan theatre is not my idea of the simple artistic life, but she's about to become a 'runner' in the feature film of 'Tinker Tailor . . .' which starts shooting in late Sep: God knows what she'll make of being yelled at by unit managers & working 16 hours on the trot . . .

Much love to you both, as ever,
David

P.S. Did I tell you I passed on a K? All right for public servants, not good for artists, writers & the like.

~

The polymath Irish historian Owen Dudley Edwards was editor of the Oxford Sherlock Holmes.

TO PROFESSOR OWEN DUDLEY EDWARDS

As from: Tregiffian
St Buryan
Penzance
Cornwall

20 November 2010

Dear Owen,
Thanks so much for your generous and fascinating letter. The 'Traitor' has had a good time in the States, & is selling happily – in Europe, particularly in Germany, even more happily – and here, decently, & Christmas will help: in so far as any of that matters. But actually it <u>does</u> matter, because novels with any

10. Jessica Cornwell, le Carré's eldest granddaughter. Her non-fiction book *Birth Notes: Fragments of Motherhood* was published in May 2022.

sort of pretention to serious content are having a really hard time these days, and publishers are jumpy. What it must be like to be a debutant writer, Heaven only knows: my son, who writes as Nick Harkaway, got huge rave reviews for his first novel, and sold a pittance, both here & in the States. So called 'big' authors – i.e. the mega sellers like Grisham & Co – are looking at a 30–40% reduction in sales. The E-book world is opening up fast, but many publishers – including my own, Penguin – are demanding such a large piece of the cake that the literary agents (including mine) won't play, with the result that sales go by default. These are not complaints – writing continues to be extremely kind to me – but simply a report from the front that is scarcely spoken aloud & is worth knowing about.

I was tickled by your reference to Graham G. – and no, tempting as the job is, I'm not about to become an Anglican bishop, despite the prospect of excellent accommodation & a decent pension. (And since I don't believe in anything very much, I am excellently qualified.) I knew Greene a bit, & was in awe of him, but I never really believed in his Catholic convictions. As a literary tool, they work to a point, but God is really best denied in fiction – Camus & Co – and morality left to struggle without him. Does anyone remember that Greene stood the <u>wrong</u> side of the Berlin Wall & said he'd rather be there than here? He who lived in Antibes and fell in love with Central American dictators? Novelists on the whole make pretty daft politicians, but Greene was in a class of his own . . .

I shall treasure your letter, and I thank you again for it. What is at my bedside just now? 'A Tale of Two Cities' & the 'Sherlock Holmes' short stories. Which shows you how up to date I am! – And R L Stevenson <u>always</u>.[11]

With best wishes,
David

---

11. Le Carré's favourite readings to his children included Stevenson's short story 'The Bottle Imp'. He named Sir Arthur Conan Doyle's 'The Speckled Band' as the first crime story he read.

~

The Swedish director had approached producer Tim Bevan after hearing his Working Title company were to make Tinker Tailor Soldier Spy. *His BAFTA-winning film was utterly unlike the television series, a 'marvel of compression' of the 349-page novel, a period piece of suffocating male betrayal, with Gary Oldman as a melancholy Smiley.*

TO TOMAS ALFREDSON

Tregiffian
St Buryan
Penzance
Cornwall

12 July 2011

Dear Tomas,

I was going to wait until I had seen the very last cut of 'Tinker Tailor . . .' with all its bells on, but I'm not sure we shall be in London much before the release, and anyway, I've seen enough to know that you have produced a wonderful work of art, a true filmic masterpiece: the film of the film, the best thing made of my work since its television elder brother, and perfect in its own right. I did not need the enthusiasm of everyone else who has seen it, or of the actors who performed in it, to tell me how good it is – or to tell you how intensely I have enjoyed its subtleties and shades. (But it's thrilling to have it all the same! – Colin Firth's letter, Jonny Geller's, and my sons' paeans of admiration, do not depress me!)

I think what I relish most is the arc of narrative by which the story sustains itself: the passions and unmaskings of the last minutes, and the coming-together of all the strands. (Only you could have put a bee in Mendel's car.) Of course, there are quite extraordinary passages of virtuoso acting & directing: Gary's conversation with the empty chair, Tom Hardy's Brando-esque monologue from his own chair; the heart-breaking moment of lovers' eye-contact between Prideaux & Haydon, followed quickly by the lover's revenge; they will be revisited by film buffs for years to come, I am sure. But what we all warm to is not the individual, but the whole, and that is finally what makes the film so strong. This isn't a bunch of performances, but one great achievement, & I am extremely proud to have provided you with the material to work your magic with. Gratitude – obviously. Joy – also obviously. But with them, my most sincere admiration & congratulations.

Ever,
David

~

Gary Oldman had emailed to thank le Carré for 'remarkably generous and flattering words' about the film.

to GARY OLDMAN

By email

31 August 2011

Dear Gary,
It was from the heart. In the original piece I wrote that even if nobody else in the cinema liked it, I would still be clapping. My agent, silly bugger he, made me take it out on the grounds that it encouraged catastrophe. I love the movie, love your Smiley, and that's a constant. Came back from Germany last night after

collecting a gong[12] [. . .] the place was hopping with excitement about the movie. We had arranged for the hacks who interviewed me to see it in advance, and they were captivated by it. I've got a hundred quid at 10–1 on winning at Venice. If I win, I'll buy you lunch. It's a beautiful, beautiful performance.

Best to you and yours,
David

[*The next month Oldman wrote 'what about those box office numbers, eh?' Le Carré replied, on 22 September 2011.*]

Numbers very nifty indeed, Control. One feels a trifle exposed.

Yes, much eager talk about SP.[13] My sources tell me that Robyn, Tomas, Peter and Tim[14] are all reading it under the bedclothes. I pitched a better way into the story to Tim – based on the 'Get Karla' feeling that we have at the end of TTSS – and he visibly nibbled. My very strong feeling, and I suspect yours, is that any sequel to TTSS must be as splendid, absorbing and original, and as bloody difficult, as its predecessor, not just a TTSS2.

Much pressure on me to evangelise the movie in the States, but I have to resist. I'm back at the drawing board working on a much neglected novel that I had meant to have finished by now, and if I leave it any longer it will simply disappear between the floorboards.

Cornwall sunny and serene. Good blackberries.

---

12. Le Carré travelled to Weimar to accept Germany's Goethe Medal, awarded to individuals who have 'performed outstanding service for the German language and international cultural dialogue'. The city was home to Goethe and Schiller and other writers of Weimar Classicism. After the publication of *Absolute Friends* in 2004, reader Dr Christoph Werner of Weimar wrote to ask about le Carré's knowledge of the city. 'Weimar was my Rome,' he replied.

13. *Smiley's People*.

14. *Tinker Tailor* producers Robyn Slovo, Peter Straughan, Tim Bevan and director Tomas Alfredson. A sequel in the form of a film of *Smiley's People* was delayed first by competing projects and then over rights issues.

Love to you and yours, and I hope they are cheering you to the rafters.

Best,

David

∾

A Californian living in France, Burroughs was a fan and wrote to le Carré over fifteen years, enclosing reviews, sketches, once a bottle of local wine. In 2011 he sent In the Heart of the Sea *by Nathaniel Philbrick, the story of the ramming of the whaling ship* Essex *by a sperm whale, thought to be Melville's inspiration for* Moby-Dick. *Burroughs mused about his search for identity in France.*

TO WILLIAM BURROUGHS

Tregiffian
St Buryan
Penzance
Cornwall

13 October 2011

Dear Bill,

Thanks so much for the Philbrick, which I haven't read, & thanks also for the touching letter, one of a line of many.

From here, I find myself wondering whether my own search for identity (which never stops) has been misplaced all along. It cannot be right not to have known my mother, but only that she walked out on me when I was five without leaving a forwarding address, & I'm starting to resent it very deeply. Strange too to learn, through my self-appointed biographer, one Adam Sisman, no slouch, of other matters related to my <u>father</u>: most notably that while serving one sentence, at the age of 27, he was tried for another offence and given an extra 8 months of <u>hard</u>

labour, a kind of 'enhanced' imprisonment – for what, God knows – but it somehow hurts terribly that people set out to make life hell for him. Talk about worlds within worlds.

My best to you, Bill, and your family, & your kind. Very right to be embarrassed when people make a fuss of you. Think what you'd be if you weren't.

As ever,
David

~

Le Carré's brother, Tony, was still pursuing his dream of publishing a novel.

TO TONY CORNWELL

9 Gainsborough Gardens
London, NW3 1BJ

4 February 2012

Dearest To,
Strangely, I was on the point of picking up my pen to write to you, even this weekend, when your letter arrived, for which many thanks. And of course, when the time comes, we – better, I think Jane, but we both – will be there to edit. I suggest we do that on your terms, but also on ours: in other words, I don't think we shd be there for content or style, but only for the physical presentation: punctuation, paragraphing, chapters, and the simple issue of comprehensibility, which sometimes becomes a blindspot for the author. Beyond that, I don't think we shd be questioning V. Wolfe's use of adverbs, or yours! – & least of all, the poetic vision or the interplay. Those things are yours alone, & you don't need our hot breath down your neck.

With us, all goes almost too well – giddying at times, & more than is easily dealt with in a continuing writing life. The sequel to the film of TTSS is underway with the same director, writer & cast, & two other books – 'A Most Wanted Man' & 'Our Kind of Traitor' are also being prepared for film. AMWM will shoot in September in Hamburg with Philip Seymour Hoffman in the lead; OKT will follow, all being well. But the glory is that my two eldest sons, Simon & Stephen, have formed their own production company & are making a really good fist of it. Meanwhile, I have a novel that is past the critical halfway mark, & planned for publication early next year, & I like it very much. I guess it will be my last long book.

Other news: our son Nick (Harkaway) looks like having scored another critical bullseye with his new novel 'Angelmaker' (Knopf in the US) and he has a non-fiction book about the Internet coming out in May. We are very proud of him, & he has handled the Father Thing with great elegance.

As I write, TTSS the movie has 3 Oscar nominations & 11 BAFTA nominations, the UK equivalent, & of course the whole system is shot through with prejudice & worse. But do I want to win a bent race? Ask Ronnie, but it's a no-win as far as the Oscars are concerned (except just possibly for best adaptation from a novel) & it's dicey on the BAFTA front because of 'The Artist' which I loved. Anyway, it's all good dirty fun.

If you live long enough in this country, and are not rude about the Queen, you get to be distinguished, but I have refused national honours, thank God, will never be Sir D, Lord D or King D, & have settled for a D.Litt from Oxford in the summer, which entails dressing up like an elderly salmon with a hat.

It's been very odd to have a book[15] exhumed from nearly 40 years ago, & rather destabilising: 'hey, hang on a minute, I've done a couple of things since!' And it's also odd to have an 'Inspector Calls' in one's life, in the form of nice Adam Sisman, going around ringing doorbells from one's past, & not always

15. *Tinker Tailor Soldier Spy* was first published in June 1974.

coming up with very edifying results: my love-life has always been a disaster area, & without Jane I w<u>d</u> long ago have gone down with the ship. But somehow it's a gift of truth, of a sort, to my children, & one I could never hope to deliver myself. With luck, the grim reaper will edit me out before he (Adam) gets around to publishing.

So how was it all, this 80-year-old-life? A total porridge really, with love of family the one abiding, triumphant discovery. I'm a late-developed father & grandfather, & fortunate enough to have had the time, & the woman, to show me the light. God knows what our parents made of their lives by the time they reached the end of them: mystification may be the one thing they had in common.

I'm so glad – <u>we</u> are so glad – that your courage paid off, & you are healthy, if not up to Olympic standard. So far, so am I, quite bouncy, but with the odd recent wake-up call: nothing dramatic. I send you my love, dear To, & all my wishes for a continued, creative, & happy long life.

As ever,
David

P.S. If you read nothing else, read 'The Hare with Amber Eyes' by de Waal, an exquisite non-fiction journey into his tragic family past.

~

Roger Hermiston's book The Greatest Traitor: The Secret Lives of Agent George Blake *was published a year after this letter.*

TO ROGER HERMISTON

As from: Tregiffian
St Buryan
Penzance
Cornwall

12 April 2012

Dear Mr Hermiston,

Thank you for your letter of 10th April. I'm not sure I have much to tell you about Blake. I had just finished a long training course. We were summoned by Hooper,[16] head of training, to be told our futures were uncertain, & that he must say something he never in his life thought he wd have to say: there was a traitor in our ranks who had been unmasked, & his name was George Blake. Then he wept & we all went home while our personal security was assessed: had we been blown, or were we still employable under cover?

A few months later the wraps came off Philby & there was more tearing of hair. Peter Lunn was at that time Head of Station in Bonn, & I was his subordinate. Yes, the Service was shaken to its foundations by Blake, & he was in many ways a much more capable & controlled double-agent than Philby, with much less in his past to unseat him, & a greater clarity of intent. But I never met him, and had only anecdotal evidence about him of the same quality as your own, I suspect. I'm not sure whether your 'discussion' wd be on air, or for something you're writing, but I'm not keen to say more than I know, or more than I should, for public consumption! His book, which I'm sure you read, is lucid & well written, unlike Philby's crabbed little hand. For some reason I always liked Blake the man a lot better than I ever liked Philby.

---

16. Robin Hooper. See note to letter to John and Miranda Margetson, 24 October 1991, p. 306.

If you think you need more than this, do please say so, but I doubt if I've anything to add – except, what idiot would <u>ever</u> have reemployed Blake with fanfares after so long in enemy hands, and give him the Berlin tunnel and a bunch of networks to betray? Answer, the hugely over-rated White.[17]

Best wishes,
David Cornwell

17. Sir Dick White was director-general of MI5 from 1953, when le Carré was at Oxford, and head of MI6 from 1956 to 1968. It was actually White's predecessor at MI6, Major General John Alexander Sinclair, who welcomed Blake back to its ranks like a conquering hero, from captivity in Korea, where he was recruited by the KGB. White's biographer, Tom Bower, says his management of Blake's interrogation was 'masterly'. Le Carré's comment here might reflect the early hostility of serving MI6 officers to White's appointment.

A DELICATE TRUTH

As to corporate power and its complicity: I believe it was Mussolini who said fascism should more appropriately be called Corporatism because it is a merger of state and corporate power ... The delegation of government responsibility to self-interested corporate identities has run mad in my country as well as the United States.

– by email to the Italian cultural journalist Irene Bignardi, for an article in *La Repubblica*, 5 July 2013

But basically for heaven's sake, it's a book, it's a story, and the power of story is of course far greater than the power of fact, alas ... if it didn't entertain we wouldn't be here now.

– to Philippe Sands at the Hay Festival, 31 May 2013

Buoyed by the critical success of Alfredson's *Tinker Tailor Soldier Spy*, with films of *A Most Wanted Man* and *Our Kind of Traitor* in production, the eighty-one-year-old le Carré was writing 'at the top of his game', said the *New York Times* – still walking the Cornish fields, if not the cliff paths. His very British story was set in Gibraltar, London, and amid the country life of Cornwall. *A Delicate Truth* was premised on two British whistleblowers – one young, one old – exposing a covert military operation handed to a private security contractor based in the United States, in which the victims were a Muslim mother and child. A taut thriller with a sharp political edge – New Labour in the War on Terror – it was received as the best le Carré in years.

TO TONY CORNWELL

As from: Tregiffian
St Buryan
Penzance
Cornwall

18 June 2012

Dear To,

All of a sudden, peace breaks out: I just turned in a new novel, & have nothing to do but wait – & nothing to lose but my chains, which are gradually easing, but, like me, must wait.

[. . .]

The novel I just turned in is presently called 'A Delicate Truth' and took 2½ years & a lot of false turns & heartache – nothing quite so bloody difficult since 'Tinker Tailor' . . . or is it age? You must be asking yourself similar questions as you bang away at your own opus: am I just stuck, or running out of gas? Anyway, I had several bad periods of that kind, not helped by being 'discovered' as a Euro-star & getting hauled off to make grand speeches about fuck all; but in the end, I'm proud of what I wrote, & confident that it will piss off enough of our political establishment to keep me smiling for a day or two. At my age, the <u>literary</u> establishment is as set in its ways as I am: those who thought I was never any good think I'm even worse, & those who thought the sun shone out of my arse now wear a Hawaiian tan of complete conviction. But I'm not sure I'll do the long novel again: perhaps a bit of theatre, or just fool around with short pieces & give Jane a few good years while we're both intact. We're off to Switzerland for 3 weeks' r. and r. on Sunday, as soon as I've collected my D.Litt from Oxford University, alongside The Lady from Burma,[1] who is dropping by to collect hers, after picking up her Nobel in Stockholm last Friday. It's rather moving, because in an interview she gave a

---

1. The Burmese politician Aung San Suu Kyi.

few years back, when she was still under house arrest, she said she passed some of her time reading me.

[. . .]

I think of you very often, & of our extraordinary, separate lives, always with great affection, & pain. We visit Jean occasionally, and witness the odd flash of venom that we (or I) remember so vividly. She's 94, I think, and has all her marbles, and human force. I like her – so it goes – a little less each time around: who else can I say that to? It's not the way charity is supposed to flow . . . Charlotte has completed her time as Prof. of Drama at USC & is back in London preparing to open her own drama school. (Theatre in Britain is one of our few flourishing industries.) And Britain herself? The rich are obscenely rich & untouchable, cultureless, & without social conscience. Unfortunately they are also the predominant force in government. (Familiar ring?) I believe – pray even, though I don't know who to – that we are close to a healthy return to Socialism of the pre-Blair sort, shorn of union power because they haven't any, and because the blue-collar class is dwindling in the face of immigrant (cheap) labour from Europe & the former colonies. Infrastructure, social services, & social courtesies, are all dismally afflicted by the disparity between rich & poor, & the gulf grows & grows.

So it goes, dearest To, & we send you both our love, and all power to your writing elbow.

With much affection,
David

~

TO JONNY GELLER

By fax

London

8 September 2012

Dear Jonny,
[. . .]

<u>Paper</u>
I made a strong point to you, that I think should be universally applied to hardback of serious fiction & non-fiction. I keep a large store of hardbacks of my stuff to sign & send to charities. Already books of 4–5 years ago are turning brown. This does not apply to US products. So why ours? If I made this point to Weldon,[2] I need to know it will have your support, or I'm wasting all our time. I think it's as important to <u>all</u> decent writers, and to the trade in general, that a guarantee of durability be attached to hardbacks – otherwise, they're just paperbacks in disguise. If books have to be re-costed on this account – well, tough. My suspicion is, hardback buyers w<u>d</u> happily pay the extra £1 to know that their children can read the same book, & if the publisher made a virtue of this assurance, he would have the support of the (very small) hardback-buying public.
[. . .]

As ever, with amitiés,
David

~

TO ANTHONY BARNETT

By email

22 September 2012

Subject: A triumph – your comments

---

2. Tom Weldon, CEO Penguin Random House UK.

Dear Anthony,

Thanks so much. Your comments are pure gold, and exactly what I would have hoped you would provide. I look forward to addressing them shortly. John Reid or someone like him is a perfect metaphor for [Fergus] Quinn.[3] Curiously, I feel at present that the two weakest characters in the story are, unusually for me, the two baddies: in the case of [Jay] Crispin, I was determined not to have a man so monstrous that he threw the story out of kilter. In the end, the villain must be the institution we have created rather than its creators.

So again, huge thanks. I will in due course send you a revised version that reflects, if not fully, your suggestions and comments; and with it, a draft of the Acknowledgements that I would like to put at the end of the book. If Judith has already started reading the book,[4] I would normally say perhaps wait till the next draft, but perhaps she should go on with the present one and then enjoy the effect of your advice later!

This is a fairly chaotic time for us as the shooting of A Most Wanted Man starts on Monday and we shall be hopping between London and Hamburg over the next few weeks, while at the same time I continue to work on the book. But once we are out of the wood, we much look forward to catching up with you and Judith over a meal.

Love to you both from us,
David

In the acknowledgements of the book, le Carré wrote: 'To writer, activist and founder of openDemocracy, Anthony Barnett, for educating me in the manners of New Labour in its dying days.'

---

3. Barnett had offered advice on the character of le Carré's 'bellicose New Labour minister', Glaswegian Fergus Quinn, who orders the covert Operation Wildlife in Gibraltar. John Reid's ministerial career in successive Labour governments included stints as armed forces minister and defence minister.

4. Professor Judith Herrin, award-winning historian of Byzantium.

∾

Mary Mount was le Carré's publisher at Viking Penguin from 2009 until he died. After le Carré expressed concern about the pages of his Viking hardbacks ageing too quickly, Mount wrote that a different paper would be used, without wood pulp, in future and offered to send him a sample. Viking published Claire Tomalin's Dickens biography using the paper planned for A Delicate Truth.

TO MARY MOUNT

By email

10 October 2012

Subject: Re: Paper

Dear Mary,
Fascinating and thank you. No need to send a copy of Claire T's Dickens, as I have one, and will immediately scurry off and examine it in a new light. Thanks again for taking all the trouble.

The 'final' draft should be with you by now. A new Minister, a better defined Crispin, a more explicit disaster (Jeb's speculation about why the mercs fired) and the two Crispin scenes beefed up, as also the Toby–Oakley scene in Canary Wharf. And a lot of enemy adverbs raked out, and a general clean-up.

Best,
David

∾

DEAR ALL

By email

16 October 2012

Subject: Beard warning

Dear All,

The director of the film of A Most Wanted Man asks that I grow a beard for my appearance as an elderly, debauched alcoholic seated in a disreputable bar. Unkind souls may wonder why I need a beard for a part that I have played with success for many years without one, but such is art. Predictions vary. It will be white, it will be red. It will be bushy, silky, bellicose, or nothing more than downy pubescent fluff. In any event, I ask you not to comment on it, and rest content that it will be removed on the 15th November.

love, d

This email, titled 'Beard Warning', was sent to the family and friends. Tom Bower replied: 'Can't wait to see the genuine alter ego!' Le Carré asked his secretary Vicki Phillips to find him a barber immediately after the shoot finished in Hamburg, which she did.

∾

TO IAN McEWAN

9 Gainsborough Gardens
London, NW3 1BJ

6 May 2013

Dear Ian,

Just to say it properly: thanks, from the heart, for the generous and – for me – timely words, from a voice I greatly respect.

It's a rum business, being a successful British writer, as you know as well as I do. Sometimes it needs gallantry in the face of the enemy, sometimes you wonder whether you <u>are</u> the enemy, sometimes you feel you're living under cover on enemy territory. And allies, when you need them, seem to be busy elsewhere. But when I read your words, a lump came to my throat, which was very unBritish indeed! Not so much age, as a kind of exhaustion at being asked for the last fifty years whether the Mossad is better than the CIA, & what it's like – oh Christ! – to be a spy.

Thanks again.
Ever,
David

Ian McEwan met le Carré for lunch while he worked on his new novel, Sweet Tooth, *with a female MI5 agent as its lead character. He told a* Daily Telegraph *interviewer, in an article published on 3 May 2013: 'I think he [le Carré] has easily burst out of being a genre writer and will be remembered as perhaps the most significant novelist of the second half of the twentieth century in Britain . . . Most writers I know think le Carré is no longer a spy writer. He should have won the Booker Prize a long time ago. It's time he won it and it's time he accepted it. He's in the first rank.'*

∾

TO GEORG AND CHRISTIANE BOOMGAARDEN[5]

22 October 2013

Dear Georg, dear Christiane,

Thank you so much for your long letter, and your news,* which sounds all good. And I'm glad you took a look at 'A Delicate Truth', which in the light of present revelations has acquired a certain topicality, particularly in Europe. Its reception does matter to me, not just for reasons of vanity, but because I know that in my country, we have all the levers available for a secret state without its masters even knowing what they're running. The spies are far too big for their boots, they never have enough, they're nowhere near overseen by any elected body, and our feeble or indifferent politicians are clay in their hands. You see I'm an excellent ambassador for my country! Yet the spies' record is appalling, and their craven performance at the time of the Iraq war will <u>never</u> be forgiven, at least by me. In my day, we were told we were little apostles for truth, pledged to speak fearlessly to power. Wow. Rant over. But of course it's almost funny, if it weren't so outrageous, that the CIA tapped into your Chancellor's cellphone (and don't imagine that if they did, we didn't!) but again we have to wonder who else was doing what to whom and – ultimately – to what end?[6]

[. . .]

I hope 'retirement' – which for real people is a fantasy anyway – becomes you both, & you feel none of the withdrawal symptoms supposedly associated with it. For my part, I look forward to hearing how you both saw us during your most distinguished stay, and perhaps you will tell me a little.

---

5. Georg Boomgaarden was Germany's ambassador to the United Kingdom from 2008 to 2014.

6. *Der Spiegel* magazine had just reported that US spy agencies had been monitoring Chancellor Angela Merkel's mobile phone since 2002.

I love my country deeply, but fear for it also; & sometimes I really do despair. But not for long.

Our love to you & yours – as ever,
David

[*in left margin*] *which arrived, God help me, on my 82nd birthday

~

Le Carré and Ben Macintyre first met at Ascot, where le Carré was revisiting the days when he carried cash bets between Ronnie and his bookmakers as a young man. In 2007 le Carré endorsed Agent Zigzag, *Macintyre's first book on an espionage theme, as 'superb. Meticulously researched, splendidly told, immensely entertaining and often very moving.' The younger writer was 'utterly thrilled', and their friendship continued in walks on Hampstead Heath and lunches at Sheekey's.*

TO BEN MACINTYRE

9 Gainsborough Gardens
London, NW3 1BJ

11 November 2013

Dear Ben,
In principle, as the FO would say, I'm prepared to consider the BBC interview, but the problem will be timing. I now have a volume of memoire – including obviously the Philby–Elliott piece – and we are juggling dates with Sisman about whether his biography (oh Jesus) goes first, or I do. I'm shooting for Spring (me) & him Autumn, but it's all a bit delicate & I don't want to upstage him by mistake, so I may hold off till Spring next year. The next two weeks will bring clarity.

If it's to be the interview, then we'll have to agree terms of engagement because I'm absolutely sick of TV, and particularly of women putting their fingertips together & leaning back and saying, head shrewdly on one side, 'And what do you say to those people who say you're talking through your arse?' The last one I had (from the BBC) did pretty much that, & I hope she's been eaten by bears. I need to <u>perform</u>, not be browbeaten.[7]

Let me have the book as soon as you can – that's <u>fun</u> – and with it, if possible, your tentative dates for publication, and interviewing me, and airing the piece. I meanwhile will try & sort my own mess.

Best as ever,
David

~

Le Carré began his work in Suffolk for what would become Silverview.

TO JOHN AND MARY JAMES, ALDEBURGH BOOKSHOP

Tregiffian
St Buryan
Penzance
Cornwall

11 December 2013

---

7. Anne McElvoy had interviewed le Carré with a live audience for BBC Radio 3's *Night Waves* programme, to mark the fiftieth anniversary of *The Spy Who Came in from the Cold*. Le Carré's sense of discomfort in the broadcast was palpable.

Dear John and Mary,

A quick note to tell you that we have booked ourselves into the Brudenell Hotel from 14th–27th February, where I will be writing. As we confided to you, I am using Aldeburgh and the surrounding area as the setting for my novel, and it would be wonderful if we could spend a little time with you and drink in the atmosphere. I have a bookshop at the centre of my novel, and would love to pick your collective brains about the ups and downs of running one. Once I have written the book, I will have the pleasure of offering you an early read in the hope that you will correct my errors and sharpen my aim.

As we mentioned to you, I greatly prefer to function incognito wherever I can, and we would be grateful for your protection in this respect. And if John feels like the odd walk, I will have my boots handy.

We wish you a very happy and successful Christmas, and greatly look forward to renewing our acquaintance.

With all good wishes to you and yours.
Yours sincerely,
David

~

TO WOLFGANG CZAIA[8]

Tregiffian
St Buryan
Penzance
Cornwall

12 December 2013

---

8. Wolfgang 'Wolf' Czaia, was a star German test pilot and author who flew gliders from the age of fourteen. He exchanged letters with le Carré for a decade.

Dear Wolfgang,

Forgive this typed letter, but I am under siege.

Thank you so much for my piece of the Berlin Wall. As somebody who saw it go up, I feel I have a proprietorial interest. I was in the distant Bahamas when the Wall came down, and was not able to accept Willy Brandt's invitation to come to his knees-up in Berlin. I sat alone and bemused on a millionaire's island, with nobody but his staff to share my disbelief.

Thank you again, have a great year, and an end to all walls, with or without a capital letter.

Yours sincerely,
David Cornwell

~

TO PROFESSOR ROGER WILLIAMS, CBE[9]

c/o Curtis Brown Group Ltd
Haymarket House
28/29 Haymarket
London, SW1Y 4SP

22 July 2014

Dear Professor Williams,

Thank you for your letter of 8th July. Forgive this dictated reply, but I am away at present, researching a novel.

My use of the alarm bells right at the end of A Delicate Truth is, I'm afraid, deliberately enigmatic. I wished it to signify everything that we bring on our heads when we raise them too far above the parapet. By sending out his transmissions at all, Toby Bell had invited the fury of the establishment and such is the speed of interception these days that they are

---

9. Presumably the prominent hepatologist Roger Stanley Williams, CBE.

coming to get him. Mercifully, we are allowed to hope that he got his message out to the world in time.

I hope this clarifies – or further obfuscates! – your interpretation of the final pages of the novel.

[. . .]

With all good wishes.
Yours sincerely,
David Cornwell

~

TO U. P. KARLSSON, A FAN FROM SWEDEN

c/o Curtis Brown Group Ltd
Haymarket House
28/29 Haymarket
London, SW1Y 4SP

5 August 2014

Dear Mr Karlson,
Thank you for your letter of 19th July.

I am not quite sure why Swedish characters keep popping up in my novels, unless it's because often, in very outlandish places, a Swede has popped up, usually working for an aid agency, often drunk and often very amusing. I have to confess that I have been very little in Sweden, but the Swedes I have met have always made a pleasant impression on me.

Thanks so much for your kind words, and for reading me so faithfully. I hope you will enjoy the new novel that I am just completing.

Yours sincerely,
John le Carré

∽

TO SIR TOM STOPPARD

Tregiffian
St Buryan
Penzance
Cornwall

27 October 2014

Dear Tom,
Finished the novel, read it, wasn't convinced, wasn't moved, revisited too many old themes, & decided to dump it.

Now I feel much better, just a bit surprised. My agent, who hasn't read it – nobody but my sons have – is surprised too. Is this age? Freedom? Just the mis-application of energy & two years? Actually, I think, the last, as I am writing away happily at something else.

Love to you both, & I hope NY was a success.
Ever,
d

P.S. Jane predictably stalwart & supportive as ever.

'I felt for you,' Stoppard responded, 'without knowing what to feel – but ultimately admiration for strength of mind, I think, qualified by regret that – undoubtedly – so many treasurable beautiful babies must have been tossed out with the thematic bathwater.'

Le Carré's reasons for withdrawing Silverview *varied by the hour, along with whether it was 'dumped' or simply 'shelved'. The book was kept at his home office, and he left the decision to publish or not with his heirs.*

∽

to MIKHAIL LYUBIMOV

> *Tregiffian*
> *St Buryan*
> *Penzance*
> *Cornwall*

> 27 April 2015

Dear Mikhail,

Thanks so much for your letter, and your interesting news. How remarkable, and how exciting, that your movie is shot.[10] Is your first night in Moscow? And where else apart from Moscow? Do please send me a disk when it's out.

Meanwhile I too live in the fantasy world of film. We are in the middle of shooting a six-hour TV adaptation of The Night Manager for the BBC and some American oligarch broadcaster. We are packed with stars you've never heard of, but everyone is very impressed and the project is hugely expensive. *Our Kind of Traitor* is shot and, as far as I've seen, seriously wounded, but perhaps it will improve with all the usual technical devices. No date for release yet, but looming. *A Delicate Truth* has been scripted and the script will be repeatedly revised. And then of course there is *Smiley's People*, which the filmmakers have bought, but about which they preserve a mysterious silence.

How strange that we old spies end up writing books and making movies. I suppose it keeps us off the streets. Like you, perhaps, I simply don't understand the Ukraine situation. Khrushchev gave it away to a point, and it seems to have been in the middle air ever since. The people look terribly ugly and the oligarchs are in London. If you can explain it to me, do.

We are all well. Grandchildren proliferate. We shall vote Labour on May 7th and pay the price in punitive taxation.

---

10. Lyubimov's novel *The Life and Adventures of Alex Wilkie, Spy* was made into the film *Soul of a Spy* in 2015.

Our election is a comedy of irrelevance. The great issues are discussed by the press and the public, but not by the political parties. Whether we are in Europe or out of it is less important than whether Mr Miliband has one or two kitchens in his house in London. So it goes.

My warmest wishes to you and to all whom you love.
David

In 'Smiley Mike', an unpublished chapter of The Pigeon Tunnel *in which Mikhail Lyubimov's adventures as the head of the KGB's London station are related, le Carré wrote that Lyubimov 'remains an aristocrat of the old Russian intelligence establishment, born a Czekist, son of a Czekist and the grandson of a third. Czekists don't change their spots that easily. Mikhail is also Ukrainian, and for Ukrainians of his stamp, whether we like it or not, Russia is the Ukraine as the Ukraine is Russia.'*

~

After setting aside Silverview, *le Carré started work on a play,* Ronnie Boy; *it went through several drafts. The work drew on the dark and funny episodes of le Carré's early life; it opens with a writer, David, interviewing his mother, Olive, about his father. He sent* Ronnie Boy *to Stoppard, who in February 2015 told le Carré in an email: 'The play is marvellous and an easy read, so speedy and full of fun, a real pleasure.' He said le Carré had at one bound freed himself 'from the supposed constraints of theatre and theatre narrative'.*

Le Carré had cooled on Adam Sisman's biography; while he praised the quality of research in the early part of the book, particularly Ronnie's early misadventures and imprisonment, he found the reconstruction of his own life intrusive.

TO SIR TOM STOPPARD

9 Gainsborough Gardens
London, NW3 1BJ

1 June 2015

Dear Tom,

Just returned from a not very successful three weeks of writing in the chalet in the Bernese Oberland – torn between the play, of which more later, and some kind of piecemeal autobiography, begun a couple of years back & then abandoned in the face of Sisman's opus, due out this October [. . .]. My advice on that whole subject, probably too late & certainly impertinent: if you're alive, don't go there, they're happier in the kingdom of the dead.

Of the play: after one ½ hr session with Goold,[11] I rejigged the first act quite considerably, and thought it quite good, certainly more organised, & more introspective and – to my ear – funnier. The proposition, you may remember, was the Olivier next autumn (2016). I have/had no problem with the 2nd & final act but thought it w̲d̲ be helpful, even necessary, to get his take on Act I, particularly the stage devices it employs of, among others, having our narrator also as a player on stage.

I suggested to Goold that I send it to him as a basis for discussion and got a 'can't wait', so sent it. Three weeks go by, I press for an answer, or a date to meet. He replies that he's tied up with a 'Greek program' (?) & after further delay tells me that the National is full up for 2016, & we w̲d̲ have to go elsewhere. His only comment on the text was that he had read it cursorily & it 'seemed to be on the right lines.' End result: we haven't spoken, on the phone or directly, no further correspondence except, from my side, the rather insincere suggestion that, when I've done Act II in time, I'll let him see the whole thing;

---

11. Rupert Goold, artistic director of the Almeida Theatre. Le Carré was hugely impressed by Goold's direction of Patrick Stewart in *Macbeth*.

but by this time I'm thinking, this isn't the way things shd be going. Rejection, disappointment, etc., we handle as part of the job, but opaque silence is no way to communicate & it pissed me off in the way bad manners do.

Meanwhile, not on Goold's account, I find myself worrying about the very personal nature of the material, & whether I actually want to deal with the publicity and fuss in my lifetime, particularly after the Sisman opus, which will cause some kind of kerfuffle of its own: one after the other feels a bit excessive. So my present plan might be: finish the play to my own satisfaction, & leave it in my estate for someone to pick up if they feel like it – notably, my sons, heirs, assigns, etc., & their burgeoning production company, if it still burgeons.

Either way, I'll finish up the autobiographical pieces, if only as some sort of antidote to Sisman, and that will come first, for publication next year [. . .]

In the meantime – may I send you Act I to mull over in yr own good time? We can send it electronically or in paper form, whichever you prefer, & there's no earthly hurry. Jane tells me you're locked into a screen adaptation of 'Arcadia', which sounds a lovely idea. In any case, I won't send till I hear from you.

Tomorrow to Mallorca to play a cameo part in 'The Night Manager', then on Sunday to Cornwall for a hard spell on the book, but always delighted to be interrupted, should you decide on a swoop to Cornwall. Jane & I had a very happy time in the chalet, which I built 45 years ago in the Bernese Oberland & have since given to the boys, so we go off-season when the village is empty. Living small & making fires and reading & being content.

Read 'Scoop' again & thought what a blessing it must be as a writer to be an unrepentant, unredeemable snob. Oh for such certitudes!

Our love to you both, as always,
David

P.S. This comes in place of the phone call I sh<u>d</u> have made but kept putting off, I suppose because of the play stuff. d.

Le Carré had hoped the Ink Factory would produce Ronnie Boy. *Stoppard predicted Goold would be thrilled by the play; it appears Goold saw it more as a film than a play. On 20 June 2015 le Carré emailed Charlotte that 'I put the play aside in a huff for reasons I will relate elsewhere, and am frantically preparing an autobiographical book of new and past writings.'*

THE NIGHT MANAGER:
'THE VAPOUR OF CELEBRITY'

I suppose that in an odd way I was shocked, not least because twenty years ago I had given up the movie rights for dead.

– from le Carré's new afterword for *The Night Manager* in 2016

The second half of the novel . . . doesn't work in the novel.

– le Carré, when screenwriter David Farr nervously suggested that the second half of the novel might not work for the television drama

After years of frustration with efforts to film *The Night Manager*, the six-part television series directed by Susanne Bier and written by David Farr, and produced by le Carré's sons Simon and Stephen, won three Golden Globes and two Emmys. It moved the setting of the six-hundred-page 1993 novel from Latin America to the contemporary Middle East, with a reported $30 million budget. The 'primary love story' of the novel, said Bier, was between the characters of the arms dealer Richard Onslow Roper, played by Hugh Laurie, and his nemesis Jonathan Pine, played by Tom Hiddleston. 'Although it reconstructs my novel and places it in the contemporary world, my name is conspicuously attached to it, and that has added to the vapour of celebrity,' le Carré wrote to his friend Vladimir Stabnikov.

то SUSANNE BIER

9 Gainsborough Gardens
London, NW3 1BJ

31 August 2015

Dear Susanne,

I have written lavishly, and entirely truthfully, to both Tom and
Hugh, to express my profound thanks for their superb performances. Over the next couple of days, I must say the same
to the peerless Elizabeth, the other Tom, to Alastair – on & on
it should go, because there isn't a single weak performance in
this wonderful film.[1] But they are all your creation, just as the
whole film is, and I can't tell you how greatly I admire it. The
central ambiguity of the relationships between Pine & Roper
is wonderfully depicted: now mutual suspicion, now mutually
narcissistic, and sometimes it's as if Roper is almost consciously
in love with his own executioner. Are Pine's sins, cumulatively,
the equal of Roper's? – sometimes it seems so. And between
them, the extraordinarily poised Jed, their prize, their victim,
their battle ground, and the Bosola who is Corkoran, the Devil
with all the best lines – & the greatest insight, and the scari-
est mind.

I wanted to come laden with gifts this evening, but so far
my imagination has failed me in the daze of admiration that
overcame me with the film. Over dinner, I expect we shall all
have our little gripes, our pet blemishes. But I need to tell you
in advance of that obligatory ceremony that you have made a
truly marvellous movie, exquisitely paced, delivering all the
required satisfactions in its consummation; that you have given
to each of the three central characters from the novel a depth
and a meaning beyond anything I could have hoped for. How
often have I been able to say that? Very seldom indeed – maybe

---

1. The cast of *The Night Manager* included Tom Hiddleston, Hugh Laurie, Elizabeth
Debicki, Tom Hollander and Alistair Petrie.

in my whole writing career, only a couple of times. But in the entirety? – then we must go all the way back to the Seventies, and Alec Guinness & the cast around him, & the mood of the time. Thank you so much – and my admiration once again.

Ever,
David

~

TO HUGH LAURIE

By email

29 August 2015

Subject: TNM

Dear Hugh,

Finished watching it a couple of hours ago at Simon's house on a large but not overlarge TV. The first thing to say is that it's one hell of a movie: beautifully performed and directed, epic in scale, light miles (years?) from anything I've seen coming out of television in the last decade, let alone British television. In a class of its own, lucid, chapter by chapter, tense internally and externally, the action well paced, and all of it rising to a skilfully engineered crescendo that ties up all the ends, except perhaps the question of how Pine is going to explain that little matter of $300 million in his current account to the Inland Revenue.

And not a weak performance anywhere, just stunningly well acted.

And Roper mysteriously wins. Even thrashing around in the back of the police van on his way to the gallows, he somehow comes over as a fellow who's been done hard by. Partly because we love him for his audacity, his urbanity and his wit; and partly because he's the captain of the ship we've been cruising in with so much pleasure for so long. But partly also because by the end we have wondered too often along the journey whether Pine isn't enjoying himself a bit too much, and whether his sins, put together, are not in their own way the equal of Roper's.

As to the art of it: Jesus, Laurie, bloody breathtaking. The interaction between Pine and Roper infinitely subtle, ambiguous, complicit, occasionally homoerotic. At times it's as if Roper enjoys being a partner in his own destruction, just for the pleasure of dealing with someone as shitty and intelligent as himself. And Jed between them is sheer delight: not a note out of tune from her anywhere, and the triangle exquisitely squared by Corky, the devil who has the best lines, and susses Pine from Day One.

As to lines, whatever you all did to the script, it sings like a linnet, particularly in the last 3 eps.

Gripes? A few, which I've passed to Simon,[2] but I don't want to mark your card before you see it and form gripes of your own.

Your own performance? From where I sit (which is a pretty isolated spot, I admit, not hugely informed), it has to be the performance of a lifetime. See what you think. Sequel? Along the lines we discussed, if you're still drawn, I am, because Roper in that context strikes me as a dramatic goldmine, and Laurie and Roper, as now constituted, are a perfect match. But I'm under-equipped to write it. As Dan Moynihan told my US publishers when they offered him the chance to spread his literary earnings over several years, I'm too damned old to buy green bananas.

If I've failed to say it loudly enough: I'm exalted by your incomparable Roper, impressed beyond my pay grade, and very grateful. Loved your visit, loved meeting Jo, sorry it was such a scrappy affair, but we prevailed. Did I say I'm very excited? Well, I am.

---

2. Simon Cornwell, executive producer on *The Night Manager*.

Best to you both,
David

~

TO MIKHAIL LYUBIMOV

By email

11 September 2015

Berlin is a city and a war grave. I never felt it so deeply as on this last 48 hour visit to research a possible remake of SPY WHO ... Even, in some awful way, a place that treats war as some kind of permanent addiction, and is taking a quick breather before the next one comes along. Glad to hear of your ups and downs in the film trade, but particularly glad that the books have been given extra life. Off to LA next week for family wedding and talks with the moguls. I'll keep you abreast of the memoir. Jane in low water with health problems, but swimming bravely. Old Age was supposed to happen to grown-ups, not us.

As ever,
David

~

TO BERNHARD DOCKE

By email

1 December 2015

Subject: The world and all that

Dear Bernhard,

Very good to hear from you. Wow, what times. On the one hand, Germany an example to the world for its openheartedness and the grandeur of its gesture;[3] Sweden running an honourable second; and my own dismal little government shaping and indeed poisoning public opinion, which as usual is in a better place than their own. And on the other hand, your Trumpisti and nationalist ostriches raging against these unwashed un-Germans. But most awful to me, the Hungarians, who fled in their thousands in 1956 from the Bear, slamming their frontiers shut against fellow refugees.

And now we're bombing Syria to avenge the spilling of European blood after we have consistently turned our backs [on] the consequences of our own disastrous meddling.

We are in pretty good shape, barring the predictable indignities of age. Work and writing swimming along. I'll send you a rundown shortly. I'm writing this from the hospital where Jane is recovering well from an operation that we hope will release her from the great pest.

Our sincere love to you all. More soon.
As ever,
David

～

TO VLADIMIR STABNIKOV

Subject: Re: Private

---

3. 'We can do this!' Angela Merkel declared in August 2015, a year in which Germany accepted about a million refugees.

Dear Vladimir,

Well, here I am, writing. And what I should be writing to you is a response to your generous words in the two emails you have sent me, the first ebullient and the second a little sad. I should be writing that, while you were profiting from the experience of bear-leading me around Russia, I was hugely profiting from your energy, generosity and enthusiasm.

Each novel I have written has been a complete life. The novels that I wrote about Russia were lives that you enabled me to lead. And when I moved on to other lives: to the Middle East, to Africa, and to Latin America, other people opened doors for me and I was again the beneficiary of kind strangers who became kind friends. I shall always remember your central position in providing me with insights, experiences and introductions that I would not have had without you, and I have indicated these here and there in the memoir I am publishing this autumn.

Put together, my life seems to be nothing but the mosaic of a huge variety of unfinished engagements, like a kind of spiritual journey on the Trans-Siberian Express. I am very conscious of stopping nowhere long enough in my eagerness to advance, and Russia is surely the place where I would have preferred to linger longest. I hope that in my new book, that sentiment comes through.

Which brings me back to expressing once more my thanks for the great debt I shall always owe you for opening my eyes to so much. And if, as you say, I did the same for you, then we should be very pleased with one another.

Because I have kept writing and have lived to a great age and am British, I am presently enjoying a kind of premature immortality which is unlikely to survive my death. The television version of The Night Manager is causing a great sensation in Britain and will soon be networked in the United States; it has also been sold to a hundred and thirty other countries. Although it reconstructs my novel and places it in the contemporary world, my name is conspicuously attached to it, and that has added to the vapour of celebrity. The result is an enormous post I cannot deal with and ludicrous propositions to appear on every kind of platform. As my reputation gets larger, I shrink.

None of which should prevent us from meeting up when you come over for the London Book Fair, which I sincerely hope will be possible. Give us your dates and the occasions when you are free, and we shall do our best.

As always,
David

~

Tom Bower's Broken Vows: Tony Blair – the Tragedy of Power *was published in January 2016.*

TO TOM BOWER

By email

21 March 2016

Subject: Congratulations

Dear Tom,
Well, congratulations. A massive piece of work, revelatory and cumulatively shocking. I think you have managed splendidly to convey the extraordinary convergence of decisions forced on any Prime Minister at any time, the random mixture of trivial and monumental – and Blair's scary incapacity to recognise which is which. Some of the passages remind me of the Nixon Papers when his sofa cabinet is busily conspiring a cover-up, and a Shakespearean messenger arrives to inform the President that the Italian Lira has collapsed. Nixon replies: 'Fuck the Lira' and resumes his conspiratorial conversation with his acolytes.

Of course it is a partisan document and unashamedly so. I don't mind that at all. In fact, it reflects an honesty found in few historians. I have just finished Andrew Roberts' *Napoleon* and he determinedly looks for excuses for his hero at every turn. You have done the reverse, which consoles me, because I feel that in your book I have met exactly the Tony Blair I wanted to find: an extraordinarily deft orator, a plausible and intuitive liar, self-delusional, self-loving, self-serving and self-forgiving.

I wanted more of his childhood, more of his parenthood, but I know a lot now about his Rosebud. It was an extraordinary journey that you made and I am glad to have shared it.

As ever,
David

~

The writer, editor and Wodehouse biographer Robert McCrum sent le Carré a copy of 'Wodehouse in Wonderland', his speech to a Wodehouse convention. It observed how Wodehouse detached himself from the troubling, exterior world – whether that was the Second World War or even possibly his own sexual impulses – in 'a kind of artistic solitary confinement . . . with a unique compulsion to pacify the pain of everyday life by living in the Elysium of his imagination'. There was 'no sex, no deaths, and no suffering', McCrum wrote, in the Wodehousean paradise.

TO ROBERT McCRUM

Tregiffian
St Buryan
Penzance
Cornwall

30 July 2016

Private, personal & all that

Dear Robert,

Thank you so much for sending me your piece on Wodehouse, which I found moving and true, and in some way very personal, & relevant to my own defence systems. Like you, I expect, I continue to rely on Wodehouse in ways far deeper than the Master wd care to acknowledge. As he found his own escape mechanism, so he provided us with one: or me, at least! I don't remember whether, in your excellent biography, you thought of Kenneth Grahame[4] as a possible additional influence on Wodehouse: paradise, & decent fellows, & the Wild Wood beyond. I try to imagine how he would have bewildered a biographer, diddled & confused him, & sent him away empty, never to return.

[. . .]

And so it is with my work – or the stuff I'm writing at the moment. The Spy stuff that I invented was also a paradise, if a pitch black one, and I find myself in age returning to it, or sticking with it, in blithe despair, as it all returns to me.

Again, my thanks, and my congratulations on nailing the old eel before he disappears into the mud.

We don't know each other really, except through our writing, but in that sense I feel I know you better from this piece.

Best wishes,
David

~

---

4. It was Jeannie Cornwell's repeated readings of Grahame's *Wind in the Willows* that introduced seven-year-old le Carré to books.

TO AL AND ANNE ALVAREZ

16 September 2016

Beloved Al & Anne,

It's time I thanked you both for your very kind messages – some on the machine in London, we learn too late – and all the support you have <u>always</u> given to my work, & the tolerance & affection along with it. TPT is doing good business [. . .] This time we landed butter side up; which is great for foreign publishers particularly, & for all the US critics who are waiting to be told what to think. I owe you so much over the years – Anne for the never failing sympathy, & Al for the stern & beautiful intellectual rigour, and faultless writing to go with it.

I am struggling with my Ur-novel, a kind of Rosenkranz & Guildenstein version of the 'Spy who . . .'[5] that imagines how everyone in 'real life' might have behaved if this weren't a <u>noir</u> novel, but a novel of humanitarian concern & fallibility. It's a thriller turned inside out, therefore, the inside being the compassion & the inadequacies & the fuck-ups that we all experience, and suppress. And the false gods we appoint, such as, taking a name at random, George Smiley . . . So it's a gas to write, and I have promised myself to complete it by Christmas, & it looks as if I shall. We are very happy together here, & the summer has been long & gorgeous. When I faltered on the novel, Jane scooped me up. And when I said, 'fuck it, let's go & be bored in London instead' she said, 'get on with your work & watch your language.'

Anyway, we all write too few letters these days. And this one is really to say, thank you, & we love you, and we'll be up in late October. And again, we love you.

David

---

5. *A Legacy of Spies.*

ᴛᴏ MARY MOUNT

By email

8 November 2016

Subject: ALOS

Dear Mary,

Thank you for your wonderful letter. The book[6] was a pest to write at first, and heaven knows how much I wrote and threw away. But then it cheered up once it became Guillam's story, and the pleasure of waking those sleeping characters made up for everything. I didn't dare reread the old books, just made do with remembering them, so there are glaring and quite funny discrepancies that by and large I can't fix. So I shall have to write an artful postscript, or find some other way to spike the guns of the pedants of Tunbridge Wells.

Thank you again for your kind and perceptive letter. As you can imagine, the book was quite a sweat at my great age, but the decision to go into hiding for the publication of The Pigeon Tunnel seems to have paid off.

As ever,
David

In 2016 Macintyre published SAS: Rogue Heroes – The Authorized Wartime History.

---

6. In *A Legacy of Spies*, le Carré returned to the characters of the Smiley trilogy for the first time in twenty-five years.

TO BEN MACINTYRE

As from Tregiffian
St Buryan
Penzance
Cornwall

15 November 2016

Dear Ben,

Thanks so much for the book, the kind dedication, & yr letter. I'm halfway into the book and completely gripped by it. The writing ever better, the character-drawing superb. What a planet . . . of course we heard of your divorce, and greatly sympathised. My own was heartbreaking, although conducted with great decency on both sides; & we both remarried shortly after it. But the wounds don't heal, or they don't for me; which is to say, I reproach myself constantly, while at the same time celebrating my release. (Ann, my first wife, died a while back after a long re-marriage.)

Glad you liked 'The Pigeon Tunnel' – it's had a good time, but in the way books disappear from one's memory, so did TPT while I completed a new novel, out next September, which I like, not always the case. We are off to Cornwall now, back in London for Christmas with children & grandchildren, then Germany probably. But it would be lovely to meet up, & when we return, I'll suggest something.

Let me say again how much I admire your writing, how well the story emerges from the research, how lucid and unflinch-ing the human portraits. Our GP in Cornwall sneaks off to Hereford now & then to teach the boys (& girls) of the S.A.S. how to handle ill-health & wounds in the field: 'In 3 weeks I have to turn them into doctors.' I shall be giving him yr book for Christmas. Our very best to you & yours –

Ever,
David

TRUMP AND BREXIT

My response to the political scene is vehement: I hate Brexit, hate Trump, fear the rise of white fascism everywhere and take the threat very seriously indeed; the craving for conflict is everywhere among our pseudo dictators.

– to the German journalist and novelist Yassin Musharbash,
4 April 2018

Amid the result of the Brexit referendum of 23 June 2016, and the election of Donald Trump on 9 November 2016, le Carré finished work on *A Legacy of Spies*. The novel that followed, *Agent Running in the Field* – his last – was read as an indictment of Brexit Britain.

'We are shattered and deeply ashamed by Brexit, and cannot yet believe there is no way back,' le Carré wrote to Bernhard Docke on 5 July 2016. 'What a pathetic cocktail of lost illusions and false hopes.'

TO NICHOLAS SHAKESPEARE

16 December 2016

Dear Nicholas,

So glad the Brouilly hit the spot. And really interested in your sudden aversion to the contemporary novel, which kicked in with me, without the help of Mumbai 'flu, about twenty years ago. I read old masters, a few, & a fairish amount of non-fiction. But my darkest secret has always been dyslexia – I read at a snail's pace, much as I w<u>d</u> read aloud, with the effect that impatience, & what Hemingway called the 'automatic shit detector', kick in almost instantly. If there is anything that explains instant literary success, it must be access, & recognition, two things I find too often denied to me when I'm trying to read.

The new novel I turned in a few weeks ago has found favour with the publishers, whatever that tells us, & I'm now embarking on my usual journey of post-facto research & rewrites: Brittany, Germany, Poland, Czecho, in quick order, to be completed by the end of February, theoretically, for September publication. Post-completion boredom has however already set in, and I can't wait to return to London (Monday) and get bored there, before leaving for Berlin in mid Jan. Betweenwhiles, I can hardly believe the depths to which the US is about to sink, or has sunk already. Our supposed great ally is a rogue state run by a thin-skinned, truthless, vengeful, pitiless ego-maniac – I forgot narcissistic – & we must <u>never</u> imagine he has a rational, temperate nature underneath the skin, & we must <u>never</u> forget how he came to power, so reminiscent of Our Dear Führer in so many ways that it dries the mouth.

Brexit? An act of economic suicide mounted by charlatans, but ultimately inoperable & retrievable in fact if not in name. Or so I hope. Meanwhile, planned penury for the huge underclass . . .

Love to you all – your parents too – for a great Christmas, & God knows what New Year –

David

~

to ROLAND PHILIPPS

> *9 Gainsborough Gardens,*
> *London, NW3 1BJ*

16 February 2017

Dear Roland,

Thank you for your wonderful and generous letter. I'm so very glad that the book worked for you – particularly you – and that you understood it so well. Your editorial points are all well taken, and I will address them together with the other stuff coming in [. . .].

And of course, as you guess, the book does mean a lot to me, and lives on, and will remain a moving target till the last minute, as usual. I am particularly keen to supply Millie McCraig[1] with a cat, & a bird table. The latter was supplied to her by Mendel & Guillam as a birthday present, with Mendel's pokerwork notice on it: 'No bird turned away'. It's one of the places where she stores microfilm in cassettes.*

But otherwise, of course, I'm in limbo, trying as ever to come to terms with the publicity package being prepared, one foot in the TV adaptation, one very much not, and fussing

---

1. In *Tinker Tailor Soldier Spy*, Millie McCraig keeps house and mans the microphones at the house where the Circus's mole meets his Russian handler. 'She was a wiry Scottish widow with brown stockings and bobbed hair and the polished, wrinkled skin of an old man.' A professional eavesdropper, 'inclined to treat all menfolk as transgressors', with a 'deep and lonely stillness'. She returned in *A Legacy of Spies*.

about what to write now. Last night I wrote the Circus psych-
iatrists' retrospective assessment of Bill Haydon, and woke up
feeling I was going a little strange ... Then I think 'short
stories' as if they were some kind of easy way out, but the reality is that every short story that grabs me turns out to be the
seed of a novel. And a lot of themes and set-ups that look good
too often turn out to be re-treads of stuff I've done with more
or less success.

Went for a long walk on the Heath this morning & got picked
up by a trio of Swedes who couldn't find Kenwood House.* The
woman of the party turned out to be Lena Wickman's sister, &
I was able to tell her how ashamed I was at having turned down
an invitation to dinner with Arthur Koestler, with whom she
was then living.[2] But that's only the beginning: I failed also to
meet Noel Coward, PG Wodehouse, and Kapuzinszky, when
offered the opportunity, & I can't even remember why; except
possibly that I was so suspicious of fame that I took it out on
other people.

It was a wonderful evening at Wiltons; so happy & bubbly.
And the Donald McL story is a marvellous subject.[3] I just read
a surprisingly well-written account of the Noel Field[4] affair,
by Kati Marton, called 'True Believer', that runs parallel to the
Donald experience, and is about equally noble, & totally misplaced intentions. The big change (viz Koestler) came when
people realised that the Comintern had been replaced by
Russian nationalism & Stalinist ethnic cleansing of the middle
class –

Love to you both – & thanks again,
David

---

2. Lena Wickman was a Swedish literary scout, employed by publisher Jack
Geoghegan, who sent him *The Spy Who Came in from the Cold*.

3. *A Spy Named Orphan*, Philipps's account of the Soviet spy Donald Maclean, was
published in 2018.

4. Field was a Boston Quaker who joined the State Department and spied for the
Soviet Union under Stalin.

[*in left-hand margin*] *And I've done some more work on the Smiley–Guillam scene at the end.

[*in left-hand margin*] *my usual rôle on the Heath

$\sim$

TO MARY MOUNT

By email

20 February 2017

Dear Mary,

Thanks for yours. Glad you like the revised text. It was a very snowy journey to Prague,[5] very eerie, freezing cold, and disturbingly unchanged from 55 years ago: spooky empty villas, abandoned castles, a sense of Eastern Europe's bloodlands.

I am making small changes all the time, and still awaiting the reaction of my hosts in Brittany. And of course Ullstein on the new material. And Seuil.[6] But we are in good time, and I would like to get the text squared away to everyone's satisfaction so that I can start thinking of something new. The hardest thing at the moment – and it was very much the case with the revisions – is to think of anything at all except Trump. Maureen Dowd today in the NY Times is pure balm, but only for as long as it lasts . . . and May, just awful all the time.

Best,
David

---

5. Le Carré had traced the route that his character Tulip took from East Berlin to Prague in *A Legacy of Spies*, and visited locations for the novel in Czechoslovakia. His narrator, Guillam, lived on a farm in Brittany. The trip he mentions to Prague, taken fifty-five years earlier, when he was still an MI6 officer, is not documented in the le Carré archive.

6. His French and German publishers, Ullstein Verlag and Éditions du Seuil.

~

Le Carré met Yassin Musharbash – a journalist specialising in Islamism and jihadism, who had recently published a book on Al Qaeda – over a glass of champagne in the Café Einstein Unter den Linden in Berlin in 2007. 'He was looking for a researcher who could help with the fine-tuning of how Islamists think and speak and plot and how German intelligence agencies operate,' Musharbash recalled at le Carré's memorial. Le Carré asked him to equip the Islamist characters in A Most Wanted Man *with plausible life stories and dialogue, and even to devise a fictional terrorism financing scheme. He later carried out some fact-checking and research for* The Pigeon Tunnel *and* A Legacy of Spies.*

In 2017 Musharbash, the son of a Jordanian father and a German mother, wrote to le Carré outlining his plans for a new book, ahead of a move back to Berlin from Amman, Jordan. Le Carré's late correspondence with Musharbash is remarkable for its frankness and intensity. 'David and I had two separate threads of correspondence going: emails for everything practical; written letters for the more personal,' he said.

TO YASSIN MUSHARBASH

2 May 2017

Dear Yassin,

Son Nick & you should meet, then part to your separate pubs, cafés, shebeens or wherever you each write best that day, because he says exactly the same: he likes the chatter round him, likes to hunker down in the places where he is known & tolerated: in short, very Parisian, very between-wars. Myself, it's <u>movement</u> that does it: taking the concept for a walk, scribbling intermittently in a notebook, walking again, going back to my desk & writing it up. But I must have the desk in my sights all the time.

Good to hear you're back in the Fatherland in July. In my view, you should on no account give up your journalism, at least till your novels have taken off, & probably not even then. Colleagues, chatter, crises, the warmth of human contact, are all grist to your mill, I'm sure; & you c<u>d</u> easily become becalmed & scared without them, as I did. The self-healing takes a long while, & is painful for family.

I'll send you a proof – the novel has much changed, as it always does, & is – dare I say it? – much better. No editor, just time, and a timely chat with my friend Tom Stoppard a while back.

And this time, exceptionally, I've decided to dive into the deep end of publicity: NYT serialisation & interview, 60 Minutes, Annie Liebovitz for Vanity Fair, presenting the book at the Royal Festival Hall in London on Sep 7th & a month later at the Elbphilharmonie in HH.[7] And a BBC profile for TV. So in short, what Joseph Brodsky said to me when he heard he'd won the Nobel: 'Now for a year of being glib.' I suppose it's pretty much my swansong, even if the swan thinks it can still fly. Anyway, that's how the media thinks of it, so I'll go along with that. In betweenwhiles, I'm planning a novel, of course.

I'm sure we'll meet before year's end – 'The Spy Who . . .' is still on track, I gather, and the Lord is in his heaven, even if not in America much these days. How can a country live without a conscience? The most endearing thing about Germany is, that it's aware of its past, & keen to correct it. Britain? Forget it. America? Russia? As if.

Love to you all. See you in autumn maybe. Join me in HH if you can, for the harbourfront beano. [. . .]

Ever,
David

～

7. Hansestadt Hamburg, the Hanseatic City of Hamburg.

Stoppard and le Carré had exchanged warm correspondence in the 1990s after The Russia House, *but the bond grew stronger in le Carré's later years. In the 2010s the two men swapped drafts of novels and plays. Stoppard reluctantly turned down a dramatisation of* Absolute Friends *for the BBC but told le Carré that* A Delicate Truth *was 'one of the top le C's to the last sentence'. Both men experienced major biographies published during their lifetime; of his friendships with other writers, Stoppard's biographer Hermione Lee wrote, 'his loving bond with David Cornwell was of the first importance.' Stoppard's detailed critique of* Agent Running in the Field *is in the le Carré archive; his analysis of* A Legacy of Spies, *which presumably preceded this letter, is not.*

TO SIR TOM STOPPARD

> 9 Gainsborough Gardens,
> London, NW3 1BJ

> 25 June 2017

Dear Tom,

Well, thanks again! I have met your points wherever I could. In the end, I felt that Millie should keep her secrets to the end, & I shouldn't signal them. I think it's such a house of secrets anyway that there's enough in the air, and in Guillam's head, for us to accept the surprise package at the end without too much surprise. We knew it all along even if we didn't know we knew. I have given Lotte full measure; you were dead right about her importance. She is now positively blazoned. I have made Christoph's age more elastic – the perpetual adolescent of authoritarian German parents, fathers (stepfathers) particularly. I have deleted Guillam's reflection that the priest might be marrying Tulip to Guillam, instead of burying her. And I caught – thank you again – the footnote on 'theatre'. I've also fiddled a bit with Smiley at the end in order to make his plan of action sound more vigorous, & risky to himself; he will testify, & he will tell the court, if there is one, exactly what happened.

It was <u>wonderful</u> to have your help, & I shall always be grateful for it. Thank you once again, so much. Our love to you both, & let us meet soon.

Ever,
David

~

FitzPatrick, a le Carré fan for forty years, living in the Netherlands for thirty, wrote of the betrayal felt by UK migrants in the EU, 'by the petty nationalists and the deceitful press'.

TO KEITH FITZPATRICK

Tregiffian
St Buryan
Penzance
Cornwall

29 July 2017

Dear Keith FitzPatrick,
Thanks so much for your very touching letter. Your feelings about Brexit spoke into my heart. Just now I w<u>d</u> rather be Dutch, German, French, or for that matter Polish, than a Brit subjected to this truly shaming process in which we are engaged. If it's not too late, grab a copy of today's 'New York Times' & read the front-page opinion piece by a London Times correspondent.[8] She says it all perfectly.

---

8. 'No Dunkirk Spirit Can Save Britain from Brexit Defeat' by Jenni Russell.

I'm very glad that my books have given you pleasure. I trust the new one, out in September, will not disappoint. I didn't expect Smiley to pop up again but, when he did, he was irresistible.

Yes, we are betrayed. Not by our country, which voted for a lot of things it didn't want or understand, but by a handful of jingoistic adventurers and imperialist fantasists, backed by a lot of dark money and manipulation: populism led from above, when was it ever otherwise?

Best wishes, & thanks again for writing –
David Cornwell
(John le Carré)

~

Michael Jayston played Smiley's right-hand man Peter Guillam with crisp, laconic style in the television series of Tinker Tailor Soldier Spy. *He became the reader of audio versions of twenty-one le Carré books. Jayston wrote to le Carré on 17 September 2017 that reading* A Legacy of Spies *brought back 'countless memories . . . like meeting an old friend I hadn't seen for ages'. The retired Peter Guillam is the narrator of the book, which Jayston called 'a masterpiece by a maestro of masterpieces'.*

TO MICHAEL JAYSTON

9 Gainsborough Gardens
London, NW3 1BJ

4 October 2017

Dear Michael,
Lovely letter! Thanks so much. Yes, let's meet & curse the world together. But not quite yet, as I'm off to Germany to strut my

stuff in the new vast concert hall in Hamburg – a kind of RFH replay, but in German – then the German press, then a freak out in Cornwall. So maybe in late November? It was just so good to know you enjoyed the book – & the memories it brought back. To be truthful, that's what happened to me in the process of writing it, & I shed a tear when it was over.

Your readings have entered the soul of my fans & yours. That alone should be grounds for a great lunch together!

Love to you and yours.
As ever,
David

Jayston first read a shortened version of Tinker Tailor Soldier Spy *for an audiobook after the television series, and le Carré was then asked if Jayston could do* Call for the Dead. *'He can do all my books,' le Carré replied. Jayston typically read the unabridged version of the novels, while le Carré read the abridged – and went 'over the top with the posh voices, because he hated them', Jayston observed. In later years le Carré read the full versions of* A Delicate Truth, The Pigeon Tunnel *and* Agent Running in the Field. *The actor Paterson Joseph read the abridged version of* The Mission Song. *It appears le Carré never authorised an audio version of* The Naive and Sentimental Lover, *specifically ruling it out in 2011 and 2017.*

∼

TO SIR TOM STOPPARD

9 Gainsborough Gardens
London, NW3 1BJ

21 December 2017

Dear Tom,

I felt quite useless when you called by on Monday evening: nothing to give, not Christmassy at all, choked up with the Californian calamity[9] and all the kids passing through, and Geller waiting to be heard. So I feel I failed your expectations, which were to wish us a merry Christmas and – of course – receive our heartfelt wishes in return, which come in full measure with this letter, if belatedly, to you both, with our unconditional affection and admiration.

And of course, I felt very strongly – since you told me – that you are on the scent of a new play, and probably, if you're anything like me in that regard, feeling pretty desperate from all the waiting and not finding. And meanwhile – and what could be grander? – your past achievements come back to accuse you, because they are simply not to be put to rest – and never will be. Or so it goes for me, with considerably less reason in my case. If I had simply gone on writing my first novel for the rest of my life, my readership would have been quite happy. But nothing I've written withstands my own scrutiny, which I suppose is what makes Sammy keep running – in this case, to Cornwall on the 28th December, there to hunker down till, I hope, it's more or less done.

But I just felt, as you left, that I'd failed you in some way, and failed myself with it. Which is probably no more than a convergence of too much stuff at the worst time of year for family dramas.

Have a wonderful Christmas, our love to you both, have an amazing trip to the Maharajah and beyond. I couldn't help a wry smile, because my papa worked several Maharajahs in his time, and conned his way into the confidence of a Maharajah of Drangadra,[10] obtaining for himself a little palace on the

---

9. Stephen Cornwell's family's home was burned to the ground soon after the Thomas wildfire broke out in southern California.

10. Meghrajji III, last ruling maharaja of tiny Dhrangadhra-Halvad, in western India. He lived in Ajit Niwas Palace, in Gujarat, and kept a sky-blue Jaguar in Oxford.

estate from which he pursued his ambition to open a football pool in the subcontinent . . . not at all, I am sure, with any success.

Don't please bother to answer this, make nothing of it – I just felt I had to write and assure you both of our love and good wishes.

Ever,
David

~

Philippe Sands had asked 'What should I be thinking about the Salisbury matter' and mentioned an unexplained visit to Moscow by Boris Johnson in December 2017. Sergei Skripal, a former officer of the GRU, the Russian military intelligence agency, and his daughter, Yulia, were left critically ill in the Novichok poisonings in Salisbury; Dawn Sturgess later died as a result of the attack.

TO PHILIPPE SANDS

By email

22 March 2018

Subject: things

Dear Philippe,
I have no doubt it was a Russian killing. I think it was done by the GRU, probably with Putin's consent, but not necessarily. The GRU as a military organisation is not as closely controlled by the Kremlin as the FSB. Evidence is largely empirical, but they have done a lot of it, and a lot of it has been ignored or not recognised for the sake of convenience. But inside the intelligence community, the scale of the killing is well known.

The Russians are proud of it, and the British chattering classes completely misread the value of it as Putin was going into the election.

I think May has protested too much for two reasons. She has seen a golden opportunity to sideline Corbyn, look tough, raise the bar on chauvinism, and distract us from the massive concessions she is making to Europe on Brexit. But as far as our allies are concerned, insofar as we have any left, she has dug herself in too deep and is still digging.

The subtext is of course the reckless money-laundering operations that the City has performed on behalf of the oligarchs, and the great big blind eye that we have turned on Russian kleptocracy. God knows what Johnson thinks he's doing in Moscow, but he thinks there's something in it for him somewhere, and I suspect that, whatever it is, it's Trump related.

Best
David

~

TO JOHN AND MARY JAMES,
ALDEBURGH BOOKSHOP

Tregiffian
St Buryan
Penzance
Cornwall

25 May 2018

Dear John & Mary,
Thanks so much for your lovely letter, & invitation to the festival.

Yes, oddly, we watched M. Portillo's piece on Orford Ness, & would love to join you on a tour.[11] At the moment our cup is, to say the least, full to bursting. I'm hull-down in a novel that I am hoping against hope to finish in the late autumn. On Tuesday I fly to Prague to play a cameo in the TV version of The Little Drummer Girl, join the cast & crew for the wrap, and over the same period discuss earnestly the adaptation of 'Spy Who . . .' plus 'Legacy of Spies' in a joined-up TV series for the Beeb, then back to Cornwall to scribble. 'Spy Who . . .' is supposed to shoot this winter.

So as to March: in principle we would love to come, and the only proviso is: will I have finished the novel, or will it over-run? So a question: on the assumption that you want to add my name to the list of authors attending, when is the deadline for an answer? We would stay at the Brudenell but pay our own way rather than burden you with the cost, and yes, please, an enormous fee to charity, my favourite being Médecins Sans Frontières, simply because I've seen them at it.

A worry I always have about literary gatherings is that I read no modern fiction at all and don't read the literary prints, so I have absolutely no idea who the big lit. cats are, or what they've written. Non-fiction and old fiction, to a point. But in lofty debate about Modern Literature with a capital L, I'm a washout. The only festivals I'm conscious of attending were set-piece speeches – bar Hay, where Philippe Sands compèred.

I would prefer not to bring a prepared speech, but you'll tell me what the format is. I remember only Hay – and Lancaster, of all places. At Lancaster I entered a strangely silent auditorium. Some grins, no applause. It turned out that an hour earlier, in the same auditorium, before the same crowd, Anthony Burgess had declared that any society that accepted me as a serious novelist had reached the last stage of literary decadence. He

11. Michael Portillo explored the history of Orford Ness in *Portillo's Hidden History of Britain* on Channel 5.

was hoping we might meet for a jolly chat in the bar afterwards, but I had a subsequent engagement.[12]

I trust you have been watching the Thorpe story on T V. I only recently read the book. The adaptation is a sheer delight. My favourite character thus far is Jeremy's Mum. If Craig has a moment, her biography is the one we all want.[13]

Our love to you both. We enjoy your company so much. Family headaches all round us, the way it goes. One of my twin great-grandsons has Romanov bleeding problems. Daughters-in-law pregnant everywhere. A son and two delightful grandchildren presently in situ here. I have my own lovely little writing house, which is where I sit now. I'll swim with them later. Swingball with Tom.[14] And sunshine galore.

Let us know about the deadline for yr announcement.
Love from us both –
David

~

12. Bill Swainson, whose friend Michael Reynolds was the organiser of Writing '78, the first Lancaster Festival of Literature, vividly remembers le Carré reading from *Tinker Tailor Soldier Spy* to a packed room in a former factory. 'It was a terrific but also very calm reading, you could have heard the proverbial pin drop, and afterwards my father, who loved the Smiley books, and later the T V series with Alec Guinness, asked him at the signing which of his other books he'd recommend. Dad came home with a paperback copy of *The Naive and Sentimental Lover*.' The memory of the event had also plainly stayed with le Carré, forty years later.

13. *A Very English Scandal*, adapted from John Preston's book of the same name, starred Hugh Grant as Jeremy Thorpe and Patricia Hodge as his mother, Ursula. Craig Brown's book *Ma'am Darling: Ninety-nine Glimpses of Princess Margaret* delighted le Carré.

14. Le Carré's grandson.

TO WILLIAM BURROUGHS

Tregiffian
St Buryan
Penzance
Cornwall

23 July 2018

Dear Bill,

Thanks for yours, and please forgive this typed response: I am in the late throes of the novel. The family bad news has brightened. I am now the great-grandfather of two decent-looking twin boys, and my son's projected journey into surgery looks as though it will be resolved one way or another this coming August.

Well, I would be puzzled to know, if I were in Putin's position, how to run Donald Trump as my asset. I have no doubt that they have obtained him, and they could probably blow him out of the water whenever they felt like it, but I think they are having much more fun feeding his contradictions and contributing to the chaos. The terrifying thing is, the closer he draws to Putin, the more he lies and denies, the stronger his support among the faithful. You don't need to own Trump as an agent. You just have to let him run.

We are moving to London for an unknown period while I change the atmosphere around the book. I hope to have completed some kind of first draft by the Fall.

All very best to you, and stay in touch.
David

∿

A friend of nearly fifty years, from time to time the Hampstead shipwreck-hunter Rex Cowan sent le Carré eccentric left-wing pamphlets he picked

up second-hand. More recently Cowan had bought up some poten-
tially embarrassing letters le Carré had written to Willard Morse, a
Maine obstetrician, which had appeared for sale on the internet. Cowan
returned the letters to le Carré, and it seems they were destroyed.

TO REX COWAN

9 Gainsborough Gardens
London, NW3 1BJ

26 October 2018

Dear Rex,

I'm in bed with a bug & other nuisances, hoping to get to Cornwall next week. I have 'The Burning Question of Trades Unionism' beside me as I write, & the gorgeous Hampstead autumn in my bedroom window. I have a suspicion that Daniel de Leon* is not his name, & English is not his first language. I shall pursue him on the internet. I smell German in the composition.

I was ill and took myself to the Wellington Hospital at night where you get a spot diagnosis for £100. The doctor told me he was very sorry, & I was dying, too late to operate. I thanked him for that useful piece of knowledge; my son Simon got hold of my consultant, who was notionally retired; the consultant said the doctor was exaggerating, & suggested I think of something new to write. I told him that was a tall order, since I had just turned in my new novel two weeks back. He said he would read it. So it goes. In sum, if I die, this is an excellent moment to do so. All my kids are happy, I have three great-grandsons. Then I read that arch-cunt Martin Amis on the pains of reaching 70, & I think, bugger him, I'll reach a hundred.

Love to you, thank you for being a loyal friend –
Ever,
David

P.S. Rex, please don't bubble. I <u>refuse</u> to die in public – too vulgar.

[*in the left margin*] *Could it be our beloved L Trotsky?

Le Carré was off-target in his Henry Higgins guesswork, but not entirely. Daniel de Leon, the American Marxist theoretician, was born in Curaçao, in the Dutch Caribbean, on 14 December 1852. His first language was apparently Spanish, though his father was a surgeon in the Royal Netherlands Army.

∼

TO STEVEN ISSERLIS[15]

The cellist Steven Isserlis introduced himself to le Carré on a train; he teaches masterclasses every spring at the International Musicians Seminar in Prussia Cove, not far from le Carré's home in Cornwall.

> *Tregiffian*
> *St Buryan*
> *Penzance*
> *Cornwall*

26 November 2018

---

15. Le Carré and Jane were at Isserlis's recital on the eve of his fortieth birthday, in 1998. Most of the correspondence with Isserlis, who regularly sent le Carré copies of his CDs and at least one book, was handled by Jane. This letter was an exception: le Carré's contribution to a sixtieth-birthday book of memories and anecdotes. Isserlis played the Sarabande from Bach's Cello Suite No. 5 in C minor in a video recording for their memorial.

Dear Steven,

Spies tell me you are about to be 60. Fake news abounds. It is only yesterday that you swept into our lives only to discover that I was tone-deaf, a condition no musician is ever able to accept. But Jane loves your music, & we endured. I came to a couple of your recitals & did not disgrace myself. Sometimes, when I listened hard enough, I deciphered conversations amid your playing, questions, answers, flippant dismissals and periods of idle meditation. At such little moments, your activities made sense to me. And with those little moments of joining came the greater friendship, which we treasure, and shall celebrate with the enlightened world with great gratitude & GUSTO!

As ever, with love,
David

~

TO SIR TOM STOPPARD

19 December 2018

Dear Tom,

First & foremost, our love & best wishes to you both, and to all you love & have around you over the holiday. We have been more than usually dilinquent about Christmas cards & the trimmings: the sequel to 'The Night Manager' is suddenly happening, or starting to, with the old gang minus Tom Hollander, whose part I so carelessly dispatched. And at last I have completed the much-needed revisions to 'Agent Running in the Field', prompted, I have to say, almost exclusively by your generous & extremely precious editorial suggestions. I believe I have addressed all the points you made, with the provision that some (very few) seemed on closer examination too elusive or disruptive; and in just a few cases, I couldn't agree fully or share your concerns. But your contribution has been invaluable, & again I thank you for it. The most radical transformation is in the 'lean' of Ed's motive towards Trumpism rather than Brexit, although Brexit still looms of necessity. But Trump gets it big, & Brexit relatively small. Rather than burden you over Christmas, I will send you the revised text in the early new year, for you to dip into, & perhaps relish the influence you have had on the whole. My last 'advisor' is Philippe Sands, who has yet to tell me of Ed's exposure to prosecution for what he has done – but I have anyway raised the ante by giving Ed more to betray.

In the end, I have to confess, 'The Little Drummer Girl' on TV left me feeling deeply dissatisfied – of that more, one day. We are staying in London over Christmas – with the Nicks as our guests – & because I have medical stuff that requires me to be around until Jan 4th, when we shall go to Cornwall (by train) for a couple of weeks, then back to London for more of the same: not a great drama, but a confining one at the moment.

We think of you both constantly, and always with the greatest fondness. And I shall be forever in your debt for the loving care – also <u>tough</u> care, thank Heaven – that you devoted on my novel: not for the first time.

As always,
David

Sir Tom Stoppard sent six typed pages of notes to le Carré on Agent Running in the Field *after three readings of the book. 'You keep your cards close to your chest, and deal them out in reverse order, but such are pleasures (as in Drummer Girl too),' he wrote. His comments ranged from wondering what secrets were left to betray about Brexit to 'why does it always have to be sherry?'*

∼

TO SIR TOM STOPPARD

3 January 2019

Dear Tom, dearest both,

Well, that's the thing: my oncologist (for it is he . . .) asked me 'how much do you want to know?', and if I'd had your presence of mind, I w<u>d</u> have replied, with you, 'nothing that might ruin my week'. I am now subjected to once-monthly shots of novichok or similar, and gruellingly cheery intimacies with the oncologist, while my extremely worthy GP in Cornwall tries to keep up. In search of unruined time, we head to Cornwall tomorrow am, but the GP is waiting. The only hope is a third house. Jane plays Sabrina's part,[16] to equal perfection, but thanks to novichok I swing around like an eel. We place our hopes on Cornish air, which on present predictions will be delivered at around three degrees below Centigrade. The new draft of Agent . . . on its way to you but NO HURRY.

<u>Our love</u> as always,
David

≈

John Westerby, a sports writer, whose family came from West Yorkshire, wrote to ask: 'Was there a real-life Westerby with whom you had made acquaintance?'

16. Tom Stoppard and Sabrina Guinness married in 2014. He told an interviewer that she printed his emails for him to write responses, and typed and retyped his plays.

TO JOHN WESTERBY

9 Gainsborough Gardens
London, NW3 1BJ

4 April 2019

Dear John Westerby,

Thanks for your letter. I wish I c<u>d</u> give you a more substantial answer. Names somehow offer themselves out of the blue, first names & surnames alike. Only occasionally, when it's a helpful reference, do I take a 'real' name and bowdlerise it a little – e.g. Toby Esterhase,[17] a poseur offering himself as Hungarian aristocracy. In the case of Jerry, I know, in retrospect, of no such reference, except that the first name belonged to my cricket coach at prep school: a big, bumbly, falsely genial man who had 'done a little of this & that' – probably jail! – before being mysteriously excused military service. Yes, I gave him a bit of blue blood, and a mass of loyalty, to Smiley, to the Service, & country. Not so simple these days!

If you're near us in Cornwall, send a card & come to tea – but the card first in case we're not there, or I'm tied up writing.

New novel out in October.

Best wishes,
David Cornwell

∽

In this late letter to the former soldier, diplomat and novelist Alan Judd, twenty-five years after they first met, le Carré wrote of how he missed the 'Office' – 'both Offices – in their way'.

---

17. Le Carré suggested Esterhase's name was a deliberate misspelling of 'Esterhazy' because Toby had pretensions he couldn't live up to.

TO ALAN JUDD

Tregiffian
St Buryan
Penzance
Cornwall

18 May 2019

Dear Alan,

Thank you so much for your letter. It's all a bit of a muddle. First they told me that the cancer had spread into the bone in a big way, & my life expectation was very short. I also had pneumonia, which didn't help. Then I found myself in the presence of a kind of Ur-oncologist who rules a whole Kingdom in Harley Street, & he subjected me to injections and pills, nothing generally available. In 3 months my PSA, whatever that means, tumbled from a stately 110 to 15.6, and the oncologist is urging me to write another book, but I think that's bravado. But realistically, he doesn't cure anything, as he's the first to say, he just keeps it at bay; & the symptoms, mainly breathing, don't quite go away. But life is beautiful again, and actually complete in all its components: new novel, which I hope to see published in October, healthy children with good marriages, scads of grandchildren, 14 standard and 3 great-, and those books – which, as you rightly suggest, are none of them half as good as I would like, but there we are.

I was extremely touched by the generosity of your letter, and thank you for it most sincerely. It has been such a strange journey. A couple of years ago I got hold of my Stasi file & it had four German press cuttings in it, & nothing else. So weeded, I assumed, either by the Stasi, or the Gauk commission,[18] or the Brits, who all had a hand in going through the stuff. Or maybe,

---

18. After the reunification of Germany the former Lutheran pastor and civil-rights activist Joachim Gauck was named head of the agency that gave individuals and groups access to the Stasi files.

it really is all they had. But my <u>father</u> had a royal Stasi file: a conman by profession, but also an arms dealer (for which he was imprisoned in Indonesia) he went to the East Germans & offered himself as an intermediary and enabler for, one assumes, third country arms sales.* They were impressed, & sent an agent from Vienna, name redacted, but a Herr Doktor somebody, to visit him at his offices in Jermyn Street & report all he saw, including (by diagram) the location of the telex machine & the safe. Infuriatingly, the file stops there. And stuff about him still flows in: people he conned in remote places, letters from his former jailer in Hong Kong, etc. And now Errol Morris, the American documentary maker (The Fog of War etc.) wants to make a documentary about the two of us, our parallel lives, etc. So this morning, to watch him at work, Jane & I tuned into Netflix and saw 'Wormwood', a 4-hour documentary Morris made about the murder of the scientist Frank Olson by his own people, the CIA. Really worth an afternoon of your time. And the central figure is Olson's son, Eric, who has made a life-obsession of his father's murder, just as secretly I've made a life-obsession of my father's incurable criminality. Google Ronnie Cornwell & you get, under profession, 'associate of the Kray brothers'. He was also the associate of Rachmann & other lovelies. So what do you do with only one parent, a father yet, and how do you balance love & evil, loyalty & betrayal, or an upright posture that is actually vengeance in disguise?

Morris for obvious reasons wants to go quietly, and will buy 'The Pigeon Tunnel' film rights, which is immaterial, and I find him very compelling and sympathetic as an interrogator – <u>very</u> smart, and aged 73, so I expect I'll fall for it, & regret it. But I'd regret it more if the plan flops, as most movie plans do.

I miss the Office, always have done – both Offices – in their way. In a sense they are the only places, apart from writing. I'm sure you feel the same, & with much more reason. It's a gorgeous sunny afternoon, no wind for once, and I'm so intensely grateful for my life that I can't help smiling. I shall always treasure your letter, & our times together, and I thank you again, & send you both my love. All being well, we shall hold a great party in October, & I hope that you & Judy will be there. Anthony (Rowell) & Carrie have already accepted!

Ever,
David

[*in left margin*] *while I was serving in Bonn!

~

Tom Bower had just reread Tinker Tailor Soldier Spy *and called it 'superb'.*

TO TOM BOWER

By email

29 June 2019

Dear Tom,

I'm very touched that you took another look at Tinker. For better or worse, it feels like history now; and a bit of mine too, since I lived through the big betrayals while I was still inside the tent, and the tent itself was in a state of decay. As I received your email I had just finished George Packer's biography of Holbrooke,[19] which I found hugely impressive, and was reflecting on the reasons why really brilliant people so often fail in politics. But Holbrooke didn't exactly fail; he stopped a war and

---

19. George Packer's 2019 *Our Man: Richard Holbrooke and the End of the American Century*. Holbrooke's shuttle diplomacy helped to end the war in Bosnia with the 1995 Dayton Accords, and he was President Barack Obama's special representative on Afghanistan and Pakistan.

preserved his humanity to the end. But by then he had made so many enemies that no one would have him in the room.

Thanks, we both fare well. I try too hard to improve my walking range, but down here the terrain is a bit risky, and I am under draconian orders on no account to fall down. So oddly, the Heath is a better bet. Today is gorgeous at last. On Thursday Errol Morris and his team descend on us to conduct a recce ahead of shooting in September. All a bit weird.

I would like to send you, under the usual seal of secrecy, the uncorrected proof of my new novel. Is it safe to post it to you in Hampstead, say on Tuesday? At present, Penguin are making reviewers sign the OSA first.

I still think of poor Jim Prideaux. How many of them there must have been who never made it back.

With much affection,
David

~

The Irish novelist and critic John Banville interviewed le Carré in the spring of 2019 for a Guardian *article linked to the publication of* Agent Running in the Field. *Their meeting coincided with le Carré's decision, after Brexit, to seek Irish citizenship through his Irish grandmother. That summer he and Jane took a holiday to explore his Irish roots. He wrote to John Banville from Ballymaloe House, in east Cork, a country-house hotel and restaurant on three hundred acres of farmland.*

TO JOHN BANVILLE

By email

16 July 2019

Subject: lunch, etc.

Dear John,

Just an interim message. We are enjoying wonderful weather in what is surely the best hotel we have ever stayed in: secure in its style, unfussy, quietly very efficient and food to die for.

There was a hilarious scene at Dublin Airport on Sunday morning. Jane and I presented ourselves at the Avis desk to collect our hire car, all arranged. An embarrassed desk clerk then told us that we are of such great age that he required letters of reassurance from our doctor and our insurance company. No such letters were at hand. Then a charming sequence: it was as if everyone at the airport had taken our problem to heart. Men rushed about, one telephoned his brother, who was a part-time taxi driver, another described the problem to a group of taxi drivers and sought the best bid to drive us to Ballymaloe. We would have taken the train, but that would have meant we missed a crucial cricket match on television, cricket being our weakness. A driver appeared, the deal was struck and for some three-and-a-half hours we were treated to an extraordinarily erudite and informative history of British misdemeanours in Ireland. And here we now are, finally provided with a car from a less fastidious hire company, and enjoying every hour.

It was a wonderful lunch. One to remember. We hugely enjoyed your company and loved the passion and the knowledge with which Patricia[20] spoke of her homeland. Our visit here has taken a strange turn for me: Ireland really does feel like the home of my ancestors, and at a time like this it has a great pull.

With best wishes to you both,
David

In an email to his granddaughter Jessie from the hotel, le Carré called the Ireland experience 'extraordinary. You walk the

---

20. Patricia Quinn, Banville's long-time partner and former director of the Arts Council of Ireland.

*pedestrians-only streets of Dublin on a Saturday evening and
become aware of an unfamiliar smell: hope.' Ireland was a very
young country newly released from perpetual strife, bankruptcy,
Catholic exploitation and British imperialism, he declared, where
the North was seen as a poor sick cousin living on outdated dreams.
'What do they think of us? You can hardly blame them for chort-
ling with bemused glee.' At the age of eighty-seven, he rejoiced in
his Irish roots.*

~

To SIMON, STEPHEN, TIMOTHY AND
NICHOLAS CORNWELL

By email

21 July 2019

Subject: My Granny[21]

Went to her birthplace yesterday, a tiny crossroads on a hill
overlooking beautiful unspoiled countryside. The village of
Ichinillin[22] today consists of two houses, both new, one of them
a shop on the site where the old shop had stood; the ruin of
one tiny cottage that just may have been hers. Went to see the
local archivist and she told me that the Wolfe family house for
my grandmother, her twin sister, two brothers and the parents was 25 feet long and – wait for it – 6 feet high. It was
graded as a superior habitation, would have been of rough
stone and a rush roof. The family were farmers and members
of the Church of Ireland, which was a broad version of the

---

21. Ronnie's mother, Bessie, le Carré's 'pure Irish' grandmother, and from whom, his
brother, Tony, suggested, the touch of blarney came.

22. Inchinattin.

Church of England that included Methodists. Its membership lived in clusters for comfort and security. My grandmother and her twin sister migrated to England two years before the outbreak of murderous religious conflict. The archivist suggested to me that their father may have smelt trouble coming. He died before his wife, and the brothers took over the farm. My great grandmother's maiden name was also Wolfe, so it's presumed that my great grandparents were cousins, or even more closely related, since marrying within the cluster was mandatory. The countryside around was some of the loveliest I have seen in Europe: uninhabited, large gentle hills and valleys descending to the sea. It was easy to imagine the twin sisters growing up in these idyllic surroundings. The church where the family worshipped was a good half day's ride away. The region saw some of the very worst of the potato famine and religious violence, and there are plaques to its many martyrs to English oppression. After spending silent minutes at her computer, the archivist looked up with a charming smile and said: 'welcome home'.

To Zurich tomorrow, thence to Mallorca.

Love,
Pa

~

To DAVID GREENWAY

9 Gainsborough Gardens
London, NW3 1BJ

2 October 2019

Dear David,
Well, we were both wrong. Eleven Supreme Court judges concluded unanimously that Johnson was wrong and had lied to

the Queen. And, amazingly, the mother of parliament, after a long after-lunch sleep, woke up and started to do her job.

Thanks very much for the Gopnik piece.[23] There is a wonderful new biography of Sorge with the rather silly title *An Impeccable Spy*. I warmly recommend it.

I am in the middle of an amusing spat with Dearlove,[24] a very unsatisfactory former chief of SIS who took it into his head to trash my work at a literary festival. I responded in today's *Times* and I expect there will be more of the same.

Enjoy your trip to Prague. I may go there later in the year to present my new book.

I'm afraid your Prince will never get his lands back.[25] My late Swiss agent owned a whole chunk of the Sudetenland, including a couple of palaces. He visited them after the Wall came down. Neither palace was occupied and the lands were overgrown. Nobody had dared live there.

Looking forward to seeing you on 18th.

With love to you both,
David

∼

23. Adam Gopnik's article 'Are Spies More Trouble than They're Worth?'('Spy vs. Spy vs. Spy' was the title in the print edition) appeared in the *New Yorker* in 2019 and used Christopher Andrew's *The Secret World: A History of Intelligence* as a starting point to ask, 'How intelligent is national intelligence?' The legendary Soviet spy Richard Sorge passed on details of Germany's planned invasion of Russia in 1941, but Stalin threatened anyone who dared to take his information seriously.

24. The former head of MI6 Richard Dearlove called le Carré's writing 'so corrosive . . . that most professional Secret Intelligence Service officers are pretty angry with him'. In a rebuttal in *The Times*, le Carré promised that 'when my new novel comes out next month, Dearlove and his notional colleagues are going to be mad as bed-bugs.'

25. Prince William Lobkowicz did get his land and several castles back, along with a fabulous art collection and original scores of Beethoven, whom the family had financed. He was luckier than le Carré's agent Rainer Heumann.

606

Le Carré accepted the Olof Palme Prize, named for the murdered former prime minister of Sweden, in Stockholm in January 2020. He said in his acceptance speech, 'Reading and thinking Palme makes you wonder who you are and who you might have been and weren't, and where your moral courage went when it was needed.' Le Carré gave the $100,000 prize to Médecins sans Frontières.

TO PIERRE SCHORI, CHAIRMAN, OLOF PALME MEMORIAL FUND

> *9 Gainsborough Gardens*
> *London, NW3 1BJ*

> 8 February 2020

Dear Pierre,

I think it was your own stately passion that awoke me to the task: a thing our children quickly noticed and admired in you. After that, there was Palme, and the sincerity of your devotion to his principles & memory. So please take the credit for your leadership & inspiration as I ploughed through draft after draft of the speech & endured all the frustrations that should properly have been invested in a novel! But we got there – it really was <u>we</u> – and you were pleased with the results, and I was pleased that you were pleased, and the rest followed.

All of which amounts to a most heartfelt thank you, and a thank you also to Maud, who so clearly shares your energy and convictions. The children (as we still presume to call them although in so many ways they are older than us) were moved in all the right ways, full of respect for the cause, bonding now with the Palme's, now with the Bonnier's,[26] not to mention the distinguished politicians and writers who made up the assembly.

---

26. Albert Bonniers Förlag publish le Carré in Sweden, and the Palme and Bonnier families hosted events for le Carré and his sons and grandchildren.

On the Tuesday, we went to the British Embassy for lunch and a talk to the assembled staff (5-eyes, so Australia & New Zealand also invited) and it all turned out to be a bit of a marathon, and the better for it.

And somehow it was entirely right that we just got under the wire: on arrival in London we kept an appointment with my oncologist who ruled that the medication I had been taking had run its course, with the result that we spent the next two days in hospital preparing for something stronger – all unpronounceable names, but Jane retains them all – with the subtext that I must remain grounded in London, no travel until I am released. So a mercy that it's all happening after the event and not before. Also the side effects are more unpredictable and include – Heaven help us – memory loss, so goofiness. C. P. Snow once told me that human intelligence was simply a matter of memory, as if imagination played no part. (Apparently he also spent much time in Stockholm lobbying for a Nobel, to no effect.)

Britain is in the hands of far-right Trumpists, as every small new event indicates. Journalists suspected of unsound sympathies are excluded from official press briefings, which now take place, not in the people's parliament, but at No. 10, on Johnson's home ground. Cowardice & bullying go hand-in-hand, & Johnson is a practitioner of both. The Democrats in America are making prize asses of themselves, Putin is appointing himself Ruler for Life, so we look like having a pretty awful decade. Which means we're back to where we were – and to the question that I know is much in your mind in Sweden – where <u>are</u> the stand-up men & women, where <u>is</u> the voice and where is the fulcrum of resistance? There is none in America, there is none here, there is none in Sweden. So where is the battleground? Where do we sign up?

Pierre, it has been a wonderful journey, & you led it. We send love & thanks to you, to Maud; and to the team, and your fellow judges, more thanks. It was the journey of a lifetime, a novel of education in itself, and let us hope we have spread the name and meaning of Palme further & wider than before.

As ever,
David

~

Daniel Ellsberg, who leaked the Pentagon Papers *to the* New York Times *and the* Washington Post, *was the previous winner of the Olof Palme Prize.*

TO DANIEL ELLSBERG

As from Tregiffian
St Buryan
Penzance
Cornwall

11 February 2020

Dear Dan,

Home at last from Stockholm, which was icy cold but wonderfully warm, to your three books, for which I thank you warmly, along with their over-generous dedication. Your presence in my life has been extraordinary ever since Pierre told me they had given me the prize. You weren't just a tough act to follow, you were definitively impossible to follow, as I indicated in the first few minutes of my speech. And what a place to speak, and what an audience! Like you, I have never considered myself a Social Democrat, whatever that means, and I don't like the misty word 'liberal' either, which from country to country changes its spots at will. I like 'humanist', but it sounds like too much of a job, like 'I do humans'. But I <u>do</u> know that what you did was emphatically right, and I loved it coming from the heart of a loyal American, just as Snowden is a loyal American, except that America won't let him be loyal. They didn't want you to be either.

When will I read your books? Slowly and carefully over time. I read at a snail's pace, am absurdly dyslexic; probably I read at speaking speed, which is how I try to write. And intermittently, because at last I am into another novel, theme to be discovered, but it's about being human. I begin with a minimum: a couple or three characters awaiting development, collision in the air, and a vaguely political context. After that, to quote Capote, I'm not a writer but a re-writer.

Your 'case', as the spooks would have it, fascinates me, and all the more so because I keep comparing it with what would happen here, or more accurately, what <u>hasn't</u> happened here, save perhaps in the case of the young woman at GCHQ, whose name escapes me, who had the guts to blow the whistle on a seedy effort by the US State Dept. – or was it the CIA? – to persuade <u>us</u> to persuade/bribe/bully <u>third world</u> representatives to the UN to vote in favour of the Iraq war.

The business of 'going public' here is precarious to say the least. Newspaper proprietors are for the most part unwilling even to cross the road unless it's closed to traffic, & the D-notice and the threats attached to it are disturbingly effective. I wrote one novel (The Mission Song) where the whistleblowers got to an internet café in the nick of time; but did the lucky newspaper (I was thinking of the Guardian even) risk putting its head so far into the lion's jaw? Just rambling.

Dan, the purpose of this letter is to tell you that I am a totally unworthy successor; that your contribution to the world is diamond-real, and mine is merely imaginative; and that it was a joy to follow in Palme's footsteps (and you actually <u>met</u> him!), with your shadow beside me.

With fraternal greetings,
David

LOCKDOWN

We're totally isolated here, but you might say we have been for fifty years, so what's the difference?

– to Philippe Sands, by email, 3 June 2020

We feel happy and, wherever we can, determined to live every day just the way we used to before the cancer and the plague struck.

– to Tom Bower, by email, 24 September 2020

Le Carré's last public appearance was at the German ambassador's residence in London's Belgrave Square on 3 March 2020. The 'Berliner Salon' was a Q&A with Nicholas Shakespeare, the former *Telegraph* literary editor, biographer and novelist to whom le Carré had offered writing space at his home in Cornwall to develop his work – on condition he never wrote about him.

Le Carré earned sustained applause from an audience including diplomats, journalists, publishers and friends, from the former cabinet secretary Lord Robin Butler and Tom Tugendhat M P to the British-German television journalist Matt Frei.

On arriving at the residence, guests were invited to wash their hands, according to the twenty-second rule. There were nearly three hundred people crammed into close rows of seats across three rooms, and no one wore masks. Lockdown followed just a week later.

'Life is without resolution for most artistic people,' le Carré said. 'I think the great thing is you go to the edge of your talent every time and see what isn't beyond, you try and go a bit further. I would just like to, it sounds maudlin, I would just like to die with a pen in my hand.'

In September 2020 David, Jane and his half-sister Charlotte shared a Zoom call in which they joked about their cancer diagnoses, but the humour was strained; Charlotte's situation was bad, and Jane's was deteriorating. Le Carré's own treatment was no longer having much effect; but weeks later he received an experimental lutetium therapy which seemed to work heroically well. That outcome felt very unfair to him as Jane deteriorated, and he had to ask himself if he might unexpectedly outlive his wife.

Le Carré's old friend Sir John Margetson died on 17 October 2020. Le Carré's eulogy for him, recorded in Cornwall and played at Margetson's funeral in Woodbridge, Suffolk, was his last public speech.

The threads of many of his most important correspondences wound together in those days.

TO NICHOLAS SHAKESPEARE

By email

26 April 2020

Subject: A wonderful evening

Dear Nicholas,

Yes, everything already feels like a last time. I marvel at the hands we shook and the droplets we inhaled and the abandon with which we didn't socially distance ourselves. In fact I marvel that, with the Germans so far ahead of us in their preparations and restrictions, the Embassy held the function at all. But it was the last in the series. Ambass and his Frau[1] were retiring and Johnson was going to international rugby matches and Cheltenham was having its horse races, so who's counting? And now the recent past is already a foreign land and the future unborn, and we float in the middle.

We're fine, really fine. Old honeymooners on a cliff. I seem to be writing and Jane shadows me on the machine, the housekeeper is furloughed, the garden is running slowly wild except for the vegetables, which our saintly gardener continues to tend, food is delivered to the door by friendly hands and Jane religiously washes every washable surface of it. Our children and grandchildren are inevitably our obsession and frustration, but we're all good about communicating. Weather outstanding, not a footfall on the coastal path, scarcely an off-shore fisherman, very brash birds, a lot of coupling and baby rabbits.

Jesus, what an unholy mess. We could get a decent, egalitarian society out of it, or a mad Brexit crashout and a king sized Tory fanatics' fuck up.

---

1. Dr Peter Wittig and his wife, journalist and writer Huberta von Voss-Wittig, hosted the 'Berliner Salon' event.

All the very best to you both. What an evening to remember. My love also to your papa. He must have been very proud of your deft handling.

Love,
David

~

TO CHARLOTTE CORNWELL

By email

26 April 2020, 23:55:33

Subject: YOUR BIRTHDAY!

Dearest Sis,
Just woke to it after a chaotic day: happy happy birthday! Let's talk tomorrow and hug each other virtually.

Goodnight, granny, and very much love,
your loving bro,
David

Charlotte's first grandchild, Frank, was eighteen months old.

~

Sam Joiner, who works for the British Antarctic Survey, wrote that 'in these strange and dark times' le Carré's books 'have transported me to somewhere else, into a world of intrigue and depth . . . so thank you'.

TO SAM JOINER

Tregiffian
St Buryan
Penzance
Cornwall

27 April 2020

Dear Sam Joiner,

Thank you so much for your very touching letter of 20th April. The rare ones, like yours, are a real shot in the arm for a writer of 88 trying to make some sense of the gone-world and the unborn one. A thrilling, frightening, daunting time to be alive, but if we learn to build a better world in consequence, maybe worth all the trauma. I'm torn between trying to write about the immediate present – but how, when I can't even walk the streets – or the immediate future, not my thing at all. So I tell myself to write good stories about a world I knew, and not be so egg-headed. If you haven't read it, perhaps try 'A Perfect Spy' and follow it with 'The Pigeon Tunnel', which contains the essay about my father Ronnie, a con-man.

Thank you again for the shot in the arm. I'm reading War & Peace for the first time. If that isn't shaming . . .

Best wishes,
David Cornwell

∼

TO ALAN JUDD

Tregiffian
St Buryan
Penzance
Cornwall

19 May 2020

Dear Alan,

Thanks for yours. Glad to hear you're writing, know your subject, & life goes well. We scribblers are the lucky ones, at least theoretically. I've been self-isolating here for the last 50 years, so the only changes are pretty minimal, & positive: assistant banished to her house, housekeeper furloughed, the gardener forages for food in Penzance (supplies irritatingly short, & quality noticeably lower – why?) and a big silence over the cliff – nobody on the coastal footpath, no inshore fishermen out to sea. But I find the news, whether here or from America, blinding & overpowering none the less, and if I'm not careful I get the serious blues. But I <u>am</u> writing, got off to a good start, then hit the deep snow, which is pretty normal. So just now I'm learning all the wrong ways to tell a story, and advancing, I hope, finally on the right one, the only one. Health <u>weird</u>. After a straight sentence of imminent death last Christmas – no earlier,* time escapes me – delivered by the Wellington Hospital doctor, I am in the stern hands of an oncologist of fame, whom I can now, thank God, only consult by telephone. Anyway, a mass of pills, an occasional injection with a horse-sized needle, and apart from spells of giddiness and the occasional presence of the black dog, I'm fine. We miss family hugely, but nothing to be done. The spring weather has been memorably benign this far, which is great for us, and tantalising for poor people in crammed tight spaces. My children, & their children, in London barely go out at all, on the grounds that too many people don't socially distance. But they have gardens . . .

Was there ever a government this bad & this shallow? I doubt it. Was there ever an American president so consistently evil? I doubt it. Fascinating to discover, by one disastrous appearance after the next, that Boris Johnson cannot muster empathy. It will be his downfall. But then who?

All our very best to you both – lovely to hear from you –
David

[*in margin*] *the winter before

~

Hampstead neighbours, le Carré and Philippe Sands bonded over their opposition to the war in Iraq. Sands hosted le Carré's first and only appearance at the Hay Festival in 2013.

TO PHILIPPE SANDS

By email

3 June 2020

Dear Philippe,

[. . .] We're totally isolated here, but you might say we have been for fifty years, so what's the difference? I think it's the sense that the place has been emptied of its recent past by some natural catastrophe, which in a way it has. Until a week ago, not a soul on the coastal footpath that runs at the foot of our land, no small boats out to sea. And the wildlife running riot in the sun and clear air, crows, hawks, rabbits, gulls all in boisterous turmoil. A lonely police helicopter patrolling the beaches. Kind people collect our food for us, our assistant Vicki works from home, the housekeeper is furloughed, I have mastered the mysteries of a Dyson vacuum cleaner. Sir Keir is doing a lovely job of demolishing Johnson, who resembles a wan, spiritless version of his former nasty self. Of empathy, not a sign. So strange and Greek that he and the unspeakable Trump are losing their populist allure in tandem, and both dangerously casting round for diversions. Are we allowed to hate? I wish. As the weeks go by I increasingly resemble the Michael Frayn character who was the author of the first page of fifty novels. Can anyone write in this?

We send our love to you all. You are the best, and from here just now, about the only good reason to return to Hampstead.

As ever,
David

∾

TO JONNY GELLER

By email

8 June 2020

Subject: A Question

Dear Jonny,

I suspect this may be happening to many of your authors, but it's certainly happening to me: not so much a bloc as a kind of sterile bewilderment.

Having launched myself on the Smiley reminiscences with a nice opening chapter, which you saw, I have gone through half a dozen versions of the first story, written a lot of pages in the process, and nothing has stirred. I wouldn't think of sending you samples: better to lock them away marked 'discarded' for the Bodleian. The first version was set in Trieste, the second in Vienna, both in 1961. The switch was no help, the plot became a tangle and the characters were stillborn. I have tried other Smiley stories – a whole list of them – but nothing resonates any better. I kept being reminded that Smiley was prettily put away in Legacy, so let him rest. And I discovered that the six hours of SPY/LEGACY screenplay, however imperfect they turned out to be, took their toll. And what the hell am I doing in 1961 anyway?

I took a look at other possibilities. Why not some polemic about the dying of Western democracy? But that's just parroting what is being said every day across the world by commentators better qualified than myself to say it. Autobiography? God forbid. First came APS,[2] then TPT,[3] now Errol. That's enough of me to last several lifetimes. I have thought long and made notes about scenarios for novels, but take a second look and the themes are disturbingly familiar. Eighteen months back, I was all set to take myself off to the bloodlands of Eastern Europe and do a story about the rise of the new dictatorships in the ashes of the old. But time has passed, things got in the way, and even if I could get there now, I doubt whether I would have the puff for a long distance run from a standing start.

All the same, age is no excuse. Spirit and ambition are intact. It's the imagination that has gone on strike, perhaps because the unimaginable is happening all around us every day. I used to pride myself on writing against adversity, or on the back of it. [. . .] I was supposed to die but didn't. All the more reason to get on with it. But now I'm stuck.

It's a great time to call it a day, if that's what I'm doing. ARIF[4] is a decent last novel, TPT was a decent memoir, Stockholm a wonderful swan song. A good body of work to look back on, and the last thing I want to do is emulate Greene and go out on something second rate. At 88 I really don't feel downcast, and neither does Jane on my behalf. I've had an amazing run and we'll put our remaining years to good use, not a regret.

Or is there a way to go that I haven't thought of, and you have? We know each other pretty well by now, and I trust your advice.

Best,
David

~

---

2. *A Perfect Spy.*

3. *The Pigeon Tunnel.*

4. *Agent Running in the Field.*

TO SIR TOM STOPPARD

9 Gainsborough Gardens
London, NW3 1BJ

1 July 2020

Dear Tom,

Lovely to get yours. I have spent far too much time since the opening of 'Leopoldstadt' fretting about the unfairness of its curtailed run – and shall we ever see such a fine production again? Answer, gradually conceded: yes, we will, in all sorts of different forms, over the next decades & longer. But what a blow all the same.[5]

After a lot of wrong directions – now if ever is the time for the great political novel, etc. – I finally settled to a format that pleased me – linked short stories from the Smiley years, as told by his Watson, P. Guillam. And the scene that presently absorbs me – & you wd write better than I – is set in 1989, with the Wall just down, when Smiley finally decides he is ready to meet his old nemesis, Karla, settled under another name with his mentally sick daughter in a village not far from yours. What vision, if any, do they now have in common? Who will be the leading voice in the (theoretically) post-ideology world, what is doable, what is pie in the sky?

It seems to me that we have experienced three moments in our lives when the world could have been usefully re-ordered: 1945 (and the Marshall plan, etc., weren't such a bad shot), 1989 (when no voice, no leader, & no real inclination towards world united manifested itself) and now. Anyway that's what I was brooding on until Jane fell ill, & then collapsed last week. Our Cornish GP (no private medicine in Cornwall) is a prince, & did what he could; 111 did excellently, appearing with flashing lights at 1.0 am with a driver and a doctor in full gear, but the prospect of getting consultants and procedures in place in less

5. *Leopoldstadt*'s sold-out opening run ended in its eighth week at Wyndham's theatre with the coronavirus lockdown.

than a couple of months over all was not inviting, particularly as it involved shuffling Jane between 3 different hospitals in 3 different towns in dense holiday traffic. Son Simon sprang into action, drove down from London, & next day – the Sunday – we somehow bundled Jane into the back of his car & by the next morning she was in the London Clinic, being attended by the same surgeon who operated on her breast cancer. As I write, I collect her tomorrow, bring her home for the weekend, and we go together to the consultant to hear the result of his tests, & his recommendations. He will by then have zoomed with his fellow oncologists. You're not allowed to visit your spouse in hospital but yesterday the consultant wangled it, and gradually panic gives way to relief that she is being so well looked after – her relief particularly – and I need hardly say that she was showing all the courage & good humour that deserts me in similar situations. So at the moment, we're just terribly grateful to be out of the panic zone, and conducting sensible conversations and addressing sensible choices, and steadying ourselves for Monday. And I of course am in London, being lavishly cared for by my sons in masks, and their equally wonderful wives, also in masks. Hence this unforgivably long letter.

Maybe I would start the Trinity story even earlier – just on a whim – when Einstein spots the scale of anti-Semitism in Berlin and jumps ship, never to return. I love the notion that the Germans delivered the world's best brains to the [Allied] powers, Einstein among them.

My love to you both – our plans as of now obviously uncertain.

David

Stoppard was writing the film script of Shockwave, *for director Cary Joji Fukunaga, about the atomic bomb dropped on Hiroshima, based on Stephen Walker's non-fiction 2005 book* Shockwave: Countdown to Hiroshima. *He told le Carré he planned to start it in 1938/39. Albert Einstein, already the public target of Nazi*

anti-Semitism, gave up his German passport in early 1933, just as
Adolf Hitler became chancellor.

≈

to BEN MACINTYRE

Macintyre had published Agent Sonya, *the story of the extraordinary*
Soviet spy Ursula Kuczynski, who passed Karl Fuchs's atomic secrets
to the Russians while posing as an Oxfordshire housewife.

By email

31 August 2020

Subject: SONYA

Dear Ben,
Just finished it, and need to tell you, it's absolutely terrific; an
elegantly assembled, scrupulously researched, beautifully told
compulsive read, and an extraordinary slice of history. Of
course I knew some of the players and had read the recent
work on Fuchs by the Oxford physicist, name escapes me, and
the rather more down to earth biography of Sorge. You got
Skardon dead to rights, and Hollis too: boring, mediocre, and
so perversely bad at the job that you still have to wonder.[6] And
living his own little secret life with his PA, Val Hammond, so
a walking character defect in his own right.

But best of all you made us over time love and admire Sonya
herself, and pity her final disillusionment, which in some ways
mirrors our own. What guts, and what nerve. And the men

6. Richard Sorge, Agent Sonya's lover and recruiter in Shanghai; MI5's Jim Skardon,
who failed to expose her; and Roger Hollis, director-general of MI5, interrogated on
unproven accusations of being a Soviet agent.

wimps or misfits beside her, save for her one great love, Sorge, a manic genius, and ultimately like herself in there for the living theatre as much as for the ideology.

I have just (reluctantly) handed the book over to Jane, who has been struck down with an inoperable cancer, and is currently undergoing chemo with great bearing. She collapsed suddenly in Cornwall, where we had just decided to live permanently, but somehow we bundled her up to London for treatment. We can't wait to get back there, but for the time being we are lost in a labyrinth of medics. So suddenly life stops.

Jonny tells me that you are a happy man these days, and somehow the book conveys that: a really good, positive voice that draws you on and shares the odd laugh with you without getting on your nerves. I believe it's called style.

Bravo again, surely your best to date, and that's a high bar.

All best to you and yours,
David

~

TO NICHOLAS SHAKESPEARE

By email

Cornwall

1 October 2020

Dear Nicholas,
Well, all pretty good considering [. . .] we are in Cornwall for a start, Jane is receiving her chemo sessions here at home, and they are vastly more agreeable than the London variety, incidentally and improbably with the modern equipment that the London hospital lacked. We can sit together, I can take her cups of tea, and the chemo nurse is efficient and caring. So the

week's graph is less gruelling for us both. I also manage to write between times. My own cancer has entered a different stage and I begin a new therapy in a month, in London, but then returning immediately to Cornwall.

But I tell you: it's a rum time to be thinking of dying. It's the feeling of going down with a sinking ship, piloted by lunatics and disaster addicts. How did we ever get here in such short order? It would be great to talk. We are not gloomy. We count ourselves hugely lucky, and are very happy together, even on Jane's down days, which kick in like clockwork 48 hours after an infusion. Let me know how your novel is selling. The market is so flooded that books seem to come and go like mayflies.

Much love to you both, and thanks for thinking of us.
David

∾

Lyubimov had emailed to wish le Carré 'very happy returns of no corona days' and to sound him out on a book 'especially for English readers: my work in GB and against it'. He would be shocked by le Carré's news.

TO MIKHAIL LYUBIMOV

By email

Cornwall

18 October 2020

Subject: Life and the other thing

Dear Michael,

Good to hear from you. The short answer to your question is, yes, I think your book as described might work in blessed Britannia. Healthy irreverence about the Cold War is long overdue. If you can put together a first chapter, well translated by a native English speaker, and a synopsis, I can make sure it gets a fair reading by a top agent (mine). It's a tough market and we have to be professionals.

Our home news is not too bright. Jane has developed an inoperable cancer and is undergoing a severe course of chemotherapy. The wonder pills I have been taking for the same complaint have run their course, and the next stage is to nuke me with an experimental radioactive infusion every six weeks. But we prevail, the kids are being wonderful, I am entering my 90th year, Jane is 8 years behind, we have been married for half a century and never been closer. And I continue to write most days.

Our love to you and yours,
As ever,
David

~

At le Carré's birthday on 19 October, he had celebrated his newly affirmed Irish citizenship, wrapping himself in the tricolour.

TO ALISON GERAGHTY, HEAD OF FOREIGN BIRTHS REGISTRATION, IRELAND

Tregiffian
St Buryan
Penzance
Cornwall

26 October 2020

Dear Alison Geraghty,
Thank you so much for your letter and my certificate of citizenship. I would like to thank you and your team for this

great honour. You have given me back my long friendship with Europe and belatedly made me a child of Ireland. I was brought up to a large extent by my grandmother, who was born in Ireland and came to London as a lady's maid in the early 1900s. While I was waiting for my application to be processed, I visited the tiny house of her birth and the church where she worshipped. I felt a great emotional connection.

Thank you all so much. I am now waiting for my Irish passport. When it comes, I intend to fly from Newquay to Cork and seek out my ancestors.

Thank you again.

Yours sincerely,
David Cornwell (aka John le Carré)

~

TO YASSIN MUSHARBASH

Tregiffian
St Buryan
Penzance
Cornwall

23 November 2020

Dear Yassin,

I owe you a better letter than that – here's a try. In answer to your question, I never tired of writing until now. I am trying my damnedest to feel the rat gnawing, but nothing takes my mind off Jane, whose condition changes (worstens?) by the hour. With cancer, one gradually learns, there are no facts, no predictions, no diagnoses, no cures, that stand scrutiny. Oncologists tell you that at some point. Jane's, as good as any other, made the statement at their first encounter.

[. . .]

Everything is waiting. We have never been so close – yet far apart too, because death – looming or simply out there – is a very private matter, & each of us does it in their own way.

Of the joy of writing – yes, you are absolutely right about finishing. It's everything. If you can't see the final frame of your novel when you enter it, don't go there, is my experience. How many first chapters have I not been sent, with the question, 'can I write?' Answer, show me your last chapter, & maybe you can. Please thank the family for my chocolates, biscuits and goodies, please thank them <u>all</u> for their kind wishes, & the beautiful paper stars. I'll be happier next time.

Ever,
David

~

TO DAVID GREENWAY

Tregiffian
St Buryan
Penzance
Cornwall

25 November 2020

Dear David,

I don't know why I sh<u>d</u> have become an optimist in old age, but my personal view is that Trump will poison himself with his own sickening doctrine, and be revealed by the lawsuits awaiting him. We have followed y<u>r</u> election as if it were our own, and of course the parallels are hypnotic. We too have a ridiculous leader with no regard for the law, consequences or parliament.

The fact that he is an Etonian classics scholar is extraordinarily irrelevant. He's an Etonian oik,[7] part of the destroyer's movement, a Trumpist through & through. Brexit will ruin us, but it's his baby, so to hell with sanity.

The rejoicing here knows no end. Trump insulted us, & terrified us with his populism. He set the stage for the worst things happening in the world right now, from Eastern Europe to the Middle East.

Our home news isn't great. Jane has been very ill. The chemo <u>seems</u> to be working, but they're changing the cocktail, and the side effects are grim. She has constant pain, but bears all nobly.

The Nicks, all four, will join us for Christmas, Covid permitting. My poor sister Charlotte is dying (also of cancer). Mountain Face & family are slowly working their way back to normal – a rebuilt home, a very ill son restored to health, big Thanksgiving reunion of vast family, a new dog.[8] We live all the time in Cornwall now. The medical scene is not posh, but seems pretty adequate so far, & it's what Jane wants. Today is perfect: cold winter sun, deep blue sea. Wild ponies now inhabit the cliff, but aren't finding it easy.

Our love to you and yours – to JB particularly – and let's raise a glass on Jan 20th. Jesus, what an escape . . .

David

∿

In December 2020, le Carré was working on a book he provisionally called *The George Smiley Years*, which included a last meeting

---

7. In 1957 le Carré observed the use of the word 'oik' for the other classes at Eton.

8. Le Carré and Greenway nicknamed his son Stephen Cornwell 'Mountain Face' for his habit of predicting the mountain weather. Stephen's family's home in Ojai, California, was rebuilt after having burned to the ground in a California wildfire.

between Smiley and Karla. One night he took a fall, and a week later developed a fever. On 8 December, protesting that he had more to do, he reluctantly agreed to go to hospital.

The last email from le Carré's iPad, sent from hospital, was to his agent Jonny Geller. 'Simon will tell you the circumstances. In case we don't get to talk, thanks for all of it,' he wrote. 'You did a great job, and I learned to cherish your family and admire you greatly as a friend and agent.'

Coda

John le Carré, David Cornwell, died on 12 December 2020 in the Royal Cornwall Hospital, of pneumonia. The one book at his bedside, packed hastily for his hospital visit, was *The World of Jeeves* by P. G. Wodehouse. His wife Jane was in a separate ward in the Royal Cornwall, but under Covid rules the couple were not allowed to meet. In her hospital bag she had brought a blanket, some personal items, and a brown A4 envelope containing correspondence, shorthand notebooks and pens, and an undated message from David torn from a telephone pad. She died at home, of cancer, on 27 February 2021.

You are the
only woman
This is the
only place
(In the end,
we have to
know the one
thing.

Our year was
extraordinary, but
we didn't say
goodbye to it
properly: so
much effort,
at such cost,
such reward.

Chronology

1931   19 October – David John Moore Cornwell is born in Poole, Dorset, to Ronald Thomas Archibald Cornwell and Olive Moore Cornwell, née Glassey. His brother, Anthony, is two years old.

1934   Ronnie Cornwell is jailed for fraud and obtaining money and goods on false pretences.[1] Le Carré has a childhood memory of waving at him in Exeter Prison, but conceded it was probably imagined.

1936   His mother, Olive Cornwell, disappears from his life when le Carré is aged four or five;[2] he is sent to board at St Martin's Preparatory School, Northwood, Middlesex, aged five.

1936   Ronnie Cornwell is declared bankrupt with debts of £20,000.

1938   At the age of seven, after a stomach operation, 'a lady who later married my father' reads him *The Wind in the Willows* two or three times, and everything seems 'to fan out from there'. The lady was the recently married Jean (Jeannie) Gronow, née Neal. Ronnie Cornwell avoided all books except those by great lawyers.

1939   Goes on to board at St Andrew's School Pangbourne, Berkshire.

1944   December – Ronnie and Jeannie Cornwell are married.

1945   September – goes to board at Sherborne School, Dorset; Jeannie accompanies him on his first day.

1948   At Sherborne he wins the English Verse Prize with his poem 'The Dream of the Deserted Island', plays 2nd XI cricket for the school and plays the Soothsayer in a production of *Julius Caesar*. At age sixteen, over the objections of his housemaster, he leaves Sherborne to study

---

1. Adam Sisman's 2015 *Le Carré: The Biography*. Le Carré was impressed by Sisman's diligence in digging up details of Ronnie's chequered career.

2. Le Carré commonly said his mother disappeared when he was five; Tony Cornwell gives their ages on her departure as four and six.

German at Bern University. He is recruited there by the British intelligence services for the first time, to report on left-wing student groups and run minor errands as a 'mule'.

1949   Leaves Bern to visit post-war Germany, including Bergen-Belsen concentration camp.

1950   January – meets Alison Ann Sharp, his future wife, in St Moritz.

After basic training for his National Service he joins the Intelligence Corps at Maresfield Camp, Uckfield, Sussex.

December – ski racing with the Downhill Only Club in Wengen, Switzerland.

1951   Is posted as a military intelligence officer in Austria. Spends a summer weekend with Ann on leave.

1952   Ski racing at St Moritz and Klosters.

Sells *Cricketer* magazine around the UK for Ronnie with his Sherborne friend and future best man Robin Cooke. Ronnie Cornwell stands for election in Yarmouth as a Liberal; le Carré helps with campaign.

October – goes up to Lincoln College, Oxford. A former Sherborne history master and chaplain, the Reverend Vivian Green, is now a tutor and chaplain there.

1953   January – Ann leaves for several months in the US. Le Carré is recruited by MI5 to spy on left-wing groups at Oxford.

August – at Maresfield Camp, he plans to meet Ann on her return.

Christmas at Ronnie Cornwell's home Tunmers with Ann.

1954   February – meets his mother, Olive, in Suffolk, for the first time as an adult.[3]

May or June – formally engaged to Ann. Ann is indoctrinated by Dick Thistlewaite, le Carré's MI5 controller at Oxford, and signs the Official Secrets Act. David plans to join MI5 on leaving Oxford in 1955; he says later he was beginning work on his first novel.

---

3. Ann Martin personal memoir.

July – Ronnie is declared bankrupt with debts of £1,359,000. Le Carré's account in Oxford at the Westminster Bank is closed.

September – now lecturing at Maresfield Camp.

October – with Ronnie failing to pay his son's bills, le Carré leaves Oxford to teach German, Latin and, according to Ann, boxing at Millfield Preparatory School (Edgarley Hall).

On 27 November David and Ann are married by Vivian Green. They spend one night in a Clifton hotel. Ann gives up her job working on a religious magazine in London. After the wedding they move to Cumhill Farm, Pilton, then in early 1955 to a nearby cottage, with a privy in the garden. Le Carré produces a play, and paints. Their dog, Bobby, gets hit by a car and learns to walk on two legs.

1955   April – after a belated honeymoon in Paris, decides to return to Oxford. Meets James and Susie Kennaway. Continues to draw and paint, decorating a hall for an Oxford ball.

1956   After graduating with first-class honours, goes to Eton in September to teach French and German.

1958   After five terms at Eton, gives notice and joins MI5. He finds a house at Great Missenden, leaving at 7.30 a.m. every day for London and returning at 8 p.m. Ann gives up her job as a sub-editor on *Home* magazine to look after Simon, their first child. The Cornwells drink Cyprus sherry and Lyons Continental coffee.

Begins writing on his two-hour commute on the train. George Smiley and John le Carré are both born, he later says, on the first page of *Call for the Dead*, in a small back room on the third floor of Leconfield House in Curzon Street, where he and his colleagues recruited agents, male and female, to run operations against Communist subversion.[4]

1959   September – the family move to Prince of Wales Drive, Battersea, to a first-floor flat with four bedrooms. At MI5 le Carré has met John Bingham, one inspiration for Smiley; Vivian Green is another.

Le Carré and Ann go to Nottingham for a weekend for him to meet one of his trade-union agents.

---

4. 'An Evening with George Smiley', Royal Festival Hall, 7 September 2017.

1960   After the birth of their second son, Stephen, le Carré returns from work and tells Ann he's changing jobs to MI6. Paints the nursery with fairy-tale scenes. The family take a Nigerian lodger.

Call for the Dead is accepted for publication by Victor Gollancz for an advance of £100; le Carré gets the news as a fresh recruit for MI6, with his friend and fellow trainee John Margetson. In June he is officially appointed to the Foreign Office: diplomatic cover for his intelligence work.

1961   June – *Call for the Dead* is published.

July – le Carré and his family settle in Bonn, where he is officially serving as second secretary, with their first home in the borough of Bad Godesberg – later used as the setting for a bomb attack in *The Little Drummer Girl*.

1961/2   Visits the Berlin Wall and later, with Ann, goes to Dachau. The family drive a Hillman Husky. An East German couple arrive at the house whom Ann assumes to be spies; le Carré hates the attitude of some diplomats towards the 'friends', or spies. Ann goes to Yehudi Menuhin's first concert in Bonn since the war. Le Carré works on *The Spy Who Came in from the Cold* in the bedroom. His father, Ronnie, memorably appears at their home on the banks of the Rhine in an amphibious motorcar.

1962   Dick Franks, future head of the Secret Intelligence Service, becomes le Carré's head of station. Alfred Hitchcock inquires about making a television film of *Call for the Dead*.[5]

May – lectures a crowd of seven hundred in Oberhausen on British foreign policy.

July – *A Murder of Quality*, in which Smiley investigates a murder at a class-ridden English public school, written in a style close to a conventional detective novel, is published. (The following year a Hollywood film reader assessing le Carré's books wonders if the novel was actually written before *Call for the Dead*.)

---

5. Letter to Jeannie Cornwell, 16 May 1962.

October – in the Cuban missile crisis, the Cornwells know Bonn will be on the front line of any Russian attack. Their third son, Timothy, is born a week after tensions ease.

In the winter the Rhine freezes over. Joins the annual Königswinter Conference between German and English officials.

1963   February – escorts Fritz Erler, deputy leader of the SPD, to London; he continues his Foreign Office work through a year in which his life is transformed.

March – Victor Gollancz writes declining to increase le Carré's royalties on *The Spy Who Came in from the Cold*, but offers £175 instead of £150 on publication; the *Express* later reports his final earnings on the book at about £500,000. Le Carré leaves Gollancz for his next novel, and frames the letter on his wall.

The Spy earns strong reviews and sales in England and is hailed for its flavour of authenticity around a complex operation targeted at the hated East German intelligence chief, Mundt. Le Carré insists he took no part in any undercover work in the East, but drew the story purely from his imagination and old hands 'who'd done little bits of it'. Paramount Pictures buy the film rights. The Foreign Office posts le Carré to Hamburg for six months.

1964   The *Sunday Times* names John le Carré as David Cornwell. US publication, by Coward McCann Inc., turns the novel into a No. 1 global bestseller. *Time* and *Life* magazines send photographers to Hamburg. Le Carré resigns from the Foreign Office.

Le Carré and family rent the top floor of a stone villa in Agios Nikolaos, Crete. Travels to London, New York and Paris.

September – the family leave for the Greek island of Spetses.

David Bailey and Polly Devlin interview Ann for an article on spy-writers' wives. Works on *The Looking-Glass War*.

November – the Cornwells move to Vienna.

1965   January – meets Richard Burton and Elizabeth Taylor on the set of *The Spy Who Came in from the Cold* in Dublin; he tells Ann he's been having an affair with Susie Kennaway, married to James Kennaway, the Scottish novelist.

March – the family return to England, ending up in a new home in Somerset.

June – *The Looking-Glass War*, a bleak story of a futile spy mission to East Germany and of failing marriages, is published; le Carré calls it 'a novel I had written in pain on the island of Crete'.[6]

September – in Chicago, hears that Ronnie is in prison in Jakarta.

December – the film of *The Spy Who Came in from the Cold* is released.

1967   *The Deadly Affair*, a film of *Call for the Dead*, starring James Mason and Simone Signoret, is released. It is nominated for five BAFTA awards but wins none.

1968   October – *A Small Town in Germany*, in which the staff of the British Embassy in Bonn witness the return of the nationalist right in Germany, is published. The film rights are sold, with le Carré to script; in February 1969 the book is No. 1 on the US bestseller list; the *New York Times* calls it 'an exciting, compulsively readable and brilliantly plotted novel'.

1969   March – London Weekend Television transmit their biographical documentary *The Spymaker Comes in from the Cold: An Interview with John le Carré*.

June – has finished a television play and is working hard on *The Naive and Sentimental Lover*, inspired by his relationship with the Kennaways, then and now his only novel that fully abandons the framework of a thriller. The deeply strained relationship between the novel's Aldo Cassidy and his wife, Sandra, evokes parallels with le Carré's own marriage.

Around this time his father, Ronnie, threatens to sue him, le Carré will say, over the portrayal of Cassidy's ne'er-do-well father, and for being given insufficient credit in the LWT interview. Le Carré has started building a chalet in Wengen, where he ski raced as a young man.

On 13 October buys Tregiffian Cottages in West Penwith, the westernmost toe of England. Over the next twenty-five years, turns the three clifftop cottages into his Cornish retreat, adding a writing studio and library, and creating an artist's garden of enclosed lawns and formal

---

6. 'Book into film into what', unpublished additional material for *The Pigeon Tunnel*.

gardens, using more than 160 tons of granite in bouldered stone walls. In 2000, after a planning dispute to prevent nearby building, with the farmer from whom he bought the land, he donates the half-mile of cliff land below the house to the National Trust to save it from 'human predators'.

1971   Le Carré and Ann divorce. *The Naive and Sentimental Lover* is published; it gets 'a rough time critically', in his own words.[7]

It is the first le Carré book Alfred Knopf publishes in the US. Le Carré's then girlfriend Valerie Jane Eustace (Jane) has introduced him to Bob Gottlieb, who will edit him at Knopf and publish milestone novels, including *Tinker Tailor Soldier Spy* and *A Perfect Spy*.

1972   February and March – travels to Kenya, Singapore and Hong Kong; he returns to Africa later in the year with his children and goes on safari. On 2 May le Carré and Jane are married, and their son, Nicholas, is born later that year. Ann marries the diplomat Roger Martin on 24 August, her fortieth birthday.

1974   *Tinker Tailor Soldier Spy* is published. The story of Smiley's hunt for a Soviet mole inside the Circus marked le Carré's recovery after three uncertain books, with poor reviews for *The Naive and Sentimental Lover* in particular. It is considered one of his masterpieces, a watershed for le Carré's life and work, alongside *The Spy Who Came in from the Cold* and later *A Perfect Spy*.

Preparing work for *The Honourable Schoolboy*, goes on a six-week tour of Asia. Travels to Berlin with his sons Simon and Stephen to see the Wall.

1975   On 29 June Ronnie Cornwell, le Carré's father, dies, aged sixty-nine. Le Carré returns to South-East Asia, where in Hong Kong he has met one of his father's jailers. In Thailand, Laos and Cambodia his chief guide is the journalist David Greenway. Liar dice, played at the Hong Kong Foreign Correspondents' Club, becomes a family game at le Carré's Swiss chalet.

1977   *The Honourable Schoolboy*, with the character of Jerry Westerby spearheading George Smiley's attempt to suborn Karla's operations in the Far

---

7. Letter to J. Welch, 20 November 1979.

East, is published. The novel is featured on the cover of *Time*. 'Le Carré's new novel is about twice as long as it should be,' declares Clive James, in the *New York Review of Books*. *The Honourable Schoolboy*, with *The Naive and Sentimental Lover*, sometimes appears an 'odd man out' in the le Carré canon; but in Westerby's journeys through the metropolitan hinterlands of Hong Kong and the steamy jungle of the Golden Triangle, the second book in the Karla Trilogy shows le Carré at the height of his powers.

Visits Jerusalem and goes 'swanning about the Middle East' but in the event delays his planned Middle East novel.

April – Francis Ford Coppola suggests filming *The Naive and Sentimental Lover*, but nothing comes of the project.

1979   The BBC television series of *Tinker Tailor Soldier Spy* is released, starring Alec Guinness. *Smiley's People*, the final book in the Karla Trilogy, is published. 'Smiley will stand for a long time as the common man's Sherlock Holmes of the spy business,' le Carré tells his agent George Greenfield[8] – but puts Smiley to bed, for now.

1981   Tells friends that he has turned down a CBE.[9] He has been havering between writing his 'daddy book', drawing on his relationship with his father, or tapping into a novel on Middle Eastern terror.

1983   In the event *The Little Drummer Girl*, in which an Israeli anti-terror team recruit an English actress to hunt down a Palestinian bombmaker, is published first. Le Carré's research includes a meeting with the Palestinian Liberation Organisation leader Yasser Arafat as well as Israeli military figures such as General Shlomo Gazit, former head of the Military Intelligence Directorate. A film starring a miscast Diane Keaton follows in 1984.

1986   Publishes *A Perfect Spy*, an autobiographical novel exploring a father–son relationship in which the central character, Rick, is emphatically modelled on le Carré's father, Ronnie, and in which his son, Magnus, works for MI6. The *New York Times* calls it 'a first-rate espionage novel, perhaps the best of his already impressive oeuvre'. Philip Roth describes

---

8. Letter to George Greenfield, 29 October 1979.

9. Letter to Sir Dick Franks, 4 August 1981.

it as the best English novel since the war. Stephen Schiff, writing later in *Vanity Fair*, calls it 'one of the most penetrating depictions in all literature of the links between love and betrayal'.

1987   Beginning research for *The Russia House*, set in post-Cold War Russia, visits Russia for the first time, but declines the chance to meet Kim Philby. He will spend time on the East Coast of the US, fixing the American characters in the book.

1988   Accepts the Malaparte Prize, the Italian literary award. Graham Greene had refused it.[10]

1989   Olive Hill, le Carré's mother, dies, aged eighty-three. He is with her on the night she dies. *The Russia House* is published; in October work begins on the screen version, starring Sean Connery and Michelle Pfeiffer, with filming in Leningrad. The name of the Russian scientist, who wants to publish secrets of the Soviet arsenal, is changed from Goethe in the book to Dante in the film.

1990   George Smiley returns in *The Secret Pilgrim*, a group of stories linked to Smiley's speech to a graduating class of trainee intelligence officers.

December – the film of *The Russia House* is released.

1991   March – visits Egypt, researching *The Night Manager*. 'An empty Luxor, an empty Aswan, empty museums in Cairo, a magical tour, somewhat fraught by the general fear of flying, empty or unoccupied cars and so on. But wonderful,' he tells Vivian Green. Visits the charismatic Dutch arms dealer and collector Henk Visser, condemned to death for his role in the Dutch Resistance in the Second World War, as part of his research into the arms business.

The film of *A Murder of Quality*, starring Denholm Elliott as Smiley, and a teenaged Christian Bale, is broadcast on television in the UK and US. Elliott was recruited to the role after Anthony Hopkins pulled out at the last moment; le Carré visits Sherborne School for the first time in twenty years when the film is shot there.

---

10. Shirley Hazzard's 2000 *Greene on Capri*.

1992   October – the first draft of *The Night Manager* is completed. The novel, in which a former hotel night manager is recruited to bring down an arms dealer, is published in 1993.

1993   September – visits Russia again, with his son Nick, the future novelist Nick Harkaway, researching *Our Game*; preparations for a film of *The Night Manager*, never completed, get under way.

A planned 1994 trip to the Central Caucasus Mountains, where closing chapters of *Our Game* are set, is called off.

1995   Eighteen months after he began researching the North Caucasus as the setting for his novel, *Our Game* is published, with war having already broken out in Chechnya. 'Once again le Carré has predicted the news,' Knopf chief Sonny Mehta tells booksellers. 'I remember a group of us sitting around an atlas while le Carré showed us where Chechnya and Ingushetia and Ossetia were. Sadly those names are now in our headlines.' Begins research in Panama for his next novel.

1996   September – Hollywood studio boss John Calley, a good friend of le Carré, begins to explore a film of *The Tailor of Panama*; the book, in which a half-Jewish English tailor is drawn into a conspiratorial plot by a wayward British intelligence agent ahead of the handover of the Panama Canal to Panama, is published the following year.

November – goes to the Scilly Isles, off the coast of Cornwall, with Frank Gibson, to write about the family's multi-generational archive of shipwreck photographs.

1997   Travels to Turkey twice, researching key scenes for his novel *Single & Single*, and to Georgia twice in the following year.

1998   After twenty-seven years, leaves his US publisher Alfred A. Knopf for Scribner's.

1999   January – goes to Panama, location scouting with *The Tailor of Panama* director Tony Scott. Scott is subsequently replaced as director by John Boorman.

April – while le Carré is researching his next novel in Kenya, his friend the aid worker Yvette Pierpaoli is killed in a car crash in Albania. He met her in about 1974, researching *The Honourable Schoolboy* in Asia.

Single & Single, another exploration of a son wrestling with a deeply corrupt father, is published.

November – embarks on a UK theatres tour to promote the book.

2000   May – goes to Canada to research 'big pharma' for *The Constant Gardener*; meets the Canadian researcher and campaigner Nancy Olivieri. The book is serialised in *The Times* and sells over one hundred thousand copies in the UK on publication in December.[11] The *Guardian* journalist Hugo Young writes to tell le Carré it is 'one of the very best of your recent books'.[12] Michiko Kakutani pans 'this disappointing novel' with its 'paper-doll victim' in the *New York Times*.

2001   February – the film of *The Tailor of Panama* debuts at the Berlin Film Festival, with le Carré and Jane present. It is widely released in the spring.

May – le Carré and Jane take an early holiday in Bavaria, searching for altars by Tilman Riemenschneider, the sixteenth-century German sculptor.

October – celebrates his seventieth birthday in Siena.

2003   January – le Carré's essay fiercely criticising the build-up to the invasion of Iraq, 'The United States of America Has Gone Mad', is printed in *The Times* and syndicated worldwide. In the meantime he is struggling to finish his new novel.

December – *Absolute Friends*, reviewed as 'an angry disquisition on contemporary geopolitics'[13] in which le Carré's leading character loathes Tony Blair for taking Britain into the Iraq War, is published; le Carré reads it for the BBC's *Book at Bedtime*.

2005   May – the film of *The Constant Gardener*, starring Ralph Fiennes and Rachel Weisz, has its Leicester Square premiere.

November – le Carré accepts the Commandeur de l'Ordre des Arts et des Lettres at the French ambassador's residence in London.

---

11. Le Carré to John Calley, 6 January 2001.

12. Hugo Young to le Carré, 29 December 2000.

13. The *Guardian* review 'Spies and Lies', Steven Poole, 20 December 2003.

2006   Makes a late research trip to experience the Congo, ahead of the publication of *The Mission Song* in September.

2008   September – *A Most Wanted Man*, set among the Muslim community in Hamburg, where le Carré was once posted, is published.

2009   Le Carré's son Nicholas, writing as Nick Harkaway, publishes his first novel, *The Gone-Away World*.

After thirty-eight years and sixteen novels with Hodder & Stoughton as his UK publisher, le Carré moves to Penguin, saying the chance to work with the 'classic paperback house' was 'unmissable'.[14]

2010   Le Carré's sons Simon and Stephen found their film company, the Ink Factory.

His friend John Margetson writes of regret that le Carré has turned down a knighthood.[15] Adam Sisman begins his first interviews for le Carré's biography. Shortly after the publication of *Our Kind of Traitor*, filming begins on *Tinker Tailor Soldier Spy*, directed by Tomas Alfredson. Jon Snow of Channel 4 comes to Cornwall for 'last interview' with le Carré.

2011   August – accepts Germany's Goethe Medal for his contribution to 'the development of coalescence, peace and creativity in Europe'.[16] 'I am not into medals otherwise,' he says, 'but this one makes a nice pair with the Légion d'Honneur, and that is my lot.'[17]

September – the film of *Tinker Tailor Soldier Spy*, starring Gary Oldman as Smiley, is released. It wins the Alexander Korda Award for Best British Film at the BAFTAs.

Celebrates his eightieth birthday in Cornwall.

2012   June – receives his Honorary Doctorate of Letters from Oxford University alongside Aung San Suu Kyi. Turning to le Carré in her speech, she says: 'When I was under house arrest I was also helped by

---

14. *Evening Standard* press account.

15. Correspondence with John Margetson (see p. 518).

16. *Guardian*, 21 June 2011.

17. Email to Bernhard Docke, 6 September 2011.

the books of John le Carré – they were a journey into the wider world.'[18] Le Carré, who has repeatedly turned down national honours, tells Tom Bower in an email that 'Oxford was a great joy to me – probably the only one I ever wanted, which I didn't know till they offered it.'

2013   April – *A Delicate Truth* is published. Critics greet the novel as a 'remarkable return to mid-season form'[19] by the eighty-one-year-old le Carré. It explores the outsourcing of defence and intelligence operations to private contractors.

2014   *A Most Wanted Man*, starring Philip Seymour Hoffman and co-produced by Simon and Stephen Cornwell, is released.

2016   February – *The Night Manager* television series, starring Hugh Laurie, Tom Hiddleston and Olivia Colman, also produced by le Carré's sons Simon and Stephen through the Ink Factory, is broadcast. It wins three Golden Globe awards.

        May – the film of *Our Kind of Traitor*, also an Ink Factory production, starring Ewan McGregor and Stellan Skarsgård, is released, to mixed reviews.

        September – *The Pigeon Tunnel*, le Carré's memoir, a mix of old and new writings, is published, partly in response to Adam Sisman's biography, published the previous year. *The Pigeon Tunnel* is a *Sunday Times* No. 1 bestseller in the UK.

2017   September – *A Legacy of Spies*, le Carré's return to Smiley, Guillam and the back story to *The Spy Who Came in from the Cold*, is published. Le Carré, aged almost eighty-six, hosts a nearly two-hour sold-out launch event at the Southbank Centre, 'An Evening with George Smiley'. The book is a No. 1 *New York Times* bestseller, half a century after *The Spy Who Came in from the Cold* became his first to top that list.

2019   October – *Agent Running in the Field*, called le Carré's Brexit novel, is published.

---

18. *Oxford Mail*, 21 June 2012.

19. Robert McCrum, *Observer*, 20 April 2013.

2020   January – receives the $100,000 Olof Palme Prize in Stockholm for his 'engaging and humanistic opinion-making in literary form'. He donates the prize to Médecins sans Frontières.

October – receives his Irish citizenship through his 'pure Irish' grand-mother, Bessie, Ronnie Cornwell's mother.

12 December – dies at the Royal Cornwall Hospital, of pneumonia after a fall.

2021   27 February – Jane Cornwell dies at home in Cornwall.

October – *Silverview* is published.

Acknowledgements

This book ought by rights to have a co-editor, and that person would be Vicki Phillips, for seventeen years secretary to David and Jane Cornwell. She helped to organise the archive at Tregiffian, and commanded all roads leading into it. She was the Connie Sachs of this operation, though maintaining, quite unlike Connie, a magnificent calm, and a meticulous order in the filing system. Her work was invaluable.

My half-brother, Nick Cornwell, the author Nick Harkaway, has in the complicated matter of my parents always brought a dose of clear-sighted brilliance washed down with common sense and love. He was generous with his input at all stages of this book, particularly with the introduction. My brother Simon Cornwell, as my father's literary executor, was a guide at every stage.

Roland Philipps, my father's friend and former editor at Hodder & Stoughton, extended that friendship to share his own letters, seek out more from the Hodder archives, and offer swift and skilful early reads of the selection.

There were particular collections of letters that propelled the story of my father's life forward. Nancy Cranham offered the illuminating correspondence with her mother, Charlotte Cornwell, and grandmother Jean Cornwell. Lady Miranda Margetson was patience itself in allowing me to access the letters to my godfather, Sir John Margetson. Nettie and Trevor Cornwell sent copies of the letters to my father's brother, Tony, and filled in their background.

Sir Tom Stoppard kindly furnished several letters in a remarkable and warm correspondence, while William Shawcross battled gamely and somewhat fruitlessly through a flooded storage space. Nicholas Shakespeare and Gillian Johnson hosted us in Wiltshire, and provided a heartfelt guide to my father's letters to him.

Respect is due to the remarkable Susan D. Anderson, who

determined that the fascinating letters to her should be published with her name attached. Susan: thank you.

The German journalist Yassin Musharbash offered, alongside his own correspondence from my father, his translation skills, and kindly advised on the German context and use of language in his work. Alex Williams shared my father's faxes to their mother, Olive, with the help of her grandson Max Perrin. Anne Alvarez opened access to my father's correspondence with her and her husband Al Alvarez. Richard Greene, biographer of Graham Greene and editor of his letters, pointed me to the Greene correspondence held in the Burns Library at Boston College.

The coronavirus pandemic and its restrictions on travel and the use of public spaces meant that more of the early searching for letters, in addition to those archived at Tregiffian, was done remotely from my desk. It relied on the generosity of librarians and archivists to provide copies at a time when their institutions were under particular pressure.

They were, particularly, Elizabeth L. Garver, French and Italian Collections Research Associate of the Harry Ransom Center, University of Texas at Austin, for facilitating access to letters including the correspondence with Victor Gollancz. Rachel Hassall, Archivist, Sherborne School, shed an extraordinarily well-informed light on my father's schooldays and the complex attitudes to them that stayed with him for decades; Lindsay McCormack, Archivist, Lincoln College, opened a window on his Oxford career.

Dr Colin McIlroy, Curator (Modern Literary Manuscripts) at the National Library of Scotland, kindly assisted with research on the Kennaway material. Thanks also to Andrew Riley, Senior Archivist, of the Churchill Archives Centre at Churchill College, Cambridge; Catherine Flynn, Senior Archivist, Penguin Random House Archive and Library; Annie Price, Archivist, Special Collections, University of Exeter; and Rachel Foss, Curator of Modern Literary Manuscripts, British Library. Bodley's Librarian, Richard Ovenden, wrote movingly about my father and Jane's partnership after their deaths; my thanks to him as well as to Oliver House and Rachael Marsay of the Bodleian Libraries; Hannah Smith, Assistant Librarian, of the

Eton College Library; Alexandra Mitchell, Archivist at the Library of the University of Salford, Manchester; and Genevieve Maxwell, Senior Reference Librarian, the Academy of Motion Picture Arts and Sciences. John Wells, Senior Archivist, Department of Archives and Modern Manuscripts at the Cambridge University Library, helped me to the Hugh Thomas materials; I thank the Syndics of Cambridge University Library for allowing their use. Emma Davidson, Librarian, the Henry W. and Albert A. Berg Collection of English and American Literature, at the New York Public Library, sought out correspondence with Herbert Mitgang.

For helping to provide letters or agreeing to their use – including those that sadly did not make the final selection – I am grateful to: Eric Abraham; Anthony Barnett and Judith Herrin; Buzz and Janet Berger; Susanne Bier; Kai Bird; Tom Bower; Caroline Brown; Margaret Bullard; William Burroughs; Sir Bryan Cartledge; Adrian Churchward; Sherman Gilbert Cochran; Robin Cooke; John and Margaret Cooper; Nettie Cornwell; Susan Cornwell; Trevor Cornwell; Rex Cowan; Steve Crawshaw; Justin Dell; Jeremy Deller; Charlotte Dennett; Bernhard Docke; Owen Dudley Edwards; Ehud Elizur; Ralph Fiennes; Robert Forrest; Stephen Fry; Jonny Geller; John Goldsmith; Robert Gottlieb; Richard Greene; Michael Hall; Dr August Hanning; Luke Harding; Graham Hayman; Henry Hemming; Prof. George Hewitt; Bruce Hunter; John and Mary James; Michael Jayston; Sam Joiner; Lieve Joris; Alan Judd; Matthew Keegan; Julie Kentish-Barnes; Jane S. Kerr; Mayuree Laolugsanalerd, Guest Relations Director, Mandarin Oriental Hotel, Bangkok; Hugh Laurie; Michael Lyubimov; Ian McEwan; Annabel Markova; Glenda Moakes; Nancy Olivieri; Tony Palmer; Neil Pepper MBE; Emmanuele Phuon; Martin Pick; Vladimir Pucholt; Anna Rankin; John Roberts; Barbara Rosenbaum; Julian Ryder-Richardson; Stefan Schaller; Andreas Seiter; Petronilla Silver; Robyn Slovo; Andrew Stilwell; Harry Tangye; Inigo Thomas; James Van Sant; Federico Varese; Lord William Waldegrave; Emma Warren; John Westerby; Rob and James Whyte; David Wilkinson; Michela Wrong; Anita Osnat Yoshpe.

Pam Wells and the *Sandakan* author Paul Ham filled out my

knowledge of Rod Wells, my father's fellow trainee at MI6, a legendary figure. Simon Bingham supplied the drawing of his father, John Bingham, by mine, though sadly no letters have emerged. Others who helped with my queries included Len Deighton, John J. Geoghegan, Michael Attenborough, Tim Bryars, William Scoular, Sebastian Ritscher of Mohrbooks, Philippa Heumann, and Heather J. Sharkey of the University of Pennsylvania. I'm grateful to Alice Pitman, who supplied the article about my father written by her father, the journalist Robert Pitman.

At my father's home at Tregiffian in Cornwall, Wendy Le Grice first began work on his archive. Brenda Bolitho, Gordon Ewing and Carl Swadling were instrumental in the care of my parents and their home.

This book is dedicated to my father's great-grandson Noah David Cornwell Hughes. David and J. B. Greenway, my father's close friends, are his other great-grandparents, and were generous with their letters and their time. Noah has had a tumultuous start in life, a drama shared by his extraordinary parents, Annie and Paul, his aunt Eliza and his grandmother the writer Alice Greenway.

It has been a privilege to work with Viking publisher Mary Mount, and with my father's agent and friend Jonny Geller. Donna Poppy's accomplished copyediting caught or clarified several critical errors; any that remain are mine.

This book has been a journey completed with a leg in plaster. I could not have started, and certainly not have reached the finish line, without the endlessly patient encouragement of my partner Anna Arthur. To her I owe my love, thanks, and my tenuous sanity.

Manuscript Sources

Entries are listed in the order in which they appear in the collection.
Items within each entry are as follows: recipient, date, format and source.

All handwritten letters to Ann Sharp, le Carré archive in Cornwall
All handwritten letters to Vivian Green, le Carré archive
All letters to Jean Cornwell, Nancy Cranham
All letters to Sir John and Lady Margetson, Miranda Margetson

R. S. Thompson, 24 June 1945: handwritten letter, Sherborne School Library
R. S. Thompson, undated, but summer 1948: handwritten letter, Sherborne School Library
R. S. Thompson, 5 May 1952: handwritten letter, Sherborne School Library
Kaspar von Almen, 3 October 1954: handwritten letter, copy provided by Adam Sisman
Kaspar von Almen, undated, likely early 1955: handwritten letter, copy provided by Adam Sisman
Robin Cooke, 7 October 1955: handwritten letter, Robin Cooke
Kaspar von Almen, undated, likely June 1956: handwritten letter, copy provided by Adam Sisman
Hilary Rubinstein, 21 January 1961: handwritten letter, Victor Gollancz acquisitions, 13-12-017-P, Correspondence 1960–1983, Harry Ransom Center, University of Texas at Austin
Ronnie and Jean Cornwell, 8 August 1961: handwritten letter, Nancy Cranham
Dick Edmonds, 8 August 1961: handwritten letter, Anna Rankin
Hilary Rubinstein, 28 April 1962: handwritten letter, Victor Gollancz acquisitions, 13-12-017-P, Correspondence 1960–1983, Harry Ransom Center, University of Texas at Austin
Dick and Rachel Franks, undated, likely spring 1964: handwritten letter, Franks family

James Kennaway, undated, likely 1964: handwritten letter, National Library of Scotland

Victor Gollancz, 30 May 1964: handwritten letter, Victor Gollancz acquisitions, 13-12-017-P, Correspondence 1960–1983, Harry Ransom Center, University of Texas at Austin

Graham Greene, 4 August 1964: handwritten letter, Graham Greene Papers, MS.1995.003, Le Carré, John, 1964 August–1982 September, John J. Burns Library, Boston College

James Kennaway, undated, likely 1964: handwritten letter, National Library of Scotland

Susan Kennaway, undated: handwritten letter, National Library of Scotland

Susan Kennaway, undated, likely mid 1965: handwritten letter, National Library of Scotland

Stephen Cornwell, 12 October 1965: handwritten letter, le Carré archive

Literaturnaya Gazeta, May 1966: *Encounter* magazine

Graham Greene, undated: handwritten letter, Graham Greene Papers, MS.1995.003, Le Carré, John, 1964 August–1982 September, John J. Burns Library, Boston College

C. P. Snow, 21 July 1968: handwritten letter, C. P. Snow, Box 83.4 John le Carré Letters, Harry Ransom Center, University of Texas at Austin

Charles Pick, 2 November 1968: handwritten letter, le Carré archive

Vladimir Pucholt, 19 November 1969: handwritten letter, Vladimir Pucholt

Charlotte Cornwell, 10 January 1970: handwritten letter, Nancy Cranham

Charles Pick, 7 November 1970: handwritten letter, le Carré archive

Buzz and Janet Berger, 8 January 1972: handwritten letter, Buzz and Janet Berger

Graham Greene, 7 November 1974: handwritten letter, Graham Greene Papers, MS.1995.003, Le Carré, John, 1964 August–1982 September, John J. Burns Library, Boston College

Graham Greene, 12 November 1974: handwritten letter, Graham Greene Papers, MS.1995.003, Le Carré, John, 1964 August–1982 September, John J. Burns Library, Boston College

Jane Cornwell and 'A', undated, likely 1975: handwritten letter, le Carré archive

Timothy Cornwell, 26 September 1975: unsigned typed letter, le Carré archive

H. Hale Crosse, 2 October 1975: unsigned copy of typed letter, le Carré archive

Mrs Pirkko-Liisa Ståhl, undated, likely August 1977: unsigned copy of typed letter, le Carré archive

Peter Rainsford, 28 August 1977: handwritten letter, Andrew Stilwell

Gerald Isaaman, 7 February 1978: unsigned copy of typed letter, le Carré archive

Sir Alec Guinness, 27 February 1978: unsigned copy of typed letter, le Carré archive

Sir Alec Guinness, 3 March 1978: handwritten letter, British Library Add. MS 89015/2/7/5

Arthur Hopcraft, 18 August 1978: handwritten letter, AHP/1/18 Arthur Hopcraft Papers, University of Salford Archives and Special Collections

Sir Alec Guinness, 27 June 1979: handwritten letter, British Library Add. MS 89015/2/7/5

Observer, 6 October 1979: unsigned copy of typed letter, le Carré archive

Sir Dick and Rachel Franks, undated, likely early October 1979: handwritten letter, Franks family

Mary-Kay Wilmers, 27 November 1979: copy of signed typed letter, le Carré archive

Buzz Berger, 29 November 1979: copy of signed typed letter, Buzz and Janet Berger

Anthony Sampson, undated but likely late 1979: handwritten letter, Bodleian Libraries, Oxford, MS. Sampson dep 20.

Sir Dick and Rachel Franks, 15 December 1979: handwritten letter, Franks family

Betty Quail, 18 March 1980: copy of signed typed letter, le Carré archive

Morton Leavy, 14 July 1980: copy of signed typed letter, le Carré archive

Sir Dick Franks, 4 August 1981: handwritten letter, Franks family

Hugh Thomas, 25 January 1982: handwritten postcard, CUL MS Add. 10195, Cambridge University Library

Sir Alec Guinness, 27 January 1982: handwritten letter, British Library Add. MS 89015/2/7/5

John Cheever, 7 April 1982: copy of unsigned handwritten letter, le Carré archive

Yuval Elizur, 3 May 1982: handwritten letter, Ehud Elizur

Graham Greene, 6 September 1982: handwritten letter, Graham Greene Papers, MS.1995.003, Le Carré, John, 1964 August–1982 September, John J. Burns Library, Boston College

Max Reinhardt, 26 September 1982: handwritten postcard, Graham Greene Papers, MS.1995.003, Le Carré, John, 1964 August–1982 September, John J. Burns Library, Boston College

Sir Dick Franks, 24 January 1983: handwritten letter, Franks family

Margaret Thatcher, 2 March 1983: handwritten letter, Churchill Archives Centre, Thatcher Papers, THCR 1/3/10: courtesy of the Margaret Thatcher Archive Trust

Hazen and Jean Stevens and Jo Anne Stevens, 29 April 1983: handwritten letter, Scott Stevens

Al Alvarez, 3 May 1986: handwritten letter, British Library Add. MS 88602

Ella Haymes, 3 May 1986: unsigned copy of typed letter, le Carré archive

Philip Roth, 8 December 1986: handwritten letter, Philip Roth, Mss22491, Le Carré, John, 1984–1992, undated, Library of Congress

Jane Cornwell, 13 March 1987: handwritten letter, le Carré archive

John Roberts, 12 May 1987: handwritten letter, John Roberts

Vladimir Stabnikov, 12 June 1987: handwritten letter, Irina Sedakova

Nicholas Greaves, 31 January 1988: copy of handwritten letter, le Carré archive

David and J.B. Greenway, 11 August 1988: handwritten letter, David and J.B. Greenway

Olive Hill, 11 July 1988: handwritten fax, Alex Williams

Olive Hill, 4 August 1988: handwritten fax, Alex Williams

Olive Hill, 8 September 1988: handwritten fax, Alex Williams

Bruce Hunter, 27 January 1989: handwritten fax, le Carré archive

Olive Hill, 24 March 1989, handwritten fax, Alex Williams

Vladimir Stabnikov, 9 March 1989: copy of handwritten letter, le Carré archive

W. J. Weatherby, *Manchester Guardian*, 11 October 1989: unsigned copy of typed letter, le Carré archive

Sir Alec and Lady Guinness, 7 December 1989: handwritten letter, British Library Add. MS 89015/2/7/5

Bob Gottlieb, 25 September 1989: handwritten letter, le Carré archive

Sir Alec Guinness, 7 June 1990: handwritten letter, British Library Add. MS 89015/2/7/5

Nicholas Shakespeare, 19 April 1991: handwritten letter, Nicholas Shakespeare

John Calley, undated: handwritten fax, original in le Carré archive

Sydney Pollack, 16 December 1991: handwritten fax, original in le Carré archive

Michael Attenborough, 24 January 1992: typed fax with handwritten P.S., original in le Carré archive

Peter Osnos, 26 January 1992: fax, le Carré archive

Derek Tangye, 23 February 1992: copy of handwritten fax, le Carré archive

Tony Cornwell, 24 April 1992: handwritten letter, Nettie and Trevor Cornwell

Don Chapman, 20 August 1992: unsigned copy of typed letter, le Carré archive

Philip Roth, 11 October 1992: handwritten fax, original in le Carré archive

Tina Brown, Editor, *New Yorker*, 12 October 1992: signed typed letter, original in le Carré archive

Michael Attenborough, 3 November 1992: handwritten fax, original in le Carré archive

Philip Weiss, 23 January 1993: signed typed fax, original in le Carré archive

Eric Abraham, 3 March 1993: handwritten fax, original in le Carré archive

Sydney Pollack, 28 July 1993: signed typed fax, original in le Carré archive

Stephen Fry, 13 September 1993: unsigned copy of typed letter, le Carré archive

J. E. C. Kuitenbrouwer, 21 October 1993: unsigned copy of typed letter, le Carré archive

Gerald Isaaman, undated, likely mid 1990s: handwritten fax, original in le Carré archive

Nicholas Elliott, 9 November 1993: unsigned copy of typed letter, le Carré archive

Mikhail Lyubimov, 15 November 1993: unsigned copy of typed letter, le Carré archive

Alice Mary Dilke, 4 March 1995: handwritten letter, Sasha Markova

Editor, *New York Times*, 22 March 1995: signed typed fax, original in le Carré archive

658

Jack Burkhardt, 19 November 1993: unsigned copy of typed letter, le Carré
archive

Nicholas Cornwell, 26 November 1993: handwritten letter, Nicholas
Cornwell

Jeff Danziger, 4 March 1994: copy of signed typed letter, le Carré archive

Eric Abraham, 29 March 1994: copy of signed typed letter, Eric Abraham

Wendy Le Grice, undated: handwritten illustrated note, Wendy Le Grice

Martina Wiegandt, 15 April 1994: copy of typed letter, le Carré archive

John Keegan, 28 April 1994: handwritten letter, Matthew Keegan

Horst Gerkens, 29 April 1994: unsigned copy of typed letter, le Carré archive

Mark Wilcocks, 1 July 1994: unsigned copy of typed letter, le Carré archive

Pusya Jopua, 15 November 1993: unsigned copy of typed fax, le Carré
archive

Professor George Hewitt, 4 May 1994: copy of handwritten fax, le Carré
archive

Vladimir Stabnikov, 11 July 1994: copy of typed fax, le Carré archive

Marianne Schindler, 11 July 1994: unsigned copy of typed letter, le Carré
archive

Edward Behr, 1 August 1994: typed fax with handwritten P.S., original in
le Carré archive

Susan D. Anderson, 24 August 1994: unsigned handwritten letter, 14-04-
002-P, John le Carré Collection, Harry Ransom Center, University of
Texas at Austin

Sonny Mehta, 19 September 1994: handwritten fax, original in le Carré
archive

Bob Gottlieb, 22 September 1994: copy of handwritten letter, le Carré
archive

John Calley, 30 September 1994: copy of typed fax, le Carré archive

Yvette Pierpaoli, 19 December 1994: signed copy of handwritten fax, le
Carré archive

Sonny Mehta, 21 November 1994: handwritten fax, original in le Carré
archive

Sonny Mehta, 21 November 1994: typed fax, original in le Carré archive

Sonny Mehta, 20 December 1994: typed fax, original in le Carré archive

Alan Judd, 24 June 1995: handwritten letter, Alan Judd

Anatoly Adamishin, 6 February 1996: unsigned copy of typed letter, le Carré archive

Alan Judd, 6 February 1996: handwritten letter, Alan Judd

Anatoly Adamishin, 21 February 1996: typed fax, original in le Carré archive

Alan Judd, 27 February 1996: handwritten letter, Alan Judd

Stephen Long, 14 December 1999: unsigned copy of typed letter, le Carré archive

Dick Koster, 3 April 1995: handwritten fax, original in le Carré archive

Helen Goldfield, 10 April 1995: copy of handwritten letter, le Carré archive

Stephen Fry, 4 May 1995: copy of handwritten letter, le Carré archive

Jane Cornwell, 10 May 1995: copy of handwritten fax, le Carré archive

Matthew Bruccoli, 19 October 1995: handwritten letter, MS-05128, le Carré Correspondence, undated, 1980–2005, Container 7.4, Harry Ransom Center, University of Texas at Austin

Douglas Hayward, 2 February 1996: unsigned copy of typed letter, le Carré archive

Sydney Pollack, 13 June 1996: handwritten fax, original in le Carré archive

Susan D. Anderson, undated: handwritten letter, 14-04-002-P, John le Carré Collection, Harry Ransom Center, University of Texas at Austin

Jack Carley, 12 March 1997: unsigned copy of typed letter, le Carré archive

Jane Cornwell, 27 April 1998: handwritten letter, original in le Carré archive

John Calley, 7 September 1998: handwritten fax, original in le Carré archive

Tony Cornwell, 13 December 1998: handwritten letter, Nettie and Trevor Cornwell

Sir Tom Stoppard, 4 February 1999: handwritten letter, Sir Tom Stoppard

Tony Cornwell, 30 May 1999: handwritten letter, Nettie and Trevor Cornwell

John Calley, 27 September 1999: handwritten fax, le Carré archive

John Calley, 17 February 2000: typed fax, copy in le Carré archive

Stephen James Joyce, 3 March 2000: unsigned copy of typed letter, le Carré archive

Pierce Brosnan, 5 March 2000: copy of handwritten fax, le Carré archive

Sue Lawley, 9 July 2000: copy of handwritten letter, le Carré archive

Nancy Olivieri, 22 May 2000: email, Nancy Olivieri

Nancy Olivieri, 18 July 2000: copy of typed letter with handwritten P.S., Nancy Olivieri

Janet Berger, 8 August 2000: handwritten fax, Buzz and Janet Berger

J. R. James CMG, British High Commissioner, Nairobi, 11 September 2000: handwritten fax, original in le Carré archive

John Boorman, 22 September 2000: typed fax, original in le Carré archive

Stanley Mitchell, 6 January 2001: copy of handwritten letter, le Carré archive

John Calley, 6 January 2001: handwritten fax, original in le Carré archive

Roland Philipps, 19 January 2001: copy of handwritten letter, Roland Philipps

Andreas Seiter and Katharina Amacker, 11 April 2001: copy of typed letter, le Carré archive

John Calley, 11 June 2001: copy of handwritten fax, le Carré archive

David's sons and Jane, 11 June 2001: handwritten letter, original in le Carré archive

Al and Anne Alvarez, 4 August 2001: handwritten letter, Anne Alvarez

John Boorman, 2 October 2002: copy of handwritten fax, le Carré archive

Jane Cornwell, 21 February 2003: handwritten letter, le Carré archive

Anthony Barnett, 1 January 2004: handwritten fax, original in le Carré archive

Dr and Mrs August Hanning, 28 December 2005: copy of handwritten fax, Dr Hanning/le Carré archive

Nancy Olivieri, 17 February 2006: handwritten letter, Nancy Olivieri

Stanley Mitchell, 19 April 2006: copy of handwritten letter, le Carré archive

Hugh Thomas, 10 May 2006: handwritten letter, CUL MS Add. 10195 Le Carré letter 10 May 2006, Cambridge University Library

Charlotte Cornwell, 17 May 2006: email, Nancy Cranham

Ralph de Butler, 14 September 2006: handwritten letter, Ralph de Butler

Nicholas Shakespeare, 14 November 2006: handwritten letter, Nicholas Shakespeare

Bernhard Docke, 9 February 2007: email, Bernhard Docke

Tony Cornwell, 15 May 2007: handwritten letter, Nettie and Trevor Cornwell

Douglas Jackson, 23 April 2008: handwritten letter, Douglas Jackson

Robert Forrest, 16 June 2008: handwritten letter, Robert Forrest

Dr August Hanning, 24 December 2008: handwritten fax, August Hanning

Dr August Hanning, 18 January 2009: handwritten fax, August Hanning/ original in le Carré archive

Federico Varese, 21 April 2009: handwritten letter, Federico Varese

Roger Martin, 3 June 2009: copy of handwritten letter, le Carré archive

Federico Varese, 3 July 2009: email, Federico Varese

Ralph Fiennes, 7 October 2009: copy of handwritten letter, le Carré archive

Al Alvarez, 26 October 2009: email, Anne Alvarez

Jonny Geller, 31 March 2010: copy of handwritten letter, Jonny Geller/le Carré archive

Tony Cornwell, 18 May 2010: handwritten letter, le Carré archive

Al Alvarez, late May 2010: handwritten postcard, Anne Alvarez

Adam Sisman, 15 July 2010: copy of handwritten letter, le Carré archive

Professor Owen Dudley Edwards, 20 November 2010: handwritten letter, Professor Edwards/le Carré archive

Tomas Alfredson, 12 July 2011: copy of handwritten letter, le Carré archive

Gary Oldman, 31 August 2011: email, le Carré archive

William Burroughs, 13 October 2011: handwritten letter, William Burroughs

Tony Cornwell, 4 February 2012: copy of handwritten letter, le Carré archive

Roger Hermiston, 12 April 2012: handwritten letter, Roger Hermiston

Tony Cornwell, 18 June 2012: copy of handwritten letter, le Carré archive

Jonny Geller, 8 September 2012: handwritten fax, Jonny Geller/original in le Carré archive

Anthony Barnett, 22 September 2012: email, le Carré archive

Mary Mount, 10 October 2012: email, Mary Mount/le Carré archive

Dear All, 16 October 2012: email, le Carré archive

Ian McEwan, 6 May 2013: handwritten letter, Ian McEwan, Box 33.5, John le Carré Letters, Harry Ransom Center, University of Texas at Austin

Georg and Christiane Boomgaarden, 22 October 2013: copy of handwritten letter, le Carré archive

Ben Macintyre, 11 November 2013: handwritten letter, Ben Macintyre

John and Mary James, 11 December 2013: typed letter, John and Mary James

Wolfgang Czaia, 12 December 2013: unsigned copy of typed letter, le Carré archive

Professor Roger Williams, CBE, 22 July 2014: unsigned copy of typed letter, le Carré archive

U. P. Karlsson, 5 August 2014: unsigned copy of typed letter, le Carré archive

Sir Tom Stoppard, 27 October 2014: handwritten letter, Sir Tom Stoppard

Mikhail Lyubimov, 27 April 2015: unsigned copy of typed letter, le Carré archive

Sir Tom Stoppard, 1 June 2015: handwritten letter, Sir Tom Stoppard

Susanne Bier, 31 August 2015: copy of handwritten letter, le Carré archive

Hugh Laurie, 29 August 2015: email, le Carré archive

Mikhail Lyubimov, 11 September 2015: email, Mikhail Lyubimov/le Carré archive

Bernhard Docke, 1 December 2015: email, Bernhard Docke/le Carré archive

Vladimir Stabnikov, 4 March 2016: email, le Carré archive

Tom Bower, 21 March 2016: email, le Carré archive

Robert McCrum, 30 July 2016: copy of handwritten letter, le Carré archive

Al and Anne Alvarez, 16 September 2016: handwritten letter, Anne Alvarez

Mary Mount, 8 November 2016: email, Mary Mount/le Carré archive

Ben Macintyre, 15 November 2016: handwritten letter, Ben Macintyre

Nicholas Shakespeare, 16 December 2016: handwritten letter, Nicholas Shakespeare

Roland Philipps, 16 February 2017: handwritten letter, Roland Philipps

Mary Mount, 20 February 2017: email, Mary Mount/le Carré archive

Yassin Musharbash, 2 May 2017: handwritten letter, Yassin Musharbash

Sir Tom Stoppard, 25 June 2017: handwritten letter, Sir Tom Stoppard

Keith FitzPatrick, 29 July 2017: handwritten letter, Keith FitzPatrick

Michael Jayston, 4 October 2017: handwritten letter, Michael Jayston

Sir Tom Stoppard, 21 December 2017: handwritten letter, Sir Tom Stoppard

Philippe Sands, 22 March 2018: email, Philippe Sands/le Carré archive

John and Mary James, 25 May 2018: handwritten letter, John and Mary James

William Burroughs, 23 July 2018: unsigned copy of typed letter, le Carré archive

Rex Cowan, 26 October 2018: handwritten letter, Rex Cowan

Steven Isserlis, 26 November 2018: copy of handwritten letter, le Carré archive

Sir Tom Stoppard, 19 December 2018: handwritten letter, Sir Tom Stoppard

Sir Tom Stoppard, 3 January 2019: handwritten letter, Sir Tom Stoppard

John Westerby, 4 April 2019: handwritten letter, John Westerby

Alan Judd, 18 May 2019: handwritten letter, Alan Judd

Tom Bower, 29 June 2019: email, le Carré archive

John Banville, 16 July 2019: email, le Carré archive

Simon, Stephen, Timothy and Nicholas Cornwell, 21 July 2019: email, le Carré archive

David Greenway, 2 October 2019: unsigned copy of typed letter, le Carré archive

Pierre Schori, 8 February 2020: copy of handwritten letter, le Carré archive

Daniel Ellsberg, 11 February 2020: copy of handwritten letter, le Carré archive

Nicholas Shakespeare, 26 April 2020: email, le Carré archive

Charlotte Cornwell, 26 April 2020: email, le Carré archive

Sam Joiner, 27 April 2020: handwritten letter, Sam Joiner

Alan Judd, 19 May 2020: handwritten letter, Alan Judd

Philippe Sands, 3 June 2020: email, le Carré archive

Jonny Geller, 8 June 2020: email, Jonny Geller/le Carré archive

Sir Tom Stoppard, 1 July 2020: handwritten letter, Sir Tom Stoppard

Ben Macintyre, 31 August 2020: email, le Carré archive

Nicholas Shakespeare, 1 October 2020: email, le Carré archive

Mikhail Lyubimov, 18 October 2020: email, le Carré archive

Alison Geraghty, 26 October 2020: unsigned copy of typed letter, le Carré archive

Yassin Musharbash, 23 November 2020: handwritten letter, Yassin Musharbash

David Greenway, 25 November 2020: handwritten letter, David Greenway

Index

Notes are indexed by locators, followed by the letter 'n' and the respective note numbers. Relationships indicated in parentheses are with reference to John le Carré unless mentioned otherwise.

674

SILVERVIEW
JOHN LE CARRÉ

Julian Lawndsley has renounced his high-flying job in the City for a simpler life running a bookshop in a small English seaside town. But only a couple of months into his new career, Edward, a Polish émigré, shows up at his door with a very keen interest in Julian's new enterprise and a lot of knowledge about his family history. And when a letter turns up at the door of a spy chief in London warning him of a dangerous leak, the investigations lead him to this quiet town by the sea . . .

Silverview is the mesmerising story of an encounter between innocence and experience and between public duty and private morals. In this last complete masterwork from the greatest chronicler of our age, John le Carré asks what you owe to your country when you no longer recognise it.

> 'A compelling character study of a supposedly retired spy . . . Such was his rare command of language and unique understanding of how the world really works that I finished the book with a sense that the only real grown-up in the room had left'
>
> Jake Kerridge, *Daily Telegraph*, Books of the Year

> 'Le Carré at his finest, revealing character and backstory through dialogue with an economy and grace beyond most writers'
>
> Mick Herron, *Guardian*

> '*Silverview* has all the old magic . . . it offers a rewarding postscript to the long-distance spellbinders *The Little Drummer Girl* and *Absolute Friends*'
>
> David Bromwich, *Times Literary Supplement*, Books of the Year